Encounters
with
American
Ethnic Cultures

ENCOUNTERS WITH AMERICAN ETHNIC CULTURES

Edited by
Philip L. Kilbride
Jane C. Goodale
Elizabeth R. Ameisen
(in collaboration with Carolyn G. Friedman)

The University of Alabama Press
Tuscaloosa and London

The paper on which this book is printed meets the minimum requirements of American National Standard for Information Science-
Permanence of paper for Printed Library Materials, ANSI A39.48–1984.

Library of Congress Cataloging-in-Publication Data

Encounters with American ethnic cultures / edited by Philip L. Kilbride,
Jane C. Goodale, Elizabeth R. Ameisen in collaboration with Carolyn G.
Friedman.
      p.   cm.
Bibliography: p.
Includes index.
ISBN 0-8173-0471-1 (alk. paper)
  1. Ethnicity—Pennsylvania—Philadelphia Region. 2. Minorities—
Pennsylvania—Philadelphia Region. 3. Philadelphia Region (Pa.)—Social
life and customs. 4. Philadelphia Region (Pa.)—Ethnic relations. I. Kil-
bride, Philip Leroy. II. Goodale, Jane C. (Jane Carter), 1926–. III. Ameisen,
Elizabeth R.
      F158.9.A1T6   1990
305.8′00974811–dc20   89–33864

British Library Cataloguing-in-Publication Data available

To Frederica de Laguna:
a "Master of Ethnography,"
Founder, Colleague, Teacher, and Friend
of the Department of Anthropology
at Bryn Mawr College

Contents

Preface

We are pleased to present in this volume some of the papers prepared by students as Senior Conference reports in fulfillment of their B.A. major in anthropology at Bryn Mawr College. The students are drawn from both Bryn Mawr College and Haverford College, and each school is represented among the papers presented here. The department was established as a separate major by Frederica deLaguna in 1967, since which time it has offered a major at the B.A. level and both the M.A. and Ph.D. degrees. Two of the graduate students, Elizabeth Ameisen and Carolyn Friedman, worked on the present project, having both participated in the Senior Conference Seminar while undergraduate students.

The Senior Conference in cultural anthropology is a year seminar that seeks to familiarize students with fieldwork experience "off campus" somewhere in the urban, periurban, or suburban areas of Philadelphia. In 1983 we decided to focus our concerns around the concept of "ethnicity." Thus, all students study theoretical material on this concept along with materials devoted to fieldwork methodology. Each student also reads pertinent historical and social science books or articles on "his" or "her" ethnic group. Actual fieldwork includes about five months, but this, of course, varies given particular circumstances. Not unsurprisingly, students ranged from wildly enthusiastic through equally intense, but more negative emotions such as fear or even, in a few cases, anger, were expressed. We have learned that, though fieldwork is at the heart of anthropology, it is not everyone's "cup of tea." As is commonly the case, vagaries of good or bad fortune while in the field contribute to any given student's academic and affective experience throughout the course. Overall, however, among the roughly sixty-five students who have participated in our seminars, the vast majority wrote papers of fine quality. The present selection, we feel, includes only those among the best, but we could easily double their number without sacrificing in any way the quality of work. We hope that the readers of this volume will agree with us about the merits of these undergraduate papers, which would show, should our view be sustained, that good American anthropology can be done in one's local area and by young students to boot! (One paper, however, by Carolyn Friedman, includes some material from her undergraduate paper that was added to her M.A. thesis.)

We would like to thank Dr. Janet MacGaffey, who taught with Dr. Jane Goodale in 1984–85, during Dr. Kilbride's sabbatical year in Kenya. Our gratitude is also extended to Dr. Jean DeBernardi, who taught in 1986–87 with Dr. Kilbride during Dr. Goodale's leave in Australia. It is difficult to determine how we, the instructors, have influenced the development of each project from the initial step of "bowing in" to the field through final write-up and oral presentation. We, of course, hope that something "rubbed off"— if nothing else than perhaps our enthusiasm for fieldwork and intellectual fascination with cultural analysis.

The present collection of essays (with two exceptions) was selected during a graduate seminar in 1985–86 that was participated in by four of the major contributors to this volume (two papers were added from the year 1986–87). All Senior Conference papers were read, with common, but not always unanimous, agreement on the "best" papers to include. Moreover, we tried to be broad in ethnic and topical coverage; thus, some of the "best" papers could not be included. As often happens, the academic year 1985–86 ended with Dr. Goodale's departure for a year to Australia, along with Carolyn Friedman, who graduated and left for the Peace Corps in West Africa. Dr. Kilbride undertook, along with Elizabeth Ameisen, the final task of the preliminary editing of the papers and preparing two introductory chapters. Dr. Kilbride wrote four of the section introductions and the Conclusion. After her return, Dr. Goodale provided significant and essential input for the final draft. In particular, the theoretical introductory chapter was expanded by her to include material on teaching, and she wrote the introduction to Part IV. Our work was greatly aided by two anonymous reviewers, who made excellent suggestions.

We can only hope that all these efforts are worthy and in some way representative of the ideas that emerged from numerous discussions the editors of this book have had in seminar and the even more numerous ones that the two professors have had together and with all sixty-five students. In any case, it is believed that each study in this volume can stand alone as a significant piece of ethnic research and that is, after all, why we want to make them all available to a wider audience by publication. This is the *students'* story, not ours.

THE EDITORS

Acknowledgments

The editors wish to acknowledge the contributions of all the senior participants, who over the years have made insightful comments in various seminars. On behalf of all the contributors, we express our gratitude to the informants for so willingly accepting us as "students" of their cultural values and traditions. We are also grateful to Professor Samuel Lachs for his advice on Jewish ethnic terms. We recognize the careful manuscript editing by Robert G. Ferris and acknowledge his fine work. Finally, we wish to thank the following for hours of diligent labor in the production of the final manuscript: Genevieve Bell, Emma Durham, Stevie Nangendo, Gina Shin, Jennifer Spruill, Holly Taylor, and Sarah Woodbury.

Encounters
with
American
Ethnic Cultures

1

Introduction
Ethnic Culture Analysis—A Course of Study

Jane C. Goodale
Philip L. Kilbride

In 1972 Idi Amin, the dictator of the Second Republic of Uganda, announced on national television that he was free of "tribalistic sentiment" as was evidenced by the fact that he had fathered children in every "tribe" (more than thirty groups) in the country. Some weeks later, Philip Kilbride's wife, Janet, was questioned at a military roadblock as to her "tribal" affiliation, to which she responded with some felt but non-expressed amusement "I'm an American." In retrospect, we at the time found Amin's statement affectively neutral and "culturally appropriate" (if perhaps impractical) while a sense of unfamiliarity and bemused annoyance was elicited in us by his soldier's use of the word "tribe." It is perhaps paradoxical that many years later it now seems reasonable to argue that "the tribe" or, more precisely, some more or less comparable term needs to be conceptually worked out for application to the American and Ugandan social scene (as suggested by Amin's soldier in his question to Janet). At the same time, social and cultural life in modern East Africa (and elsewhere in the developing world) needs to be conceptually divorced from an overdependence on a "fossilized" tribal social formation idea (R. Cohen 1978). Fortunately, there is progress in the social sciences such that we can now conceptually offer the term "ethnic group" as a contemporary substitute for the older term "tribe," not only as applied to social formations in the modern developing world, but also for certain social groups in the United States and other industrialized nations. In this way, we intellectually achieve the long-pursued goal of conceptual "universalism," itself essential for a truly comparative theoretical perspective in anthropology and related disciplines.

To be sure, the term "tribe" may be historically appropriate for certain more or less bounded societies in existence prior to the modern era. Novak states: "The new cultural self-consciousness is first of all post tribal, arising in our era in which almost every culture has been obligated to become aware of many others . . . in contrast to the isolation of ancient times . . . " (1980:32). Ethnicity is an expression of diversity within and across modern borders. In Australia, for example, the aboriginal tribes are described as "a collection of persons who speak a common language, or what they themselves regard as such, practice the same custom and normally have a name by which they distinguish themselves and their language" (Hart 1930:169–170).

Jane Goodale in 1987 participated in a Tiwi Land Council meeting. It was pointed out in the discussion that one need only consult an NT telephone directory to discover that there is a suburb of Darwin called Tiwi, with a Tiwi primary school, a shopping center with a Tiwi supermarket, a Tiwi fish and chips carryout, and a Tiwi butcher. Outside the suburb are Tiwi Plumbing and Roofing, Tiwi Motel, and Tiwi Steel Fabricators. In addition to these non-island uses of the name, there are local industries called Tiwi Design and Tiwi Pottery on the islands, and a company called Tiwi Tours guides visitors through the islands and elsewhere.

Jane Goodale writes: "In 1986/87 I frequently heard media and other Territory public speakers (including Stanley Tipoloura MHA, himself a Tiwi) make reference to the Tiwi Islands, *to be found on no map*. But in spite of the increasing use of the name by aboriginals and others, I continue to ask, as I have since my first visit to Milikapiti (Snake Bay) in 1954, is there a Tiwi ethnicity, a Tiwi cultural identity? If so, in what collective and individual contexts is it expressed?" (Goodale 1988).

New terms such as "ethnic group" and "ethnic identity" are now necessary to capture the modern use, for which older "tribe" labels may once have been appropriate.

The purpose of this introductory essay is to develop the term "ethnic group culture" as an important idea for theoretical and applied application in the United States. Specific field studies follow that illustrate some of the remarks considered below. We will emphasize the "culture" concept in the newer context of ethnicity, an approach that we believe justifies continuation of the culture concept as a robust and viable "cornerstone" concept for anthropology (Langness 1975). It was our theoretical concern with cultural phenomenon that several years ago prompted our intellectual interest in ethnicity in the United States, for example, in the Philadelphia urban and periurban context.

Our colleagues in sociology have been, for many years, engaged in the study of ethnic minorities in the United States. For example, M. Weber (1968), the pioneering German theoretical sociologist, popularized in this country by T. Parsons, long ago defined the ethnic group as one that possesses a subjective belief in a common descent because of similarities of physical type or of custom and where this belief is particularly salient in the continuation of non-kin communal political relationships. Presently, sociology is mainly concerned with ethnicity as a social process having important connections with class, stratification, and politics, though ethnicity as cultural (customary behavior) process is not without interest to the sociologist (cf. Yinger 1985).

It seemed to us that the discipline of anthropology, and our experience in Africa and Australia, with its cross-cultural comparative perspective particularly concerned with cultural analysis, might also contribute insight to the study of ethnicity as a cultural process here in the United States. We took heart in R. Cohen's conclusion to his excellent review article on ethnicity, which states: "To summarize, ethnicity, as presently used in anthropology, expresses a shift to multicultural, multiethnic interactive contexts in which attention is focused on an entity—the ethnic group—which is marked by some degree of cultural and social communality" (1978:386).

In the same review, Cohen provides a rationale for research efforts such as this volume represents. Following Kunstadter, Cohen (1978:386) believes that the ethnic group is "a set of individuals with mutual interests based on shared understandings and common values. How much is shared *is an empirical question*" [emphasis ours]. We also follow Yinger, who believes that an ethnic group is "a segment of a larger society whose members are thought, by themselves and/or others, to have a common origin and to share important segments of a common culture and who, in addition, participate in shared activities in which the common origin and culture are significant ingredients" (1985:159). In sum, the ethnic group is *by definition* cultural.

The average American today experiences his or her life in a variety of social contexts. There are commonly "mediating structures," which, for example, serve to orient the individual in today's all too bureaucratic world (Burger 1977). The impersonal world of office and factory is mediated by special clubs, churches, and community organizations. Recreational facilities, bars, shopping centers, and so forth are also significant. Our national popular culture provides for most Americans common experiences that can become instant conversation pieces for even strangers. Disneyland, the evening news, the Super Bowl, and McDonald's are known by most Americans (Kottak 1982).

In spite of the growth of a common U.S. experience with Anglo values that are reinforced in the schools, there still persists a strong sense of ethnic culture in America. This life-style orientation pertaining to a subpopulation of Americans, however, varies in intensity. For some, ethnicity is a self-chosen experience, as among Irish-Americans who choose to join Irish dance clubs (Hebard this volume) or among Ukranian-Americans who become involved in Easter egg decorating (Krier this volume). For others, ethnicity is a strongly religious experience, as among the Amish or Jewish Hasidists (Part III this volume). Ethnic grouping may also be a neighborhood experience, as in "Little Italys," "Chinatowns," or Hispanic "barrios," or it may involve commuting from various neighborhoods to a common church, as in some Greek Orthodox churches in Philadelphia (Belsley this volume). In sum, ethnic experience is variously "marked" by cultural, linguistic, and social criteria, but "how so" remains a researchable issue.

For many Americans, however, ethnic background is denied entirely in the desire to achieve respectability or middle-class status. The American school system, in particular, has often extinguished ethnic languages and habits. The denial of ethnic difference would appear to be not unlike a more general denial of differences in social class, wealth, and personal attributes—all in conformity to the "average" person (how many of us are "just middle class?"). In fact, Riesman's lonely "other-directed" American (1961) and the Spindlers' (1983) point that individualism is in dialectical opposition to conformity as *competing* values in American social life suggest a characterological backdrop for the denial of diversity. Thus, all Americans are, in fact, "ethnic," but there is considerable variation in degree and kind of experience.

The most significant factor in determining ethnic experiential variation is, of course, the variable "class." Affiliation by class is not only known to cross-cut ethnic groups, but is itself an important source of variation within the ethnic group. The significance of class in American life as well as various social, cultural, and economic criteria for its composition is brilliantly treated in Warner et al.'s classic book *Yankee City* (1963). In the present volume, questions of class are secondary to those of culture, though some papers do touch specifically on class and ethnic interaction. The "Exclusivity in an Ethnic Elite" piece by Ameisen on WASPs (White Anglo-Saxon Protestants) and the work of Belsley on Greek Orthodox religious affiliation are particularly sensitive to the question of class. For "non-white" ethnics, ethnicity is often "attributed" by other features irrespective of a person's self-chosen life-style.

For American Indians, Hispanics, Asian-Americans, and African-Americans, ethnicity also involves a racial experience. American racism has been particularly harsh on those citizens who have been here the longest: the Indians; and those who came soon after the Europeans, the African-Americans. Unfortunately, racial stereotypes still structure the national view of Indians and blacks. Erroneous facts and omissions of historical events are typical in U.S. schools (Rosenfeld 1971). Significantly, the powerful WASP ethnic group has many derogatory jokes pertaining to blacks, even though they do not live by, attend school with, or otherwise associate with them (Ameisen this volume). For "racial" ethnic groups, there can be no self-chosen ethnic experience.

Whatever the merit of earlier assumptions, it is clear that those social formations once thought to be "tribes" are now clearly "ethnic" groups when viewed in the context of modernizing, "multiethnic" nation-states. For this reason, R. Cohen suggests that the term "tribe," with its assumptions of isolation, primitiveness, non-Westernness, and boundedness, among other things, be replaced by the idea of ethnic group that is conceptualized to be not isolated and is contemporary, universal, and characterized by shifting boundaries (1978:384). The effect of his program would be to subsume American ethnic groups (hyphenated-Americans) and the social formations once labeled tribal *in the same category*. This strategy requires, of course, a shift of focus in cultural analysis because the older holistic assumptions about culture, linked as they were to assumed isolated social formations, have little to recommend them in the modern U.S. context. Precisely *how* cultural analysis can be useful is, of course, the subject of the essays in this volume.

Looked at from the "outside" (or etic perspective), it is clear that ethnic-group life-styles are not usually "holistic" along exclusively ethnic lines. There is, for example, no formal African-American "government," Italian-American religion, or Polish-American economy. Most ethnic groups are thus "segmented" in the sense argued for the African-American experience when Blauner (1970) compared African-American culture with its African "tribal" and more holistic social antecedents. Nevertheless, these essays show that there is variation in the degree of holism. The separatist Lubavitchers

(Part III this volume) are more culturally holistic in ethnic life-style when compared with the more segmented experience of other groups included in this book.

Issues of culture and power are also important when ethnic groups are viewed from the "outside." The editors of this volume follow A. Cohen (1974:97), who believes that "ethnicity is fundamentally a political phenomenon as the symbols of the traditional culture are used as mechanisms for the articulation of political alignments." He contends that use of symbols is often "unconscious" by group members but in practice becomes obvious to anthropologists when they notice that only members of the powerful "elite" group are invited to the wedding, funeral, or other cultural events (events where important political alliances are maintained). Therefore, just as holism is a variable in ethnic cultural study, so also is the domain of power. This idea is illustrated by the inclusion of a study of WASP ethnic culture in this series of essays (Ameisen). It will be surprising for some to discover that there is even a WASP ethnic culture, so successful have been symbols of exclusion (as in racial jokes). WASP power maintains symbolic devices that overall serve to segregate WASPs from other ethnic groups in exclusive churches, schools, and neighborhoods.

There is, of course, some conceptual continuity with the older ideas about culture as viewed etically. The editors of this volume still assume, for example, that ethnic culture emerges as a historical process. Thus, this study offers materials that are consistent with Herskovits's (1958) argument that black American behavior and institutions show numerous "Africanisms," which constitute historical survivals from preslavery experience in West Africa. This unpopular view flies in the face of extreme assimilationist theory, which, among other things, sought to see only deficiencies in the black experience, which, it was hoped, would improve once such things as female-dominated homes, "pathological" language, and "unwholesome" ethics were eradicated. The popular current term "African-American" symbolically shows that today to argue for African cultural antecedents is not only respectable but is also scholarly correct. The consideration of African-American food customs (Friedman this volume) illustrates the centrality of a temporal dimension in ethnic cultural process. Nevertheless, the processual development is not widely recognized given the powerlessness of African-Americans and racist attitudes in America. This is seen in the following remark: "It is not possible for Negroes to view themselves as other ethnic groups viewed themselves because—and this is the key to much in the Negro world—the Negro is only an American and nothing else. He has no values and culture to guard and protect" (Glazer and Moynihan 1963:153).

Movement of populations, forced as in slavery or, for example, voluntary as in immigration, reveals not only the historical but also the structural aspects of ethnic cultural analysis. Popenoe (this volume) demonstrates that recent Cambodian arrivals to America largely conform to traditional positive Cambodian ideas about arranged marriages. In time, she speculates that this current preference will lessen (perhaps to become a future cultural "survival"?). Arranged marriages, of course, are counter to a U.S. national preference for companionate marriage. Thus, for Cambodians, there is a structural contradiction or a particular example of a more general "assimilation" versus "pluralism" tendency in American ethnic life (cf. Pettigrew 1976). The dynamic of assimilation is often quite stressful. Popenoe's essay is in a category that focuses on expressions of ethnicity by individuals and groups under culturally traumatic experiences of homelessness or enforced refugee status in an alien nation and culture.

These essays contain several examples that illustrate how such expressive things as music and material culture objects (for example, calendars [Dahlem], Easter eggs [Krier], and dance [Hebard]) are "meaningful" not only to group members themselves but also as symbolic representations of the group conceived of as a social community. Geertz (1973) emphasizes ethnicity as grounded in a primordial tie of "longing" to belong to that group alone. Symbolic attachments clearly reveal this attribute at the level of affect.

Ethnic-group symbolic elaboration and powerful affective experience are frequently associated with religion through participation in a church community. Although a number of the essays show this association, this volume will focus on ethnic religion as collective representation (Durkheim 1961) in three studies. For Hispanic-Catholics (Schoch-Spana), American-Indian Baptists (Batten), and Greek Orthodox Americans (Belsley), the church serves as a kind of master symbol and often elicits a fundamental affect whose interpretation is simultaneously "primordial," "collective," and culturally ethnic; and in a religiously affiliated school, Jewish children (Dahlem) also are introduced to these symbols at an early age.

The symbolic property of ethnic culture, however, at once orients theoretical concern to the insider's perspective or emic aspects of cultural analysis. Ethnic cultural experience is learned in the home, school, and church as well as from peers. Examples of this where relevant are provided in this book. Importantly, however, the insider's perspective illustrates a subjectivist dimension involving ethnic identity that best illustrates the *situational* context-dependent nature of ethnic cultural experience. Emphasis on this situational factor is sometimes called the "new ethnicity" in anthropological study (Bennett 1975) or an even more extreme belief that at the level of epistemology "ethnicity has no existence apart from inter-ethnic relations" (R. Cohen 1978:389). It is, of course, true that the recent search for "roots," name changes, and proliferation of ethnic studies courses in America constitute a vastly different sociocultural context for expression of one's ethnic identity when compared, for example, with America in the 1920s and 1930s. This volume will therefore consider the issue of *context* and ethnic identity where appropriate but will highlight this idea in the discussion about Irish-American, Welsh-American, and Ukranian-American experience as "self-chosen" ethnic expressions.

Finally, ethnic culture if viewed from the inside or the outside is, like other conceptualizations of culture, "interpretive." The senior editors of this book have consistently attempted to convey to our students the personal and subjective dimensions not only of fieldwork itself but also of cultural life in general. Accordingly a section is devoted to this subject, in which a male and a female student each presents his and her own view of Lubavitcher social life. Their chapters are also reminders that ethnic cultural experience, like all cultural experience, reveals a "male" and "female" point of view—a position long ago argued by Jane C. Goodale and continued at Bryn Mawr in the Senior Conference Seminar (cf. Goodale 1971).

Importantly, the editors do not argue that the materials presented in this volume are exhaustive, not even for the specific theoretical topics or ethnic communities that are treated here. For the American experience, we have already noted the primarily sociological concern to date with ethnicity, particularly involving interaction with "social" phenomena as class and politics. We have clearly chosen to emphasize the "cultural," but even then options of interpretation are possible. We have not stressed ethnic conflict, particularly given the experience, sensitivity, and skill that such an interest would require of young student ethnographers. Our approach, therefore, is by choice and circumstance primarily "symbolic," or even "Weberian," but in the Soviet Union "Marxist" materialist and evolutionary cultural perspectives are being applied to interaction between ethnicity and societal evolution. In Japan, to mention another example of "national anthropology," cultural analysis seems more inclined to ignore "ethnicity" altogether as a topic in favor of debate over "culture" or "civilization" as a cornerstone concept (Umesao and Kreiner 1984). This comparative Japanese absence of research on "ethnicity" seems best understood as a reflection of the nation's self-proclaimed ethnic uniformity compared to the Soviet Union and the United States, which are multiethnic nation states. Indeed, Japan does in fact have both Korean and Ainu minorities. Nevertheless, it is relatively homogeneous.

In summary, the studies in this volume collectively illustrate that, on the whole, ethnic culture is a group sociocultural symbolic process that is context-dependent within a temporal frame. The essays show that the ethnic communities discussed can be differentiated in terms of specific symbolic criteria based on shared meanings. A major paradox, however, is that in spite of ethnic cultural variation obvious to, for example, the comparativist oriented cultural anthropologist, American national mythology on the whole denies, as do many social scientists, even the existence of ethnic culture. This myopia has serious theoretical implications for general cultural study—not to mention practical consequences, some of which will be mentioned below. Particularly problematic is that mythic denial at the informant level has the theoretical consequence in research of making "emic" oriented research difficult or even on occasion impossible. Kochman (1981:11) noted in the context of his research on black-white cultural differences in communication styles that it is "impolite to discuss minority group differences in public. This rule emerged over a period when such differences were regularly used as evidence of minority group inferiority. To resist this minority group members felt it necessary to divert attention away from distinctive differences. Some went so far as to deny that differences existed! Liberal minded whites cooperated with minorities in these efforts, since they shared the general view that the differences were signs of minority group inferiority."

There are many reasons for the "mythic denial" noted by Kochman and many others. In America, for example, there is a national preoccupation with "upward mobility" and assimilation" that receives cultural reinforcement in the school systems. Formal education is grounded in linguistic ethnocentrism, where English (and other Anglo values) receive powerful symbolic support. Such traits as rugged individualism (Hsu 1983), seen in commitment to personal ""liberty" and "freedom," seemingly contribute to the notion that "group" determinants in behavior are either nonexistent or undesirable. Whatever the causes, it is clear that there is considerable national doubt over such things as to whether or not schools should be bilingual, have academic diversity requirements, or, not so long ago, if Japanese-Americans (and some other ethnic minorities) could even be "loyal" Americans. Nevertheless, although the editors of this volume strongly believe in the existential reality (even if sometimes denied) of ethnic cultural experience, this should not be interpreted to mean that there are not or should not be some common, even a majority, of symbolic meanings shared by all Americans. We believe, along with most Americans of all ethnic groups, that there should be a national language. This does not preclude that in some regions *all* people could be encouraged, or even required, to learn specific second or third languages of regional significance.

Moreover, it is clear that there is what can be labeled a "pop" national culture (Kottak 1982). Such things as various as "evening news," Disneyland, McDonald's, and "Monday Night Football" transcend specific ethnic cultural experiences. At the other end of "pop culture" on a cultural continuum, conceived in this volume to be "national" or "pop" at one end with "ethnic" midway, are, of course, "universal" symbolic experiences that would unite *all* human communities. For this reason, common themes such as meals and food, music and dance, and family life recur across specific ethnic experience studied by the students in the Senior Conference. One is reminded of Kluckhohn's famous statement that every person is like everyone else, some other people, and no other person. Ethnic cultural experience is, the editors believe, similar to his category of "some other people."

There are, of course, serious practical consequences for not sorting out, say in public education circles, the theoretical problematics outlined above. Failure to recognize systematically the cultural realities of pluralism, even within a framework of national cultural assimilation, often has painful consequences for individuals and deleterious effects on entire ethnic communities. The present condition of American Indians is sadly informative and needs no elaboration here. On a more personal level, many Americans now struggle to learn European languages that were not taught by their parents at home because it was considered to be shameful. On a stronger note, one reads almost daily about violence directed at blacks or Asians or racially mixed couples by other ethnic Americans, many of whose grandparents worked as domestics or in other "low"-status occupations (or even received welfare or "charity"). Schools regularly teach curricula that, often unwittingly, give the appearance that Anglo language and values are *absolutes*, not simply cultural alternatives. The editors of this volume believe therefore that ethnic cultural study should receive high priority in American public and academic life, if for no other reason than the practical. We take heart that American anthropology in its inception was designed as cultural analysis for the purpose of "freeing" the human being from the "shackles of tradition" while fostering dignity and respect to people of "other" cultures (Boas 1963). Sadly, many current anthropological problematics, agendas, and programs seem to us as without *stated* practical purpose or consequence. We attempt here and in our undergraduate major program to foster an original anthropological spirit so that it may not only exist as a "footprint on the sands of time" but as such can be revitalized (without, of course, the concept of "tribe").

Ethnic cultural analysis conceived as an empirical enterprise requires firsthand fieldwork experience. In the Bryn Mawr plan, all senior majors must take a two-semester course devoted to analysis of original data. (For those majors who elect the archaeological strand, their fieldwork is carried out during previous summers, a solution to the time problem not normally available to those in the cultural strand.) The expressed aim of this requirement is to familiarize students with the development of ethnic studies in the contemporary anthropological tradition and with methodological and analytic methods used in the anthropological study of culture in a multicultural industrial society. Through the student's personal involvement in a field investigation and its analysis, the faculty believe they achieve a greater understanding of the complex relations between ethnic group, class, gender, and cultural values in contemporary nation-states than can be achieved through second-hand accounts alone. In addition, the students gain valuable skills in the practice and experience of designing and carrying out a practical and feasible field investigation of a selected problem as well as in the analysis and reporting of results. For example, at the end of the first semester the students prepare a grant proposal along the lines of the requirements of the National Science Foundation and at the end of the second and final semester a full report of the research.

Teaching fieldwork to undergraduate students is not an easily accomplished goal, and this volume has been prepared with the hope that it will serve both the instructors and students in other institutions as a pedagogical guide as well as source book for the study of American culture. To this end, the Appendix contains course outlines that may serve as models. This Introduction will emphasize some of the issues as the faculty have encountered them over the years.

It is important to stress that the course is required, and the papers that result are the work of senior major anthropology students who have had, in addition to introductory courses, intermediate and advanced level courses that deal with ethnographic area(s), cultural and social theory, linguistics, as well as one or more topical courses. Secondly, although the general ethnicity focus was preselected, students were quite free to select the particular topical focus often related to personal interests in art, music, ritual, social issues, and so on. Thirdly, neither Goodale nor Kilbride was personally involved in research in the greater Philadelphia area and therefore provided only the minimal general advice necessary to facilitate the selection of and initial entry to a particular community or group. Students were forced by this to experience and capitalize on the common and often traumatic and "accidental" initial encounter with a member or members of a targeted group. Each of the following chapters therefore has in common fieldwork, and related issues, as a basic experiential denominator. And each student, though concentrating on expressions of ethnicity in behavior, necessarily grappled individually with the complexities (ambiguities, joys, and frustrations) of ethnographic field research.

Projects were conceptualized, data gathered, and written up during one academic year. (This course has been taught in a one-semester version, and a model of this is presented in Appendix # 2. However, the degree of frustration of the student in having to cut short fieldwork just when it was beginning to "pay off," in the opinion of the faculty justifies the two-semester plan.) Weekly group meetings analyzed the theoretical literature on ethnicity and fieldwork; and, as the year progressed, more focused discussion centered around specific issues deriving from the practice and ethics of fieldwork, ethnic cultural analysis, and interpretation as well as on the style of presentation of results.

Because "culture" was of particular interest, the faculty emphasized participant observation along with the interview as the two techniques best suited to determine the existence (or not) of patterned regularities in behavior. Each student, of course, read pertinent literature on background for his or her project in that each study was expected to be "grounded" in "the literature." The editors of this collection have elected to omit much of this background, but some of the major sources used by each author are contained in the citations. However, the editors chose to include those sections relating to method and particular research techniques and strategies by which the data were gathered and as much of the original data as feasible. In sum, the reader will find that the student research proceeded more or less along lines practiced by professional anthropologists doing ethnographic research in non-Western contexts. Nevertheless, research on American ethnic culture had some quite different methodological properties from those of the ethnographer who goes "abroad" to live for a year in a community where holistic cultural study is the objective.

First, some ethnic Americans do not live in discrete residential areas, but are scattered about the city or suburbs. Scandinavian-Americans are a good example of this. Korean families are also dispersed. Second, there is sometimes such a reluctance on the part of some individuals to recognize even the existence of an ethnic culture that some students found it difficult to raise the topic, particularly to African-American informants. Perhaps the biggest hurdle, however, is that American ethnics are, like the majority of our students, Americans and therefore all share a considerable common cultural and linguistic background. Puerto Rican Catholicism, for example *is* Catholicism, but after considerable participant work it was discovered by an Anglo-Catholic investigator (Schoch-Spana) that certain Hispanic themes could be identified in the Hispanic Mass.

Another major difference from traditional ethnography is in the domain of "power." Students felt compelled somehow to *reciprocate* for the usually graciously extended opportunity to enter the lives of informants. Students were not "powerful" outsiders with informants as is typical for overseas researchers, where reciprocity, often in the form of money, school fees, transportation, medical aid, and the like is not uncommon. In general, it was found that "just listening" was a salient reward for many informants; and, for those who requested it, a copy of the final paper was usually all our investigators could offer. Although a miniscule amount of departmental funds was available for "emergencies" such as transportation or entrance fees to "events" held out of town or beyond the students' personal finances, they mainly used their own very limited funds to carry out their projects.

The students, as in all fieldwork, faced ethical concerns. Should they laugh at racial jokes told by WASPs about blacks? Should women sit at the back of the church in a black Moslem mosque? In general, ethical issues were resolved through both group discussion and individual counseling, and it is hoped that the overall research effort can in some way repay the many gracious hosts for their willingness to cooperate. The following studies were done while the authors were pursuing a full-time course of study and while learning how to do field research. Deficiencies of time are obvious and were the greatest frustration felt by the students. Nevertheless, the studies are offered as examples of what committed students of anthropology can accomplish when one's own society is the subject of study. The editors believe that the essays are strong at the level of description and provocative concerning theoretical insight. The Conclusion of this volume will discuss comparative implications arising from the field studies and offer some suggestions for further research.

2

Methodology

Elizabeth R. Ameisen
Carolyn G. Friedman

The answer is: fieldwork and cultural analysis. The question is: What are two distinguishing features of cultural anthropology?

The assignment is: Create and conduct an original anthropological fieldwork project. The question is: How did I ever become interested in anthropology in the first place? Following are two student responses to a survey of past participants in the anthropology Senior Conference:

> "Anthropology, because of its insights, had seemed to be a constructive methodology for developing political policies that could help people teetering between a disappearing past and an uncertain future. I wanted to learn how the lessons of anthropology can help people now."

> "What fascinates me the most about anthropology is its adaptability as a discipline to yield a humanistic analysis in any field of human endeavor."

Choosing cultural anthropology as a major course of study in college might appear to be a relatively painless way to earn a degree because the array of courses and topics that the discipline encompasses is vast. This is due to anthropology's "holistic" approach, which assumes that human social experience is all interrelated in a total "design for living" or cultural system pertaining to a person's society. Anthropology therefore enables one to study such activities as art, music, dance, economics, and politics, not only in our own society but, given the discipline's comparative cultural perspective, in far away places as well. No matter what our particular reasons (almost endless) are for studying anthropology, we all share a holistic interest in behavior and a common desire to understand all people from the "cultural point of view."

Intimately connected with these professional concerns is an interest in learning about ourselves through our work. Constantly confronted with our own influence on our research and on our informants, we try to face our biases, account for them in our conclusions, and admit them, at least to ourselves. Attitudes and beliefs that we have so long taken for granted are revealed to us anew; as we attempt to observe and analyze others "objectively," we cannot help but be subject to our informants' interpretations of us (indeed, we try to learn just how our informants do perceive us) as well as the subject of our own self-interpretation. In observing others, we observe ourselves, and so we are simultaneously the observer and the observed. Anthropology is truly a *Mirror for Man* (Kluckhohn).

Our neighbors or friends from foreign countries, the *National Geographic*, our own family backgrounds, or a book we once read (which we later learned to call an "ethnography") may have initially stimulated our interest in other people (which we later learned to call "our interest in anthropology"). As anthropology students, we continue to read ethnographies. We read about the history of the discipline of anthropology and about anthropological theory. We peruse novels written by and about people all over the globe. We read about anthropologists who "do" anthropology, but somehow the "doing" of anthropology takes on a world of new meaning when we are ourselves confronted with this task.

Particularly when contemplating and planning our *first* fieldwork project, the many anthropological books and articles we have read, the discussions we have had, and the movies we have seen flash through our minds as examples of what other anthropologists have done and experienced. We remember "on-the-job" descriptions and scenarios related to us by anthropologists who have returned from the field, all of whom operated under a unique set of circumstances, encountered various dilemmas, and reacted to their field situation in their own way. Books we have read about ways to do fieldwork, such as Pelto and Pelto's *Anthropological Research: The Structure of Inquiry* (1978), make us wonder how anthropologists managed prior to the 1960s, before anthropological methodology was deemed necessary as part of the preparation for entering the field. We realize too, although not until after we have conducted our fieldwork, just how difficult it is for anthropologists and professors to teach a methodological approach like participant observation. A shift in the student-teacher relationship perhaps begins when we realize that questions we pose to our professors, even seemingly practical and "simple" questions deserving "simple" yet unavailable answers, are indeed unanswerable by anyone but ourselves through fieldwork.

When Professor Jane Goodale made her maiden fieldwork expedition in 1954 to work among the Tiwi of the Melville Islands, she went equipped, as all anthropologists of the time, with her supplies and as thorough an understanding of "her people" as possible. One important thing was missing however: an explanation of how to do fieldwork. Over the last thirty years, significant changes have been made in anthropology curricula in an effort to remedy this problem. Books such as Agar's *The Professional Stranger* (1980) outline different approaches and techniques currently being used in the field. In fact, today's budding anthropologists may read as much about field methodology as they do about ethnographic or theoretical issues. Yet, for all this reading and studying, participant observation, the cornerstone of the fieldwork experience, remains an enigma for most anthropology students. But why should this be the case? The answer seems to be that descriptions of how to do participant observation lay only a foundation for a true understanding of the process. Ultimately, one must go out into the field and experiment with the technique. Despite this fact, few undergraduate anthropology departments offer their students the opportunity to try their hands at this most fundamental research form. As a result, most students pursuing careers in this field enter graduate school without fully comprehending what it is they hope to do.

At Bryn Mawr College, the professors in the Anthropology Department decided several years ago that, in order to provide a thorough educational experience for their majors, they had to include some sort of fieldwork opportunity. In the previous chapter, Professors Goodale and Kilbride have outlined the theoretical concerns of this field method phase. We (Ameisen and Friedman) were participants in their course during the academic year 1983–84. By that time, it had developed into its present form: an introduction to field methodology that focuses on an evaluation of the applicability of different concepts of ethnicity. From the students' perspective, this combined focus was particularly significant because it enabled us to gain general fieldwork experience while also learning how to obtain data that are relevant to a particular theoretical question. Moreover, because there was an underlying theme to the course itself,

Methodology   17

we were, as a group, able to make comparisons amongst ourselves and our own work.

Not surprisingly, the course began with detailed discussions of how fieldwork is to be conducted. These discussions were based upon readings we had all done, including the previously mentioned books by Agar, Pelto and Pelto, also Spradley's *Participant Observation*(1980)—and even the classic introductory chapter to Malinowski's *Argonauts of the Western Pacific* (1922, 1984), which describes the scientific goals of all good fieldwork, particularly participant observation. Although we were all acquainting ourselves with the accepted anthropological field methods, we were also being introduced to a myriad of definitions and approaches to the study of ethnicity. Specifically, we all read an extensive volume on the subject, *The New Ethnicity* (Bennett 1975), which is a collection of essays published by the American Ethnological Society (see also Glazer and Moynihan's *Beyond the Melting Pot* [1963] and DeVos and Romanucci-Ross's *Ethnic Identity* [1975] for more information on the topic). This reading was then supplemented by articles pertaining to our particular ethnic groups.

It is difficult to determine how one goes about selecting a group of people and a topic to study; sometimes these two criteria go hand-in-hand, and sometimes one is decided before the other. A long-standing interest in either a particular topic or an ethnic group may well help us decide who and what to study: "I chose my ethnic group because I am a member of it, and I wanted an objective way in which to learn more about it and about myself"; "I chose my group because of personal naiveté and the connected genuine interest in learning about a different group." Several practical aspects should also be considered in our decision-making process: How easily will we be able to make contacts within our chosen ethnic group? Do our would-be informants live close to us, that is, is transportation to their area a problem? Do we anticipate any difficulty in having them discuss the topic we wish to investigate? Are we ourselves truly interested in learning about the topic we are considering for investigation? Do we think we will feel comfortable working among the group of people with whom we plan to work?

None of these questions are necessarily simple ones nor are they likely to be answered definitively prior to beginning fieldwork. However, basic questions such as these force us to think through our plan of action and change it from the start largely according to "gut" feelings. Getting started on our fieldwork *early* (we had only a few months to complete it) was the best way to discover any serious difficulties in working with a chosen group and a chosen topic; and, at this beginning stage, we could even make the necessary "large" changes, that is, choose a new group or topic (see Map 1 for the locations of the groups studied for this volume).

As our fieldwork progressed, we also made necessary minor changes in our anticipated approach to our study, and it is these changes that make fieldwork challenging and exciting. They come about for many reasons. Aside from practical considerations, our informants may say or do something which leads us into a new line of investigation that we never before thought pertinent to our study. Classmates working with a similar ethnic group or on a similar topic may learn something from their informants that sparks our own curiosity to discover if the same thing is being exhibited in words or in actions by our informants. No matter what the source of curiosity, we realize that flexibility and patience are important personal attributes vital to any fieldwork.

Because friendships were formed, withdrawing from the field was difficult. It was important to remember not to leave our informants dangling in any way. The unwritten rule of anthropology states that our relationships with them are always meant to be reciprocal. Just how that reciprocity is achieved is up to the discretion of the anthropologist and his or her informant. Sometimes it may simply be that the friendship is maintained beyond the time of the project itself. In other cases, the anthropologist may provide some service such as babysitting, tutoring, or arranging an introduction to a potential employer. Whatever the arrangement is, the intention is for the anthropologist to recognize, in a substantive way, that the information provided by the informant is valuable.

The reciprocal relationship between fieldworker and member of his community is particularly pronounced when each is from the same national culture and even more so if some subcultural membership is similar. We discovered that simply "listening" to our informants was significant to them, a point raised by Ablon (1982) about research in America by Americans. On a more theoretical note, our concern to do cultural analysis was probably not compromised by the common "inside" status enjoyed by most participants in our research projects.

The fieldwork techniques used most frequently were participant observation and the ethnographic interview. The details about how these techniques were used will appear in the relevant context of each chapter that follows. In general, these techniques, among other more formal ones, were the most informative given our interest in cultural analysis, particularly from the "insider's" perspective and time restraints.

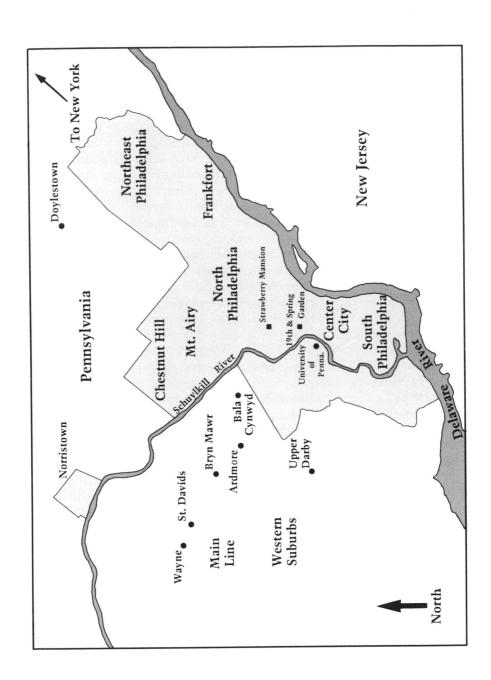

The thesis itself was also a challenge for most of us because it represented the longest, most detailed paper of our undergraduate careers. The essays ranged in length from 40 to 125 pages. This created a considerable editorial undertaking for us all, particularly the decision about how best to "pare down" our study for publication. We were allowed much flexibility in the presentation of our material, which also made the task of editing more difficult. The issue of comparability of the papers will be addressed specifically in the Conclusion to this volume. Nevertheless, we all had to include certain requisite information, such as our theoretical orientation, methodology, and evaluation of the preexisting literature on our topic. Beyond this basic framework, however, we were free to do as we pleased.

The following studies were selected from four years' worth of student theses (approximately sixty-five students participated). The editors used a number of selection criteria. First of all, we chose those that represented the wide variety of ethnic groups covered by our studies. Secondly, we selected those that touched on important theoretical issues pertaining to ethnicity. Some essays were picked because they also demonstrated the successful employment of a particular methodological technique, and others represented a unique grasp of the relevant theoretical issues. In short, we have tried to provide the reader with a sense of both the quality of work done in our class and the range of material covered without compromising the more general objective of contributing to the fund of ethnographic work on American ethnic groups through original, firsthand field research material.

Part I

Black and WASP in American Cultural Experience
The Invisible Ones

"Black" and "white" are central to the Black-American (African-American) perception of the group's experience of life in the United States. Racism and associated political and economic issues are pervasive themes in African-American novels, art, politics, and so forth, in ways that are barely known among "white" (Anglo) Americans. Although African-Americans need to take notice of the Anglos, the reverse is not the case. It is little wonder that African-Americans recognize racially different faces, whereas Anglos only show good recall for white Anglo faces (R. Malpass, personal communication). The "invisible" African-American ethnic experience is, of course, seen from the perspective of Anglos, many of whom still consider African-Americans to be devoid of anything "positive," such as a strong cultural tradition. Indeed, the "pathological" or deficit model of African-American life is commonly held—even among academics. One well-known statement, for example, which is repeated here for emphasis, asserts: "It is not possible for Negroes to view themselves as other ethnic groups viewed themselves because—and this is the key to much in the Negro world—the Negro is only an American and nothing else. He has no values and culture to guard and protect" (Glazer and Moynahan 1963:53).

African-Americans are, in fact, when compared to Anglos, bicultural. Du Bois (1903) long ago recognized that African-Americans operate in two cultural idioms, one held by most Americans and the other by those who have African roots. Du Bois's concept of "double consciousness" refers to the individuals' experience of African-American music, folklore, and religion, for example, within the context of a repressive racist society. Du Bois concludes: "One ever feels his twoness—an American, a Negro: two souls, two thoughts, two unreconciled strivings, two warring ideas in one body" (1903:17).

The second chapter in this section shows that, when a historical comparative method is applied to the African-American ethnic experience, it then becomes necessary to argue that the term 'African-American' is culturally appropriate. There are now demonstrated African cultural components in the African-American experience that are discussed in the essay as a background for appreciation of the cultural significance of food practices among Philadelphia African-Americans and Kenyans.

The first chapter in this section represents the flip side of the cultural coin described above. Many Americans, including African-Americans, are "imperfectly" socialized into the dominant value orientation of American cultural life: for example, the WASP ethnic culture. Although this culture is standardized through formal education, a national language, preferred national racial features, television advertisements, and the like, it shares a kind of "invisibility" with African-American ethnic culture. Whereas for African-Americans "invisibility" is due to a pejorative attitude toward blacks and their life-style, among WASPs invisibility stems from the view that their culture is a kind of "absolute" good, not to be compared within a relative context as simply one life-style among numerous *ethnic* alternatives. Second, WASP culture is very much an "elite" one, such that "rituals of exclusion" and secrecy are prominently exercised to maintain power. Social and cultural boundaries are sharply enforced, sometimes through such things as racial jokes, which serve to perpetuate relations of power through exclusion (A. Cohen 1974). Wealth as an ideal and material possessions are also highly valued.

Thus, the interpretation of WASP ethnic culture is intimately connected to one's understanding of social stratification, particularly class and caste, just as is so for the African-American experience. Sooner or later, as many writers have pointed out, the American national experience can be reduced to issues of race and class. This is most clearly seen in the "black-white" dialectic— some of which will be addressed in the following pages. The WASP culture is strongly associated with upper-class status, whereas African-American foods, for example, cannot be fully understood apart from issues of slavery and poverty.

3

Exclusivity in an Ethnic Elite
Racial Prejudice as Boundary Maintenance

Elizabeth R. Ameisen

Although the focus of anthropology has traditionally been on non-Western cultures, in recent years the discipline has changed and begun to expand its scope to include Western people as well. While it is certainly true that much of the work done in this "new" Western context, particularly in the United States, has continued to deal with those outside the mainstream, the so-called "minority," or ethnic, populations, some anthropological research has begun to explore the "majority," or dominant, culture. In the United States, this group, White Anglo-Saxon Protestants (WASPs), has been described most notably in *Yankee City*, by W. Lloyd Warner et al. (1963), and *The New Englanders of Orchard Town, U.S.A.*, by Fischer and Fischer (1966). As these two texts suggest, WASP culture is particularly well entrenched in the area known as the industrial Northeast. Few places within this region have, however, achieved the reputation that the Philadelphia Main Line and its particular WASP culture have acquired over the years.

Despite the notoriety of the Main Line, largely because of the area's affluence, no serious research has been done on its residents and their specific cultural configuration. To date, published material about life in the area has been of a general nature and is best characterized as unsystematic (Draper 1980; Mallowe 1983). In an effort to rectify this situation, a short-term anthropological field research project was designed and conducted. The purpose of this fieldwork was to obtain an overall understanding of the ethnic culture of Main Line WASPs, with special emphasis placed on its perpetuation. This chapter will present the data collected for this project and will examine it with respect to certain ethnographic and theoretical criteria.

Theoretical Issues

The Transmission of Racial Prejudice

Although pursuing the aforementioned comprehensive picture of WASP Main Line culture, the fieldwork here focuses on one particular cultural aspect: the process of cultural transmission, or socialization. Specifically, it examines the transmission of racial prejudice on the Main Line. There is an abundance of literature on racial prejudice in general as well as on its transmission specifically. These topics have been analyzed by psychologists, educators, historians, political scientists, and sociologists, as well as anthropologists. The result has been a truly interdisciplinary achievement, with major works such as Porter's *Black Child, White Child* (1971) incorporating the available information from all fields in order to present as complete a picture as possible. In the interest of brevity, acknowledgment will simply be made here of the many other works done on racial attitudes in America throughout this century. Of note is a book by Mildred A. Schwartz, *Trends in White Attitudes toward Negroes* (1967), and a volume edited by John Brigham and Theodore Weissbach, *Racial Attitudes in America* (1972). Each of these addresses shifts in racial attitudes in recent years with the development of the civil rights movement and desegregation issues.

Contrary to earlier beliefs that racial attitudes were "based on 'consciousness of kind,' were innate rather than learned," Lasker's work *Race Attitudes in Children* (1929) and that of others (Trager and Yarrow 1952; Trubowitz 1969) represent the development of a "learning theory" with regard to prejudice (Porter 1971:1). This shift has been upheld by all the recent research. The goal of the studies today is to determine when the effects begin and how exactly each particular factor contributes to the process. According to Porter, the consensus is that the preschool years (especially age four) are the significant period at least as far as racial awareness is concerned (1971:1). But she and other researchers (Williams and Morland 1976; McDonald 1970) assert that studies concerning the influences of sociocultural variables are lacking. Porter maintains that "we have no clear picture of the influence of social class, age, sex, contact with the opposite race, and shade of skin color on the formation of racial attitudes in young children" (1971:2).

It is with regard to these sociocultural criteria that the fieldwork described below will be particularly important. Because the WASP Main Line is almost exclusively middle and upper class, research on the social-class variable was made possible. In addition, the racial homogeneity of the Main Line facilitated the investigation of the effects of contact with other racial groups on the development of racial attitudes.

Perpetuation of an Ethnic Elite

Beyond the preliminary investigation of the relationship between the Main Line and the variables described above, particularly social class and out-group contact, the issue of function becomes significant. In other words, what purpose does racial prejudice serve for the people who transmit it? Recent work in the area of anthropological definitions of ethnicity and ethnic groups (*The New Ethnicity: Perspectives from Ethnology*, Bennett 1975) introduces new concepts that relate directly to this research on the Main Line.

If, as Levy puts it, an ethnic enclave is "a group of people who share fundamental cultural values expressed by unified cultural forms," then the process of transmitting negative racial attitudes on the Main Line takes on entirely different significance. In short, the transmission of these attitudes may reflect a conscious, or unconscious, attempt by one ethnic group to keep itself distinct from another such group (Levy 1975:26). An example of this type of separation can be found in A. Cohen's book *The Politics of Elite Culture* (1981). This work is especially important here because it adds the necessary dimension of status inequality. As Cohen defines it, "an elite is a collectivity of persons who occupy commanding positions in some important sphere of social life, and who share a variety of interests arising from similarities of training, experience, public duties, and way of life" (1981:xvi). He goes on to say that, as the elite "matures," its members begin to act together as a whole, in opposition to others outside their group. Ultimately, the elite, must socialize their children to their ways in order to maintain its elevated position (1981:xvi–xvii). The combination of the ethnic and elite aspects may be the most appropriate way of characterizing Main Line WASPs.

If they are culturally homogeneous, especially with regard to race, how is this isolation maintained? Or, rather, is it maintained actively by exclusionary processes or passively by other as yet unknown mechanisms? By looking at basic cultural patterns, for example marriage rules or postmarital residential constraints, information can be obtained about the boundaries of Main Line WASP culture. In a more general sense, the research has come full circle back to the original problem: to describe Main Line WASP culture.

In summary, the research sought three different sorts of information: data of a general, descriptive nature about WASPs on the Main Line and their culture; material on socialization processes, especially those that pertain to the transmission of racial prejudice; and information that examines the relationship between the development of particular racial attitudes and the maintenance of ethnic-group boundaries. With these goals in mind, we will now begin to examine the data on Main Line Culture.

Main Line WASPs

History

The history and development of the territory west of the city of Philadelphia, known as the Main Line, are well documented:

> The "Welsh Barony," as its first white settlers called the 30,000 acre tract they carved out of the wilderness in 1682, held little future in the eyes of William Penn and his compatriots who founded the City of Brother Love. (O'Leary 1955:3)

> The original settlers, nine men and one woman, bought their land from Penn himself. They were his "friends and social equals, brought up in manor house and castle, schooled in English, Latin, and Greek. . . . All, like Penn, were converts to the Quaker religion, "The Society of Friends." (Draper 1980:37)

Although the Welsh Quakers did become the first Main Line white residents, this territory continued in turmoil. There were boundary disputes through Revolutionary times right up until 1790 because "half of the Main Line fell within the limits of Philadelphia county" (O'Leary 1955:5). The Welsh settlers were joined in the 1750s by English, and then, German, groups—each of which claimed a part of the Main Line as their own. Settlement stopped during the Revolutionary War because much of the Main Line fell in between the warring troops.

"In 1795 the first macadamized turnpike in the world, the Lancaster Road, was opened" (O'Leary 1955:7). The new road cut through the Main Line and provided access for more people, but it was not until after 1832 when the Columbia Railroad, later the Pennsylvania Railroad, was constructed that more families made the Main Line their permanent home. Before the railroad's arrival, "the only wealthy Philadelphia families who went there were a few whose ancestors had been Welsh Quaker settlers, and who spent quiet summers there on their family farms" (Draper 1980:16). The railroad, in order to promote itself, encouraged development, and several hotels (notably the Bryn Mawr Hotel, now the Baldwin School, and the defunct Haverford and Wayne hotels) and schools were erected. "Finally several major stockholders and officers of the railroad, Mr. Cassat, Mr. Morris, Mr. Drexel, and others took the plunge and built elaborate houses along their line" (Draper 1980:17). Gradually, others in Philadelphia society followed the lead, and the Main Line developed.

Cultural Development

From the extensive historical documentation on the founding of the Main Line, we can glean very little about cultural traditions. Two things, however, can be deduced from the material available. First, it can be seen that certain residents can trace their roots back to the original group of Welsh settlers. As late as 1922, J. W. Townsend found that "some of the present residents have their deeds signed by William Penn, while their country places are called by Welsh names of places from which their ancestors migrated" (1922:7). Second, although the first real wave of permanent residents that followed the railroad out to the Main Line was made up of railroad executives, the culmination of this exodus occurred when the majority of Philadelphia society had joined these first families. Thus, the modern Main Line was founded by people who came from upper-class, wealthy traditions—whether they were Welsh aristocrats or Philadelphia's First Families—names such as Cassat, Austin, Whitney, Wharton, and Morris. Beyond this limited information, there is little data on the cultural development of the Main Line.

What material there is pertaining to the cultural characteristics of the Main Line can be found in rather abstruse sources. In 1955 the local newspaper, *The Main Line Times*, put out a compact volume entitled *This Is the Main Line*. A five-page chapter dealing with "culture and art" is sandwiched in between others concerning zoning, fire and police protection, taxes, public utilities, and water. More recently (1980), a seventy-page book of childhood recollections was published by a woman who grew up on the Main Line during the 1930s. She provides some information about rituals, such as weddings, but the bulk of her material is thoroughly random and subjective (Draper 1980). Another recent publication deals with a life-style known popularly as "preppy." The book, entitled *The Official Preppy Handbook* (Birnbach 1980), takes a satirical look at this particular cultural manifestation, which is often associated with the Main Line. This volume makes numerous specific references to the Main Line and its institutions: private preparatory schools like the Agnes Irwin School and the Episcopal Academy (1980:54–55); colleges like Bryn Mawr (118); rituals such as the Assembly and the Charity Ball (37); clothing stores to purchase the specified attire, the Talbots, Carroll Reed, Lilly Pulitzer, Joseph A. Bank Clothiers, and Eddie Bauer (154–155); and even restaurants like H. A. Winston & Co., Hillary's, and the Rusty Scupper (176–177). This source deals very generally, albeit humorously, with the affluent "preppy" life-style. Although the purpose of the book was to describe the more widespread phenomena found throughout the United States, it does discuss certain aspects of the Main Line. Consequently, it may be viewed as preliminary data and introduces an additional variable for this research endeavor. In sum, the cultural material on the WASP Main Line introduces numerous specific criteria: affluence, traditionalism, religion, and even, "prep," but nothing approaching a synthesis of these variables exists.

In actuality, the most abundant source of information about Main Line culture comes not from these factual texts but, rather, from the numerous novels and plays that depict this particular cultural manifestation. Novels such as *Main Line Girl*, by Robert Boyd (1957), *Main Line: Philadelphia Novel*, by Livingston Biddle, Jr. (1950), and *Kitty Foyle*, by Christopher Morley (1939), set somewhat forgettable characters and events against the backdrop of life on the Main Line. *Main Line Girl* "is the story of Jeanie Clay, a product of Haverlyn, a Main Line Philadelphia suburb—wealthy, inbred, snobbish, and hypocritical, devoted to 'elite' living, proper matches and addicted to the cocktail hour" (Boyd 1957: book jacket). The author of *Main Line: A Philadelphia Novel*, "Livingston Biddle Jr., grew up along Philadelphia's Main Line. Out of his own experience, he writes about one of America's wealthiest, most traditional communities—suburban Philadelphia, with its proprieties and horse-shows and insurmountable social taboos" (1950: book jacket).

Without a doubt, however, the most well known fictional presentation of the Main Line can be found in Philip Barry's *The Philadelphia Story* (1939). This play contains a description of Main Line WASPs that has contributed to the national, and even international reputation of this culture. This has, of course, been largely because the story was immortalized on film first by Katherine Hepburn; and then later, in the musical version, by Philadelphia's own Grace Kelly. In simple terms, the plot revolves around the impending marriage of a wealthy, Main Line woman to a non-Main Line man. Reporters from a New York scandal sheet have been sent to observe and write about the event. When they arrive, the butler directs them to the sitting room to await the family's arrival:

> Mike: (Entering—gazes about room—notices crystal chandelier) "He said the sitting room. I suppose that's contrasted to the living room, the ballroom—the drawing room—the morning room—the . . . "

> Margaret: "After lunch Sandy must show you some of the sights— the model dairy, and the stables, and the chicken farm—and perhaps there'll be time to run you out to some other places on the Main Line—Devins, Saint Davids. Bryn Mawr, where my daughter Tracy went to college . . . " (1939:27, 40).

The elements that *The Philadelphia Story* present as characteristic of the Main Line are much the same as those introduced in the nonfictional sources: extreme wealth, conservatism, religion, leisure activities like cricket and fox hunting, and, finally, the issue of class. The validity of these literary representations, as well as those from the factual material, will be assessed as a part of my attempt to define accurately the ethnic group known as Main Line WASPs. With regard to these, or any other depictions, we must be careful to notice who uses them. Do Main Line WASPs accept these characterizations as being valid? Or are these images that outsiders perpetuate in order to separate themselves from, or even deprecate, Main Line WASPs? We will return to these questions at a later point. However, they are important ones to raise at the outset because they are basic problems that helped guide the course of my field-work.

Methodology

The goal of this fieldwork was to obtain a considerable amount of data in a relatively brief period of time. The material sought was diverse, and consequently many different fieldwork techniques were employed. To begin with, the traditional anthropological technique of participant observation was used to gather the basic Main Line WASP cultural information. The aim of this technique is "to cover the full extent of the phenomena in each aspect of tribal culture studied, making no difference between what is commonplace, or drab, or ordinary, and what strikes him as astonishing and out-of-the-way" (Malinowski 1984:11). Clearly, the goal, as described by Malinowski, one of the pioneers of this approach, is to look at all aspects of a given culture. His reference to tribal culture can be extended to other cultures as well, with little modification in technique providing that the size of the community is taken into account.

The geographical Main Line is a medium-sized community that, as the name suggests, is linear in shape. It parallels the Pennsylvania Railroad line, known locally as the "Paoli local." The area is made up of approximately twenty small towns, though the core of the geographical Main Line is in the midsection, which includes Haverford, Bryn Mawr, Rosemont, Gladwyne, and Villanova. This section has taken on such importance for the area, and particularly for WASPs, because many of the private schools and social clubs to which these people belong are situated in this vicinity. Although the geographical Main Line would not be considered large for many research projects, given the time constraints of my work, it was necessary to limit the focus. Consequently, the bulk of the research was conducted in this middle area. This is not to say that the entire region was not considered, but because, as has already been mentioned, many of the key institutions are situated in the mid-part, this area received more attention.

As Malinowski implied in the statement above, a fundamental aspect of the participant observation process is what might be called "submersion." Knowledge of special events such as funerals or weddings must be coupled with the commonplace, day-to-day occurrences that constitute daily life. As a researcher, I was especially fortunate because I live, and grew up, right in the midst of the community I was studying. Although this may have some drawbacks, which I will discuss in a moment, this was, I feel, important in that it enabled me to participate in and view the daily lives of Main Line WASPs in a particularly thorough manner. To give just a partial

The Bryn Mawr Hotel, designed by Frank Furness, was a summer resort for well-to-do Philadelphians in the 1880s. Today the building houses the Baldwin School and is a nationally registered historic building. (Courtesy of Elizabeth Ameisen)

list of the places and situations where I was able to work—supermarkets, department stores (including specialty stores like those mentioned previously, such as Carroll Reed's and the Talbots), dry cleaners, PTA meetings, Girl Scout meetings, churches, restaurants, bars, banks, private clubs (like the Merion Cricket Club and the Philadelphia Country Club), and public places (like the YMCA)—demonstrates the advantages of living within one's own community. In addition, I was able to attend special events as well: many parties of all types and sizes, a high school reunion, a bridal shower, a baby shower, a Christening, and funeral as well as wedding rituals. One may ask why this type of immersion was necessary. For an answer, one must return to Malinowski and the ultimate goal of anthropology: "To describe the total culture of a group of people." But "this description, as much as possible, should be made from the point of view of the people—i.e. the insider view" (Jones 1982:472).

There is no doubt that anthropology seeks the insider's view of any given culture, but much debate still persists with respect to who can best obtain this sort of information. Jones, in an article entitled "Towards a Native Anthropology" (1982) explains well this conflict within the discipline. In anthropology, American "students are generally taught that a person working among his own people cannot maintain the degree of objectivity desirable, hence research experiences must be gained initially in another culture . . . however, the rule that the student should not work in his own culture seems to be reversed when it comes to the foreign student, the 'native' who is studying for a Ph.D. in the United States. It is an undeniable fact that most African students in American Universities are Africanists who have conducted fieldwork in their own society and are specialists in their own people" (1982:472).

It is difficult to say where or why this obvious bias began, but it has become sufficiently well entrenched, regardless of its origin. It is only fair to admit that native anthropologists may potentially lack objectivity, or be unable to separate themselves from a certain study group. On the other hand, it is equally possible that native researchers might have access to significant information that an outsider would not be in a position to collect. In short, each perspective has its inherent weaknesses and strengths. The important thing to remember is that all anthropologists, if they have been properly trained, will be fully aware of their responsibilities and will compensate whenever necessary.

In addition to the basic anthropological technique, participant observation, two types of interviews were conducted. First, numerous formal interviews were completed: "In this activity the ethnographer sits with an informant for the purpose of developing information on ethnographically significant points" (Honigmann 1970:71). In keeping with the project's purpose, several different types of people were interviewed formally. With regard to the general cultural material, many individuals were interviewed—among them, adults, teenagers, and children, professionals, business people, students, and religious leaders. Interviews with teachers, school administrators, librarians, ministers, and other adults who are involved with children were undertaken to get data on the socialization aspect, as well as the racial variable (Pelto and Pelto 1978:71–75).

The other type of interview, known as informal interviewing, also played a critical role in this ethnographic endeavor. Agar uses several criteria to distinguish the informal, from the formal interview: "First, you don't have a written list of questions. It's also informal because you are not taking on the formal role of interrogator . . . finally, it's informal because it happens in many different situations besides one-on-one isolated talk . . . the general idea distinguishing formal from informal interviews is, again, the idea of control" (1980:90). Most importantly, informal interviews were conducted with a number of Main Line children (1980:89–111). A handful of these youngsters were interviewed repeatedly, or at length, and served as key informants, providing information about both the culture and the private educational system on the Main Line. The formal and informal interview situations each provided different, albeit complementary, insights.

Several life histories were taken, in addition to these other methods. As described by Pelto and Pelto, life histories provide extensive, in-depth, personal accounts of individuals that can then be compared to other general material (1978:75): "To the objection that life-history data frequently cannot be checked against objective observations of real behavior, he replies that very frequently a chief anthropological concern is the patterning of peoples' beliefs and conceptualizations of past events, rather than the truth or falseness of these accounts. From that point of view, life-history materials may be more useful for examining the patterning of general values, foci of cultural interests, and perceptions of social and natural relationships than as true histories" (1978:76). In this instance, patterning is precisely the aim, specifically, to gain some long-term information on the Main Line: how things have come to be the way they currently are. This type of data was also evaluated with respect to socialization processes because, it was assumed, life histories might provide some important and unique insights.

Finally, extensive surveying was done on the Main Line (Agar

1980:61, 75). These surveys were conducted in several locations: private schools, churches, Scout troops, clubs, and neighborhoods. The goal of these surveys was to determine the racial makeup of these collectives. The information derived from these surveys will bear directly on the issue Porter (1971) raised about the effect of interracial contact on attitude formation.

In summary, several research methods were used to obtain the requisite information for this project. Each method was selected in order to uncover specific material. However, it was the mixture of all these tools that made successful data collection possible. The use of different methods is important, not only for obtaining a breadth of information, but also because this enables the researcher to compare, and cross-check for accuracy, any data received from a single, specific source (Pelto and Pelto 1978:67). The anthropological methods for this fieldwork were selected carefully and were, for the most part, appropriate for the situation. Any problems or shortcomings in terms of methodology will be discussed as the field research is presented below.

The Main Line

What's In a Name?

At the outset, the most basic problem was simply to define the Main Line. There is no doubt that one definition is that it is a geographical area: to be precise, a western suburb of Philadelphia. This definition is universally accepted by people on the Main Line as well as off. At every opportunity—at cocktail parties, in grocery checkout lines, at a local service station, students at school, and parents at home and at work—I asked, in a somewhat simpleminded way: "What is the Main Line?" This was often an ice-breaking question, one that provoked further conversation. But the initial response was always the same: "The 'Main Line' is a term representing a geographical area (western suburb of Philadelphia)," or it is "a name for a geographical area of suburban Philadelphia," or it is "a suburb located on the outskirts of Philadelphia." Beyond this initial agreement, however, every other definition was subject to dispute.

Because there was such a consensus with respect to the geographical description, one might think that there would also be a widespread understanding of how the region obtained its unique name. Yet, this is simply not the case. As stated earlier in this chapter, the area sprang up along the Pennsylvania Railroad line. The name was derived from the expression that described the run from Philadelphia out to Paoli, Pennsylvania, as "the main railroad line." It was shortened, and the area became known as "the Main Line." Although this etymology is well recorded, many of my informants were either completely ignorant of it or have chosen to disregard it as being significant with respect to defining the Main Line today.

The distinction between those who mentioned the historical relationship between the name and the railroad and those who did not was, for the most part, age-related. None of the younger people, aged twenty-five or under, mentioned or implied that the railroad was, in any way essentially related to the Main Line. In part, this may be explained by the fact that the railroad does not play the role in the lives of youngsters in the area today that it previously did. What with the expressway and other easy access routes into the city of Philadelphia, and the fact that every Main Line family has its own car (usually two) for local driving, the train is simply not used the way it once was. But this divergence also seems to reflect a difference in the perceptions of disparate age groups, particularly with respect to this question. Interestingly enough, though none of the young people mentioned the railroad, virtually all of my older informants did. All persons over the age of forty included some reference to the railroad in their current definition of the Main Line: "The 'Main Line' originally developed as towns grew up along the Pennsylvania Railroad from Philadelphia to the west" (a forty-year-old WASP female); "The name was created by the Pennsylvania Railroad operating a local train system to Philadelphia" (a sixty-one-year-old WASP male); or, "Originally towns located along the primary route (i.e.: 'Main Line') of the Pennsylvania Railroad from Philadelphia to western Pennsylvania" (a forty-eight-year-old WASP male). Unlike the younger group, the elder people stressed the importance of this particular historical relationship. It may simply be that older people are more cognizant of historical factors. However, it seems more likely that, to this group, the development of the name is synonymous with the development of the culture on the Main Line.

Affluence

Although all my informants described the Main Line as a particular geographical area, many of them defined it also as a specific cultural configuration: "The Main Line is more than just a place or area, it is an environment and a way of life (a form of society)" (a twenty-five-year-old Catholic female); it is "a name for a geographical area, and a mind set" (a forty-five-year-old Irish Catholic male); it is "an attitude of social superiority" (a twenty-six-year old WASP female). Some characterize it as "a way of life," "a set of ethics," or "a set of values." Attitudes about the way of life are mixed, among people living there and those who do not as well, and frequently people on either side expressed their feelings loudly and strongly. In an effort to determine exactly what the way of life consists of, we will begin to examine some of the characteristics mentioned in the literature listed above, as well as variables brought up in the field.

The most frequently cited aspect of Main Line culture in all research contexts is the area's affluence. Over and over again, the issue of wealth and especially ideas about money—how to spend it, how it should be made, how much is necessary, and the like—were brought up by my informants. It is impossible not to notice that the Main Line is a wealthy area. At a recent auction, when some prime land was made available by the Lower Merion School District, purchasers paid $50,000 per acre. Advertisements in the local newspaper's real estate section offer homes of various types and sizes in the area, but few fall below $100,000, with the average house price being about $225,000. It is not unusual, however, to see listings of between $600,000 and sometimes upwards of $1,000,000 for a single-family home. Add to this the cost of daily maintenance. I was told by one informant that it cost her over $13,000 to supply one year's heat (just fuel oil, no other utilities) for her thirty-two room mansion.

As I have already mentioned, every family I came in contact with throughout my fieldwork had a car; in fact, most had two cars. It is not unusual for a family with teenage children to have many cars. One family has a total of eleven, with only eight family members, including in-laws, able to drive. Of course, those families who own only two cars and those with more invariably drive very expensive, most often, foreign brands. Currently, BMWs are the rage, followed by Audis, Volvos, Volkswagens, Mercedes-Benz, Porsches, and Jaguars. The most popular American-made car on the Main Line is the Chrysler Le Baron Town and Country station wagon, though many Cadillacs can still be seen on Lancaster Avenue. Just to give some guidelines with respect to the cost of these cars, a new 1984 model 320i, customized BMW (with such features as computerized controls and internal and external thermometers) sold for $54,000 in round numbers. The newest Porsche Carrera convertible sold for between $42,000 and $45,000 depending on the extras.

Private schools in this area cost on the average over $5,000 per year for upper-school (grades nine to twelve) students, and the private nursery schools charge more than $1,000 for a five-morning-per-week program (see Table 1 for a complete listing of school fees). This is not to mention the cost of clothing (usually designer), food, club memberships, household help, and medical as well as all other normal expenses.

Table 1. Comparative Educational Data: Main Line Private Schools

School	Tuition	Total Enrollment	Minority Enrollment	Faculty Total	Minority Faculty
Nursery					
A	$1,028	280	4* (1.4%)	22	0
B	$1,450	215	10 (4.7%)	25	0
C	$1,260	60	0	12	0
D	$1,210	60	0	7	0
K-12					
E	$5,060	989	not avail.	116	not avail.
F	$4,700	860	not avail.	85	not avail.
G	$4,975	556	11 (3.1%)	59	0
H	$5,100	555	8 (1.4%)	82	0
I	$5,100	488	42 (8.6%)	82	0

*Approximate number
Source: See text.

It was actually difficult to confirm in statistical terms the extent of the Main Line's affluence compared with other communities throughout the country. While doing my research, a particular statistical comparison, based on 1980 Census Bureau figures, was quoted repeatedly. The census figures apparently were used to compare zip codes to per capita income levels. Several people mentioned the study in passing, saying that the Main Line was in the top ten wealthiest areas in the country. Three informants stated categorically that the zip code for the town of Gladwyne, Pennsylvania, which is 19035, had the highest per capita income in the entire United States. One informant said Gladwyne was actually the fourth highest recorded, the only place in the entire Northeast to make the top ten, and was surpassed only by three communities in California: Beverly Hills, Bel Air, and Palm Springs. All four of these informants attributed the information to a newspaper article, though they differed with respect to which newspaper had contained the piece. Two said it was in the *New York Times*, one the *Philadelphia Inquirer*, and the fourth was unsure. My attempt to view this article in these two sources was unsuccessful.

In an effort to confirm the information in another manner, I examined the financial statistics from the 1980 census, but this did not begin to clarify the situation. I discovered that census figures are not evaluated in terms of zip codes (which are merely a numerical way of sorting for postal delivery), but rather by much larger groupings: cities, with a certain minimum population; counties; boroughs; and states. The smallest, bounded, legal configuration that appears in census figures is the township. Although it is possible to look at the per capita income by township, this is done by state, rather than across the country. In order to make such a comparison myself, I would have needed to have access to all fifty individual state census volumes, which I did not. Ordinarily, a library has only its own state and perhaps one or two other surrounding states. In addition, the Main Line is a geographical region that is comprised of numerous towns, and actually parts of it belong to different townships.

The most centralized, and that which contains the town of Gladwyne, is Lower Merion Township. Looking at these figures proved helpful in that the median income for families in 1979 was $38,129, surpassed only by one other township in the state, Upper St. Clair Township (Census Bureau figures, August 1983: Vol. 40, pp. 38–44). Comparison of population figures for the two townships, however, reveals an important factor: the total population for Lower Merion Township was 59,651 (the second highest population in the entire state), but Upper St. Clair had only 19,023 citizens. When we turn to the mean income figures, the picture changes considerably. The mean family income in Lower Merion Township in 1979 was $51,608, by far the highest in the state. Despite the fact that these figures are different from those presented by my informants, they do indicate that, at least within the state of Pennsylvania, Lower Merion is a very wealthy community.

One of my informants (a twenty-five-year-old Catholic female

Main Liner) summed up the relationship between wealth and the Main Line: "Although I understand that it [the Main Line] developed as an area from which upper-class Philadelphians could escape the evils of a growing city, it has become more than just a place to live. It has evolved into a way of life and a type of thinking. On the Main Line, values are high with the motto being 'a good life requires a good education, a respectable job, and a deserving place in society.' Of course this suggests that only the rich live on the Main Line. We know this is not true, but only the rich live the Main Line way of life."

Class Structure

Perhaps the greatest philosophical dilemma with respect to the Main Line revolves around the question of class. The original development of the area was accomplished by wealthy, aristocratic Welsh Quakers; and then, later, the upper class from Philadelphia, particularly the railroad moguls. There is little doubt that these families were wealthy, but they were also an undisputed part of the upper class in America. Before proceeding, it seems necessary to provide at least an initial, working definition of the phrase "upper class." To use Baltzell's terminology, there are "two aspects of high class position, an *elite* and an *upper-class*. The *elite* concept refers to those *individuals* who are the most successful and stand at the top of the *functional* class hierarchy. . . . The *upper-class* concept, then, refers to a group of *families*, whose members are descendants of successful individuals (elite members) of one, two, or three or more generations ago. These families are at the top of the *social class* hierarchy; they are brought up together, are friends, and are intermarried one with another; and, finally, they maintain a distinctive style of life and a kind of primary group solidarity which set them apart from the rest of the population" (1958:6–7).

We can look at one family, the Biddle family, to provide an example of this upper-class phenomenon. The first members of the family emigrated to America from London in 1681. They were William and Sarah Kempe Biddle, and they brought with them their two children, William aged twelve and Sarah aged three (N. Biddle 1931:3). The successors of this first family came into prominence by the time of the Revolutionary War. Among the signatures on the Stamp Act of 1765 were those of Owen and Clement Biddle (the great-grandsons of William and Sarah). When the war finally came, several Biddles took leadership roles. Clement Biddle, in particular, was a colonel and worked closely with his friend George Washington (Baltzell 1958:42–77). Between 1754 and 1923, sixty-three Biddle men served the United States in the military, many of them becoming commissioned officers and receiving decorations.

The Biddles were also involved in other important endeavors. Not long after the end of the War of 1812, "in 1816, Congress chartered the Second Bank of the United States" (Baltzell 1958:89). Following several years of organizational problems, "President Monroe appointed his friend, Nicholas Biddle, to its presidency in 1823. . . . As President of the Second Bank of the United States, Nicholas Biddle was the czar of American finance for more than a decade" (1958:89–90). In a listing of "Proper Philadelphia Families and their elite Members" from 1682 to 1940 as drawn from the *Dictionary of American Biography* and *Who's Who* (1940), nine Biddles were included:

Clement (1740–1814)	Merchant, Patriot
James (1783–1848)	Naval Hero
Nicholas (1750–1828)	Naval Hero, Literature & Pres of Second Bank
A. J. Drexel	Author, Marine, Pugilist
A. J. Drexel Jr.	Diplomat
George	Artist
Francis	Lawyer, New Dealer
Gertrude	Civic Leader
Clement M.	Merchant

The Biddles typify both the elite and the upper class as characterized by Baltzell (1958:72).

According to a forty-five-year-old Catholic male, the first thought of the Main Line "is of both wealth and the upper class, then of large estates with maids, butlers, and gardeners—of private schools and exclusive clubs. All this is a tradition of many generations." Although the statement by this informant is accurate, things have changed on the Main Line. For the most part, the current descendants of the founding families do still live there, but they must now coexist with many newcomers. Essentially, the large estates have become too expensive to maintain, and consequently have been parceled off and developed. Of course, the two groups have one significant element in common: money. But, to return to our original dilemma, what is the relationship between money and class on the Main Line?

There is considerable conflict of opinion with regard to this question. Many of my informants felt it was important to make a distinction between the two: "By and large, the people are upper middle class or quite wealthy" (a twenty-two-year-old Jewish female). The term "nouveau riche" was mentioned over and over again, as well as criticisms of what the term implies, such as "frivolous," "ostentatious," and "designer clothes." In an effort to understand the distinction, if any, between the two factors, and who makes the distinction, I began to ask my informants to define each. Those who made the distinction were most often people who have resided on the Main Line for more than one generation. In fact, no WASPs that I encountered failed to make this distinction, even if they did not consider themselves to be upper class.

In talking with young people, this division was especially obvious. Children who have themselves grown up on the Main Line, but whose parents did not, mostly equate upper-class status with wealth. I asked one of my informants: "Does being rich mean you are upper class?" She responded, "Upper class is really a state of mind, but being rich is what lets you get to that place" (a sixteen-year-old Catholic female). Her response was representative of the wealthy newcomers. One of her classmates, however, felt differently: "A lot of these new kids think they are upper class but they're not. All they have is a whole lot of money. And besides, they aren't upper class because they don't know how to act" (a sixteen-year-old WASP female).

The class issue was one of the most difficult problems I encountered in my research. The WASPs on the Main Line feel they have a monopoly on the upper class; and the newcomers, most of whom are not ethnically WASP but rather Jews or Catholics of various ethnic backgrounds, assume that wealth is the sole criterion for upper-class status. Without addressing the issue of prejudice completely at this point, it is safe to say that it is operating on both sides of this debate. Because I was seeking an emic perspective, I looked more closely at what Main Line WASPs felt was relevant rather than at the other groups. To put it somewhat simplistically, Main Line WASPs generally consider themselves to be upper or upper middle class. Few respondents said they were squarely in the middle class. An interesting, new phenomenon has also had an impact on their attitudes about class. Although the non-WASPs frequently equate wealth and upper-class status, the WASPs, many of whom have experienced financial losses over the last twenty years as evidenced by the dismantling of all the old estates, now disassociate financial status with class. So we actually have WASPs with little, if any, fortune left still considering themselves as upper class. In the truest sense of Baltzell's definition, this is correct because the fundamental aspect is diachronic. This would also make it impossible for any other ethnic group to be a part of the Main Line upper class inasmuch as these new groups have only recently become part of the Main Line.

As a forty-six-year-old Irish Catholic male said, "The Main Line is an aristocratic elite social class who have traditionally held the power in Philadelphia. . . . Main Line families have controlled major banks and the railroad as well as the larger cultural institutions. This rule has espoused conservative values and the preservation of its own advantages against the outsider." This informant acknowledged that Main Line WASPs do form an "aristocracy," to use his terminology, and he also introduced a point of view that may explain the failure of WASPs to recognize or accept others into the upper class. For now, we will leave this problem, as we examine the other facts of Main Line culture, but we shall return to this question, and particularly this last informant's perception of the problem, at a later point when more pertinent information has been provided.

Religion

Religion is another significant factor with respect to Main Line culture. The acronym WASP, obviously, contains a reference to religion, namely Protestantism, though it does not make any further distinction. Because Pennsylvania is known as the "Quaker State" and the area around Philadelphia, William Penn's bastion, was founded by groups of Quakers, we know that the original religious influence was from this group. But, in actuality, this influence was at its strongest prior to Revolutionary times.

At the beginning of the eighteenth century, the Quakers were the most significant group numerically in Philadelphia. But, because of the lack of religious constraints in the city, many other people were drawn to this colony. In the 1720s, there was an influx of Scotch-Irish Presbyterians, followed in the 1730s by Germans. According to Baltzell, "The Society's failure to proselytize, and its frequent expulsion of members for 'marrying out of meeting' or for 'disunity,' contributed to its failure to keep pace with the city's growth. By 1750, Philadelphia was the Quaker City in name only; less than one-fourth of its inhabitants were members of the Society of Friends" (1958:238). But the Quakers that remained accumulated significant fortunes in trade and finance. This was the group that built their summer and country homes on the Main Line. Yet, according to Baltzell, there was a conflict of values between the Quaker faith and "the more conspicuous forms of worldly display so dear to the hearts of the aristocratic classes" (1958:240).

As a result, many of the members of this Quaker oligarchy, particularly the second and third generations, changed their church affiliation to the more dramatic and ritualized Anglican church. Penn's own sons had switched to it by the late 1700s. "Towards the middle of the century, it was said in Philadelphia that one could be Christian in 'any church, but not a gentleman outside the Church of England.' After 1750, 'Quakerism had to share wealth and influence with the Church of England. Though never so numerous as the Friends, Presbyterians, or even the Lutherans, the Anglicans became definitely the congregation of wealth, fashion and position'" (Baltzell 1958:240).

A similar transition occurred on the Main Line. The first Quaker Meeting House was built in 1695 and was central to the community throughout this early phase. In 1715 the first Episcopal church was erected. The church, St. David's in Wayne, not surprisingly was composed entirely of Welsh Quakers who left the Meeting House as their peers in Philadelphia had done. Of course, the Main Line itself did not really develop until the mid-1800s, so the church was small and rural. With the arrival of the railroad and the exodus of Philadelphia's upper class, four new Episcopal churches were built on the Main Line: the Church of the Redeemer (1852), the Church of the Good Shepherd (1871), St. Martin's (1887), and St. Asaph's (1888). "The Church of the Redeemer was built on a hill overlooking the old Bryn Mawr Hotel in Lower Merion Township: the construction of these Episcopal churches marked the beginning of the suburban trend" (Baltzell 1958:258–259). In 1860 there were 29 communicants at the Church of the Redeemer. By 1900, there were 318, and finally 831 by 1940. The total number of Episcopalian communicants on the Main Line went from 109 in 1860 to 2,854 by 1940. "By 1920, the urban churches in Philadelphia reached their peak in number of communicants. By 1940, however, the fashionable suburban churches became the center of upper-class Episcopalianism" (1958:261).

By the 1940s, Baltzell contends, churches were not as significant in their parishioners' social lives as they had been in the previous century (1958:236). Yet, an analysis of religious affiliations as related to social class revealed that many of those in the Philadelphia upper class (as designated by their listings in the *Social Register* and *Who's Who*) maintained ties with their churches. After 1940 there is little information about religion on the Main Line until the present work.

What role does religion play in the lives of Main Line WASPs today? This is a difficult question to answer. My informants, of course, identify themselves, and are identified by others, as WASPs. This is a concise ethnic identification, but I wanted to determine if the P (Protestant) in the acronym was still as important as it used to be. Baltzell's discussion of the lessening of religious significance raised this question. Over the last twenty years, if anything, this alienation from religion, throughout the United States, by all faiths, has been accelerated. It was not surprising to me then to discover that religion has a far less obvious role in Main Line WASPs' lives today as well.

This is particularly true among young people. Out of all of this group that I spoke with, only one girl mentioned being religious, and stated that religion and participation in church activities were important to her family and herself. Many people said they went to church only sporadically through the year, and usually on holidays. In large measure, however, the younger informants were dependent upon their parents in terms of religious decisions. If their parents are churchgoers, children have little choice but to go too, albeit often reluctantly.

When individuals do become old enough to exercise their freedom of choice, around eighteen years of age on the Main Line, few continue any religious activity. Of my informants between the ages of eighteen and thirty, none attended church of their own accord. When asked why this is so, respondents gave two basic answers. First, many said they simply did not like going to church: "It's boring!"; "I went all the time as a kid because my parents made me go, but I really don't get anything out of it"; and "You don't have to go to church to be religious." The other answer most frequently given is more closely related to the age of the informants: "I work all week; the only time I have to relax and enjoy myself is the weekend; usually I go out with my friends on Saturday nights and I just don't get up early enough on Sunday to go to church." Essentially, these people feel that they have other priorities at this time in their lives. In both cases, there tends to be a return to church by the late twenties to early thirties. This is generally precipitated by a major life event that occurs during this phase in people's lives. The event, of course, is usually a wedding. Of all those I heard about from my informants (I asked most of them about their own as well as those of their friends and acquaintances), only two were conducted outside of a church.

Marriages fall into two distinct categories on the Main Line today with respect to religious type. The first are those between Main

Line WASPs who share the same faith. Their only dilemma may occur if their families do not belong to the same Main Line congregation. They must then choose between the two or select one of their own. In most instances, the wife's family's church becomes the young couple's. This seems to happen because the wedding is held in the bride's church inasmuch as it is her family that pays all the wedding costs. Among Protestants, children generally follow the faith of their mother, so a couple may be more likely to settle into the wife's congregation.

The second type of marriage involves people who belong to different faiths. I am referring specifically to marriages occurring between two different Protestant faiths. Marriages between Protestants and non-Protestants, especially Catholics and Jews, are often problematic, though they are becoming more and more common. The difficulty with each of these other faiths is that they generally require that children born of such intermarriages be raised in their faith, and may even insist that the spouse convert as well. I came into contact with only one such mixed marriage that did not create severe problems for the couple and their families.

Marriages between persons of different Protestant religions can also cause difficulty. The reason is that one of the two must switch, if not their religion, certainly their allegiance to a particular church. This happens because spouses always belong to the same church. I did not encounter a single couple who attended different churches. This may reflect the modern notion of church membership. In the past, churches determined the size of their congregation by the number of individual members or communicants that they had. Today, all the churches I visited spoke in terms of the number of families in their congregation. In any case, some decision must be made by the couple. As mentioned above, children tend to take the faith of their mother. This may explain the fact that a man tends to switch to his wife's church.

Someone suggested that men may simply be less religious on the Main Line. I found no evidence to support this contention. Rather, men seemed to participate less in the more visible church activities, like rummage sales or church suppers. Instead, they often make their important extra-religious contributions in other ways, such as assisting in financial planning. I feel that a husband switches to his wife's congregation, not because he is less religious, but because it is expected of him for the reasons stated above.

A wedding, as both a cultural and religious milestone, marks the arrival of the couple into, and the acceptance of them by, the adult community. The subsequent birth of the first child cements this relationship, particularly in the church. It is highly uncommon for children not to be christened within the first few months of their lives. Even adults who do not attend church feel compelled to christen their children. Likewise, they tend to return to the church as the children age. One informant put it this way: "I had religious training as a child, and I feel it is my responsibility to provide the same for my children." Because this woman had already told me that she did not like going to church herself, I asked her if she thought her children would feel differently. "They will go because I tell them to; it's an important part of growing up" (a forty-year-old WASP female).

The majority of my informants who were over the age of forty felt themselves to be religious, and so stated. This religiousness manifested itself in several common ways: regular attendance at church; active participation in its affairs; frequent discussion of religion, church functions, and other related concerns; and, finally, conscious efforts to direct the family (children specifically) into religious participation. Religious values are also espoused, but these will be presented in a more general discussion of all sorts of values in the following section. As a result of this strong religious sentiment, the association of religion in general with Main Line culture is very strong among older people. They feel that religion was integral in the founding of and also the current way of life.

Although there is now considerable acceptance of all the Protestant denominations on the Main Line, there is what might be called a hierarchy of social status with respect to church affiliation. Episcopalians and Presbyterians are the two significant denominations numerically, as well as with regard to status. These are followed, in descending order of importance, by Lutherans, Methodists, Quakers, and Baptists.

In addition to this denominational hierarchy, there is a further distinction made within each group: the ranking of individual churches. Church A is the premiere Episcopalian church on the Main Line. Its long history as the church for the upper class has persisted to the present. Currently, it has 750 member families; it is a large and wealthy congregation.

Presbyterian Church B is the most significant within that denomination. Although a neighboring town has its own Presbyterian Church (Church C), one informant told me that "over 75 percent of the Presbyterians in [this town] go to the Presbyterian Church B." He went on to tell me that this has little to do with the churches themselves, but instead reflects the status factor. Church C, a small one that had been founded in 1874, catered particularly to the chauffeurs, gardeners, and other servants employed on all the surrounding estates. Church B had been established only a year earlier, but its congregation was made up of the families who owned, rather than worked on, these great estates.

Despite the fact that these distinctions are no longer valid, each church's philosophy seems to manifest some of its original purpose. The small church has only 150 families and is an informal one with an emphasis on community involvement. Church B has over 3,500 members and is much more highly formalized. These opinions are generally acknowledged by all my informants, but, when discussions become specific, few admit that they join a church for the social status. In talking about others, however, they often state: "Can you believe —— and ——! They drive all the way to Church A just so they can say all week, 'Yes, we belong to *the* Church A.' Or 'I saw so-and-so at Church A on Sunday.' They just want to make connections and appear as if they belong to the Main Line." It is interesting that both Church A and Church B are located in the same town; in fact, they are right around the corner from one another. The location of these two churches supports my contention that the midsection of the Main Line (where these two churches are found) is the critical part and represents the core community of this particular cultural configuration.

In summary, religion and religious activity are in important ways fundamental to Main Line culture. As with other factors, however, their influence and significance are different among disparate age groups. The historical impact of churches on the founding of the Main Line is often emphasized by my informants, as well as their influence on the system of private education. But churches on the Main Line fulfill more than just spiritual needs, they also meet social needs in terms of social status and contact for their parishioners.

Values

Virtually every one of my informants talked about a value system that is unique to the Main Line: "I see it as a representative of ethics. These ethics: (1) date people of equal wealth, (2) marry wealth and in the same faith, (3) attend and throw many parties, (4) dress rich, (5) be a club member, (6) play tennis, (7) vacation always, (8) any other material bull that ignores other's feelings" (a seventeen-year-old WASP male); "Main Line people prefer to send their children to private schools and believe that no matter how sick they are, they should work—very puritan attitude. Main Line people do not believe in being ostentatious with their money, though whatever they buy is the best" (a twenty-two-year-old Jewish female); "Ideals. Snobs. Prestige. Fast cars. Expensive Houses. Prejudices. Money. Good schools. Nuveau Riche [sic]. Luncheons. Designer clothes. Overrated. Transparent. Shallow. Frivolous. Material. Ostentatious. Absurd. Gossipy. Unpardonnable [sic]. An area: No. A way of life for people who do not want to deal with real issues of life" (a sixteen-year-old male); "Nowhere else in the world possibly can one find so many people obsessed with money and material objects. The people here make no bones about this either. The competition is open and vicious. Those who have the best cars and wear the best clothes are popular. . . . Unfortunately this competition takes its toll" (another sixteen-year-old WASP male).

It is difficult to interpret these statements and the values described because they are somewhat contradictory. Some of the informants claim that Main Line people are ostentatious and frivolous, but others state the opposite. Some maintain that they follow the "Protestant work ethic"; others speak of parties, tennis, and other pastimes. Despite these contradictions, certain underlying assumptions do seem to be shared. For one, all the informants emphasized that the accumulation of wealth is critically important to Main Line people in one way or another. The way in which money is spent may differ, whether it be for a fast car or a big house, but everyone is agreed that obtaining money, and lots of it, is an important goal. But how is this different from any other group, for most people want to have money. In fact, an astute foreign-born informant who has lived on the Main Line for approximately twenty years said that it is not the desire to obtain lots of money that is unique to the area. On the contrary, she said, "All that is is the American Dream, which is hardly unique to the Main Line. It's actually the motivating force behind all of American society." Rather, what seems to differentiate Main Liners from others is their *successful* pursuit of wealth.

The old saying "The rich get richer" best describes the situation on the Main Line. Family fortunes accrued over generations are carefully tended to ensure further growth, even at times to the detriment of other seemingly important factors. Take for instance a very well known, well-to-do family that we will call the Baldwins to protect their identity. Mr. and Mrs. Baldwin each came from prominent wealthy families, and their marriage was a match well made. He took over his family's already large holdings and proceeded to increase them significantly over his lifetime. Mrs. Baldwin's family money was divided equally after the death of both her parents, though the family estate (over eighty acres of prime Main Line real estate) was controlled by her older, spinster sister.

Upon Mr. Baldwin's death, he bequeathed $300 million to each of his three children and another sizable portion (I could not obtain this figure) to his wife. Mrs. Baldwin's sister subsequently died, leaving her estate to her sister. The decision was made to sell Mrs. Baldwin's family home to pay off the inheritance taxes. Several investors were interested, but one man wanted to preserve the grounds and mansion, restoring much of the natural beauty. When he had difficulty acquiring funds, he contacted one of the Baldwin children to negotiate an investment opportunity. The Baldwin offspring refused, saying she wanted no part of the investment despite the fact that it would have meant preserving the estate. The way it was described to me, the investment was too small to warrant her involvement. There was no mention made of the fact that the children's grandfather had designed the house, built it, and landscaped the property with trees from around the world—or that the family had lived there for eighty years. Currently, half the property, all woods, has been sold off and developed. The rest of the estate, too, has been sold and is merely awaiting construction to begin. Perhaps it is the attitude involved that distinguishes Main Line values from similar ones elsewhere. It could also be said that it is this attitude which enables the people to accumulate the kind of wealth that others can only dream about.

Traditionalism is a value that is often associated with Main Line life. In political terms, the WASPs are Republicans, but this conservatism is manifested in all areas. Youngsters say that these traditional values are negative. For example: "These ideals are old-fashioned. Individuality of mind, thought, and life are not encouraged. Social progression is looked at as immoral" (a seventeen-year-old Catholic female). How then, does this conservatism manifest itself? In my earlier discussion of religion, I mentioned that certain values were important in this area. Religious tradition has become an important issue recently. Church A, which has been for quite a while the socially significant Episcopalian church on the Main Line, hired a female curate. This caused much upset, and finally resulted in many families permanently leaving the congregation.

In another instance, Presbyterian Church C received a new minister in 1970; the new spiritual leader was a young man who sported long hair and a beard in the spirit of the times. His sermons included lyrics from popular music and references to television. He introduced folk music, played on his guitar, into the services. He rode a motorcycle when he went to visit the sick or the poor. He was an almost stereotypical representation of a 1960s minister. Fourteen years later, he is much loved by his congregation. Earlier, however, quite a few families left the church, never to return. These two incidents demonstrate that Main Line WASPs are conservative, particularly within the sphere of religion. But their resistance to change can be seen in other situations.

To be more specific, we can look at another example of this traditionalism in a social, rather than religious, sphere. The Premiere Club was founded in October 1865 by a group of fifteen young, wealthy Main Line men who wanted to establish a club so they could play cricket competitively. The group was given some property by one of the men's fathers, and the club was founded. It was successful, membership grew, new sports were added, particularly lawn tennis and golf—all of which increased the club's appeal dramatically. Dining facilities were added, and over time the club expanded and became *the* social club on the Main Line. Essentially, everyone who was anyone belonged to this exclusive, private club: "In most major American cities there are one or two distinguished metropolitan men's clubs whose members dominate the social and economic life of the community. Max Weber, on a visit to America more than half a century ago, observed that 'affiliation with a distinguished club is essential above all else. He who did not succeed in joining was no gentlemen'" (Baltzell 1958:336).

In keeping with this tradition, the Premiere Club has remained a men's club up until the present. Although women may use the facilities and participate in club activities (the women have their own bridge club and tennis and field hockey teams), they are not in any sense members. Excerpts from the club's by-laws will demonstrate this point. Article 1, Section 1 (f), states: "'Eligible Women of the Household' means and includes only women who reside permanently in the home of a member or subscriber and who have one of the following relationships to the member or subscriber: wife, unmarried daughter, mother, unmarried sister if her father is not living, unmarried woman relative, mother-in-law, or unmarried sister-in-law if the father-in-law is not living" (Club Book 1953:23). The result has been that widows and divorced women are not permitted to use the facilities even if they have been associated with the club for years. According to Article 1, Section 3 (b): "'Family members.' Adult men and married men under 21 years of age are eligible. They shall have Full Privileges and may obtain Cards of Admission (General) for their wives and Cards of Admission (Limited) for their other eligible Women of the Household" (Club Book 1953:25).

In February 1984, at the annual members' meeting, a formal stag affair featuring everything from an oyster bar to live entertainment, a gentleman introduced the following motion: "Resolved: That the By-Laws and Amendments committee draft revisions to our current by-laws which would provide equal membership status for men and women in the Club. These revisions should be submitted for membership vote not later than the 1985 Annual Meeting. While continuing to maintain different classes of membership related to age, family status, geographical location, and club usage, the revisions should provide for full sharing by men and women in participation, office holding, financial responsibility and voting." Suffice it to say the resolution created a lot of turmoil. Many women, and men, who have for a long time found the club's policies to be unfair, praised the move and the gentleman involved. But there is fairly strong resistance to the the idea among the members and many of their wives. I talked at length with several people concerning this incident, and the proposed changes. One female informant was concerned: "I know that the young women want parity, and want to be able to use the men's facilities. They even want to have a woman on the Board of Governors. But those of us who are a little older are simply glad for the privilege of using the beautiful facilities. We don't need a woman on the Board of Governors. Women are putting themselves in places they don't belong today. The men have the last say. It's a men's club and it should stay that way." Most of the male members concur with this woman's statement; and though the resolution did pass to the By-laws and Amendment Committee, it was believed that it would be resoundingly defeated when it came up for a formal vote in 1985.

At the Country Club, an incident demonstrated that its rules are much the same as the Premiere Club's. A young, upwardly mobile couple joined the Country Club. Although she chose to keep her maiden name upon marriage, the club refused to acknowledge this and referred to her consistently as "Mrs. ———." The young woman and her small child used the pool and athletic facilities often; the husband was not so involved at the club. He died suddenly, leaving the woman a twenty-eight-year-old widow with a young son. Several months after his death, she returned to the club, assuming that she would be able to resume her activities. The management informed her that this was not so, and that her case would have to be reviewed by the board, which told her she would have to reapply for membership. Even though the membership was supposedly for the family, it was clear that the male was really the true member and that the woman was secondary.

In most segments of American society, these attitudes are thought to be outdated. In many cases, these barriers have been broken down by sex-discrimination accusations and lawsuits. On the Main Line, there are differing opinions with respect to these sorts of clubs. In the effort here to obtain an emic perspective, it must be said that the Main Line WASPs enjoy and value these clubs. Even many of the females, who are seemingly at a disadvantage, believe that the situation is as it should be.

This discussion of private clubs introduces another related element that is of particular importance. They have historically been men's organizations, but they have also been exclusively the domain of the WASP. Until very recently, this exclusionary policy was strictly maintained. Throughout my youth, I spent time at the Premiere Club. As a teen, in the years 1970–72, I attended a private dancing class that was, though not affiliated with the club's management, still held in the ballroom. There were no blacks, Jews, or any other ethnic groups besides Main Line WASPs in attendance. I asked my teenage informants today about these classes, which are still quite popular. The policy remains much the same today, though some Jewish girls have been permitted to join. This was seen by Jewish and Christian children alike as tokenism, and consequently a group of Jewish mothers founded their own exclusively Jewish dance class.

I played tennis frequently at the Premiere Club as well, and on one occasion went with a group of friends to have a match. We were all properly attired (the club requires that all-white tennis attire be worn at all times), but when we signed in we were told we could not play and were even asked to leave. We later discovered that we were turned away because one of the girls in our party had a Jewish-sounding name.

Today, the threat of legal action has begun to affect policy, albeit very slightly. I was told by several informants that there are now a handful of Jewish members at the club. Further probing revealed, however, that these members are either only "half" Jewish, that is, not actively Jewish, or merely have what are supposed to be Jewish names. Although these new members were believed necessary to protect the club, there is a fear among the other members that this will cause an influx that will bring about permanent change. An older informant explained how this precise situation had happened at another facility: "We belonged to the swim club for many, many years. Our children grew up there. Several years back though they began to admit Jews and now they've taken over the place. It's unfortunate really; the club just isn't the same. Well, we're no longer members." She would not, even when pressed, specify in what way the Jews had "taken over" or how it was not "the same," but she implied that they were not like WASPs and that they did not have the same standards of behavior or value system. Similar attitudes were either implied or directly expressed when informants were attempting to justify their exclusionary policies.

Exclusivity

The earlier discussion of the relevant theoretical issues examined Porter's work, in which she raises the question of these exclusionary practices (1971:7). Essentially, she explained that little is known about the effects of these policies, or in a more general sense the consequences of segregated living, particularly with reference to the formation of attitudes about different ethnic groups. Her study and this essay both focus primarily on racial distinctions, though I have already touched on attitudes toward Jews, Catholics, and women in my examples from the Main Line. In an effort to quantify the extent of these exclusionary policies, I attempted to complete a thorough survey of the racial composition of many Main Line institutions. Those surveyed were of various types and sizes, but primary emphasis was on those that most directly had an impact upon the children.

Education

WASPs on the Main Line believe that providing a good education for their children is perhaps the single most important responsibility of parents. Although the public school systems there are known to be among the best in the state, and perhaps the country, an extensive set of private schools has developed on the Main Line. As a twenty-six-year-old WASP said, "To be a 'Main Liner' it is imperative to never do as the common folk do. You *mustn't* send your children to public school (no matter how good they may be)."

Main Line children today begin their education at a very early age. Preschools, nursery schools, and Montessori schools all accept children at the age of two and a half, though some schools that have day-care certification take youngsters as early as eighteen months. On the Main Line, because public education does not begin until kindergarten, all preschool programs are privately owned and operated. These schools are variously affiliated. Many are associated with local churches, but others follow specific educational philosophies, particularly those of Maria Montessori and Jean Piaget. Regardless of the type of school, however, they are all private and as a result require that parents pay tuition. These costs vary from school to school, but they are prohibitive for families with small incomes. At Nursery School A, tuition costs are $1,028 for one year; at Nursery School B, $1,210; at Nursery School C, $1,260; and at Nursery School D, $1,450. These schools do offer limited financial aid, but there are not sufficient funds to help more than a few needy families.

In talking to teachers and administrators at these various schools, it was clear in their minds that these high costs were in large measure acting as an unintentional exclusionary mechanism for minority populations on the Main Line. But these educators said another factor was also significant in limiting the number of minority students at these private nursery schools: geographic accessibility. As one informant, the director of a Montessori school, put it, "When you are dealing with very young children, few parents want to put them in schools very far from home. First of all, the children are only in school for about three hours and having to drive long distances is just impractical given this time frame. But also, parents of young children want to be close to their children's school in the event of an emergency." Schools are generally built therefore in, or near, the residential communities they serve. With this in mind, information about the racial composition of these institutions provides not only a picture of them, but also of the neighborhoods in which they are situated.

Nursery School A is made up of twenty-eight classes, each with between 9 and 12 students, approximately 280 total. Minority representation is roughly 1.4 percent. Nursery School D has only 60 students, all of whom are white. Nursery School C has an enrollment of 60 without any minority students. Nursery School B currently has 215 students, though 63 of these are in a pilot elementary program. The preschool program has a 3.2-percent minority enrollment. In addition to the low minority student enrollment, I found no minority faculty in these schools. This information was especially relevant when compared with the policy statements provided in school brochures. Here is one example: School A "was founded on the basis that it would always be open to all children regardless of race, color, or creed" (1984 brochure). (See Table 1, p. 39.)

There are many other nursery schools on the Main Line, but these four were selected for research because they were mentioned most frequently by my informants as the schools where their children are either: currently enrolled; have been enrolled in the past; or will in the future, given a choice, be enrolled. These schools sit atop a hierarchy of private nursery schools and provide much in the way of social status for the students and their families. In large part, this status comes from the fact that these schools act as feeders for the other exclusive private schools. Of course, the prohibitive tuition costs also reinforce the status perception associated with these institutions. It is clear that certain factors act to limit minority enrollment. Despite the fact that the school philosophies do not encourage exclusion in any way, this nonetheless is the end result.

In further pursuing an understanding of the educational climate on the Main Line, research was done on five independent schools, referred to here as Schools E through I. Founded long ago, one each in the years 1785, 1869, 1884, 1888, and 1894, they have been an integral part of the area's development. All of them consist of grades Kindergarten through Twelve; two are coeducational, one is all-male, and two are all-female. As with the preschools, yearly tuitions are considerable, in 1984 ranging from $4,700 to $5,100 (the cost of both of the all-female schools).

My attempts to determine minority enrollment figures were not thoroughly successful. Two schools asserted that such statistics were not available. Of the three schools that provided figures, School H has a total enrollment of 555, including 8 minority students (1.4 percent of the total student body). School G has 556 students, 11 of whom were minorities (3.1 percent). School I has the smallest overall enrollment, with 488 students, 42 (8.6 percent) of whom were minority students. In addition, School I has a Jewish population representing 27 percent of the total, bringing its minority enrollment to 36 percent. When questioned about these figures, the Director of Admissions said, "We look for diversity as much as possible. I'm happy to say there is no such thing as a typical School I girl." Nevertheless, this school is penalized in various ways by the surrounding community for its liberal admittance policy. Parents comparing schools have been known to reject it simply on this basis and make no bones about their reasoning. At the time of my research (1984), there was an incident that drives home the problems School I faces.

During the field hockey season, on the eve of the big game between the two schools, School H had a pep rally. One of the common elements of these events is the making of signs such as "Beat School I" or "Go School H." The students then form a caravan with their cars and drive over to the opposing school, where they display the signs. Coincidentally, the School I Parents' Association happened to be holding its fall meeting that evening, so many of the parents witnessed the events that took place. In keeping with tradition, the caravan arrived at the School I grounds with horns blasting and lights flashing. The noise attracted the parents' attention, and they went out to observe the goings-on. What they saw was quite a shock and fueled a controversy that was still raging six months later. The School H signs did not feature the usual innocuous themes, but instead read "Kill the Jews!"—a reference to a sizable portion of the School I student body. Although shocking to many people, some viewed it merely as an adolescent prank. This was not seen as surprising in light of the attitudes that are commonly attributed to School H.

Given this situation, one might easily ask how and why School I persists in a policy emphasizing diversity. I found that this high percentage was not achieved easily, but has required considerable effort on the part of the administration. School I is the only one that actively recruits minority students. This is done through the faculty of the Philadelphia center city public schools. When teachers feel they have qualified students, they contact School I and work together to make the arrangements. But even this recruitment is not as effective as School I would like. Some factors tend to discourage minority interest. First of all, the common problem of costs is present at the school: the 1983–84 tuition was $5,100. Fifty-three students (10.8 percent) receive some financial assistance. For the most part, the school provides only 50 percent or less in the way of financial help to each student, thereby stretching the available dollars as far as possible.

The second problem is more complex and much more difficult for the school to overcome. An administrator described it this way: "Blacks at School I are educationally, economically, emotionally and geographically disadvantaged." *Educationally*, because the city schools are well behind School I. *Economically*, not only in terms of tuition, but also in students' comparisons with their Main Line classmates, who make no bones about the fact that they have a lot of money. (Roughly twenty students in the junior class at School I received cars for their sixteenth birthdays.) The economic inequality is compounded by the fact that the School I Parents' Association holds fund-raising functions, such as a recent auction, where tickets cost $150 per couple, prices that are obviously way beyond the income of most average families. This creates a real sense of isolation for the students and impotence for their parents, who feel unable to participate or contribute in the same way other parents at School I do. *Geographically*, the students are disadvantaged because they have to leave their home neighborhoods and travel sometimes an hour or an hour and a half, one way, just to get to school. And, finally, they are *emotionally disadvantaged* because they have to work twice as hard just to play catch-up academically—all the while having to cope with all the other problems mentioned above.

The administrator describes the situation in this way: "The whole thing can be frustrating especially for a fourteen year old who is vulnerable. We are asking an awful lot and demanding a tremendous amount of trust from a teenager when we say 'give me four years of your life and I promise it'll be of benefit to you.'" In short, it is an awful lot to overcome. School I is trying to avert this situation by bringing minority students in at the lower-school level rather than waiting until high school. However, these elements undoubtedly discourage many minority students and their parents from coming to School I—or, for that matter, any of the other schools mentioned.

One might now, at the conclusion of these educational data, wonder why so much emphasis has been placed on the gathering of this kind of information. I concluded that it was important in two ways, particularly in light of the theoretical questions examined here. In a basic sense, these data demonstrate the level of interaction between Main Line WASPs and black children. Because Porter believes, and I can now concur, that exposure may be a critical factor in the formulation of attitudes with respect to other people who are different from one's self, the fact that, at least in these nine schools, the level of interracial interaction is very low is clearly significant. It could still be debated whether this is done consciously or unconsciously, but we know that the elevated tuition costs at each of these institutions may preclude minority enrollment. Of course, the schools argue that these costs are necessary to maintain the level of academic excellence to which they aspire. This rationale must be taken seriously when we discover that at a school like School H the average cost per student who is not covered by tuition is $588, a total of $326,340 for the entire student body for one year —all of which must be obtained from other sources.

There is a further question that arises when blaming the exclusivity on financial factors; namely, this assumes that all the minority students are poor, urban kids who cannot afford to attend these schools. As one can deduce from my interviews with administrative personnel, this is their assumption as well because they associate minority enrollment with financial aid and transportation costs. In reality, there is a strong basis for these conclusions. At several schools I researched, however, they mentioned the one or two wealthy black families who live on the Main Line and can obviously pay the full expenses. A striking example is a well-known black professional basketball player who has children in two of these schools. But, comparatively speaking, most of the black students do come from outside the community, and cannot afford the tuition costs required. This information also indicates something about the racial makeup of the Main Line itself. I have implied throughout this work that this area is primarily populated by white people. One of my goals was to try to corroborate my assumption with some statistical figures. These data support my contention about the racial makeup of the Main Line's population. We will return to this question shortly when we discuss neighborhoods in a more specific way.

These educational data also directly relate to the following theoretical question: In what ways are these institutions acting to reinforce the standards and values of the predominant ethnic group on the Main Line: the WASPs? To begin, we can look at some of the school philosophies. School E has these objectives: "To demonstrate the importance of a belief in God as revealed in the life and teachings of Jesus Christ, using as a vehicle the teachings and practices of the Episcopal Church . . . To teach that our American republican form of government based on democratic principles requires the concern, participation, and, on occasion, sacrifice of every citizen" (1984 brochure).

The following are excerpts from School F's statement of philosophy: "The vigorous democratic growth of this country owes a great debt to our nation's private, independent schools. Although these schools do not educate the majority of this country's children, they send forth an impressive number of graduates who assume positions of leadership in their communities, their states, and their nation. . . . In an era of increasing federal interest in public education, the independent schools continue to represent the strong, traditional, republican ideal" (1984 statement). These two statements reveal that the schools are supporting certain religious and civic values that correspond to those attributed earlier to Main Line WASPs.

In addition, these schools all emphasize their responsibility in training their students to assume leadership roles in their communities. The first step in this process is preparation for college. Of course, these students do not simply attend any college, but rather the best in the country. During the period 1980–84, School E sent graduates to: the University of Pennsylvania (22), Princeton University (8), Cornell University (7), Duke University (7), Harvard University (6), Yale University (5), Brown University (4), as well as many other fine schools. Since 1967, School F has sent many of its graduates to: the University of Pennsylvania, Princeton University, and Trinity College, in Connecticut. School G's graduates from the class of 1983, some 59 in all, went to: Amherst (2), Brown (1), Duke University (6), MIT (1), Middlebury College (1), Oberlin (1), Princeton University (1), Swarthmore College (1), University of Pennsylvania (2), to name but a few. From 1979 to 1983, most School H graduates have attended: Brown University (2), Bryn Mawr College (2), Colgate University (5), Cornell University (6), Duke University (7), Harvard (8), Mt. Holyoke (4), Ohio Wesleyan (8), Sarah Lawrence (2), Smith (2), University of Pennsylvania (12), Vassar (3), and Yale University (4). Over the last three years, 34.2 percent (51 out of a total of 149 students) of School I's students went to Ivy League schools and 8.7 percent (13) to the 7 "sister" schools. Three of the Main Line institutions, E, H, and I, have a 99-percent college attendance rate, and School F has a 100-percent rate (figures for School G were not available). An administrator from School F said that colleges welcome its graduates because, within four years following graduation, 97 percent of them had completed their college education.

These figures reveal that students who attend these Main Line institutions are likely to be accepted by the best colleges and universities in the United States. Essentially, these people move from one prestigious institution into another—schools that are attended by people very much like themselves. One cannot overestimate the importance of the friendships and alliances formed at these schools, not to mention the level and quality of education that is provided.

To summarize, the private preparatory schools on the Main Line provide their students with the academic qualifications necessary to be accepted by the country's finest colleges, thus enabling them to obtain the highest level of training, which increases future job opportunities as well as potential earning power. The schools encourage WASP values in the area of religion and political thought. Socially, because the student populations are so thoroughly homogeneous, bonds between like people are formed and reinforced for later use in the adult community. One of my informants said that the old adage, "It's not what you know, but who [sic] you know!" is characteristic of the Main Line. In this instance, whom these children know are basically other children like themselves: Main Line WASPs.

Religion

Now that we have looked at the schools and the significance of the private educational system, we can begin to examine some of the other important institutional influences on Main Line youths. Although we have already discussed the role of religion in the lives of people in the area, there is another facet of church life yet to be described. It seemed to me that the racial composition of the Main Line churches might also have a bearing on how children perceive other types of people.

On the one hand, the church is a place where significant social interaction can occur: families attend church together and they meet other similar families who are their friends. But the church is also a place where morality and values are taught—in this case, Christian values. What becomes the message if these children see only other white children in their churches? They might easily conclude that whites are meant to interact only with other whites. But it might also appear that the preachings in church—the values espoused—belong exclusively to the white community. Earlier, I touched briefly on the exclusiveness of the Main Line churches, some of which provide higher social status than others. What I did not mention, however, was the relationship of race to this status situation.

My research concentrated on three specific churches in order to obtain statistical information on race. These churches were centrally located, in Bryn Mawr and Gladwyne, and were selected precisely because of their high social position within the community. The first, Church A, has been described at length above. For our present purposes, it currently has 750 families who are members. They have many activities, including a junior and senior choir, Sunday school and adult Bible study classes. I observed the congregation on five separate occasions throughout an eight-month period. During this time, I never once saw a black or other minority attend the services. I might add that the services were very well attended; there were always several hundred people present. It might be argued that observing a church five times is not a fair test and that these conclusions are merely preliminary. I was able to ask a handful of members if my conclusions were valid, however, and they confirmed that to their knowledge there are no black members of Church A. A similar pattern was revealed at Church B. The present congregation totals 3,500 individual members. I was in attendance three times, and, as with Church A, I observed no minority participants. In the case of Church B, several reliable informants concurred with my assessment.

The last church that I examined was Church C. When I was a youngster, this was the church to which my family belonged. Consequently, I arranged to interview the young, very popular, minister with regard to the racial issue. I was especially interested in talking to him because I was aware that he has always been a progressive force within the community. The irony, of course, is in the fact that this liberal minister's church is situated in Gladwyne, Pennsylvania, perhaps the wealthiest community on the Main Line. Later the minister said that he was painfully aware of the lack of diversity within both the surrounding community and his church as well. He says that he views Gladwyne as a "ghetto," in the true sense of the word, meaning an aggregate or concentration of like people.

Historically, the church, as previously described, catered to the servants working on the large Main Line estates. This tradition has resulted in a segregation of the members, with 75 percent of Gladwyne's Presbyterians going to the more illustrious Church B. Despite this split, Church C's congregation, currently about 150 families, is still predominantly white. The Reverend and his family have brought some of their own minority friends to the church, but they are a very small group.

In the last few months, the minister instituted a new trial program in an effort to correct the minority problem. With the help of Shoemaker Junior High School, a West Philadelphia middle school, this minister has formed a biracial middle-school youth group at his church. The group is comprised of ten inner-city black youths and ten youths from Church C. Although he believes these sorts of attempts are important, he remains cautious, and acknowledges that the current group is already having some problems. The black children leave their home environment, travel out to the all-white church and participate in a variety of activities, most recently, a church supper. The minister reported: "It was amazing! These kids, in totally alien surroundings, came right in, got their plates and food, and sat right down and began talking. They enjoyed themselves." The white youths are the ones manifesting the problems. He said quite honestly that they are nervous and uncomfortable; they do not know how to act. Instead of facing or admitting their feelings, they simply take the easy way out, with lame excuses: "I'm bored" or "This isn't any fun."

The minister concluded by saying that this church will never be racially mixed because the community is not mixed in this way. He says he has succeeded in encouraging other sorts of diversity; the congregation draws families from all over the geographic Main Line, there are numerous divorced families in which both partners have remained in the church, and there are unemployed members as well as several emotionally disturbed adults. The minister's goal is to make Church C an open, welcoming place for all sorts of people, particularly those who are not wanted in other churches. This might someday include minorities, but he is doubtful that such a change will occur, at least within the near future.

In questioning other informants, I inquired about their specific churches, and virtually everywhere received the same answer: few or no minority members. This included a Lutheran church in Ardmore, a Methodist church in Gladwyne, and two Catholic churches, one in Bryn Mawr and the other in Gladwyne. I went on to ask my informants why they thought this was so. They unanimously agreed that it was because the blacks have their own churches. In fact, this is the case. There are several (three that I am aware of) exclusively black churches situated in the black neighborhoods in Ardmore and Bryn Mawr. The result is, of course, that Main Line children do not interact with nonwhite children in their churches. The message being transmitted to youngsters troubled the minister: "It does look bad; it gives these children the wrong idea about the way the world really is. It's our responsibility to help them learn about the real world and I don't think we're doing a very good job right now."

Neighborhoods

It is difficult to talk about neighborhoods in an area like the Main Line. The houses are often set far apart from one another and well back off of the road. There are few residential areas that even have sidewalks. Main Line WASPs speak of neighbors, the group of people who live in the houses immediately surrounding one's own home, and towns: "I live in Gladwyne," rather than a certain neighborhood.

The only neighborhoods on the Main Line are located in the lower socioeconomic areas, such as downtown Bryn Mawr or Ardmore, or, the farther one gets away from the central zone of the Main Line—for instance out in Berwyn or Paoli. It is important to note that even these neighborhoods are different in character from the average middle-class neighborhoods of say Havertown or Media, which surround the Main Line. Essentially, these areas lack the aspect of unity that is characteristic of neighborhoods as we have come to know them.

One informant said that Main Line people have no pride in their neighborhoods; they have pride in their homes, but have transferred their collective or shared sense of pride to institutions like the schools and churches. Living on the Main Line provides a considerable amount of status in itself, but additional prestige can be accrued in accordance with an individual's address. The towns on the Main Line form a hierarchy in themselves with regard to status. Gladwyne is currently at the pinnacle of this system, followed by Bryn Mawr, Haverford, Rosemont, Villanova, and Ardmore. Next come St. Davids, Wayne, Strafford, Berwyn, and Paoli on the western side; and Wynnewood, Penn Valley, Narberth, Merion, Bala Cynwyd, and Belmont Hills on the eastern side. Basically, the farther one moves away from the central area, in each direction, the prestige decreases. There are neighborhoods, in the traditional sense, on the Main Line, but these do not belong to WASPs. I have previously alluded to the fact that there are black neighborhoods in both Bryn Mawr and Ardmore. There are other ethnic neighborhoods as well: an Irish-Catholic one in Bryn Mawr, an Italian one in Belmont Hills, and a Jewish one in Penn Valley.

For the purpose of this study, I wanted to examine the demography of Main Line WASP communities. Specifically, are the children exposed to people who are ethnically or racially different from themselves in their home communities? Basically, I asked all my informants to describe their residential areas. None of them mentioned having black neighbors. They had Italian, Polish, Irish-Catholic, and Jewish neighbors, but no blacks. Several informants were quick to point out that there are blacks who live on the Main Line: "There are plenty of Blacks on the Main Line; just look at Bryn Mawr or Ardmore." Or, they talk about the exceptional blacks: "Dr. J. lives right on the Main Line. They have a lovely house in Villanova." Further probing in this area revealed an uneasiness with respect to this question. When asked how they would feel if a black family moved into the neighborhood, responses were quite hesitant, if not downright antagonistic.

Two separate incidents illustrate the point. In Gladwyne for many years, there was a small parochial school and convent that were affiliated with the large Catholic parish there. Within the last year, the property on which the two buildings stood was put on the market and ultimately sold to a Jewish group. The group intends to build a synagogue on the property, which borders on a residential area. When the news of the sale got out, three of the houses that back up to the property were immediately put up for sale. In a different situation, an informant described her neighbor's reaction when she decided to sell her house. The neighbor was fearful that she might sell the house to an unnamed, undesirable element that would cause the community's property values to drop. My informant had no doubt that her neighbor was referring to blacks.

The Main Line is so large that conducting neighborhood censuses was not possible, but I made sure that I interviewed several people from each town to assure some balance. I did discover that Main Line WASPs like to live in closed communities. With respect to the issue of interracial contact, we can see that Main Line neighborhoods, such as they are, do not facilitate this type of interaction. The area is largely homogeneous, with a handful of ethnic pockets scattered intermittently through it. The residential pattern, therefore, follows the schools and churches in terms of racial exposure.

Racial Attitudes

Now that we have examined the question of interracial contact on the Main Line, we can examine the attitudes that WASPs expressed with respect to other racial or ethnic groups. Stated another way, we will now attempt to discover whether racial prejudice is an attitude that is transmitted to the WASP children. A brief exploration of the term "prejudice" will help clarify it and its meaning as used here. In literal terms, the word means simply "a prejudgement." But, as Berry puts it, "prejudice is hardly a judgement, for a judgement is an operation of the mind which involves comparison, discernment, examination of facts, logical processes, and good sense" (1951:369). The commonly assumed definition of prejudice is more accurately that which belongs to the word "antipathy": "a wide range of attitudes itself, including hatred, aversion, dislike, enmity, and various other hostile and unfavorable feelings." As used here, prejudice will mean "an antipathy based upon faulty and inflexible generalizations. It may be felt or expressed. It may be directed toward a group as a whole, or toward an individual because he is a member of the group" (Allport 1954:9).

Throughout my research, attitudes and opinions about other racial groups were expressed to me in many different situations. In most instances, I did not need to introduce the subject; it came up quite freely. The most frequent way that racial attitudes were expressed was through the telling of racial jokes. (For a partial list of the jokes that were collected, see Table 2.) At every group function, parties, weddings—everyplace except at funerals—racial jokes were told. The vast majority of the time, they were told by men, though both men and women laughed freely in response. This same pattern was reflected by the children. None of the young females told these sorts of jokes, yet their male counterparts did so often.

Some theorists have asserted that men are more prone to racial prejudice than are women (Berry 1951:367). Although the information obtained seems to support that hypothesis, I do not believe this is actually the case. On the contrary, I think Main Line WASP men and women are equally susceptible to these feelings, as evidenced by the fact that both sexes seem to enjoy these jokes equally. I concluded that the difference between men and women as joke-tellers reflects more about what is seen as appropriate behavior for males and females than about the attitudes held by the two sexes. One of my student informants commented on this situation: "My brother, who goes to School G, comes home every day with a new racist joke. They are really awful. That doesn't happen at School I with the girls in my class because they are much less open about that sort of thing and would be too embarrassed to tell those sort of jokes even if they had similar feelings. Of course, blacks are much more prevalent at School I and that would make it more difficult to tell those kinds of jokes."

This joke-telling is done without any knowledge of the recipient's views. There does not appear to be a need for previous personal contact between the two individuals before these jokes are told. In short, the teller assumes that everyone present shares his or her view and will find the joke funny. This assumption was borne out because I never heard anyone, no matter how offensive the joke, criticize the joke or the teller for presenting it. The only negative responses were "Oh, that was really bad," followed by laughter. These jokes are told freely in front of children of all ages. The only occasion for hesitation in this respect occurs when the jokes pertain to sexual matters or use profane language. Profanity, in this case, does not include the use of words like *nigger*, *jiggaboo*, *pickaninny*, or pejorative terms used to refer to other ethnic groups. It has been asserted, by some researchers, that the telling of negative ethnic jokes does not necessarily signify prejudice and that it may instead simply be a mechanism for relieving anxiety or tension about different sorts of people.

I have to disagree with this hypothesis, at least with respect to the children on the Main Line. The jokes usually describe blacks in stereotypical fashion, referring to them as lazy, dishonest, and untrustworthy. Children, particularly young ones, accept these depictions as being valid and incorporate the qualities ascribed into their own definitions of black people. I encountered some situations in which the children had accepted certain negative terms—one example was the word "shiftless"—and applied them to blacks in general, without even knowing what the words meant.

Table 2. Racial Jokes

What do you get when you cross a black and a groundhog?
   Six more weeks of basketball season.

What do you call a black millionaire physicist?
   A nigger.

Why do blacks wear high-heeled shoes?
   So their knuckles don't scrape the ground.

Did you hear about the little black kid who got diarrhea?
   He thought he was melting.

What do they call a woman in the Army? A WAC.
What do they call a black woman in the Army? A WACcoon.

Why do blacks always have sex on their minds?
   Because of the pubic hair on their heads.

Did you hear about the new black French restaurant? Chez What?

What are three French words all blacks know? Coupe de ville.

Why do blacks wear white gloves?
   So they don't bite off their fingers when they're eating Tootsie Rolls.

How many Ardmore youths does it take to shingle a roof?
   Nine, if you slice them thin.

What did Lincoln say after his five-day drunk? "I freed WHO?"

"Gag me with a coon."

Another way that racial attitudes are presented is through statements or in simple conversation. According to Porter, "Adults often discuss matters pertaining to racial issues with one another, assuming that the child playing nearby has neither the interest nor the intellectual capacity to follow their conversation. But young children can and do listen to discussions, and studies have shown the particular potency of such overheard conversations for attitude change" (1971:14). In the course of my research, I heard hundreds of pronouncements that were racially or ethnically related: "We had to get to the restaurant before six o'clock, before all the Jews get there"; "I never liked basketball; what's to like? Six jiggaboos running up and down the court chasing after a ball"; "My boss sent me down to a store in North Philadelphia, a small auto parts business; I was afraid to get out of the car. There wasn't a white face around for miles." These remarks, like the jokes, are most often negative and derisive. Interestingly, however, they are not made as openly as the jokes are. Casual remarks may be made, but the really negative statements, those in which the word "nigger" or "nig" are used, are reserved for more intimate circumstances. I was able to observe my informants as they maneuvered their way through different social settings and watched as their opinions changed with each switch.

This is not an unfamiliar situation for me because I grew up watching relatives doing exactly this. Inside the family, it's "niggers and Jews"; with the neighbors, it's the same; but at parties, they suddenly become "the blacks." It is important to note these changes because they demonstrate some awareness on the part of the informant that the use of certain epithets may be unacceptable in a given circumstance. I became aware, however, that simply changing certain terminology does not necessarily alter the basic message. In one situation, an informant said, "The niggers are all just plain lazy; they just don't want to work," but in another instance his response was: "The trouble with the blacks is that they just don't have any ambition; they just don't want to work the way the rest of us do."

Because adults are generally more relaxed and informal in their immediate circles, their children tend to be exposed to their most intimate, strongest attitudes with little restraint. Children may also notice, as I did, the differential attitudes and wonder about the inconsistencies. It is impossible to say whether the recognition of these inconsistencies increases or decreases the impact of the statements involved.

In addition to attitudes, parents may express their feelings through actions, what Porter calls "subtle behavioral cues" (1971:

14): "The white mother who presses down the locks on her car doors as she drives through a ghetto area is indeed providing highly effective instruction about race" (Porter 1971:15). This door-lock incident was reiterated in my own research. A young informant, aged sixteen, in describing the fact that life on the Main Line is sheltered, said, "When we, any of my friends or I, go through Philadelphia everyone would lock their doors."

Other less subtle forms of behavior are also present on the Main Line. One incident frequently cited has to do with eating arrangements. On the previous Thanksgiving, an informant reported that her mother invited the maid to stay for dinner because she did not have any family in the area with whom to share the holiday. When dinner time came, the maid was asked to serve the family and then told to help herself, in the kitchen. The children were horrified: "Mother, how can you do this; it's Thanksgiving!" She replied "What's wrong? She's having a nice meal for free. She wouldn't want to sit with us anyway. She'd much rather be out there in the kitchen."

My research showed that this type of behavior was common, especially in situations where black people are employed in white homes. They often must eat alone in the kitchen, and, though their expected payment for service includes the provision of a meal if they work during normal mealtime hours, on many occasions they are given only leftovers from the family's meals. Because this discussion had raised the issue of household help, it is important for us to consider it in another way as well.

Virtually all my young informants mentioned that their families had black household help. The jobs, including everything from cook to maid to laundress to babysitter, were all filled by black women, most of whom are Americans, though recently there has been an influx of Haitian and other women from the Caribbean islands. It seemed surprising to me that today, given the poor economic climate in America, that all of these workers would be black. One of my older informants tried to provide an explanation: "It's the work they do best. Besides, at least you know where you stand with them. I'd feel strange having another white woman come in and do this work for me. I just wouldn't know how to handle her."

Nowadays, few people can maintain a sizable household staff; the average Main Line WASP family has one maid who comes in one to three times a week to do the "light" household work. The wealthier families today have a maid, a cook who comes in to prepare the meals, and a houseboy to do the heavier housework, such as washing windows, waxing floors, and odd jobs. Most of the other work is done by outside services of various kinds, such as gardening and rug and upholstery cleaning. There are even chauffeuring services to pick up children at school and bring them home. Most of these jobs, unless they require some special skills, are held by blacks or other minorities.

Given all the negative influences described above, one might ask how the Main Line children feel about the situation. Are they prejudiced? Because we are dealing with a rather large group of people, it would be impossible to say that all Main Line WASPs are prejudiced. But, as with everything else, here we are pursuing patterns of behavior and thought that are commonly found. In order to obtain some comparable data, I tried to speak with many youngsters in the same age category. I concluded that high-school students would be an appropriate age group for me to consider. In fairness, I had more access to young women than young men, though I did talk with some of the latter. With most of my informants, I was able to obtain data from both casual and formal situations. That is, I observed behavior and listened to conversations, but I also asked certain specific questions. My young informants did not view themselves as racist or prejudiced at all. Many compared their parents' generation with their own: "My parents are really prejudiced. They don't like any other kinds of people," or "Both my parents are entirely prejudiced; my mother thinks all blacks are thieves or something like that; they're all dumb to her. I don't share my parents' feelings because I like to judge people on their own personality." There is an element of adolescent rebellion present at this stage. When I asked one informant why she thought she had not picked up more of her parents' beliefs, she replied, "My brother picked up more of their beliefs than I did. I reject my mother's attitudes because I hate my mother and I don't want to be like her in any way." Interestingly enough, this rejection had to do exclusively with the parents themselves, not with any evaluation of the attitudes presented.

Despite their pronouncements to the contrary, Main Line WASP children said and did things indicating that they had absorbed the negative attitudes that seem to surround them. To begin with, I observed little voluntary interaction between the WASP teens and their black counterparts. In school, the black students, because there are so few of them, group together without respect to age or grade—attending classes, eating lunch, and at most other times. The WASP students stay away from the group as much as possible. Some of them never even talk to the black ones. Others do so only when absolutely necessary, as in class or at some other function.

Finally, some of the white students talk to the blacks, yet do so in an entirely different way than they talk to everyone else. One informant said, "I talk to the blacks just like they were anyone else, like I was talking to one of the ABC (A Better Chance) students about a class trip to see Michael Jackson, you know, attacking his body, ripping off all his clothes. God, he's so cute!" Without even realizing it, my informant told me that the only way she felt comfortable talking to a black student was if they talked about something that would be of interest to the black—like another black. It is important to note that a WASP will occasionally befriend the black students; in doing so, she relinquishes her social status and is never treated by the WASPs in the same way again.

Outside of school, I was told, there is never any interracial contact. From a very early age, social activities are entirely segregated. As young children, the black students are never invited to any of the white birthday parties. On the Main Line, these parties are generally extraordinary affairs: the food is catered, clowns hired, and ponies procured for rides. As a rule, these gatherings are quite large, with the child's entire class invited to attend—everyone that is except for the black students. This early pattern is repeated over the years and lasts even into the teen years with boy/girl parties. The negative sentiments are so strong that when a public function does occur where blacks are invited, particularly class events, they consistently do not attend. One teenage informant, a junior at school I, told me that neither of the two black students in her class had ever participated in the annual class dance. With the junior prom fast approaching, I asked if they would be present. "I don't know for certain, but I doubt that they will. They've never come before," was her response. This sort of exclusionary behavior matches that of the parents, with the same results: segregated social groups and activities and negative, generally derogatory, feelings about blacks and other "outsiders."

I mentioned earlier that the young females did not make use of the typical epithets that are associated with a racist ideology. Not so for boys. The words "nigger" and "coon" were used repeatedly in my hearing, though not directly in my presence, except in jokes. These pejorative terms are used by boys as young as nine years old. I overheard a group of boys talking: "Did you see the Grammy show last night? I couldn't believe Michael Jackson. I don't know, I just hate Michael Jackson."

"Aw it's just 'cause he's a nigger!"

"Yeah, I guess so."

I encountered a group of youths in an Ardmore record store, which apparently did not have the record they wanted. As a result, they left the store, saying loudly for all to hear: "That f——ing nigger doesn't know his a—— from a hole in the ground. Dumb nigger!" The reference was to the salesclerk, who was black. It is not too difficult to imagine that a lot of this is young male bravado, trying to impress the other fellows. Yet, the attitudes being expressed are strong ones, not easily dismissed because they relate directly to underlying real feelings held about blacks in general by these youths.

As a final test of my young informants' beliefs, I asked them a series of hypothetical questions about their future lives. Among these questions were: Would you every marry a black person? Or a Jewish person? What would your parents do, how would they feel? How would your friends react? The responses to the Jewish questions were mixed. "I might marry someone Jewish; it depends on who [sic] I fall in love with. My parents wouldn't mind." One girl said that she could never marry somebody Jewish, that she had dated a boy of that faith seriously for six months and that their cultural backgrounds were just too different. In addition, she said her father was furious that she was going out with a Jew. She concluded that in all likelihood if she were to marry one, her father would disinherit her.

The responses to the black questions were consistent: "I could never marry anybody black; my father would kill me," or "I'm just not strong enough to do that; some people can and I wish them well, but not me. No way." One woman responded: "My father hates my husband; they just don't get along at all. I remember overhearing him say once, 'Well, at least she didn't marry a black guy.'" Sometimes, reality can imitate the hypothetical, and we can observe the consequences. Recently, the son of a well-known and respected Philadelphia family married a black woman. They have virtually been ignored by his family and Philadelphia society in general. When the couple attended a charitable gala last fall, they were ostracized; no one wanted to associate with them. Comments ranged from "I can't believe he married her, can you?" to "I can't believe he brought her here; does he really expect us to welcome her, treat her as if she belongs here. I think he's just plain crazy!" This last remark is indicative of the feelings that most Main Line WASPs have about these things. The young man has committed an unforgivable breach; surely he must be crazy. It is certainly possible to say that Main Line WASPs, like most groups, prefer to marry people who share the same ethnic and cultural background as themselves. But the strength of the negative responses in even a hypothetical setting suggest that prejudice is acting in this instance as well.

Now that the common pattern has been described, I want to introduce briefly the deviant element. There are Main Line WASPs who are not racially or ethnically prejudiced. They have black friends and associate freely with them. But these individuals generally do not participate fully in Main Line WASP life. They intentionally shun the private clubs and exclusive churches. Often, they begin at one of the private schools, but become dissatisfied and leave to go to other "freer" schools; the Friends' schools are very popular with this group.

I talked with two of these deviant individuals at considerable length; I was especially interested in how or why they had rejected the racist ideology that is so pervasive on the Main Line. All these informants concurred that two factors made it impossible for them to accept the negative attitudes: the fact that their parents had not encouraged, in fact had rejected, prejudicial feelings themselves; and these informants had from a very early age enjoyed close personal relationships with blacks or Jews, including strong, affective ties. As a twenty-five-year-old WASP female said: "I was raised by Hazel; she worked for my family from before I was born. Her mother worked for my grandmother before that. Even though she worked for us, she was always part of our family. Everyone treated her that way. My mother never permitted anyone to say a harsh word to her, or treat her differently from anyone else. Now that I have a family of my own, I don't see Hazel very often any more. But we talk on the phone, talk about the kids, you know. I really love her!"

Another informant, a thirty-two-year-old WASP female, described a similar event in her life: "My parents were never prejudiced at all. When my father was in the army, he volunteered to be the commander for the all black unit. He said he wanted to work with them. No one else wanted the job, but he did. . . . As a child, dad used to go down South to visit his grandmother for the summers. She had a chauffeur named Sanford who my father just loved. He was like a second father to him, took him fishing, played with him. For some reason, Sanford came North to visit once, and my father's mother made him sleep in the basement and wash his hands in a washbasin instead of in the sink. My father was crushed. I think he's seen all he ever needed to see about prejudice."

If we take this deviant material and add it to the other material we have, the evidence seems to indicate that parental influence, as well as interracial contact, affects significantly, possibly conclusively and irreversibly, the attitudes that young children acquire with respect to other racial and ethnic groups.

In summary, we have seen that racial attitudes can, and are, transmitted in various ways: through jokes, conversation, and all sorts of behavior. Of course, attitudes can be positive, negative, or even, I suppose, neutral. On the Main Line, these attitudes are generally ones that support racial prejudice or negativity about other groups. In rare instances, individuals have been able to avoid these feelings with parental support, but, for the most part, Main Line WASP children accept the negative racial evaluations that their culture presents to them. We can now turn to an examination of the role that racial prejudice plays in the maintenance of Main Line WASP culture.

Perpetuation of an Elite

Berry, in *Race and Ethnic Relations*, contends that a distinction must be made between prejudice, feelings and attitudes, and discrimination. He defines the last of these as differential treatment accorded individuals who are considered as belonging in a particular category or group" (1951:371–372). Presumably, Berry feels this distinction is important because prejudice may in itself be bad, but, without the accompanying discrimination, it would cause little damage to the opposed group. On the Main Line, I have demonstrated the existence of both prejudice and discrimination, as just defined. Berry goes on to say that groups that are prejudiced and act in discriminatory ways seldom acknowledge their reasons for these approaches. Instead, they formulate rationalizations for their behavior:

> Rationalizations of racial prejudice and discrimination by dominant groups, wherever they are encountered and whatever be the terms in which they are expressed, invariably fall into four categories: 1) self-defense. The dominant group maintains itself, its values, its status, and its way of life. 2) subordination and superordination are universal, natural, inevitable, normal phenomena. They have been regarded as sacred and divinely instituted. 3) the fault lies with the minority group itself, for it is either innately and biologically inferior, or it is addicted to immoral, filthy, dishonest, treacherous habits. 4) prejudice and discrimination or what appears to be so, are in reality but a manifestation of worthy, unselfish, altruistic motives. Differential treatment is actually in the best interest of the minority itself (Berry 1951:393–394).

Essentially, I encountered each one of these explanations in my work, and have touched on them in the data already presented, though on the Main Line the first two types of rationalizations seem to be predominant. These two seem to feed off one another: our way of life is superior, and therefore we must fight off any attempts to infiltrate our community by other ethnic or racial groups. Thus far, these Main Line WASPs have been largely successful, as can be seen from the racial composition data from various Main Line institutions that were presented earlier. To repeat: "An elite is a collectivity of persons who occupy commanding positions in some important sphere of social life, and who share a variety of interests arising from similarities of training, experience, public duties, and way of life. To promote these interests, they seek to cooperate and coordinate their actions by means of a corporate organization" (A. Cohen 1981:xvi). In particular, Main Line WASPs may be seen as constituting an ethnic elite that has cooperated to form a private school system as well as a status hierarchy with respect to church affiliation and exclusive social clubs and institutions—all of which consistently exclude blacks and other ethnic groups from participation. This exclusion prevents these other groups from sharing in the best that Main Line life has to offer. Further, by instilling in their children attitudes of racial prejudice, Main Line WASPs can guarantee that their culture will be perpetuated as it currently exists. In this sense, and from their point of view, prejudice and discrimination are necessary to ensure that the way of life they know will continue.

Conclusion

The purpose of the fieldwork project described here was to begin to examine Main Line WASP culture in a systematic way. Although the time constraints made a comprehensive picture impossible, extensive data were obtained, particularly with respect to socialization influences. In describing Main Line culture, I selected several key variables that seemed most relevant to an emic understanding of this life-style. These included: affluence, religion, and class. My goal was, however, also to determine the process that helped transmit these values to subsequent generations of Main Line WASP children. In examining the institutions that most directly have an impact on these youngsters, a consistent pattern of exclusivity was revealed. It has been facilitated by attitudes of racial antipathy as well as discriminatory processes.

4

Africans and African-Americans
An Ethnohistorical View and
Symbolic Analysis of Food Habits

Carolyn G. Friedman

*There is such a thing as Afro-American culture and every black
person in the country knows it*
(Rose 1970:xxii)

Not all people—white and black—know or believe that African-
American culture exists. Those interested in this debate must look
back in history to uncover the basic facts. Documents of Spanish
colonial administrators, dating from the year 1502, contain the first
references to blacks. This is when the New World traffic in African
slaves is thought to have begun. Six percent of the more than
9,500,000 who were forcibly transported across the Atlantic between 1502 and the 1860s were brought to the United States (Fogel
and Engerman 1974:15). The focal point of the transatlantic slave
trade was along the West African coast between Senegal and Angola
and, though some slaves were captured in the interior of the conti-
nent, the majority of them were taken from within 300 miles of
the coast (Meier and Rudwick 1966:5). Did African slaves brought
to the New World, and the United States in particular, leave behind
all traces of their cultural heritage? Do African-Americans today
possess and exhibit a unique culture, certain dimensions of which
reflect having come from Africa?

E. Franklin Frazier ([1939] 1966; [1949] 1957a; 1957b), a sociologist, argues against African survivals among African-Americans. As
a result of belonging to different tribal groups, being transported

long distances, sold randomly on the slave markets, and "broken into" slavery before arriving on plantations, African slaves lost all their cultural heritage. The brutal slave system robbed black men and women of their cultural traditions, forced them to adopt the dominant white culture, and kept them from developing a new cultural tradition. Frazier ([1949] 1957a:3–4) does not deny that slaves brought to the West Indies, where their conditions were less harsh, were able to retain some of their African heritage, but slaves brought to the New World, in what became the United States, responded somewhat differently: "During the process of adjusting themselves to American civilization, the majority of the Negroes have sloughed off completely the African heritage" ([1949] 1957a:21).

Those scholars who have pursued Frazier's line of argument point to the close contact U.S. slaves had with Europeans and the lack of firsthand contact with Africa because many slaves, by the 1700s, were born in the American colonies (Fogel and Engerman 1974: 23–24). The "liberal" sociologist Gunnar Myrdal (1944:237–240) deserves much credit (and I use the word sarcastically) for characterizing the American black as "an exaggerated American," with "pathological" American values. Similarly, Glazer and Moynihan (1963:53) state, in *Beyond the Melting Pot*, that "the Negro is only an American and nothing else. He has no values and culture to guard and protect."

In *The Myth of the Negro Past*, Herskovits ([1941] 1958) presents Africanisms he sees existing among contemporary New World Negroes in both secular and religious life. Some examples include modes of speaking, sitting postures, singing, dancing, codes of polite behavior, and concepts of time—all of which represent uninstitutionalized survivals. Africanisms that may be viewed as institutionalized survivals include cooperative and mutual-aid efforts in economic and political endeavors, family organization (including ways Africans have adapted to a monogamous society, with all its implications regarding "illegitimate" children—in the *American* sense), the mother-child and father-child relationship, and the institution of marriage itself ("common-law relationships" are seen as Africanisms, for no state or religious approval is, by tradition, necessary). As for Africanisms in religious life, Herskovits ([1941] 1958) notes the prevalence of emotional displays, Baptist "shouters," and the belief that good and evil are both attributes of the same power rather than existing in a dichotomous supernatural relationship to each other. Finally, Africanisms may be seen in the arts and language of New World Negroes.

Unlike some European communities and families that transferred their societies to America intact, enslaved Africans could not do so; this circumstance helped shape the unique African-American ethnic experience. Yet, all notions of life in Africa were not simply "sloughed off." "The daily job of living did not end with enslavement, and the slaves could and did create viable patterns of life *for which their pasts were pools of available symbolic and material resources*" [my emphasis] (Mintz 1970:7–8).

We cannot expect African-American culture to appear exclusively African or American, for neither categorization in and of itself is accurate. Many African cultures, integrated into American society, make up the African-American subculture, members of which experience life by drawing from both cultural traditions. The black historical experience—life in Africa, American slavery, and institutionalized racism—is what is shared by African-Americans (Wheeler 1973).

Slavery, as vicious as it was, did not repress the African-American "durable fiber of humanity" (Mintz 1970:9). Creative freedom thrived because there was and is among African-Americans "a will toward expression" (Ellison 1964:254–256) that is more important than any aspect of cultural content. "Style" and "soul" indicate and reflect personal qualities of the individual and a concomitant sensitivity in social relationships that is valued by and binds the African-American ethnic group (Aschenbrenner 1976; Ladner 1971). Disregarding African-American culture in favor of explaining black behavior in terms of socioeconomic class distinctions results in a failure to see black and white lower-class families as different: "It masks the distinct Black culture due to the disproportionate number of black families in the lower class" (Wheeler 1973:5–6). Only when the culture concept is adhered to can "class" distinctions be accurately understood within their cultural contexts; when class differences serve as the controlled variable, "unexplained" behavior may then be attributed to one's culture (Roberts 1966).

The contributors to *Ethnic and Regional Foodways in the United States*, edited by Brown and Mussell (1984a), all grapple with the problem of how the group under study defines its boundaries. Stating the problem this way points to the significance placed on *internal* definitions used by the group, that is, what are its markers of self-identification? "This approach is significant because foodways in subcultural groups are rooted in tradition but express dynamic aspects of in-group culture through a process that is highly charged with meaning. Foodways bind individuals together, define the limits of the group's outreach and identity, distinguish in-group from out-group, serve as a medium of inter-group communication, celebrate cultural cohesion, and provide a context for performance of group rituals" (Brown and Mussell 1984b:5).

Blacks who migrated northward from the Southern United States brought with them such foods as "pigs' feet, chittlins, hog jowls, corn bread, and other foods that were called 'soul foods.'" These same foods "were actually familiar to innumerable Southerners, white and black" (Hooker 1981:337). Joyner (1971:171) poses the question of how one accounts "for the transformation of these cheap, filling foods [i.e., corn bread, fatback, collards, and chitterlings], long staple dishes of both blacks and whites in the rural south, into one of the very symbols of black identity?" Following Herskovits, we will consider food from a cultural history perspective.

Data

Having informally introduced myself to African-American foods with friends and at restaurants, I began gathering data from twenty-three informants, relying heavily on participant observation and informal, open-ended interviews. I found it easy to strike up a conversation with someone about food because it is a topic with which everyone is familiar and which people often speak about casually. Some material that is reported here was gathered in East Africa during a research trip in the summer of 1984. Previously, I had spent my junior year in New Orleans, where I first became familiar with African-American foods.

"It's Just Food"

"What is soul food?" I thought that question would be a fairly simple way to start a conversation with my African-American informants, but clearly something was wrong with my question when they would look at me, wrinkle their foreheads for a moment, raise their eyebrows questioningly, and perhaps chuckle a bit in what seemed to be disbelief at my having posed such a query. Another momentary pause was followed by a listing of foods that fit under the heading "soul foods":

Clay: "Soul food is greens, every part of the pig that's been left over after most of the meat's been removed, black-eyed peas, grits, potato salad, sweet potatoes, rice. All that's soul food."

Selma: "Soul food? That's greens, black-eyed peas, lima beans, potato salad, sweet potato pie, pig feet, chitlins, hot biscuits."

Crystal: "Grits, pigs' feet, greens (collards, turnips, kale, spinach, mustards), potato salad, chitlings, hog maws, pigs' tails, pig snouts, corn bread, hush puppies, hoppin' johns. *You all call them soul foods.*" [my emphasis]

"You all" meant me. "It means white people" (Crystal). No wonder! Here I was, a white woman, asking a black person to explain to me a word that white people had attached to her ethnic group's foods. It is not that African-Americans never refer to the food they commonly eat as "soul food"; rather, they tend to use this term when speaking with people who are not of the same ethnic background. As Clay so succinctly put it: "Blacks call it soul food because other people understand that. Some call it 'home cookin', but mostly we don't call it anything. To us it's just food."

"Home cooking," "southern cooking," "down home cooking," and "I just call it food" were all responses given to my new and improved question: "What name do you give to all the foods you eat?" Having now learned some of the ways my informants did so, I felt I could re-ask my initial question using the very terms with which they had provided me. (The "I just call it food" response was to make more sense a bit later.) Posing my question again with the new terms I had learned did not, to my frustration, produce a different sort of answer. The new question only changed the non-verbal response to a sigh or a head shake, or maybe another laugh, but the verbal response remained the same: "It's the foods I just told you."

Finally, I started asking for exhaustive lists of soul foods until my informants told me that "all foods are soul foods." Indeed, this is true, I discovered, at least before you prepare them, add anything to them, or cook them. Every food is soul food insofar as it can potentially be prepared a certain way. Yet, even that "certain" way, is really very uncertain because the preparation of any soul food is an extremely flexible undertaking; my informants rarely agreed on just how any one item of food should be prepared. I collected, in the short time spent in the field, five different recipes for corn bread alone.

Cornmeal, from which all corn bread is made by my informants, is used to prepare grits in Louisiana and in Kenya to make *ugali*, the staple food. The food that makes a meal a meal is white cornmeal. Supermarkets in black neighborhoods, I have subsequently noticed, all carry it, whereas I have found it much harder to find in those that cater to a white clientele and usually stock yellow cornmeal.

All my African-American informants told me they preferred white to yellow cornmeal because it looks and tastes better (see also Cussler and de Give 1942:58). Kenyans have a similar preference and regard yellow maize flour as animal food. Maize meal was in especially short supply in Kenya in 1984–85, and yellow corn was all that the country was able to import. Many people, however, did not want to buy this yellow maize flour because it was regarded as unfit for human consumption (Professor Philip Kilbride, Bryn Mawr College, verbal communication).

A similar shortage of white cornmeal during the summer and early fall of 1943 in Mississippi provided the occasion for Dorothy Dickens (1945) to study the effects of such shortages on the consumption of corn bread and foods that "just go naturally with corn bread" among the families of white and black children. Although yellow cornmeal was available, white corn bread was preferred, but more so by the black than the white group. Whereas 43.5 percent of the families of white girls and white boys made corn bread as usual, using yellow meal, only 29.5 percent of the families of the black children did so. Green, leafy vegetables (for example, turnip and collard greens and cabbage) were most often named by all respondents as those foods which would not be eaten if corn bread were unavailable; next in importance were lima beans, cowpeas, and string beans. For all these items, the black response was stronger. Although very few children said their families ate no corn bread at all (12 percent of white respondents, 8.5 percent of black respondents), the overall importance of corn bread and foods eaten with it is clear. "All this suggests that choice of cornbread may be determined by what other foods are available, while the choice of other foods, in turn, is determined by the availability of cornbread" (Dickens 1945:288).

Several aspects of the probable connection between a preference for white cornmeal or cornflour among Africans and African-Americans come to mind, but they are difficult to resolve. First, corn and cassava, both eaten in Africa, are of American origin (de Garine 1972:159). Second, in sub-Saharan Africa, "there is a tendency to replace yam, millet, and sorghum with cassava, maize, or rice . . . [and throughout the world] there seems to be a tendency to replace the traditional unrefined, dark cereal flours with refined, white wheat flour or polished white rice for reasons of taste, convenience and prestige" (den Hartog 1976:103).

Assuming this is a worldwide phenomenon, we must look historically at the particular circumstances of Africans and black slaves. Colonization and slavery, the form of human repression in Africa and the United States, respectively, were in part combatted by attempts of each population to maintain a sense of humanity in the face of such repression, and foods may have been one way of doing so. Although I cannot find any data that address this point, I wonder whether yellow corn was commonly fed to animals in the United States during the time when slavery was prevalent? If so, it may well be that slaves were expressing their humanity through the use of white cornmeal, with the yellow being reserved for animal feed. In Kenya, this is clearly the case. Furthermore, my African-American informants like to eat corn bread on a daily basis, and also enjoy biscuits made of white wheat flour, particularly on weekends. White wheat flour is readily available in the United States, but my informants choose to make a commonly eaten quick bread out of white *cornmeal*. The preparation of biscuits undoubtedly derived from the availability of wheat flour and ovens (in which foods may be baked) in the United States. Corn bread could also be made because of the availability of ovens. In Africa, where ovens were not available, foods could not be baked (Bascom 1951:49; Begrie 1966:8).

Cornmeal is not the only staple food used in Africa today or historically; finger millet, plantains, cassava, sweet potatoes, and sorghum are also common (Bascom 1951:50; Karp and Karp 1977:103; Lawrance 1957:118–125; Richards 1939:37; Winter and Beidelman 1967:192–193). Aside from the possible historical connection associated with white cornmeal, we might note as well the importance my African-American informants gave to the texture of "heaviness" of foods and a similar importance given to this quality of foods by Africans. While I was in Kenya, Adija and Ruti both told me how much they missed the *ugali*, made of finger millet and cassava, that they ate while growing up in rural western Kenya. I ate some of this *ugali* while in that area, and the texture was quite different, that is, somewhat coarser, than that of *ugali* made from maize meal, and it was also "heavier." *Ugali* made of finger millet and cassava is, however, more time-consuming and difficult to prepare; being thicker than *ugali* made from maize meal, it takes a strong-armed woman to mix it in the cooking process. Ease of preparation was stressed by Adija as the main advantage to maize-meal *ugali*, but she preferred the taste, texture, and "heaviness" of finger millet-cassava *ugali*. Throughout Africa, the texture of staple foods and their ability to "fill the stomach" has been noted (Bascom 1977:83;

Newman 1980; Richards and Widdowson 1936:172; Sharman 1977:107).

A distinction between the lightness and heaviness of foods is made by my African-American informants, who characterize them according to how they "sit in your stomach." Blacks, they say, like to consume "heavy" foods and whites relatively "light" ones. Such "stick-to-the-ribs" food was certainly important for the hard-working black slave (Jerome 1975a:46). The use of cornmeal over wheat flour, by African-Americans, reflects a preference for heavy foods among Africans and African-Americans. Corn bread made with cornmeal *is* heavier than "corn-bread" prepared solely with white wheat flour. The staple foods used by Africans and African-Americans may be different and are in part based on the availability of particular items, but the result is the same: a *heavy* staple food.

Ovens available in the United States, but not in Africa, have already been mentioned as a reason why the heavy staple corn bread was prepared in a way unlike heavy staple foods in Africa. But baked bread is just one of the forms cornmeal may take. It is also made into corn pone, hush puppies, cornmeal mush, hoecake, grits, corn fritters, crackling bread—all made from a choice of several main ingredients: white cornmeal, water, salt, and milk. These foods are variously fried, boiled, or cooked over an open fire (Jeffries 1970; Prudhomme 1984; Soniat 1981; my African-American informants; people I met and foods I ate in New Orleans). Like the different names given to each dish made from cornmeal by African-Americans, the Yoruba of West Africa give a separate name to and have a distinctive taste for foods made from cassava that differ only in minor detail, such as cassava meal porridge and cassava starch porridge (Bascom 1951:50).

Cornmeal prepared in the ways just mentioned corresponds to common cooking methods in Africa: frying, boiling, steaming, and stewing (stewing is reserved for the preparation of meats, poultry, and vegetables) (Bascom 1951:49; Begrie 1966:8; Lawrance 1957: 118–125). Based on his one and one-half year study of sixty-three women in African-American households in Milwaukee who had migrated there from the rural South, Jerome (1975a) found that boiling and frying were the two most common cooking methods. Haag (1955:920), offering further evidence, notes that Southern United States cooking practices are partly characterized by frying foods in fats: "Frying is common throughout Africa, especially on the Guinea Coast and in the Congo Basin that contributed most of the American Negro slaves. . . . It is possible that various frying techniques would thus enter the cooking complex of the southerner. In addition, such cooking would soon attain a cultural value that would make it desirable to those who could not afford slaves."

We have come full circle: food habits of slaves were influenced by African ones in the ways thus far discussed, which in turn influenced those of African-Americans today. But, along the way, white American food habits, in the Southern United States particularly, were also affected; and today "regional" food habits (Gutierrez 1984) illustrate this phenomenon. Slaves from Africa, in part, influenced this "regional" food pattern.

Staple foods consumed by Africans and African-Americans are generally not eaten alone; rather, they are eaten with a vegetable or meat stew (regarding Africans, see Bascom 1951:50; Karp and Karp 1977:103; Lawrance 1957:118–125; T. Richards 1939:37, 46; Winter and Beidelman 1967:192–193; regarding slaves, see Fogel and Engerman 1974:110–111). Dickens's (1945b) study, previously mentioned, shows the importance of foods eaten in combination by African-Americans—namely corn bread and greens (see also Gladney 1972:4). Styles (1980:174) states that "the pro-vegetable attitudes (mess of greens) culturally inherited from and reinforced by the [slave] masters still prevail among Blacks." Eating a leafy vegetable and a heavy staple food, for example, a "mess of greens" and corn bread, at the same meal, seems to have derived from Africa, even though corn bread per se is not consumed by people there.

Flora, an African-American informant, related an incident involving food and a group of black singers who had performed at the local college where she worked. Preparation of food for them had been organized by her. Greens was one of the foods prepared "and I'll tell you those greens went fast. You know foods like greens reminds black people of somethin'." Corn bread was the item Flora mentioned first when I asked what other foods they had eaten on that occasion.

A further and all-revealing piece of information was related to me by an African-American with whom I spoke on March 30, 1986. Bill, thirty-six-years of age, grew up in a small farming town in Alabama and was working toward a degree in computer science at a college in Philadelphia. Corn bread and greens were often prepared by his grandmother when he was a young child, and his family would eat these two foods together, using their fingers. "You a real 'A Lebo,'" his grandmother would sometimess tell him after he had finished all his food. Not until he went to Nigeria several years ago did he realize what she meant. His first meal in that country consisted of "somethin' like thick grits and greens," and he ate with his hands just as everyone else did. The other Nigerians were amazed at the ease with which he used his hands to eat and commented on it. He told them he had often eaten greens and corn bread with his hands as a child in Alabama. While in Nigeria, he also learned of the Igbo ("A-Eebo") group of people.

Food in Africa is commonly eaten with one's fingers (Lawrance 1957:118–125), as I discovered for myself when I was in Kenya and as all my African informants now living in the United States have told me. Almost every Kenyan meal I ate, moreover, consisted of maize-meal *ugali*, either a meat or chicken stew and a vegetable stew made with *sukumawiki*, a green very much like collard greens. Consumption of the staple with a vegetable stew, that is, greens, and eating with one's hands are fairly clear examples of African influences on the food habits of African-Americans. Flora's "somethin'" that greens and corn bread reminds African-Americans of is their cultural heritage.

Turning to African-American ethnicity as reflected by food habits, we see that some foods are used more frequently by blacks than by whites and each group may associate these foods with "black people's food." Whitehead (1984), for example, conducted an in-depth study of eight households in a rural southern community of North Carolina; four were of lower socioeconomic status (SES), two black and two white; and four of somewhat higher, that is, middle, SES, two black and two white. Lower SES black and middle SES white "key kitchen persons" (KKPs) referred to such pork products as neck bones, fatback, feet, ears, and tails and to such chicken components as necks, feet, giblets, and backs as well as black-eyed peas and dried beans as "poor people's food." Lower SES whites and middle SES blacks, however, considered the same items to be "black people's food" (1984:115). For

middle SES blacks and lower SES whites, the reference to such food as black is an indicator of dietary content as an ethnic marker. However, for the former it indicates "ethnic inclusion;" while for the latter, it indicates "ethnic exclusion." For the middle SES black KKPs, the more humble parts of the pig and chicken are a part of the "soul food" menu, a consumption pattern they perceive themselves to share with lower SES blacks as an indication of their ethnic identity. For lower SES whites, however, the association of such foods with blacks is a negative one, and they refer to such foods as "nigger foods." For them not to eat such foods is a mark of superiority (1984:115–116).

Viewed positively or negatively, inclusively or exclusively, the foods listed above are markers of African-American ethnicity. Pork products offer a clear-cut example; some of these, such as bacon, sausage, chops, hams, shoulders, and ribs, were consumed by both whites and blacks in all SES groups and termed "mainstream" (1984:118). But other pork products are clearly "ethnic," such as chitterlings, neck bones, pigs' feet, pigs' tails, and fatback because Whitehead (1984:118) found *no instances* of ethnic pork products consumed in either lower or middle white SES homes."

Hinted at by Whitehead's findings is the status symbolically attached to "black foods." Slavery fostered this lower-status symbolism attached to the foods blacks eat, as my African-American informants told me:

Crystal: "Years ago when they killed a pig, we got the entrails and they got the hog . . . they kept the turnip tops and we got the greens."

Maisie: "All we had to eat when I was growin' up in South Carolina was what was thrown away and we did a lot with it. We grew a lot of what we ate too."

Serena: "Some black people are shamed or embarrassed to tell white people that they eat all parts of the pig. I guess they think their foods aren't as good. But you know, for a long time whites laughed at our food and that's why it's so nice that a white girl is interested in our food."

Selma: "Eatin' soul foods had been a survival technique. Blacks had to eat what was left over. Now they don't."

"Throw-away" foods, "leftovers," and "scraps" that nobody else wanted were taken by slaves and made into "something good." Foods that white masters considered inedible were, out of necessity, considered to be edible. Blacks, in the eyes of whites, ate food unfit for human consumption; they ate "low-status" foods in order to survive. Leftovers are commonly eaten in Africa, as Africans now living in the United States have told me, for little food is wasted, particularly when it is not abundant. Leftovers from dinner were commonly served for the morning or evening meal the next day in the household where I stayed in Kenya (see also Lawrance 1957:118–125).

African-American adult informants who spent part of their childhood in the South told me, however, that many white southerners, poor whites especially, ate a lot of the same foods that they did.

However, whites did not prepare them in the same way as blacks: "Blacks eat the same foods as everybody else. . . . we just season 'em different" (Cora). It is from this very piece of information that we receive the first glimpse into why African-Americans do not contradict themselves in saying that "all foods are soul foods." The actual foods themselves, uncooked and unprepared, were used not only by African-Americans but also by whites. The difference arises when the way in which these foods were prepared is considered. Some typically eaten by my African-American informants are also thought to be consumed quite often by southern and northern whites, including chicken, sausages, string beans, and potatoes. Other foods, however, such as pig parts, are thought to be eaten by whites less frequently. Although emphasizing preparation, my African-American informants also see a difference between the two races in frequency of use of foods commonly associated with blacks. Crystal states that "nowadays white people think 'soul' food's a new thing. Some white people fry up chitlins and serve 'em as an hors d'oeuvres. But we eat 'em as a main meal and some people eat 'em boiled."

"Soul food, is how it's prepared"

Clay: "Soul food is food that's had somethin' special added to it. The same food is different every time."

Clay: "It's when a food is spiced up that it's soul food."

Brenda: "Soul food is plain food with a special taste."

Dera: "Soul food is spicy because in the old days people wanted to make the basic, plain food they had, taste good. Salt, which brings out the flavor in foods, was expensive (and one of the reasons we were sold into slavery in the first place) so we had to use a lot of other spices too."

The importance of how an item is prepared and of the types of ingredients used in its preparation was revealed to me only when I asked informants if they had ever eaten any food that was not soul food. Dera provided an example: "Southern cookin' is a seasoning. It's food that's highly spiced. You would cook a cabbage by boiling it in water and then addin' a little butter to it. Very plain. But we cook it with some ham bones to give it flavor" (see also Jerome

1980). Typically, ham hocks, fatback, or any little bits of pork are cooked with vegetables to provide flavor.

The type of "other" ethnic foods most enjoyed by informants also reveals the nature of soul food. Chinese and Italian foods were the only two ethnic ones informants ever mentioned as those that they either went out for (no informant seemed to prepare Chinese food at home) or occasionally made at home (spaghetti, for example, which was identified as an "Italian" food). These two types are enjoyed because they are like soul food:

Clarence: "Chinese food has good spices. . . . I like shrimp fried rice."

Cora (Serena's daughter): "My sister makes a good spaghetti. Her sauce is real spicy and thick, not like those sauces you get out of a can."

Crystal: "I like Chinese food. I like the way they do their spices."

Selma: "Chinese food is a favorite ethnic food of mine. I like the way they spice it. I love sweet and sour pork."

Salt is the spice commonly and liberally used by my African-American informants in the form of table salt or salt pork. Serena told me point blank: "I know it's not good for me, but I use a lot of salt and don't ever let black people lead you to thinkin' they don't use much salt" (see also Whitehead 1984:118–137). Salt is also used widely throughout Africa as African informants from Sierra Leone, Nigeria, Burkina Faso, and the Central African Republic, living in the United States, told me and as my experiences in Kenya verified. (See also Lawrance 1957:123; T. Richards 1939.)

The belief that "all foods are soul foods" may seem contradictory to the experience of having eaten a food that any one of my informants told me was not soul food, but rather, belonged to a different ethnic group. But Chinese and Italian food, respectively, exhibit two important qualities of African-American and African food: spiciness and "heaviness." A twenty-five-year-old man from Sierra Leone who has been living in the United States for three years told me that when he first came to the United States he tried all different kinds of foods and liked the Italian and Chinese best. "But with Chinese food," he told me, "I am hungry after I eat it." Italian food filled him up more adequately, but he preferred the spices in the Chinese.

Soul Food: Flexibility, Creativity, and "Making Do"

Soul food, black folk cooking, is compassion food. The origin of soul food goes back to Africa, the birthplace. When the slaves first set foot upon this land, soul food took its stand! This was the food that the slave master saw no need for so, therefore, it was thrown out, and slaves took this food to their shacks and prepared it. That's why it was called compassion food, because it was cast off.
(Jackson 1969:7)

Women in Africa, African female slaves, and African-American women historically were responsible for the preparation of food, using whatever food and cooking equipment was available (Cussler and de Give 1942:238; Lawrance 1957:118–125; LeVine and LeVine 1963:158; Mead 1955:110; Richards [1932] 1948:84, 1939; Roscoe 1966:426). My African-American informants commented on the historical and present practice of "making do" with whatever is available:

Dera: "We know how to stretch foods. For instance, white people ate regular apple pie. We had a lot of mouths to feed so we layered our pies with apples and scrap dough to stretch it."

Dera: "Often we didn't have many utensils so we just made do with our hands and ate with our fingers like they do in the motherland [Africa]."

Dera, Mr. and Mrs. Jones: Eating lunch together one day at the Main Line College dining center, these informants and I served ourselves some fish chowder. Mr. and Mrs. Jones commented on its blandness. Dera added about a quarter of a teaspoon each of salt and pepper and said: "That's all you have to do is add something to it if you want it to taste like something."

Selma: "We eat a lot of leftovers. Many foods taste better on the second day anyhow. And you can put together leftovers and make a new dish."

Serena: While peeling her potatoes with a long bread knife, she commented: "I know you're supposed to use a peeler for this, but I just use whatever I lay my hands on." Serena and I exchanged some intimate details about our lives—about our families, religious beliefs, sexual experiences, and food habits. Near the end of our time together, she said to me: "You are a very passionate person and I'm not just talking about sex. You want to know the truth? You got to have passion to get by. You got to put feeling in everything you do. It doesn't matter what you do or what you want to be, you got to be the best. You got to make the best out of any situation. And food is no different. You got to cook like you know how."

"Making do," as these quotes reveal, refers not only to the preparation of meals; it is an attitude that cuts through many aspects of African-American life-style. Activity is inherent in the verbal expression "making do." African-American women prepare and cook food, and this takes time. The length of this activity seems to be one of the basic features of soul food, aside from the way it is prepared. Increased preparation time means that all the more ends up going into the food. The "more" is not only quantitative but also qualitative.

The time element was revealed to me through statements about the types of foods my informants bought. Consistently, fresh foods, particularly vegetables, are preferred over frozen or canned foods (see also Jerome 1980), and unprocessed foods over pre-prepared. If one is going out for a meal, this last preference does not apply, for, by definition, going out for a meal means you will eat food that has been prepared for you. Selma, for instance likes "to go out for something like lobster or stuffed shrimp with crabmeat—something I don't usually prepare at home or something I don't know how to make." However, if a meal is prepared at home using these "less preferred" foods, it is considered "cheating" by my key African-American women informants, whose responsibility it is to prepare the meal.

Every family member has responsibilities to meet. Informants frequently mentioned the chores they were expected to do on a daily basis while growing up, and those who have children detailed the types of chores their children are expected to do: cleaning, straightening up, taking out the garbage, and cleaning the cellar, to name a few. The idea of instilling a sense of responsibility in one's children is basic in the allotment of chores. Everyone in the family is expected to "pitch in," to "do their fair share."

"Cheating," then, in one sense, can be interpreted as accomplishing one's goal, that is, preparing a meal, in a less than "honest" way; it is getting the job done faster and with less effort. The African-American woman is the main cook in the family and she also usually raises the children. Because she acts as a role model for the children and tries to instill in them a sense of a shared lot in life, it would be hypocritical to shirk her own duties and responsibilities. I suggest that women who feel as though they are cheating in the ways described above believe they are depriving their families of a truly good performance of their "jobs." Working women are caught in a bind because, even though they may want to prepare from scratch all the food they feed their family, time may not permit it but that is an ingredient of soul food.

Serena manages to sidestep this factor by not setting a specific time at which dinner is served. She prepares it when she comes home from work, and whenever it is ready everyone eats. She gives up a strict mealtime in favor of producing a home-cooked meal, one that takes longer to cook but is considered to be of a higher quality than what might be called a "home-heated" meal of warmed up frozen, pre-prepared, or pre-packaged foods. This sort of flexibility allows Serena to "do her fair share."

The time factor involved in making soul food stems from the long time it took and takes African women to prepare foodstuffs for cooking and from the way in which slaves were forced to cook their meals. Pots of their food would cook all day long on a back burner because time would not be available to begin meal preparation at the end of a long workday. Another factor is the cooking time required for pork, which, Clarence told me, had to be "cooked a long time because it can make you sick." A long time element was involved therefore, much out of necessity, and my informants still feel that for food to be good it has to be cooked a long time. It is during this process of preparation that each African-American woman adds the "soul" ingredients to her food: "No two people can cook up the same recipe in exactly the same way. There's a secret ingredient and it's the cook, not the recipe" (Jackson 1969:7, quoting from Princess Pamela's *Soul Food Cookbook*).

"Cheating" then, in a second sense, is cheating oneself. Preparing home-cooked meals for her family members is a source of satisfaction and fulfillment for an African-American woman; it is her chance to "give" to them, to put her "soul" into the foods that they then literally put into themselves. All of this, in turn, makes her feel good about herself: "Food remains one of the Black woman's self-concept expressions. Through her mysterious, spiritual self-confidence and through her arrogance in food preparation, the Black woman gains a sense of pride as she watches her extended family —her man, her children and maybe her grandparents, sisters, nieces, and friends—enjoy the soulful tastes and textures prepared by her skillful hands" (Styles 1980:163). Fulfilling as they were their actual and symbolic role as "nurturers" by preparing food for their families, my African-American female informants expected the members of their families to be home whenever a meal was served. Missing a meal is viewed as breach of responsibility on the part of one who misses it, just as it is on the side of the mother should she fail to cook it. Yet, such a breach is not punished by withholding food.

Fifteen informants, in response to my questioning them about the consequences of not showing up for a meal (assuming you were not ill), told me in effect that it never happened; it was an unwritten law, and nobody broke it. Selma added that, if you were late for or missed dinner, you "had to eat what was left, but no one ever went hungry" (see also Cussler and de Give 1942:66–67). It is inconceivable that food would be withheld from children, I was told by Kenyans (see also LeVine and LeVine 1963:158) and African-Americans, inasmuch as it is intimately connected with meanings of survival: "Our diet is based on our background, on makin' it from day to day" (Selma). Gathering together for a meal is the culmination of *everyone's* hard work and *everyone's* "pitching in" because in the most basic sense it is survival toward which everyone is working and lending a helping hand. Food represents this survival —it is much more than biological nourishment.

A constant theme among an ethnic group whose heritage in the United States stems from times of slavery is that of daily survival, of "makin' it." Preparing foods for her family is fulfilling for a black woman in that she gives something to her family and she is "makin' it." "Making do" is, like the "giving" to her family, a personally derived feeling of satisfaction. Buying frozen or pre-prepared foods is cheating in that someone else has done the work which is really "supposed" to have been done by my female informants. However, preparing the same foods differently every time or concocting a new one out of whatever ingredients are at hand is not considered cheating inasmuch as there are no specified rules that must be followed. Cheating is not even a factor because, without rules, anything goes.

Crystal told me that she did not like foods with a lot of gravies, like eggs Benedict, because "the gravy disguises the taste. All those gravies taste the same. Gravies are only good when they're homemade. Then you make 'em however you like and they give the food flavor." She hints at the fact that foods or gravies made only a certain way or according to a specific recipe taste sterile. But, unlike such "sterile" foods (foods made one certain way, according to a specific recipe, is a feature of those that are *not* homemade), homemade foods are, in the abstract, full of the cook's imagination, ingenuity, and ability to "make do." The term "make do" is clearly connected with "soul" as used by African-Americans; I use it instead of "soul" because this is the term my informants used most often.

I did not get the impression from my informants that, at the other extreme, using a recipe was considered to be cheating. Recipes are sometimes used to prepare a specific dish that is not in the cook's repertoire. Serena recounted an incident when her employer wrote her out a recipe for *matzoh brie,* a food commonly eaten by Jews during Passover. She said it tasted terrible the first few times she made it. Once she got a feel for it, she "got rid of the recipe and started makin' it right." Rather than "cheating," using a recipe is often considered more of a hindrance than a help.

My informants cook according to a sense of taste, smell, and touch. Speaking specifically of her mother, Styles (1980:164) says: "As she mixes together a 'handful' of, a 'pinch' of, a 'dash' of [we see] that her culinary creativity is much like other Black women who defy the rules of measurement and scientific cooking precision. Many Black people of her generation never used recipes or measuring instruments. . . . Slaves were accustomed to their African cultural cooking, and . . . the European cooking techniques underwent many adaptations as the Black woman added her African cultural style. Her recipe variations were passed from generation to generation through oral history in the African tradition." Once written down, a recipe becomes inflexible; food is prepared according to a set of rules and steps indelibly printed in ink. It is not surprising that African-American women, who value flexibility, shun written, stagnant recipes. Verbal description of how a food *might* be prepared are better suited to them.

The type of "cheating" that recipe use infers is depriving oneself of the satisfaction derived from the almost game-like or "puzzle-solving-like" task of preparing good, flavorful food out of the same basic ingredients day in and day out. Each time an African-American woman does so, she feels good about herself because once again she has "made do." Although she shares with her family the food she has prepared, shares its good flavor, and shares the symbol of her contribution to the family, she does not explicitly share all of the thought and inventiveness that went into the preparation of this food—that is hers to keep and hers to feel good about. "Making do" is an attitude held by my informants that, combined with an attitude of flexibility, underlies many aspects of their African-American life-style. These attitudes are partly based on the African-American heritage of slavery. "Making do" under poor conditions and maintaining an attitude of flexibility in order to facilitate "making do" has resulted in an approach to life, the outlines of which are purposefully vague and thus always flexible.

"Soul"

"Soul" is expressed by African-Americans through their food habits but is not confined to any one sphere of life. "Soul food" is a term used by whites to denote African-American food when they want to be understood by whites. Another dimension of soul can be layered on top of this and it relates *"to the cultural values of a [this] particular cultural group"* (Leninger 1970:165).

My informants described *people* as "having soul": Selma invited me to her church to hear a singer in the choir whom she described as having soul; Clay told me that, if a woman excelled in dancing, he would say, "That girl's got soul." Maisie described a recent trip "home" to South Carolina as "soulful." All these examples demonstrate that "soul" is used in reference to a person in whom "soul" is embodied; anyone who is providing a given situation with "soul" is displaying "soul." Similarly, "soulful" is a descriptive term for a situation or circumstance that is provided with soul by people. The idea of "soul," then, is never removed from the persons who provide the "soul" or "soul ingredients." "Soul" is a living being, not an object. The phrase "soul food" as used by a white person disregards the human element for the food itself, becomes divorced from the person who has *made* it. Finally, the human quality inherent in an African-American's use of the word "soul," the idea that there is human action involved in a food's being soulful or having soul, is reflected by the terms used by African-Americans to describe their own foods. "Home-*cooking*," "southern *cooking*," and "down home *cooking*" are all *active* descriptive terms that emphasize the human action or "doing" that is inherent in a food's being soulful.

Black culture—African and African-American—stresses humanism (Aschenbrenner 1976), and "soul" is "the essentially human" (Hannerz 1973). Soul food *derives* its soul from a human being; blacks, being human, have soul simply by virtue of being black humans: "Black sisters and brothers are *all* soulful" (Styles 1980:167). Asking if a black person or black food is soulful is a moot point (1980:167–168) because if a black person prepares food it will automatically get "soul" put into it. All food prepared by blacks is soul food.

The humanistic character of black culture is expressed through the *"intent of sharing"*:

> When there is a hog killing . . . the neighbors and friends are included. Women play special assisting roles at hog killings; they usually clean the meat, do the trimmings (shave off the fat), cook some samples, give portions to neighbors, and prepare the meat for storage. Men assume the "masculine" chores like slaughtering the beast, removing hairy covering, and cutting it into major parts such as hams and shoulders. The hog-killing ritual is one of the few clearly delineated sex role activities for Black men and Black women.

> The role definition around hog killings relates to the African hunting tradition. African men were hunters and providers; women were nurturing souls for the children, men and elders. (Styles 1980:171)

Although certain roles were traditionally "male" and "female" in black culture, such as those associated with hog killing, preoccupation with basic survival has led to a breakdown in such defined roles. Still, as the black woman gained independence and autonomy, she maintained her dominance over the kitchen, the place where she could express her culinary creativity (1980:172).

Sharing food and sharing the experience of eating pervade African-American society today: "Eating soul food is a symbolic act of 'creating community.' Taking a meal in a soul food restaurant is really a highly stylistic symbolic expression of community. Solitude and privacy for individual customers is unheard of. . . . There is intimacy, in the sense of one large extended family in a state of perpetual flux. . . . The stewing pot-of-soul symbolically represents harmonious family relationships" (W. Shack 1976:127).

The ambience of the restaurants I visited during my study of African-American food habits reveals the pervasiveness of social interaction, of "shared community" in the context of an establishment. Restaurants generally provide two things: food and atmosphere. Although food is contributed solely by the restaurant, atmosphere may be contributed by the restaurant staff and the customers—I speak here of the social atmosphere, rather than the physical environment. Nonetheless, that environment may affect the social atmosphere. None of the restaurants, predominantly patronized by blacks, that I visited in 1983–84 and subsequently was physically designed in a way that "cut off" an individual or group of customers from any others.

Images of Health and Beauty

Dera: "People who are healthy have meat on their bones—not fat, muscle. Small people aren't strong."

Selma: "Blacks think a healthy person has more weight than white people do. Whites like thin bodies but blacks ask if you're sick or feelin' O.K. if you are thin."

Brenda: "I think a healthy person is not fat but full looking. Not too small or skinny."

Foods eaten by African-Americans, as well as other people, are ingested into the body and are reflected in one's physical appearance. The above quotes demonstrate an idea of beauty or health that stresses strength and full-bodiedness. There is an obvious contrast between the general opinion of African-Americans about what is beautiful and white standards of beauty, which have generally stressed thinness, petiteness, and relative weakness of women in comparison to men—though, in the very recent past, emphasis within white America has somewhat shifted to an admiration for stronger women.

A distinction between lightness and heaviness in the differential attitudes to beauty taken by blacks and whites corresponds to the same distinction made by my informants about foods. "Heaviness" of foods and their ability to "stay with you awhile" are qualities stressed by African-Americans and Africans (Jerome 1975a, 1980; T. Richards 1939:51; Styles 1980:163). Adija always encouraged me to eat more *ugali*: "Kula, kula" (eat, eat), she would say, "we can't send you back to America as thin as you are—your family will think we didn't feed you." Although Serena thought I had a healthy figure, Adija wanted to expand my healthiness. A recent article about "soul" in the *New York Times* notes the stress felt by whites as a result of constant dieting: "How, I [Claiborne] asked Mr. Honis [chef from North Carolina], could he account for the sudden popularity of soul food? 'It's because people are dieting all over town,' he said, 'and soul food is such a relief'" (Claiborne 1984).

Conclusion

I have argued in this chapter that the African-American cultural experience cannot be understood apart from a historical perspective.

Many scholars, such as Herskovits, for example, maintain that numerous historical antecedents can be traced directly to Africa. That their position is true for food, as well as many other ethnic markers, is supported by my data. At the same time, factors such as class, slavery, economic poverty, and other social variables are also important in a full understanding of the richness of African-American cuisine.

Part II

Self-Chosen Ethnicity

One of the most significant characteristics of modern American ethnic cultural experience is that for some ethnic groups the geographical integrity of the "neighborhood" is no longer a trait associated with ethnic behavioral expressions. With this dispersal of peoples who formerly resided in ethnically segregated neighborhoods and enclaves, emphasis is on ethnic identity as a more pronounced element of conscious choice. That many groups that were once bounded in space are no longer so distributed has, in fact, influenced the emergence of "new ethnicity" theoretical concerns. These seek to show that ethnicity is primarily an "interactional" or contextual phenomenon that emerges only if individuals are conscious of their ethnic "identities," which appear as a kind of social construction by the individuals through interaction with the social audience for and by whom their identities are so construed.

Thus, a kind of personal "self-chosen" ethnic experience best portrays the circumstances that typify the situation of many millions of Americans who can actually *choose* whether or not they wish to "be" an ethnic person and, at the same time, to be so construed as such by others. Self-chosen ethnicity is most common among ethnic *individuals* who are located in the suburbs in neighborhoods that are ethnically diverse. People with "self-chosen" ethnic identities are often affluent, certainly in comparison to other ethnics for whom the urban, ethnic neighborhood is still the major locus of something less than a self-chosen ethnic experience.

The three studies that follow illustrate "self-chosen ethnicity" in the Philadelphia suburban area. The significance of music (Welsh), dance (Irish), and Easter eggs (Ukrainian) demonstrates the "symbolic" nature of much of ethnic cultural experience. In the extreme instance where geographical boundaries are nonexistent and where self-chosen identification is operative, the symbolic nature of all cultural experience is graphically revealed through focus on aesthetic experience. Cooperative economic activities that constitute a significant component of economically poorer ethnic cultural preoccupations are notably absent in the following accounts. Institutional affiliations are, however, frequently maintained through the church. This section reveals the importance of Roman Catholicism, Russian Orthodoxy, and the Presbyterian church in the social lives of the communities that are described.

Political identifications are also significant, though, once again, self-choice is quite significant. Many Ukrainians, but not all, are "anti-Soviet"; and many Irish-Americans, but not all, are anti-British. The significance of ethnic *identity* emerges because each study emphasizes what individuals say about their own experience. For the three groups discussed, ethnic cultural experience is shown to be largely a matter of a person's own self-choice. Previously in Europe, however, for each group ethnic experience once emerged, in fact, as a collective reaction to political oppression. What is now self-chosen ethnicity in America often contains a persisting element of hostility for past British and Soviet imperialism.

5

Unique Americans
The Welsh-American Ethnic Group in the Philadelphia Area

Lorraine Murray

This study of Welsh-Americans in the Philadelphia area focuses on the musicality that is prominent in their ethnicity as well as cultural heritage and is revealed through their participation today in events such as the *gymanfa ganu* (hymn-sing); the *eisteddfod*, a literary and musical competition that was frequently held in earlier years; and the use of music in other social affairs.

The largest immigration of Welsh people into the United States (though there never was a major influx) occurred at the turn of the century, about 1900 to 1920. Thus, almost all my first-generation informants were in their eighties, having come from Wales as children, usually when they were about five to ten years of age. Another group are second- or third-generation, some of whom do not maintain contact with their Welsh heritage. Several of these people, however, are prominent in the overall group, whether through formal positions or just natural leadership. Most of the individuals had lived, at one time or another, in the coal-mining areas of Pennsylvania, usually the Wyoming Valley or Carbon County. The traditional Welsh economic activity for the last century or so has been coal-mining; and, whether or not they themselves were miners, many immigrants were attracted to the region by the presence of other Welsh, and, as one informant suggested, because it looks like Wales.

Theoretically, I found Barth's (1969) concept of boundary maintenance useful in that it views the ethnic group as an entity that seeks to maintain its distinctiveness and its social perpetuation by establishing and maintaining group differences. The reason behind social perpetuation is provided by Abner Cohen's theory (1974), which states that, in the process, the ethnic group becomes an interest group trying to establish a status within a polyethnic society. I feel that Welsh-Americans use their cultural uniqueness to define boundaries, no matter what that cultural content may be, and that specific cultural attributes come to be used as symbols of ethnic-group status. The way that this process operates for Philadelphia Welsh-Americans is the subject of this chapter.

Historical Background

One of the heroes of Wales is Dewi Sant, or Saint David, who was born in A.D. 530. He established a monastery there and became so well known for his saintly behavior that the people adopted him as their patron saint. The day of his death, March 1, is celebrated as a national holiday in Wales, and is also commemorated wherever in the world there is a contingent of emigrants. Hartmann says, "In America, 'the day' became the occasion for the annual rallying of the Welsh consciousness and a perennial reminder of the cultural heritage of the little motherland" (1978:28).

The original emigration of Welsh to the New World took place after the restoration of the Stuarts to the throne in 1660. That began the religious persecution of Welsh Quakers (almost all of whom fled to the New World), Presbyterians, and Baptists (Hartmann 1978:32). Even after the persecution ended, the emigration continued; many people of note in America, including important figures during the Revolutionary War, were of Welsh descent. The next big wave of immigration came during the U.S. industrial revolution. Iron, coal, and steel workers were needed, and the skilled Welsh, dissatisfied economically, saw greater promise in America, resulting in the immigration of thousands of them (1978:34).

All the while, Anglicization and industrialization had been taking their toll on Welsh folkways and music, which might have been lost were it not for the concerned Welsh scholars and educators who, during the nineteenth and early twentieth centuries, made an effort to preserve the literature and heritage. This trend of placing a high value upon the culture led to the creation of three institutions: the University of Wales; the National Museum of Wales, in Cardiff; and the National Library of Wales, in Aberystwyth (1978:35). Hartmann notes, "Nineteenth century Welsh immigrants to America reflected these trends. They came to America more alertly Welsh conscious than their colonial predecessors. They quickly introduced the *Eisteddfod* and certain of them made valiant efforts to compose literature in the Welsh language" (1978:35–36).

Eisteddfod (plural: *eisteddfodau*), explains Lake (n.d.:172), means "session. . . . It is a meeting of literati and musicians, artisans and craftsmen, who compete in a public session for prizes or certificates and awards of merit." It developed mainly in the nineteenth century but is connected by continuity to the eisteddfodau of medieval times. "The Cymry have always loved a contest," he concludes (n.d.:172). Today, the Royala National Eisteddfod is held annually in Wales, a cherished event. Hartmann quotes one Tomm Parry as saying (1978:41): "During the first week of August, the eyes of all Wales are upon the town in which the National Eisteddfod is being held and that town is, for the time being, the 'capital' of Wales." Lake says the institution "has grown out of a tremendous effort by the Welsh for a truly national cultural expression" (n.d.:172). "The essential thing to grasp," Morgan (1968:45) points out, "is that competition, for choirs, or soloists, has, for competitors and audience, the kind of excitement which competitive athletics or horse racing have."

The *gymanfa ganu* is another uniquely Welsh institution. Lake calls it "a festival confined to the enjoyment and preservation of Welsh hymnody. This is accomplished through a festival of song in which the participants are the performers, singing in four parts, and worshipping God in their fervent offering" (n.d.:280). He considers the singing of Welsh hymns as essential to the preservation of the language, along with the Bible, which was translated into Welsh during the reign of Elizabeth I [albeit as an aid to Welsh people learning English (Edwards 1972:210)], and was responsible for the standardization of the language. "Many Welsh-Americans will attest to the fact that they first learned to read the language in the Sunday Schools of the Welsh chapels. The objective, of course, was to be able to read from the Welsh bible and to learn the hymns of the great Welsh hymnodists" (Lake n.d.:220).

Although the eisteddfod and the gymanfa ganu were both brought to the United States by the Welsh immigrants, the eisteddfod has not flourished in the long run the way that the gymanfa ganu has.

Fieldwork

Through preliminary research, I learned that there were several Welsh organizations based in Philadelphia: the Welsh Society (founded in 1729, the oldest ethnic organization in the United

States), the Women's Welsh Club (part of a nationwide network of such clubs), and the Welsh Guild. I called the secretary of the Welsh Society, which is a fraternal organization, in order to obtain some preliminary information and to introduce myself. He was enthusiastic and invited me to attend the gymanfa ganu that was to be held that weekend. It turned out to be a very important event in this community, and it will be discussed at several points in this chapter. After the gymanfa, a *te back*, or Welsh tea, was served, and the secretary introduced me to many of the participants. By volunteering to help the ladies who were cleaning up in the kitchen, I met many of them and obtained the phone numbers of several. From then on, it was easy enough to widen my circle of contacts through the social network because it is a fairly small community and people, it seemed, welcomed my interest in their group. In fact, it was rather disconcerting to realize that almost everyone knew who I was, even though I had not been introduced to them, and that they knew why I was there.

Several other events like the gymanfa ganu formed the nucleus of my fieldwork schedule. The most important was probably the celebration of St. David's Day. I also attended monthly meetings of the Women's Welsh Club and the *te backs* that sometimes took place after church services. I observed the participants at those events, often following it up with informal questioning of them. In addition, I informally interviewed several.

Interviews did not make up as large a part of my fieldwork as did participant observation, partly because I lacked my own transportation, and many people lived out of the city in areas as far away as southern New Jersey and some of the more inaccessible suburbs of Philadelphia. I did conduct several interviews, which were very open-ended, without a specific agenda of questions most of the time. Usually I did not expect to jump right in with questions but to start a conversation about relevant matters and to wait for the informant to offer a more provocative subject. The people I interviewed knew that I was a student interested in all aspects of Welsh culture; and, because I realized that this was flattering to them, as the experts, I thought that they would tell me what was important to know about them. I also found that, if I asked straight questions, the informants began to doubt their knowledge; the tone had to be kept social because if the interview began to resemble an information session, people felt that I was putting them on the spot, that I wanted "the truth."

The Welsh-American group in the Philadelphia area is not a very large one; the most people I ever counted at one event were between

110 and 120 people at the St. David's Day banquet. At the gymanfa ganu I attended there were around 90, and attendance at other events was considerably smaller. The Women's Welsh Club drew about 20 at its December 1984 meeting; and, almost without exception, the members were in their seventies and eighties. This is true of most of the community, though some of the members of the Welsh Society seem to be younger men.

The children of some of these people live in the suburbs, and many live farther away. Because the Arch Street Presbyterian Church (in center-city Philadelphia), where Welsh activities are more or less focused, is geographically inconvenient for many people, only long-standing members make the effort to attend, despite the fact that many of them also live far away. Three of the more faithful participants live in New Jersey, one in Yeadon, two in Bryn Mawr, two in Chestnut Hill, two in Gladwyne, and at least three in center-city Philadelphia. Other areas are certainly represented, but these were all I was able to ascertain. Many of the Welsh-Americans originally lived in the coal-mining areas of Pennsylvania, including Carbon County and Wilkes-Barre.

Music

The main theme of this study is the role of music in Welsh-American ethnicity, for it is the strong identification of music with the Welsh that is the most immediately recognizable aspect of the culture. The historical place of music in the culture has already been discussed; this section will deal with the musical behavior of the Welsh-Americans in Philadelphia by analyzing their musical life in its contemporary state, as well as providing brief historical information.

I attended a gymanfa ganu at the Arch Street Presbyterian Church, in the St. David's Chapel. In the foyer, several kinds of literature were provided: copies of the newspaper Y Drych (self-described as "The American Organ of the Welsh People"); handbills with a brief history of the Welsh in the United States; programs for the afternoon; and gymanfa ganu hymnbooks, put together by the Welsh National Gymanfa Ganu Committee (a suborganization of the Welsh National Gymanfa Ganu Association). The day's guest conductor, Olwen Morgan Welk, was a member of the latter organization and had come from Ripon, Wisconsin, to participate. A note in the front of the hymnbook explained that the gymanfa ganu "gives an outlet for their deep and fervent religious feeling through the medium they love best, the music of human voices, blended in harmony."

The chapel was quite small, with only two columns of eleven pews each, but it held about ninety people. The conductor sat up at the front with the church's pastor, a Dr. Todd, a man named Williams, and a Mrs. Pritchard. They were placed around a central table, and behind them were American and Christian flags. The organ, which provided the accompaniment, was on the left; and a piano, to be used for the soloist's accompaniment, on the right. The people were predominantly older, mostly forty-five and upward, though some younger people and children were in attendance. They were dressed nicely but not formally, in skirts and business suits. Many of the men wore blazers with the crest of the Welsh Society on the pocket.

The program began with the singing of "The Star-Spangled Banner," which was followed by introductions and opening remarks. The singing, I noticed immediately, was loud and expressive, and this tone of enthusiasm was to be sustained throughout the two-hour program. The hymns were sung in English and Welsh: the hymnbook provided verses in both languages; and, though many people evidently did not speak Welsh, they were urged to try to do so.

During the service, many references were made to the common Welsh heritage. The audience seemed very conscious of it, as I could tell by comments that were made. For instance, when the soloist was introduced, it was mentioned that she had "three good Welsh names." When the pianist was introduced in appreciative terms, she reminded us: "Don't forget, I sing too!" This pride in singing was marked in all the participants; as I looked around, I did not see anyone who was not singing or who did not look as if he or she were enjoying it.

The conductor directed the hymns with verve. She often stopped to point out lines that were particularly meaningful, or to have the participants repeat lines or verses. She encouraged everyone to "sing the words with your voice, from your heart, mind, and soul." The president of the Welsh Guild suggested that everyone take time to think about what the songs meant to them. Clearly, this is just what was done. Choruses were repeated at will, the verses were sung in Welsh and English, and the tempo was varied to create different moods. The singing style, in short, was very emotional. One hymn in particular, "Deemster," was a showcase. The choruses consisted of men and women not only singing in harmony, but also splitting up in parts and answering one another's lines in a rather complex pattern. The conductor paused in between verses and elaborated upon what kind of expression and counterpoint she wanted; and, the next time around, this was accomplished to her satisfaction.

The gymanfa ganu seemed as much a rehearsal as a performance. The tradition of Welsh musicality is here clearly cherished, especially, I think, as an opportunity for individuals to improve and practice their singing, one of the few chances they have to do so. No one was shy when it came to singing. The people took up the songs with enthusiasm and changed tempo and dynamics to suit themselves. In fact, enthusiasm rather than ability seemed to be valued. Finally, the music seemed to bind the community together in the self-recognized Welshness, which was demonstrated in the clasping of hands and the singing of "God Be With You 'Til We Meet Again," as well as of the Welsh national anthem, "Hen Wlad Fy Nhadau." Both the importance of music and the audience's sense of community were stressed by action and by words.

The same function was served by other events that involved the singing of Welsh hymns, notably the St. David's Day banquet, which, in addition to the hired entertainment, had periods of song in between courses. The dinner will be described later because it illustrates many significant points about Welsh-Americans. What is interesting is that all the ethnic events featured singing. On St. David's Day, for example, a short ceremony was held at City Hall in front of the plaque (on the building's east facade) commemorating the Welsh in Philadelphia. It reads:

> Perpetuating the Welsh heritage, and commemorating the vision and virtue of the following Welsh patriots in the founding of the City, Commonwealth and Nation—William Penn, 1644–1718, proclaimed freedom of religion, and planned New Wales, later named Pennsylvania. Thomas Jefferson 1743–1806, third President of the United States composed the Declaration of Independence. Robert Morris, 1734–1806, foremost financier of the American Revolution and signer of the Declaration of Independence. Gouverneur Morris, 1752–1816, wrote the final draft of the Constitution of the United States. John Marshall, 1755–1835, Chief Justice of the United States and father of American constitutional law.
>
> Erected on St. David's Day, March 1, 1968.

The Police Band was on hand to play the music. After a welcome by the president of the Welsh Society, the national anthem was sung. One woman wore the traditional Welsh costume of a red cape and a black hat with white-lace edging. By the podium was a wreath of daffodils, the flower symbolic of Wales and named after St. David (Welsh spelling: Daffyd); it was decorated with red, green, and white ribbons, the colors of the Welsh flag. Dr. Todd, the society's chaplain, gave an invocation and talked about "the ancient, green and pleasant land" of Wales. He mentioned the courage of the early Welsh settlers in the United States, including the noted men named on the plaque, and thanked God, "in whom they trusted and were not put to shame." A representative from the mayor's office read a proclamation that also named the early Welsh patriots, the sixteen signers of the Declaration of Independence, and the founders of illustrious American universities such as Yale and Harvard, who were of Welsh descent. The Welsh Society was mentioned as being the oldest ethnic fraternal organization in the United States. The mayor thereby proclaimed March 1 as St. David's Day in Philadelphia to recognize the contributions of Welsh-Americans to the city. Finally, the Welsh national anthem was sung in Welsh.

The Welsh-American Connection

Several points already noted assume larger importance when considered together: the symbols that represent the Welsh and American heritages. Welsh-Americans are very aware of the dual heritage. In fact, I will try to show that an identity containing components of both is almost consciously crafted by this ethnic group.

The most obvious indicators of the process are the visual symbols at all the gatherings: daffodils, Welsh flags, dragons, red and green colors—all signifying "Wales" as well as the presence of the American flag, denoting the American side. Also significant is the fact that every event began with "The Star-Spangled Banner" and ended with "Hen Wlad Fy Nhadau."

Welsh-Americans are also interested in writings about themselves that deal with their dual heritage. Two books that were recommended to me by at least four or five people were *Americans from Wales* (Hartmann 1978), which was written by an American; and *The Welsh in the United States* (Ashton 1984), by a Welshman. Both books are quite similar; in fact, I gained the impression that my group was basically delighted that "they independently reached the same conclusion," as Mr. Williams put it. Somehow, I think there was agreement that both authors had correctly told the story of the Welsh-Americans. This follows the general trend I noted of self-explanation by the Welsh-Americans through authoritative, that is, published, texts. I was handed clippings, articles, books, and pamphlets—far too many to enumerate—all having to do with Welsh-Americans, and all confirming the same stereotypical "Welshness" concept: the love of singing, the Welsh pride, the interest in the language. A representative sample includes:

1. An article, "Cymru conquers the British," in the May 27, 1978, issue of *TV Guide*, about the successful demand of nationalists for a Welsh-language television channel in Wales (Davidson 1978).
2. *Our Welsh Heritage*, a booklet published by the St. David's Society of the State of New York. It contains bits of information drawn from all aspects of Welsh culture, including history, both Welsh and Welsh-American; hymns; the language; and folklore (Thomas 1972).
3. An article, "The Welsh Indians," in the May 1980 issue of *American History Illustrated*. The abstract reads: "Early adventurers told tales about white Indians living in the American hinterland. Were the stories true or were they more New World myths?" The article deals with a popular legend among Welsh-Americans which alleges that the discoverer of the New World was a Welsh prince, Madog ap Owain, and that his supposed descendants were the blue-eyed, Welsh-speaking Indians (Walker 1980).

The legend of Madog's discovery of America in 1170 is a long-standing one, but the evidence for its truth is flimsy and inconclusive. Yet, despite the cited article's objective analysis of the evidence as well as its hypothesis that such evidence is not a proof of the legend, the woman who gave me the article persists in believing it. She has written on the back of it: "Madoc ap Owen Gwynedd landed in Mobile Alabama in 1170 A.D. 300 years before Columbus. As proof, a picture of the D.A.R. commemoration marker of Prince Madoc landing in the Mobile Bay." Of course, the picture of the marker, put up in 1952, does not prove that any such thing happened eight hundred years ago. I do not mean to imply that the legend is generally credited in the Welsh-American community, but I consider examples of such beliefs to be indicative of the same impulse that causes the group to stress the Welsh connections of many important Americans, no matter how remote. For example, I heard several times about the Welsh origins of Abraham Lincoln. As it turned out, this was true on his mother's side, several generations back.

The legend is also significant in that it is the ultimate historical representation of the Welsh-American connection: the deliberate creation of a hybrid image. One could not hope for a more powerful symbol of Welsh importance in America than the discovery of the New World by a Welshman.

The Welsh-American culture speaks through its newspapers, *Y Drych* and *Ninnau*, which, though they do feature Welsh language and Welsh current events to a degree, concentrate more frequently on such things as American entertainers of Welsh descent; Welsh travel; and, most of all, on the activities of the many Welsh-American societies around the country. These are all topics that emphasize the American aspect over the Welsh. Conspicuously absent are substantial amounts of Welsh news, items on Welsh problems, or political information. I understand this is because the newspapers are not geared to Welsh immigrants eager for news of the homeland but to people who are very much American and interested in those aspects of their cultural heritage that are pleasant and familiar.

Welsh-Americans have been criticized for their sheltered attitude, particularly in my experience by the speaker who received the Robert Morris Award at a dinner I attended on St. David's Day, Professor Alun Hughes, of Ontario. His speech deserves discussion because it was the first really critical insight I received on the subject of Welsh-Americans and was the catalyst in my thoughts about how that community relates to Wales. Hughes is also a reliable source because he was born and raised in South Wales, and now lives in Canada, so he has seen both sides of the picture.

Hughes began by describing the garbage one can see by the roadsides of Wales, replacing the colorful flowers that used to be there. He said that the region is becoming dirty, like much of Britain, but that this fact is something which Welsh-Americans want to ignore. He said that one may celebrate Wales, but one must keep a level head about it; people in North America idealize and romanticize it. He talked about the stereotypes of happy miners singing in their Nonconformist chapels. Such images contain an element of truth, but also distort it; there is an air of decay and despair in Wales.

He remarked that the Wales of the late eighteenth century has a strong influence on the perceptions of Welsh-Americans. For example, the gymanfa ganu is extremely popular here but hardly practiced at all in Wales. America, he seemed to be saying, is the victim of a time lag in ideas about Wales because so few people see how it really is today, nor do they want the bad news. He said, "We need an idealized Wales to keep our sense of Welshness in a hostile world." Perceptions of the homeland must be kept in perspective.

Welshness in North America is taken mostly for granted. But in Wales there is soul-searching for a sense of identity in a culture becoming ever more Anglicized and nontraditional. In their ideas of Wales, he concluded, Welsh-Americans must "recognize the garbage among the flowers."

This speech was, as I have mentioned, one of the first realistic looks at contemporary Wales I had received, and it was interesting to hear such a cautionary report of social changes going on there. My thought was that my informants might not have been happy with the news, but that they would have accepted it. But a Miss Jones volunteered an opinion, when I asked her two days later about the dinner, that she had enjoyed it but that she did not like the speaker. She considered some of the things he said to be untrue, particularly that Wales was becoming dirty. The part about Anglicization might be accurate, she said, but contended that Hughes was a pessimist who probably went back to Wales expecting to find something that was not there. I interpreted her opinion as meaning that he had been soured by disappointment at the changes that had occurred since he had emigrated.

Miss Jones visits Anglesey, in North Wales, every year with her mother, so she certainly is more familiar with Wales than I. Yet, it seems probable that she, as Hughes accused many Welsh-Americans of being, is blind to all but the good in Wales. As he said, their concept of the homeland is primarily influenced by the eighteenth century and, I would add, by their own idealized recollections and impressions of the turn of this century. Welsh-Americans, in my observation, do have a static concept of Welshness and Wales that is necessary as an anchor in a fast-paced, polyethnic society. In order to remain ethnic in the face of their own assimilation, they must keep the same fixed ideals, norms, and activities because it is through such cultural material that they act out their membership in the discrete ethnic group.

St. David's Day: A Celebration of Welsh-Americanism

The St. David's Day banquet serves as a good example of many of the themes I have been discussing. It was a formal dinner given at the Union League, a Republican men's club in center-city Philadelphia, on March 1, 1985. Cocktail hour preceded the dinner, which began at 7:15 p.m. Most people were dressed formally: dark suits or evening clothes for the men, and long or short gowns for the women. As they entered, each man was given a cloth patch with a red dragon printed on it to pin to his jacket, and each woman was given a daffodil with which to do likewise. In the front of the large dining room was the banquet dais, at which were seated, left to right:

President, Daughters of the British Empire in Pennsylvania
Chaplain, the Welsh Society of Philadelphia
President, the Women's Welsh Club of Philadelphia
President, the Scotch-Irish Society
President, the Society of the Sons of St. George
President, the Welsh Society of Philadelphia
Alun Hughes, honoree and speaker
President, the St. Andrews Society of Philadelphia
President, Friendly Sons of Saint Patrick
President, the British Officers Club of Philadelphia
President, Cambrian Society of Delaware Valley
President, the German Society of Pennsylvania

As can be seen, all these people represented various ethnic organizations in the area. What I found significant, though not surprising, was the representation of two English societies: the Daughters of the British Empire and the Sons of St. George. The English-Welsh tension evidently had no place at this affair. I was confused by the presence of the German Society president but did not ask about it.

Not counting those at the dais, there were twelve tables that had room for ten people each, but not all were full. I estimated that a total of about 120 people were in attendance. In addition to the personal decorations already mentioned, each past president of the Welsh Society wore a large dragon pendant, with his name engraved on the back, hanging from a red ribbon. The current president's pendant was larger, more ornate and colorful; and, though I did not really study it, it looked like a reproduction of the society's seal.

Each table had a centerpiece consisting of a flowerpot covered in either red or green foil with two daffodils as well as the Welsh and American flags. At the head table were the following decorations: at the lectern in the center of the long table was a dragon picture flanked by two daffodil bouquets—one containing an American flag, and the other a Welsh flag; full-sized flags stood behind the table, to the left and right center. The Robert Morris Award stood on an easel to the left of the table, and the daffodil wreath was on the right. In the upper left corner of the room were a piano and risers for the hired singers.

After the president of the society and the guests filed in, "The Star-Spangled Banner" was sung. The chaplain, Dr. Todd, gave the Invocation. At each place setting were the menu/program, a list of financial contributors, and a song booklet of Welsh hymns that were to be sung at various times throughout the dinner. The dinner was not Welsh, except for the potato-leek soup, yet Welsh translations were given for the dishes. I was amused to read such descriptions as "Braised Yankee Pot Roast/*Cig Wedi Rhostio.*" Hymns from the booklet were sung between courses; I noticed most people sang just the melody, and had their eyes on the program when Welsh verses were sung.

After dinner, Williams gave the necrology, the listing of all the members who had died in the past year. Then everyone sang "Penpark," a very slow, reflective hymn. Next, the hired entertainment, the "Valley Voices," took the stage. They were a fairly talented group who sang Broadway hits of yesteryear. When their program was over, they and the audience all sang "Hen Wlad Fy Nhadau" (the Welsh national anthem) together, in English.

Next came the presentation of the Robert Morris Award to Alun Hughes. Morris was one of the early Americans of Welsh descent named on the commemorative plaque at City Hall. Dr. Bevan, the society president, read the award, and then Hughes spoke. His speech has already been discussed. After that, the society's new officers and stewards were introduced, the Welsh national anthem was sung again—this time in Welsh—and the chaplain gave the Benediction. Many people stayed afterward to socialize in small groups, but I noticed that I was one of only three or four people who went up to greet the speaker. It was then that it first occurred to me that his speech had not been too popular. After talking to him about what he had to say about Welsh-Americans, and after he had urged me to subscribe to the Welsh newspaper *Y Drych* and to take a Welsh language course, I left. Most of the other people had gone by that time.

Theoretical Conclusion

The above description of the St. David's Day banquet contains most of the elements of Welsh-Americanism I have touched upon. All the symbols were there (daffodils, dragons, flags, colors, and national anthems), reiterating the double heritage of the group.

Abner Cohen takes up this point of the interaction of ethnic groups within the social system, and he adds to his definition of them the characteristic that their members "share some patterns of normative behavior" (1974:ix). This is an important qualification because it emphasizes that to be a group a "collectivity" of people must have something in common besides a shared recognition of their being alike; there must be some content to that recognition. This does not mean any *particular* cultural content, but rather symbolic formations and activities, largely collective representations, that are "involved in psychic processes and thus can be subjectively experienced by the actors" (1974:x). They are objective, however, in the sense that they are "socially created and are internalized through continuous socialization" (1974:x).

Cohen stresses that, again, context and interaction are the keys to understanding ethnicity. He contends that the term "ethnicity" cannot be used to describe cultural differences between whole societies, but, when immigrants interact in a foreign land as members of their original societies, "they can then be referred to as ethnic groups. Ethnicity is essentially a form of interaction between culture groups operating within common social contexts" (1974:xi). The ethnic group includes not only the immigrants but also their descendants and those who identify with the group. Cohen points out that such groups can be analyzed in terms of interconnections with economic and political relationships; ethnicity "pervades almost the whole universe of social relationships" (1974:xv).

The interrelatedness of ethnicity and politicization, then, brings out a further facet of the ethnic group: the interest group, which is the vehicle through which the ethnicity is expressed in certain purposeful, directed ways. Cohen believes that interest groups can be organized in two ways: (1) on formal bases, where the aims of the group are clear and organization is planned along bureaucratic lines; and (2) when such organization is not possible, "the group will articulate its organization on informal lines, making use of the kinship, friendship, ritual, ceremonial, and other symbolic activities that are implicit in what is known as style of life" (1974:xvii). I believe that the concept of the interest group can be useful not only in the analysis of economic relationships but also in any case that involves the presentation of the ethnic group to the larger community. The manipulation of the group's unique cultural symbols can be an important tool of interaction. Cohen terms such action "political ethnicity" and contends that members of such groups make use of the available cultural mechanisms to "articulate the organization of their grouping" (1974:xviii).

Such articulation requires a consciousness of the group's position in the social system, and its result is the establishment of the ethnic group as a social entity for as many generations as continue the practice. Cohen explains: "If in a dynamic contemporary complex society a group of second- or third-generation migrants preserve their distinctiveness and make extensive use of the symbolism of the ethnoculture, then the likelihood that within the contemporary situation they have become an interest group is very strong" (1974:xxii). This, I think, aptly describes the cultural situation of the Philadelphia Welsh-Americans.

In this chapter, I have attempted to provide ethnographic data that will serve to document the persistence of an ethnic cultural tradition along the theoretical lines presented in this concluding section.

6

Irish-Americans and Irish Dance
Self-Chosen Ethnicity

Erin McGauley Hebard

Irish-Americans are a large and varied group. To attempt a study of them that is not strictly limited in scope and is not grounded in a theoretical approach would be utter folly. For the purpose of studying an ethnic group that has so successfully assimilated itself into American culture to the degree that some scholars maintain it is "becoming an invisible ethnic group" (Moynihan in Griffin 1981:ix), the concept of self-chosen ethnicity as outlined in *The New Ethnicity* (Bennett 1975) seems most productive.

William Shannon estimates that there are 20 million Americans of Irish descent (Shannon in Griffin 1981:vii), and in a census survey in 1972 some 16.4 million Americans claimed "Irish descent" (Blessing 1980:540). Given these numbers, it is obvious that the potential members of an Irish-American ethnic group far outnumber the people who so identify themselves. Irish-American ethnicity is, for the most part, a self-chosen ethnicity. In his introduction to *The New Ethnicity*, Bennett refers to "the conscious . . . construction of an identity for the individual and the group out of traditional cultural symbols" (1975:3).

My field research, conducted in the Philadelphia area over several months, supports this hypothesis. The maintenance of Irish-American ethnicity increasingly is falling to groups and organizations established explicitly for that purpose. Whereas in the past ethnicity was "tied firmly to socialization in a particular group" (Bennett 1975:5), many of the vehicles of Irish-American socialization now fit the following description by Bennett: "Many of these . . . 'networks' are self constituted groups: they emerge out of those who define themselves as ethnic and then *become* networks and *acquire* the . . . shared sense of cultural past" (1975:9).

In a study of Irish-American ethnicity as self-chosen ethnicity, several specific questions arise. Within the limits imposed by time and finances, this study attempts to examine which people identify themselves as Irish-Americans, what symbols they have chosen in the construction of their ethnic identity, and why they chose the particular symbols they did.

Irish-Americans in the Philadelphia area are numerous and are active in a variety of groups and organizations. It is beyond the scope of any single study to analyze the complexity of Irish-American ethnicity in the area as a whole. Thus, the study focuses on two Irish dance groups: one centered in the Mt. Airy section of Philadelphia; the other in Glenside, approximately four miles northeast of Mt. Airy.

It is not possible to restrict the study to these two groups alone, however, because for many people other opportunities arise for assertion of their Irish-American ethnicity. Not the least among these is politics: specifically, Americans' involvement with and attitude toward the politics of Ireland. The Republic of Ireland is a source of great pride, and the "troubles" in Northern Ireland affect the lives of all Irish-Americans in some way. Indeed, the importance of Northern Ireland as a symbol in the Irish-American identity is such that I found it impossible to avoid. That country is seldom regarded with indifference by Irish-Americans but instead arouses passionate discussion and debate.

In discussing the construction of an ethnic identity from symbols it is necessary to examine what is meant by the term "symbol." In the field, symbols may be "objects, activities, relationships, events, gestures" (Turner 1967:19). As an Irish-American, it was often difficult for me to justify according the status of "symbol" to something observed in the field; it was *obviously* a symbol. The question of how one recognizes a symbol is handled capably in "On Key Symbols" (Ortner 1973), which has helped to provide the distance necessary for me to reconstruct the recognition of symbols of Irish-American ethnicity. Ortner writes of the key symbol: "(1) The natives tell us that X is culturally important. (2) The natives seem positively or negatively aroused by X, rather than indifferent. (3) X comes up in many different contexts . . . in . . . different kinds of action, situations, or conversation. . . . (4) There is greater cultural elaboration surrounding X. . . . (5) There are greater cultural restrictions surrounding X, either in sheer number of rules, or severity of sanctions . . . " (1973:1339).

Most of the key symbols of Irish-American ethnicity are marked by several of these indicators. As previously noted, Northern Ireland and the Irish Republican Army (IRA) are marked by their ability to elicit strong reactions, their recurrence as issues in a wide variety of settings, and the cultural restrictions that enshroud them. Likewise, Irish dance is marked by many of the same indicators. It is of interest that Irish-Americans are usually more willing to label Irish dance as "culturally significant" than they are to label the IRA and its activities as such. There is, in a sense, a reluctance to acknowledge this issue, which only serves to point up its importance.

Fieldwork

My first significant contact with Irish-Americans in the Philadelphia area was unplanned. While listening to Irish folk music on a local radio station, I heard several announcements for events of interest to Irish-Americans, such as concerts and a dance. On impulse, I called the phone number provided and thus entered the local Irish dance scene.

From inside the network of the two dance groups I found myself focusing on, it was easy to widen the circle of informants. Once these initial contacts had been established, referrals led to new informants. All these people frequently introduced me to others or provided me with names and phone numbers, accompanied by the encouraging words "You must talk with so-and-so, who will be able to help you."

Spending time with informants also revealed their favorite gathering spots outside the immediate context of the dance groups. These gathering spots also proved to be additional sources of information because they frequently had bulletins announcing events, flyers about things of interest to Irish-Americans (from tours of Ireland to Irish jewelry), and Irish-American publications.

The methods of data collection used in this study are those that characterize ethnographic research. Chief among these has been participant observation. This has the threefold purpose of observing what takes place in a society or group, of noting the people and the activities they engage in, and of participating in an appropriate manner in these activities (Spradley 1980:54). The ethnographer thus assumes the role of "learner" in the group under study (Crane and Angrosino 1984:15).

This role was particularly easy to adopt in the groups I studied. My introduction of myself as a student from Bryn Mawr College studying Irish-American ethnicity was greeted warmly and designated me automatically as a "student" rather than a "social scientist." Furthermore, this role became explicit every Tuesday night when I arrived at the Irish Center for lessons in *ceili* dancing. As a student of this type of dancing, I was expected to have many questions to ask, and much information was given to me that I did not have to request as a result of my status as a beginning dancer who was unaware of the rules and the history of ceili dancing.

My informants were, on the whole, a talkative group. In one case, a two-hour discourse resulted from my introduction of myself and the purpose of my study. Simply by nodding or shaking my head at appropriate intervals, I was supplied with a short life history, including a sketch genealogy, an analysis of the history of the Irish in America, and an in-depth appraisal of the IRA and the 1981 hunger strikes. This informant then concluded the interview by handing me a large quantity of literature on Irish Republicanism for my perusal at home.

During the course of this study, a historic agreement concerning Northern Ireland was signed by Britain and the Republic of Ireland. Although some people saw the agreement as a victory for voices of moderation, it was attacked from all sides (*Inquirer* 11/17/85:12A). This pact was a topic of conversation and was a useful tool for exploring an informant's feelings regarding Irish Republicanism and Northern Ireland.

The holiday recognized across America as the occasion when "Everybody's Irish for a day," St. Patrick's Day, took place during the research period, thus enabling me to observe the reaction of Irish-Americans to the holiday. This reaction, both within the group and individually, was illuminating.

Unfortunately, the period of fieldwork missed the "Feis season." Every weekend during the summer, dance competitions take place wherever the local Irish-American population can organize them. The big one in the Philadelphia region is the Delaware Feis. Likewise, the annual Traditional Irish Music and Dance Festival of the Philadelphia Ceili Group, which takes place in early September, was not directly observed. Data concerning these events were drawn from informant recall and from printed sources, such as local Irish-American newspapers.

Irish-American Ethnicity

The impact of the emigration of Irish people to America cannot be underestimated. They were the "first major immigrant group to threaten the stability of American society" (Blessing 1980:545). Proportionally, no country has given more of its population to the United States than has Ireland (McGoldrick 1982:312). According to one estimate, there are 20 million people of Irish descent in the country today (Shannon in Griffin 1981:vii). From the beginning, the Irish maintained a strong sense of national identity in spite of the fact that there never had been an actual Irish nation. What bound these people together was a sense of national unity based on loyalty to the Catholic church and a bitter hatred of England (McGoldrick 1982:313; Downey 1983:32; Beckett 1984:137; Griffin 1981:9).

The Catholic Irish peasants who came to America in the 1846–49 period were far different from the earlier Irish immigrants. Mokyr speaks of a "political, religious, and cultural abyss" between Protestants and Catholics of Ireland (1983:124). The already settled, predominantly Protestant Irish-Americans attempted to distance themselves by emphasizing their own identity as "Scots-Irish" or "Protestants" (Griffin 1981:5). As a result, their descendants did not tend to identify themselves as Irish-Americans and today exhibit the lowest rate of endogamous marriage of any ethnic group (McGoldrick 1982:311).

The Irish Catholic immigrants in America met with a great deal of anti-Catholic prejudice (D. Clark 1973:19–21). This rejection was instrumental in the creation of an Irish-American subculture (Griffin 1981:8). The Irish fostered the Catholic church as a force in America. An associated system of schools, hospitals, colleges, orphanages, and other charities reinforced this subculture and transmitted an Irish identity to generations of Irish-Americans (Griffin 1981:8–10, 175; McGoldrick 1982:312; D. Clark 1973:88–125). Shunned by the majority of Americans and exploited by industrial capitalism, the Irish learned to care for their own and missed no opportunity to further their interests through a variety of clubs and associations, many parish-based but some with a larger regional foundation (Griffin 1981:220; D. Clark 1973:106–144).

The other important element in the identity of the great wave of Irish immigrants was an overwhelming hatred of the British. The suffering and oppression endured at their hands made pro-Irish sentiment virtually identical with anti-British sentiment. As Griffin has noted: "The Irish were more persistent in their attachment to their homeland's political interests, and more audacious in promoting them, than any other immigrant group" (1981:137).

The Irish assimilation into American society has been quite marked. According to Daniel Patrick Moynihan, Irish-Americans today are more likely to be professionals or managers than are other citizens, and are less likely to be laborers, service personnel, and factory workers (in Griffin 1981:ix). He also points out that, as recently as 1950, the opposite was true (in Griffin 1981:ix). Griffin's analysis (1981:11) highlights several factors contributing to the increasing invisibility of the Irish in America, such as increasing affluence and education that have caused many of the old neighborhoods to break up as the residents move to the suburbs and adopt an increasingly mainstream life-style. The slowing of immigration (Blessing 1980:528) has lessened immediate ties to the homeland. Commitment to Irish politics, while continuing, has not been as strong since the founding of the Free Irish State. As Moynihan adds, the breakup of the old neighborhoods means that ever larger numbers of Irish-Americans, indeed a majority, are more likely to marry a non-Irish spouse (in Griffin 1981:x).

Nevertheless, Irish-Americans, though now a part of the mainstream of American culture, have begun reexamining their roots. Many Irish-Americans are now seeking out the Irish elements of their personal history and of the American nation. Griffin notes a recent increase in the number of groups interested in traditional art, music, dance, and in the study of the history, folklore, and the language of Ireland (1981:12, 193–218).

Irish Dance

Given the importance of Irish dance music in the body of the culture's traditional music as well as the early commentary on the musicality of the Celts, it is interesting to note that there are virtually no references to dance in Ireland prior to the sixteenth century and that the Irish words for dances are borrowed words (Sadie 1980:318). The traditional dance forms generally originated outside Ireland (usually in Scotland or England); the Irish, however, have adapted these forms and made them their own, with the result that there are thousands of dances that may be considered to be "native to Ireland" (Sadie 1980:321).

There are several dance types that traditionally have involved groups. There are round dances, so called because the dancers stand in a ring to perform them; and long dances, or *rince fada*, in which they stand in lines, gentlemen facing the ladies. Both of these are referred to in English and Anglo-Irish writings from the sixteenth century onward (Sadie 1980:318). These dances are based on the steps of jigs and reels (1980:319) and are done to a variety of tunes but most frequently in single-jig or double-jig time (An Coimisiún le Rincí Gaelacha [1939;1943] 1969).

An important part of the Irish dance tradition is step dancing. This is generally a solo form (Sadie 1980:319), performed by particularly skilled dancers. Rhythms are beaten out upon the floor by the feet with the upper body unmoving; complex designs are executed with the pattern of movement through space. Ó Canainn compares the style of the step dancer with that of the *sean-nos* singer, who uses only a small portion of the possible techniques of ornamentation in a performance; he refers to this as the "normal Irish artistic restraint combined with a minute attention to intricate patterns," an apt description of step dancing (1978:75).

Step dancing originated as a way for the most skilled dancers to show off their talents. It is danced on a kitchen table, a door hitched for the purpose, a lid on the floor or on the "flag[stones] of the fire" (O'Neill [1910] 1973:116, 300, 301). The effect of dancing on a hard surface rather than the usual dirt floor was the ability to drum out the steps on a surface that reverberated, thus accentuating the dancer's ability to ornament the melody through dance (O'Neill [1910] 1973:116); the dance became an aural as well as visual display of virtuosity. Step dancing continues to play an important role in traditional Irish dance.

Irish-American Dance

As I noted earlier, my first contact with the dance groups on which this study focuses was made by phone. I was responding to a radio announcement of "an evening of Irish dance with the Dougherty Irish Dancers." In my conversation with the woman who answered the phone (whom I later found out was Mrs. Dougherty), I asked for such details as where the dance was being held and how much it cost. She responded: "This is an Irish dance, dear, a ceili. Not Irish-American dance, but Irish dance. We'll be doing Irish dance all night. Are you sure this is what you want? Are you sure you want to come?" I told her it sounded perfect inasmuch as I was studying the Irish in America. Assured of my interest, she gave me precise directions on how to reach the hall by car.

Because I was completely unfamiliar with traditional Irish dance,

I consulted a friend who is a member of a prestigious Scottish dance group, on the assumption of some degree of similarity in the two types of dancing. She suggested that I dress nicely and fairly conservatively, in a skirt or dress. She also told me to wear soft-soled leather shoes (ideally something like ballet slippers, which I did not own at that time).

Because the dance was taking place at night in a town some distance away to which I had never been, I decided to invite a friend along. Vickie was also unfamiliar with traditional Irish dance, so we arrived in a state of nervous expectation. As we entered the hall, the woman checking coats asked us if we were going to "that lovely Irish dance." It was held in a large room floored with linoleum tile; there were tables around the room for people to sit. When we paid our admission, we each received a membership card that bore the name of the dance group in Celtic script and had a space for a signature.

When Vickie and I entered the room, the dancers on the floor were doing a promenade dance, in which couples execute the steps as they move in a circle around the room; there is no interaction between them. Approximately half the people in attendance were dancing, a proportion that is typical for almost any dance at a Dougherty ceili. This particular dance was Gay Gordons, a dance of Scottish origin. The principal difference is that the Irish dancers lengthen one phrase of the dance and eliminate the one that follows.

Vickie and I sat down at an empty table and found on it a sheet listing the evening's dances and another photocopy with both the American and Irish national anthems. Two flags, American and the Republic of Ireland, flanked the small platform, where two accordion players were performing. The crowd of about eighty was predominantly middle-aged and nicely dressed. There were slightly more women than men; and, with few exceptions, the women wore dresses or skirts. Most of them also wore dancing shoes, or "pumps," a soft leather shoe not unlike a ballet slipper. Many women arrived in dress shoes and then slipped their dancing shoes out of their handbags for dancing. The men wore leather-soled dress shoes, or occasionally sneakers.

After several dances, Dave, a handsome man in his late fifties, asked me to dance. I told him that I did not know how to do so, but he said that would not be a problem because he could help me. He told me that Irish dancing was based on two groups of steps: groups of three to move forward or backward, and groups of seven to move sideways. He guided me carefully through the Fairy Reel, a dance for trios, each of which consisted of a man and two women.

It is a progressive dance, meaning that a trio stands with its backs to one trio and facing another in a long line. At the conclusion of the dance movement, trios pass through to face new trios, progressing through the line until the music ends.

Having muddled through the Fairy Reel, I found myself dancing the Walls of Limerick, another progressive dance, because Dave said it was "very easy, a real beginner's dance," and he insisted that I do it with him. Everyone we danced with encouraged me, offering tips and counting the steps for me. I was also introduced to Dave's wife, Maureen.

After I had sat out several dances, a man of about thirty-five years of age approached, introduced himself as Jim, and invited me (by name, even) to join him for the Haymakers Jig, a long dance for five couples. Everyone encouraged me, calling out instructions and offering praise. Over the course of the ceili, Jim asked both Vickie and me to dance several times. He also wrote on the back of my dance sheet when the next Dougherty ceili would be and gave me Mrs. Dougherty's name as a dance teacher. In addition, he mentioned that there was another group that held a ceili every Friday night, "not quite like this ceili . . . kind of different," and urged me to check out this other group, known as the Philadelphia Ceili Group.

About midway through the ceili, a couple of interesting things happened. One was the distribution of a flyer for a benefit "Irish-American dance" the following weekend, including an "Irish-American band" and an appearance by a local step-dancing group. Shortly after the flyers were handed out, a woman came around selling a set of "Ireland Trivia" cards that were designed to be used with games such as Trivial Pursuit. She was selling them with some difficulty because many of the people present already owned a set. The white box, decorated with green shamrocks, contained fifty cards with six questions on every card, one each from the following categories: history/politics, culture/religion, geography/science, miscellaneous trivia, people, and entertainment/sports. While Jim was sitting with us, Vickie and I played with the cards, causing him to remark that he knew "about one out of a hundred of those questions." He actually did somewhat better than that.

At the end of the evening, the remaining dancers (very few had left early) stood, either at their tables or in a group on the dance floor, facing the flags that flanked the bandstand for the singing of the national anthems. With much solemnity, we sang the Irish national anthem in English; the phrase of Gaelic in the song was a little muffled. I noticed only one person looking at the lyric sheet.

The word "soldier" seemed to receive particular emphasis in the singing. This was followed by "The Star-Spangled Banner" and a round of applause before we left for home.

One of the dances that both Vickie and I attempted was the Clap Polka, another long dance. Patterns of clapping hands with one's partner (similar to the child's game Pat-a-Cake) were alternated with a couple of polka steps. This dance took place more than halfway through the ceili and Dave referred to it as a "sobriety test." In spite of the fact that we had consumed nothing stronger than ginger ale, Vickie and I both "failed" the Clap Polka.

The next Dougherty Irish Dancers ceili was in early December and was billed as a Christmas ceili. It was held in a Knights of Columbus hall rented for the occasion. When I arrived, there were 175 to 200 people present. Compared to the previous ceili, dress was slightly more formal.

This ceili differed from the previous one in several important ways. First, the crowd contained many new faces (Nancy and Barney among them), most of them in their thirties. Many of these people were not seen at other Dougherty ceilis. It was interesting to note that those who were unfamiliar seemed more inclined to buy an Irish drink (such as a Guinness or a Jameson's whiskey) at the bar.

Secondly, there were boards of food. Whereas at the previous ceili there had been one table with some package cakes and cookies on it, this time there was an abundance of food, ranging from crudité and cheese and meat platters to a variety of home-baked cakes and cookies. There were a couple of loaves of Irish scones (soda bread), but these did not move any faster than the other food. At one point in the evening, Nancy remarked that someone's New York style cheesecake was almost as good as his tipsy cake. Barney asked what tipsy cake was, and Nancy said it was a terrific Irish dessert, a rich nutty sponge cake soaked in Irish whiskey.

One of my first dances was the Ballyvorney Set, a set dance from the town of the same name. Much later, I learned that natives of Ballyvorney, Ireland, had taught it to dancers at the Philadelphia Ceili Group. It is one of the most vigorous and taxing dances in the repertoire; and, owing to the frequent spinning (similar to spinning or swinging in a square dance), I was extremely dizzy. A set dance consists of a "body" and "figures." The body opens the dance, closes the dance, and is repeated between figures, like the chorus of a song. The figures vary, like the verses of a song; typically there are three or four of them. The Ballyvorney Set has a body that involves much spinning and six figures! It is the only dance I encountered where the music stops before each new figure so that the dancers can catch their breath. At the end of the dance, I was so dizzy I could not leave the floor. When I was able to see straight, I was gratified to find that I was not the only person waiting for the room to stop spinning.

During the ceili, there are several waltzes played. The waltzes danced at Dougherty ceilis are the standard waltz steps done to an Irish tune. About half of the tunes are accompanied by singing. Three favorites with the Dougherty group are "One Day at a Time," "County Mayo," and a medley that includes "When Irish Eyes Are Smiling."

I danced the second waltz of the evening with a spritely man in his early fifties whose dancing style I had noticed earlier. His steps seemed showy yet precise and I so remarked to Nancy. She responded: "Frank is especially good, one of the best dancers. . . . His jig step is excellent; really gets high. But he's a pain because he knows how good he is." She also told me that he had been a member a prestigious local men's dance group several years ago. His waltzing was lively but smooth.

I danced the Haymaker's Jig with a man in his mid-thirties. During this dance, something went "wrong" with interesting results. One part of the jig involves the top couple advancing down the center of the group. They link right arms and do a turn in the center of the two rows of dancers, then extend their left arms to link with the member of the opposite sex in the second couple and do a turn. They then turn each other in the center again, and then turn with the third couple and so on down the line. Although women often dance men's parts (it is not uncommon to see two women waltzing together), I never observed a man dancing a woman's part. One of Joe's friends decided to play a joke on him and switched places with his partner so that he was standing in the line of women as Joe danced his way down the center. Joe was confused when he found a man in the line of women and he made several missteps, which was unusual for such an accomplished dancer. This incident reinforced my observation that men do not dance women's parts.

During the Haymakers Jig, Joe noticed that I was counting my steps under my breath. He told me not to do that, saying, "You don't need to count. Just relax and feel the rhythm . . . you're doing beautifully."

Nancy, my female informant, proved a valuable source of commentary on the dances. During one called Shoe the Donkey, she remarked that it was of Polish origin. I could not find any written references to back this up, but the dance is noticeably different in style from the others, especially in its heavy-footedness. Likewise, during the Kerry Set, Nancy remarked: "We don't do this dance at the Ceili Group. They call it the Kerry Set but I think it should be called the Dougherty Set. It's a Dougherty dance. I've never seen it anyplace else." When I interviewed Mrs. Dougherty some time later, I remembered Nancy's comment and asked about the Kerry Set. She said that it is a very old country dance and almost nobody does it any longer. She was proud of the fact that her dancers were "saving it."

I asked one of my informants how she knew so much about ceili dancing, and she told me that she had to know a lot because she taught dancing. She told me that she would be offering a set of ten beginners' lessons for $20, starting in January at the Irish Center in Mt. Airy. When I expressed interest in the lessons, she gave me her phone number and told me to call her when I returned from my winter vacation.

During one of the breaks, I spoke with a young woman of about twenty. I had noticed her at my first ceili with her parents. She seemed to be a particularly good dancer and was much in demand as a partner. In talking with others, my judgment was confirmed —all agreed that she was a splendid dancer.

As we talked, I found that she had started dancing four years previously when her parents had joined the Dougherty Irish Dancers; they had heard of the group through friends. She is the youngest of five children and the only one who dances regularly. Her three brothers do not dance at all, but her sister, who is twenty-eight and no longer lives in the area, occasionally attends a ceili with my informant and her parents.

The final Dougherty ceili I attended was the St. Patrick's Ceili, which took place the Saturday before St. Patrick's Day. It was held in a church hall at Bala Cynwyd. The group was nicely dressed, as at the Christmas ceili, and again consisted predominantly of middle-aged couples. The band performed on a raised stage at one end of the hall, flanked by the two flags. It consisted of the usual pair of accordion players, but this time they were joined by a fiddler. Because I was now familiar with the Philadelphia Ceili Group, I recognized about eight of the regulars at this ceili.

Interpretation

The most obvious symbols of ethnicity that serve to reinforce the function of Dougherty ceilis as markers of Irish-American ethnicity are the flags and the anthems that are the focus of the closing of the event. The singing of the anthems appears to be a final assertion of a separate "Irish" identity, followed by the singing of the American anthem to signal a break from the Irish identity and resumption of the larger identity of "American."

The national anthem of the Republic of Ireland is "The Soldier's Song," written in 1907 by Peadar Kearney, with music by Patrick Heeney. The popularity of this song dates to the 1916 Easter Rebellion. Irish rebels in British internment camps sang it in defiance of their captors. The British pronounced the song seditious, but in spite of the Defense of the Realm Act, which authorized the arrest of anyone heard singing "The Soldier's Song," its popularity grew at home in Ireland. It was officially adopted as the national anthem in July 1926 (Hoagland 1947:684–686; Figgis 1968:172).

The ceilis reveal that Irish dance is a metaphor for social organization. The Dougherty Irish Dancers, like many ethnic groups, "use dances symbolic of themselves to set their group off from surrounding groups" (Royce 1977:79). Royce notes that in complex societies, dance may function as an identity marker (1977:155). That Dougherty ceilis function in this way is borne out by many observations in my data. Mrs. Dougherty's initial emphasis on "Irish dance" as opposed to "Irish-American dance" indicates a concern for the purity of the dances as "Irish." The variety of markers of Irish ethnicity present at ceilis, from the Ireland Trivia cards to the Irish scone on St. Patrick's Day, and the ever present Irish Tricolour, show an appreciation for the manipulation of easily recognized symbols, along the lines mentioned by Ortner (1973). Likewise, the prizes at the St. Patrick's Day ceili involved familiar images of Ireland.

Those who are not regular attendees at the ceilis seem to feel a need to emphasize their "Irishness" at the event. This was seen in the drinking patterns at the Christmas ceili. The nonregulars were far more likely to order a bottle of something "Irish" and take it to their table, where all could see it. They did not seem to be aware of this pattern, and the regulars did not seem to notice either. The Christmas ceili also showed some signs of ethnicity in the gifts, many of which bore such common symbols of Irish ethnicity as the shamrock.

An interview with Mrs. Dougherty provided further data on the Dougherty Irish Dancers. She had come to the Philadelphia area from County Derry twenty-five years before in order to join a cousin. She was dancing at the Irish Center when a group of women approached her with the idea of teaching dance. As she explained: "They liked my style and wanted me to teach their children. I'd never taught before and I told them so but they really liked the way I danced. So I started teaching. . . . the group sort of grew out of those people."

The Dougherty Irish Dancers were founded twenty years earlier. Many of the women who first convinced Mrs. Dougherty to teach are still with the group. She instructs both children and adults, operating out of an Irish club in the area. She teaches step dancing and ceili dancing for children, starting at about six years of age and continuing through high school. She says she loses many students to high school activities. The ratio in the early classes is about thirty girls to every boy and, as the children get older, "it just gets worse and worse."

Mrs. Dougherty is not competitive about Irish dancing and she tries to emphasize its fun aspects. She is not accredited by the Commission on Irish Dance, either for teaching or for judging, and therefore cannot send her pupils to compete in Ireland. Many teachers attempt to win accreditation and the tests are rigorous, including questions on the history of the dance and a section wherein one is given a group of dancers and an hour to teach them a dance they have not done before. Mrs. Dougherty emphasized the importance of money if one wishes to compete seriously because the travel expenses can be daunting. She said, "You can tell over the phone when they call. They're so eager . . . just the tone of voice. I won't take those pupils because I'm not the teacher those parents want. I'll refer them to other teachers who are interested in competition."

Mrs. Dougherty's adult classes are well attended. Her own dance teacher, visiting from Ireland, was impressed by their size and enthusiasm. Mrs. Dougherty claims to have a fairly even sex ratio in her adult classes. The core of the Dougherty Irish Dancers is a group of about eighty people of various ages, predominantly in their forties and fifties. Mrs. Dougherty emphasized that the group does Irish dancing and does not attract Scottish dancers. She said that with the exception of the step dancing there is very little Irish dancing in Ireland, though the dancers there are more precise in their steps.

The group advertises events in a local Irish-American newspaper and on radio station WXPN, but Mrs. Dougherty admits that this brings few new dancers: "Mostly I get calls from people who want harpers or bands and I put them in touch with the right folks. We don't get many new dancers that way. We mostly get new dancers from word of mouth or from demonstrations. At the nursing home where we performed last night three of the nurses asked for more information."

Mrs. Dougherty says that the group performs about once or twice a week and that they have a ceili almost every month outside of the Feis season. During the summer months, the group performs almost every weekend at a Feis, or outdoor all-day dance competition and exhibition.

Mrs. Dougherty stressed that the group has no religious or political affiliations. This is because people of various backgrounds join the group: "We get people from all sorts of backgrounds. They're Germans, Jews, Italians, Polish . . . all sorts. But they also happen to be Irish-Americans. So we have to be careful. We don't want to discriminate against them. . . . Almost all of them are American born."

Members of the group take a trip to Ireland every summer. They tour together for about two weeks and then split up to continue individually, returning whenever they like. According to Mrs. Dougherty, most of them "go looking for their roots—you know their grandparents or something."

Mrs. Dougherty describes the Dougherty Irish Dancers as "a social group with an ethnic focus"; the strength of that focus comes through in her words: "Ireland has a rich tradition of dance, of music, of poetry, or storytelling. Someone has to carry on that tradition. Someone *must* carry on that tradition. And I guess that's what I'm doing, carrying on the tradition. I guess that's what my life is—Irish dance."

Several factors in the interview highlight the concept of self-chosen ethnicity. The group emerged out of a number of people who had already defined themselves as ethnic and wanted to pass this identity to their children. The group's strong focus on *Irish* dance does not seem to draw many folk dancers from other traditions. The self-conscious carrying on of a tradition that is faltering in its land of origin came through again and again during the course of the interview. The group performs and thus displays dance as an aesthetic activity; the differentiation of context is evident in the wearing of costumes.

The most important piece of information is Mrs. Dougherty's comment on the composition of the group. According to her, it is composed of people who have a variety of ethnic identities to select from and have chosen to identify themselves as Irish-Americans through their participation in traditional Irish dance.

The interview with Mrs. Dougherty seemed to support the hypothesis of Irish-American ethnicity as self-chosen ethnicity. Importantly, my interviews of members of the Ceili Group provide further backing for my conclusion.

For example, Barney began Irish dancing only a year ago, when a fellow worker invited him to a Friday night ceili because "he fig-ured I'd enjoy it because I'm Irish." He so enjoyed the ceili that he began taking dance lessons from both the Ceili Group and Mrs. Dougherty. His identification of himself as Irish-American is fairly recent and has also manifested itself in studies of Irish mythology and folklore. He traveled to Ireland a couple of years ago on a pack-age tour; he has no relatives in the country to visit and "wouldn't know where to find them."

A female informant, Courtney, and her male friend present simi-lar cases of self-chosen ethnicity. Both are in their early twenties. As children, they were enrolled in step-dancing classes by parents who thought it would be a good experience. Courtney began ceili dancing because her step-dancing lessons ended on Friday nights just as the ceili was beginning. When her mother came to pick her up, she would persuade her mother to stay for the ceili. Soon both her parents had joined the Ceili Group, and her father eventually became a member of the board of directors. Other informants have told me similar tales of bringing parents and siblings into the group.

Her friend began ceili dancing after a hiatus from step dancing. He said that he had missed Irish dancing. He is an exceptionally good dancer who takes great pride in his skill. My informants have forged close ties of friendship based on their experiences together in the Ceili Group. They converse freely and knowledgeably about the history of Ireland and of Irish dance. Neither can trace their ancestors back to Ireland beyond a vague knowledge of the region from which they came. Courtney's mother has been researching the family tree for five years but still cannot pinpoint the link to Ireland.

Few informants demonstrate the concept of self-chosen ethnicity as clearly as another male informant. He joined the Ceili Group in 1979. As he explains it: "My mother and father split up when I was very young and she never told me anything about him. In 1979 my father died and I found out that his name was Casey [pseu-donym]. I wanted to feel a connection with him so I began to im-merse myself in Irish culture. . . . I found the Ceili Group through a notice in the *Inquirer*'s Weekend section and I went. . . . I've con-sciously immersed myself in things Irish, especially music and dance. I've always liked to dance."

My informant's immersion has been extremely successful. Instru-mental in the organization of the Oiche Cois Tine events, he is now a ranking officer on the board of directors of the Ceili Group. When I asked him how he organizes the Oiche Cois Tine and Ceol nah Eireann events, he paused to consider and then said, "Well, I didn't know anyone at first. But people in the Ceili Group would put me in touch with other people. There's a whole network of people out there interested in Irish culture . . . you just have to tap into it. . . . I guess you could say I'm a part of it now."

Although I could provide more information to support my central thesis that the concepts of key symbol and self-chosen ethnicity were useful in my research, it is hoped that this chapter has provided a glmpse into the important expressive domaiñ of dance as a significant marker of Irish-American ethnicity.

7

Art and Identity
Ukrainian-American Ethnicity

Jennifer Krier

During the course of my fieldwork, many people—including my informants—asked me why I had chosen Ukrainian-Americans as a group for study. Such occasions, on which these individuals turned the tables around and started asking *me* questions I had never bothered to ask myself, were tricky, and my answers were always vague. I usually ended up saying something like "Well, I just love your culture." However, in retrospect, I realize that I had been drawn to its study because I found it to be alluring.

The means by which this recognition took place can be revealed by recounting my first exposure to the culture. When a friend told me he was Ukrainian, I asked "What's that?" After he gave me a brief and ineffective geographical explanation, he said, "Okay, you know those very beautiful and intricately dyed Easter eggs? Those are Ukrainian." Something clicked; in the back of my mind, those eggs became a symbol by which my friend could differentiate and identify himself. Moreover, this approach provided me with a means to recognize his unique identity. After having learned to associate this particular art form with Ukrainian-American culture, I found myself appreciating both the art and the culture all the more.

Being both an anthropology and an art history student, and therefore interested in the relationship between art and society, I became intrigued with this example of art as an integral aspect of one's cultural identity. In previous work, I had explored the role of art in non-Western cultures in Australia and Africa and was interested in the following idea, expressed by McCarthy: "In primitive society an important element of culture is produced by uniting the desire of aesthetic expression with an inspiration which is of social benefit, and art is thus brought into a social and ritual mechanism from which it cannot be viewed in disassociation" (1958:12). This contrasted with my view of Western art, which seems to be not only purely aesthetic but also removed from access to and understanding of most individuals. In the Western world, art is very distant from the social context, and the "best" products are sold for prohibitive prices or displayed in museums with signs saying "DO NOT TOUCH."

However, my friend's remark indicated to me that Ukrainian-American art plays a role more like the one McCarthy defines for art in primitive societies. Rather than being isolated from social context like Western art, Ukrainian-American Easter eggs are so integral to Ukrainian culture that they can be effectively used as symbols that describe or identify that culture to non-Ukrainians. Their forms are not esoteric but can inspire appreciation in Ukrainians and non-Ukrainians alike; and, far from being inaccessible, I found that Ukrainian Easter eggs, as well as other traditional arts of the culture, abound in both public and private contexts and can be made by anyone who has the time or interest to do so.

In studying Ukrainian-Americans, then, I hoped to be able to understand firsthand how people use art as a symbol that expresses and describes their cultural identity, in both the private and public spheres.

Ukrainian-American Ethnicity

In reviewing the literature on Ukrainians, their immigration, and their ethnicity, I realized that the interest in expressing their identity was, at first, an in-group concern. Procko (1979) states that the first of these immigrants to come to the United States in the 1890s were at a very low level of ethnonational awareness and identified themselves with a number of terms, such as Ruthenian, Little Rusyn, and Rus-Ukraina. Priests, the only educated people among the mass of peasants, were also the only immigrants who did express a high level of cultural awareness, and they sought "to enlighten the Ukrainian people and to protect their religion, rite, and language" (Procko 1979). However, Procko documents that, with later waves of immigration, what began as cultural patriotism grew into a more politically oriented national consciousness as Russia's domination over the Ukraine became stronger.

It was during World War II that the height of Ukrainian "ethnic consciousness" was achieved in the United States. Magosci, in his article printed in the *Harvard Encyclopedia of American Ethnic Groups*, states that, rather than assimilate, the immigrants tried to create "their own world, bounded by a widespread network of churches, secular organizations, and Ukrainian-language newspapers" (1980:1008). Other literature also emphasizes the success with which Ukrainians have established their own communities in various places around the United States (Halich 1937; Chyz 1959; Lushnycky 1976; Magosci 1979). All these works stress that both the existence of a Ukrainian formal structure, such as churches, schools, publications, social clubs, resorts, and sports teams, as well as nationalistic World War II immigrants, contributed to group maintenance and the reinforcement of ethnic commitment. The fact that the authors of these studies are themselves Ukrainian-Americans illustrates that dedication to preserving the ethnonational identity is practiced in scholarship as well. In the words of one scholar: "We have not been assimilated, and . . . we can be very proud of the fact that we are here today to celebrate the centenary of our immigration. We have indeed triumphed, putting an end, once and for all, to the concept of the melting pot as a viable model of ethnic life in America" (Magosci 1979:49).

Symbolic Theory

Because much of this chapter discusses Ukrainian folk art as a "symbol" of ethnic identity, it is necessary to discuss theories of symbolism briefly. As we shall see, these theories question a functionalist understanding of the role of folk art and will lead us to more general or universal meanings of art that are grounded in ideas about psychology and semiotics.

Geertz (1973), in his discussion of "Art as a Cultural System" (1973), addresses the problem of talking about art. He asserts that, though art articulates much about a people's feeling for and patterning of life experience, art is often not talked about in a way that elucidates these feelings and patterns for an outsider. Most scholars, he contends, try to study art in their own Western-value terms of formal properties, symbolic content, affective values, or stylistic features; this leads not to an understanding of the role of art in culture but to an "externalized conception of the phenomenon" (1973:98). What is needed, states Geertz, is a "realization, that to study an art form is to explore a sensibility, that such a sensibility is essentially a collective formation, and that the foundations of such a system are as wide as social existence is deep" (1973:99).

Geertz is in keeping with the theories of folk art and ethnicity that we have discussed so far in that he stresses the collective nature of art and locates its meaning within the social context rather than in the technical process or aesthetic power. However, he differs from theorists such as Stern and Graburn in stating that his idea of art "leads away from the so-called functionalist view . . . that works of art are elaborate mechanisms for defining social relationships, sustaining social rules, and strengthening social values. . . . Anything may, of course, play a role in helping society work, painting and sculpting included, just as anything may help it tear itself apart. But the central connection between art and collective life does not lie on such an instrumental plane, it lies on a semiotic one. . . . [works of art] materialize a way of experiencing, bring a particular cast of mind out into the world of objects, where men can look at it" (1973:99). In Geertz's view, the primary role of art in an ethnic group would not be to maintain social cohesiveness or to provide a vehicle by which that group could make itself distinct. Rather, art is a means by which members of a group articulate their experience in a common world "in which men look, name, listen and make" (1973:118).

After reviewing the literature on art, ethnicity, and Ukrainian-Americans, my interest in the following ideas emerged: (1) Art has social meaning and works actively to communicate or articulate, through symbols, social experience; (2) Ethnicity is, in some contexts but not in all, self-ascribed cultural identity that serves to distinguish an individual or group of individuals from others and thus creates a dichotomy between members and nonmembers; and (3) Ukrainian-Americans have a strong sense of ethnic identity that is reinforced both internally—through religion, language, and organizations—and externally—through interaction with other American groups. A synthesis of these ideas is represented in my hypothesis that Ukrainian-Americans' practice of traditional art is a manifestation and reinforcement of ethnic identity, as well as a means by which that identity can be communicated to non-Ukrainians.

Fieldwork

The Ukrainian-American population in Philadelphia is both very large and very active. According to the U.S. Bureau of the Census, in 1970 some 49,398 Ukrainian-speaking people lived in Pennsylvania, including 21,055 in Philadelphia (Lushnycky 1976).

The hugeness of the Philadelphia Ukrainian community was both an advantage and a disadvantage in fieldwork. I knew I had a wide range of resources available to me, but I hardly knew where to begin at first. Despite the large size and social cohesiveness of the group, it is dispersed geographically; and most Ukrainian-Americans, I learned, lived in the suburbs. Not having a car, I found it difficult to center my study around a Ukrainian neighborhood. I also found access to organizations, such as women's groups, difficult, both because I was not encouraged to visit and because my transportation was limited.

Although I did attend one church regularly in an effort to become involved with a defined group of Ukrainian-Americans, my informants ended up being from various churches and areas of Philadelphia. I dealt with twelve of these informants consistently throughout the fieldwork period, which lasted about six months. My informants were divided basically between two generations—those born in the 1930s and 1940s and those born in the 1960s—and were, for the most part, second-generation Ukrainian-Americans. These sources were also divided between the Ukrainian Orthodox and Ukrainian Catholic faiths. Because I was interested primarily in the arts of women, most of my informants were of that sex. But, as we shall see later, a key informant was a man. All these individuals, save two of the younger generation, had a working knowledge of the Ukrainian language.

Crane states that folk art may be analyzed usefully on two levels: form and content (1965:118). My first fieldwork efforts involved acquainting myself with the various forms of Ukrainian folk art in its different contexts. I determined these contexts to be the church, private homes, and public arenas such as museums and shops. Although I selected these contexts primarily because they were the ones I had access to, they seemed also to reflect different aspects of artistic significance: religious (church), decorative/utilitarian (home), and commercial (shops and museums). This was an observation-oriented stage of fieldwork in which I visited shops and other places where folk art was displayed. Initially, I focused on paying attention to each setting and the way people interacted within it. I also regarded how folk art objects were presented in each setting and felt free to react to and interpret these forms subjectively; this was helpful in understanding the meaning of Ukrainian folk art to outsiders.

After regularly visiting these places for about a month, I began to make contacts. Then I was able to participate, to some degree, in the contexts of church and home. I also began to enroll in classes and demonstrations of Ukrainian folk art. As Easter drew near, these activities became more numerous. Because the bulk of my field-work took place the few months before Easter and because Easter itself is a holiday in which specific arts play a significant part, I found myself concentrating on those associated with this holiday. Indeed, Ukrainian-Americans are perhaps most commonly distin-guished as an ethnic group by their Easter-related arts. While speak-ing to a woman who was active in Philadelphia's Ukrainian commu-nity, I was told that "one of the first things that Americans think about when someone says Ukrainian to them is Ukrainian Easter eggs."

In talking to members of families and in actually participating in some family events, I tried to learn about specific aspects of the content of folk art. For example, I examined the use of the objects —whether they were, in my opinion and/or those of the family members, products of specialized skill. I also asked my informants about the meaning of the objects, and I was always careful to note patterns in their interpretations of content, and to compare contem-porary meanings of the arts to their traditional meanings, as de-scribed in the literature. I was especially interested in noting whether the content of the art forms, as they are now practiced among Ukrainian-Americans has changed significantly from expla-nations of traditional content.

Aside from learning about folk arts in the family sphere, I tried to gain more specific knowledge from specialists in the crafts. "Spe-cialist" is a tricky word, I discovered, for many people that I inter-viewed because those I thought were in this category did not so regard themselves. Therefore, I need to clarify my definition of the word "specialist": I mean those individuals who have perfected their techniques in the arts to such an extent that they are singled out from the ethnic community at large. Therefore, the craft special-ists I talked to were usually rather public figures, in both the Ukrainian and non-Ukrainian spheres.

Because my general focus on the arts centered around the artistic activities that take place during Easter, especially the decoration of eggs, my interviews were limited to those specialists who were specifically involved in Easter arts and whom I met at workshops, demonstrations, and displays of Ukrainian folk art. My encounters with specialists were usually in formal contexts, such as interviews, classes, and demonstrations. In speaking with them, I followed Brunvard's four goals for folk art fieldwork (1968:322). First, I in-quired about the materials used and the stages of construction. Second, I tried to gather information about how the skills were acquired and to what uses the finished items are put. Third, I tried to gain some sense of the artists' personalities and histories in order to understand how they see themselves in relation to the Ukrainian community. And, last, I hoped to elicit some comments from them relating to the "aesthetic appeal" of their products. Did these specialists feel that their artwork played some sort of important artistic role within the Ukrainian community?

Ukrainian Folk Art: Psanky

Ukrainian-Americans continue to practice a wide variety of traditional folk arts. Among those practiced by my informants were: embroidery, weaving, ceramics, traditional cooking, *bandura* (a Ukrainian stringed instrument), dancing, and singing. By far, the most widely practiced art was *psanky*, or Easter-egg dyeing. All these arts are exposed to the public, in shops, displays, museums, and performances, but psanky seems to be, in many ways, the most visible of the forms in the Ukrainian-American folk art tradition. It is because of the wide production of psanky and their visibility (especially in the months right before Easter) that I concentrated on them in my study of Ukrainian-American folk art.

Psanky are made from three basic materials that are unique to their form: a white, uncooked egg; beeswax; and a bright, chemical dye. The egg must be uncooked so that it will dry out without causing odor. Beeswax is used not only because it is traditional, but also because it has a higher melting point than other products and a greater ability to stick to the egg and be absorbed into its pores (Vaughn 1982). The dyes originally used to color psanky were all made at home out of natural materials, but now most people use commercially prepared and packaged aniline dyes, which are mixed with boiling water and vinegar (Vaughn 1982). The only tools used in making psanky are the *kistka*—the writing tool used to draw designs on the egg—and a candle.

Yaroslava Surmach states: "The egg, as the embodiment of the life principle, has been associated with the mythical and religious ceremonies from earliest pagan times" (1957:3). Because the egg held within it the promise of life, it became a symbol of the rebirth that accompanies spring. Pagan people, it is asserted, saw parallels between the yellow yolk and the sun (Vaughn 1982). Decorated with motifs that were symbols of the sun—such as the star, the triptych, and the swastika—psanky celebrated the coming of life, and also

Examples of psanky, the Ukrainian folk art of dyeing Easter eggs. The beautiful and intricate designs are apparent, though the rich and varied colors are not evident in this black-and-white photograph. (Courtesy of Jennifer Krier)

protected people from disaster, disease, and evil spirits (Horniatkevych 1963).

Although the tradition began in pagan times, sources assert that, with the advent of Christianity, the egg transcended its symbolism of nature's rebirth and became the representation of human rebirth (Surmach 1957). The egg was seen as the tomb from which Christ arose, and the old pagan symbols were given new Christian meanings. The sun designs now stood for the Son of God, the Holy Trinity, God's love for man. The swastika grew into the cross, which represented Christ's suffering. And new symbols also emerged—such as the fish, representing Christianity; the forty-triangle designs, representing the forty days of Lent; and designs of the Ukrainian church, representing the faith of the Ukrainian people (Vaughn 1982). Secular motifs that represented Christian good wishes—the rooster for fertility, the deer for prosperity—also developed.

Because so much time and care were spent in making psanky, they came to be viewed as religious mementos. They played, and continue to play, a major role in Easter rituals. Psanky were decorative items that accompanied the foods eaten to break the fast after Lent and were blessed, along with the traditional foods, on Easter Sunday. After Easter Mass, psanky were commonly exchanged as people greeted one another and were intended as a sign of fondness (Luciow 1973). On the Sunday after Easter, psanky were placed on the graves of the dead, who, having no calendar, must be "informed" when to celebrate Easter (Horniatkevych 1963).

Contemporary Practice in Philadelphia

In view of the ancientness of the psanky tradition, it is quite impressive that they continue to be made today. What is more, both the technique used for making them and the designs used to decorate them remain largely unchanged. Of the thirty or so Ukrainian-Americans I talked to during the course of my fieldwork, most had made psanky at least twice. People learned the craft either through their mothers or Ukrainian organizations such as churches or youth leagues. Although traditionally psanky were made only by women, in modern times men make them too. Generally, my informants did not use "fancy" equipment such as electric *kistkas* or butane torches.

Although the same traditional motifs are used in contemporary times, their meanings were not known by all my informants. Usually it was only the specialists that were familiar with the vast repertoire of psanky symbols; other individuals, when I inquired about the meanings, would rattle off a few motifs they were familiar with and then hand me a book and say, "I really can't tell you all about the symbolism of the designs." Thus, my informants usually valued psanky art in terms of its aesthetic appeal, rather than in terms of the meanings of its motifs. Specialists articulated this feeling too, and said they chose which designs to draw on the basis of beauty rather than meaning. However, on some occasions, the meaning of the design becomes most important. For example, one informant told me of an egg that she was going to make for her friend's wedding: "I'll have to throw in a few fertility symbols, just to make sure," she said.

Psanky continue to have their old role in Easter ritual. Having attended a Ukrainian Orthodox Easter service, I was able to observe the eggs in this context. At this service, people carried baskets to church that were stuffed with the traditional Easter foods such as *paska* (a special kind of Easter bread), homemade cheeses, kielbasa, hard-boiled eggs, and horseradish. Psanky and hand-embroidered cloths decorated the baskets as well, and all the items were blessed in a small ceremony that took place outside the church after Mass.

Psanky also have new roles and purposes; most notably, they are now not only given to, but also sold to and the production of taught to non-Ukrainians. Many of my informants were accustomed to giving them to their non-Ukrainian friends at all times of the year —for birthdays and weddings or as gifts. Public museums and stores also sell psanky, as well as the materials needed to produce them, making them widely available to non-Ukrainians. In visiting these places, I found that the public displayed a great interest in viewing and buying psanky. This interest was also demonstrated by the public's active participation in workshops that offered instruction in making them. Because non-Ukrainians obviously cannot value them for the religious, historical, and aesthetic meanings that are ascribed to them in Ukrainian culture, they can be seen as having new meanings in the contemporary world. These new meanings are dictated by both non-Ukrainians, who come into contact with the art, and by Ukrainian-Americans, who have given it a new public context.

Informants' Views

In the previous discussion, we have seen that folk art plays a significant part in the collective life of Ukrainian-Americans. Because its forms are ancient, it links the culture of contemporary people to that of their ancestors. It surrounds them in church, plays a part in major holidays, and decorates their homes. Examples of the art can even be bought in Ukrainian stores. Still, I observed a great variation among individuals in their relationship to art. Moreover, individuality seemed to be stressed as a cultural value. Therefore, we now consider the meanings of folk art to my individual informants, beginning with two specialists.

The Kulaks

As I mentioned before, during the last two months before Easter, non-Ukrainians are offered many opportunities to buy, view, and make psanky. Often, these opportunities are advertised in non-Ukrainian contexts, such as local newspapers, magazines, and even on television. One of the largest of these advertised events that I attended was a psanky workshop held at the Norristown Library. Having been advertised in the *Philadelphia Inquirer*, it drew a large crowd of participants, many of whom came all the way from Philadelphia. Almost all of the forty participants were non-Ukrainian.

Some had attended the workshop in previous years, but most had learned about it through the *Inquirer*. All the available seats were filled, and onlookers continued to drop by throughout the day.

The workshop was led by a dynamic couple, Paul and Natalia Kulak (I have used pseudonyms for all my informants). After showing an interesting film entitled "Ukrainian Easter Eggs," the two shared roles instructing the participants both as a group and as individuals. Aside from receiving instruction from these two, I was also able to talk with them throughout the day; and, by the end of the workshop, we had exchanged telephone numbers. They became my key informants.

Even before speaking with the Kulaks personally, I was able to obtain some idea of their relationship with and attitude toward their folk art. First, it was obvious that the workshop was an educational rather than a lucrative enterprise; people were encouraged, in the *Inquirer* ad, to bring their own materials, and the participation charge was a mere dollar. This was a great contrast to the fees of fifteen and twenty dollars I had encountered at other workshops. The Kulaks' interest in educating their pupils was demonstrated by the fact that, before the class began, they showed a film that discussed psanky's history, traditions, symbols, and techniques. The film was noteworthy for the many beautiful psanky it displayed and also for one segment in which a Ukrainian-American woman was shown making one. Her sureness and virtuosity in creation were clearly emphasized.

My immediate impressions were reinforced through personal contact with the Kulaks, who articulated both a pride in their artistic tradition and a concern that Ukrainian folk art traditions be maintained. Mr. Kulak seemed especially involved with these concerns and was acknowledged as being the better artist. This was surprising to me, for, though almost every Ukrainian-American I talked to, male and female, had tried the craft of psanky, usually women were the ones who practiced it consistently. Indeed, much of the literature also emphasizes their role in maintaining this craft, saying that the ancient art has been handed down through the generations, from mother to daughter (Surmach 1957). In Mr. Kulak's case, however, the craft was handed down from mother to son. "I learned how to make psanky from my mother," he told me. "I watched her— she never taught me. . . . And you know, the minute I started, she stopped. She didn't need to do it any more—the tradition had been passed on." Mr. Kulak acknowledged that it is unusual for a man to make psanky, for traditionally it was not "a man's business" but rather a "secret," indoor occupation for women during the long winter months.

Although Mr. Kulak picked up the craft as a result of his natural artistic curiosity, he continues both to make and collect psanky, despite the fact that this is not a usual practice for Ukrainian-American men. His interest in the art was cemented in graduate school, when he began to make psanky for sale at a local boutique. It was at this time that he taught the craft to his wife, whose mother had *not* made psanky; and together they managed to make enough eggs to provide a small supplement to their rather meager income. Although both of them have taken advantage of the lucrative aspect of the craft, they stressed that their discovery that they could *sell* their psanky was really a lucky break. Mrs. Kulak said, "My husband made the eggs—and still does—just out of his own pleasure. You know, we really hate to sell the eggs—they're a gift of love, and they're made to be given away."

Thus, although Mr. Kulak learned the craft within his household and identified this event as the passing down of a family and cultural tradition, his practice of the craft moved from a private context to a public one. Whereas he first recognized psanky's public role as of economic value, his wife's comment and my observation that the psanky workshop was obviously nonlucrative indicated that his interest in psanky's public role had changed. He stressed the fact that today, he does *not* sell the eggs—"We just do these for fun." For fun, and, it seemed to me, for something more. For the Kulaks, part of the "fun" of making psanky involves teaching the craft, as they have been doing for the last seven years, to people who are not even Ukrainian. Having learned the tradition from his mother, Mr. Kulak is concerned with "passing it on" not only to his own children (as he has done) but also to the community at large.

It was interesting to observe how the workshop participants, who can be seen as representatives of the larger community, responded to this education. Although the movie, and Mr. Kulak himself, emphasized the importance of following traditional motifs, the participants obviously felt unrestricted by such concerns and created whatever designs they wished. I observed faces, hearts, rainbows, and even abstract, nongeometrical designs. Mr. Kulak did not discourage this, but, when I questioned him about his own craft, he said, "The designs are always traditional—in other words, you don't draw a Volkswagen, because that means nothing."

Evidently, the purpose of the workshop was not to teach non-

Ukrainians how to produce perfect psanky. Mr. Kulak stated this fact in his own words when I asked him why he was involved in such workshops. He put the emphasis on sharing: "Basically, I just feel like this is something to share. Because really, there isn't much known about Ukrainians, and they've had such a messed-up story. We figure if people remember nothing else, they'll remember the word Ukraine or Ukrainian." Both Mr. and Mrs. Kulak thought that the workshops were successful in such an enterprise. It was clear that they regarded the workshop experience, rather than the mastery of the craft, as important. "Many people give up making psanky after class," stated Mrs. Kulak, "but some people keep practicing, and come back a little better the next year." Indeed, at the workshop I attended a non-Ukrainian woman had a whole egg carton full of psanky that she had made after her first workshop the year before. However, most of the participants I questioned said that they would probably not create any more of them after class.

Mr. Kulak, in his statement just above, articulated a wish to make Ukrainian culture distinct. In this light, it is important to note that the Kulaks emphasized the uniqueness of the psanky craft. Before demonstrating the technique, Mr. Kulak pointed out the ways Ukrainian psanky were different from decorated eggs made by peoples of other Eastern European countries; these differences, he said, lay in the colors, the geometric division of the designs, and the intricateness of the work: "There are two things about Ukrainian psanky that will strike you: the evenness of the line, and the brilliance of the color." The small display that the Kulaks had set up at the library exhibited only Ukrainian psanky and embroidery. And, when Mr. Kulak learned that I was doing a paper on Ukrainian folk art, he asked: "Where are you going to get unbiased [meaning non-Soviet] sources?" Thus, there was an emphasis on a strictly Ukrainian presentation of the arts.

Some of the workshop participants seemed as if they had already been made sensitive to the distinctness of Ukrainian culture through exposure to the folk arts. One of the women at my table had made psanky before, in an art class at college. Another man, whom I heard talking with Mr. Kulak, had come to "see who made those eggs and if it was really possible." The Kulaks themselves seemed to view the psanky craft as a significant form of Ukrainian folk art, in terms of its public meaning. Mrs. Kulak said, "Some Ukrainians get sick of all this psanky. They say, 'Eggs, eggs, eggs, —that's all we ever see.' But for people who have never seen the eggs before, they're really something special."

Other Informants

As stated above, one of the objectives that I constantly tried to pursue while doing fieldwork was: What does folk art mean to Ukrainian-Americans? The explanations that were articulated for me by young and old as well as specialists and nonspecialists revealed great differentiation:

> "Psanky have a lot of symbolism—they mean Easter. And Easter means life, life always."

> "Psanky is an art. It means friendship. It's an art form that has a lot to do with Church and Easter, so its meaning is that it's a tradition that people do at Easter."

> "The most important meaning [of psanky] these days is financial."

> "The artist is endangered. She has to do the arts very conscientiously. . . . the overall sentiment is a deep need to preserve here."

> "Art, religion, and nationalism are the three glues that hold Ukrainian culture together."

> "I never thought about the meaning of Ukrainian art. . . . I knew that that was my heritage, but it's not something I make a conscious effort to maintain—it's just a part of me."

It became obvious that my informants possessed a variety of attitudes about the meaning of art that seemed to defy generalization. However, I noted four aspects of meaning that were generally commented upon.

Many informants expressed the idea that Ukrainian folk art was not so much an *artistic* activity, however, as it was a *traditional* activity. Although people felt that artistic ability made learning these arts easier, they did not feel that it was a necessary prerequisite for the production of Ukrainian folk art. For example, Mrs. Kulak said to me, "I'm not an artist." When I objected by saying that she made such beautiful psanky, she said, "Yes, but that's different. It's tradition, you know. It's something that's inside of me—that's inside of all of us. But other things I cannot do."

However, some informants, such as Mia, felt that Ukrainian folk arts can be an artistic as well as a traditional expression and that the artist's work can be differentiated not by skill, but by subtle qualities of color and composition. In any case, all my informants expressed the general attitude that Ukrainian-Americans were slightly predisposed to produce fine works of traditional art and also that any Ukrainian-American could produce an acceptable piece of folk art, with time and practice.

Conclusion

Overall, my informants were not at all consistent in their knowledge of the symbolism of particular arts, though specialists usually had the broadest knowledge on this topic. Despite the lack of specific knowledge, however, all possessed a general knowledge of the symbolism of the arts—for example, that psanky are a symbol of rebirth and resurrection. They also knew that the motifs were not purely decorative but expressed particular meanings. Often, people articulated the meaning of arts according to their roles in other aspects of Ukrainian tradition—that is, holidays and customs. Thus, my field research provided support for the semiotic theoretical position concerning the social significance of art reviewed earlier in this chapter.

Part III

Interpretations of Gender and Ethnicity
The Lubavitcher Experience

Controlled comparison is a cornerstone of the anthropological experience and tradition. Although most ethnographers today acknowledge that ethnographic data are always compared and filtered through the researcher's own culture and experience and therefore should be considered as subjective interpretations of the "other," it is through restudies by two or more investigators of the same culture that the quality and nature of the interpretation can be seen more clearly. Restudies frequently reveal as much or more about the researchers as they do about the "other" culture. Redfield versus Lewis (Lewis 1963), and Freeman versus Mead (Freeman 1983) are two classic restudies with contrasting interpretations of the same cultures—albeit at different times, locations, and with other differing personal and theoretical orientations.

The chapters in this section are both studies of the Lubavitchers, a Hasidic Jewish sect. Because they were prepared a year apart, Srinivasan had the opportunity to read the earlier one by Baldinger. Although both authors chose to concentrate on Lubavitcher women, Baldinger is a male graduate of Haverford College who majored in Bryn Mawr College's anthropology program, and Srinivasan is a female graduate of Bryn Mawr. Baldinger's maleness is apparent in his use of both female and male informants concerning women in the sect, and Srinivasan interviewed women almost exclusively in gathering her data. Thus, there are gender distinctions to be seen in the information given by informants as well as minor variations in the data revealing that not all members of a religious group define basic concepts similarly. Both investigators self-identify as Jewish and were aware of the possible implications of studying one's own ethnic culture, but neither was Lubavitcher, and there were additional differences in their personal (cultural) backgrounds that are touched upon in their studies.

It is interesting to speculate (we can do no more) why both authors chose to focus on the women in this particular group. Cross-cultural gender study is well entrenched in contemporary anthropology (and an issue in contemporary American society), and both male and female students at Bryn Mawr over the years have been at the forefront of this approach. But perhaps it is also because of the particular role and identity of women within the Lubavitcher culture that, in the initial stages of investigation, signaled their importance in the movement itself: to understand the movement one must begin with the women.

Finally, the Lubavitcher Hasidic movement is the most holistic ethnic group reported on in this volume. It is interesting because members are both born to the sect and recruited from the wider Jewish population itself. This distinction is marked by the sect's use of "lifer" for those born to Lubavitcher parents, and "returnee" for those who self-select at a later time in their lives to dedicate themselves to the particular ethnic tradition that informs the lifestyle of a Lubavitcher.

8

Equality Does Not Mean Sameness
The Role of Women within the Lubavitcher Marriage

Philip Baldinger

For nearly seven months, I explored the world of the Lubavitcher Jews. They are one of more than forty different Hasidic sects throughout the world with a membership of about 100,000 Jews —and they are still growing. What delineates the Lubavitchers from other Hasidic groups is their adherence to their own particular "grand rabbi," called a "rebbe." They feel that he is "the personification of all core values that they hold dear" (Levy 1975:25).

Hasidism is an enigma to many people, Jews as well as non-Jews. The Lubavitchers in particular have been termed as "cultists" and "religious fanatics" for their attempts to proselyte nonreligious Jews. A friend of mine warned me to be wary of the Lubavitchers because her cousin, a college student, had been studying them for only a few months when she suddenly decided to shave her head and adopt their practices. Nevertheless, this sort of talk whetted my appetite to understand who the Lubavitchers really are.

I chose to look at gender roles because it is one of the most apparent aspects to outsiders as being different from their own. The men are "bearded, black-hatted, and clad in severe dark suits. The women dress to conceal their elbows and knees and cover their shorn hair with wigs" (Ostling 1986).

When I was first introduced to a Lubavitcher woman I naturally extended my hand to introduce myself. She ignored my salutation with a look of indifference. I was shocked and confused. Had I done something wrong? I was relieved to learn that I was not the first male to receive such a reaction from a Lubavitcher woman. One of my male informants quickly thereafter informed me that there is no touching of any sort between the opposite sexes unless the two people are married. In fact, as I would notice later, some Lubavitcher men say very little if anything to other women in the same room. When there is conversation between the sexes, it is usually concise and to the point. However, this is not always the case.

For example, I had the pleasure of meeting a dynamic Lubavitcher man who was equally comfortable speaking with men as well as women for hours at a time. This may have been because he is a public school teacher and has to deal with students of both sexes in addition to their mothers. But, indeed, it did seem odd to me not to see an occasional kiss or a pat on the back between a man and a woman. It seemed just as unusual when I found the women seated separately from the men during religious services.

To an outsider this may not only look foreign but also may appear to be sexist. But is it really? As anthropologists we are taught to look beyond the surface of scenarios to understand a deeper, perhaps esoteric, meaning. It is unfair and inappropriate to assign our own cultural biases to peoples who have a different culture. Throughout my experiences with the Lubavitchers I tried to keep a cultural relativist attitude to treat them fairly as well as to provide an accurate description of their way of life.

There has been a great deal written about the unequal role of the woman as compared to the man in different religions and within different cultures in general. Sherry Ortner, in her essay "Is Female to Male As Nature Is to Culture?" states: "The secondary status of women in society is one of the true universals, a pan-cultural fact. . . . the actual treatment of women and their relative power and contribution vary enormously from culture to culture, and over periods in the history of particular cultural traditions" (1974:67).

With this statement in mind, it appears that in Western culture women are taking an unprecedented stand to gain more representation in their religion and/or society. For example, in Catholicism there have been persistent attempts to allow for the ordination of women, even though the Pope has insisted that women cannot be priests. He has also pointed out that there were no women among Christ's chosen apostles (Ostling 1986). Nevertheless, Episcopalians and Anglicans in the United States, Canada, and New Zealand have granted priestly orders to women, and the mother church in England appears ready to follow suit.

Judaism has long been proud of the status it has given to women. Every phase of its history is considered to be marked by the heroism of its women—from the original four matriarchs, Sarah, Rebecca,

Rachel, and Leah, to women of modern times like Golda Meir, who was considered to be one of the finest prime ministers of Israel (Friedfertig and Schapiro 1981:54). However, within recent years, women of all affiliations (Reform, Conservative, and Orthodox) and from various backgrounds have been asking questions about their identity and purpose. Some have written books to support the idea that Judaism has granted women a "lofty" status (Meiselman 1978), but most books written today suggest that Jewish women are not equal to men. Blu Greenberg, author of *On Women and Judaism* (1981), poses the fundamental question as to how can women become more responsible, fully equal members of a holy community.

Jewish feminists vary in degree in their response to this question. Blu Greenberg, in a panel discussion with two other Jewish feminists, Susannah Heschel and Julie Greenberg, at Bryn Mawr College in January 1986, stated that it was "not a process of breaking down or diluting but rather of enhancing and building up." Heschel has added that "what is Jewish is defined in terms of what a man does so that society confuses 'human' with 'man'" (Heschel 1986). Julie Greenberg's answer to this problem is to reinterpret the Torah so that the name of the Lord is feminized to the name of a Goddess. She felt that this gave "a different perspective on the exact same history" (Julie Greenberg 1986). These women represent one side of the debate. The flip side is well represented by the Lubavitcher Women's Organization. In a handbook written by the group, their position on the debate between feminism and Judaism is elucidated:

> One might think that the increased Jewish feminist awareness of the past decade, corresponding to the general "women's movement," would be met with opposition in Torah circles. However, the recognition of the importance of the woman and of her unique qualities and powers has always been welcomed, for actually, the Torah gives the Jewish woman a lofty status. Ignorance is the greatest enemy of the Jewish people; misconceptions and outright myths about the Jewish woman have prevailed until very recently, turning many women away from the appreciation of Torah and from accepting a Jewish lifestyle. It is of crucial importance that valid, thorough information be available on this subject. (Friedfertig and Schapiro 1981:169)

Much of the literature that has been written is in response to the attack that Jewish feminists have made on what they feel is the inferior status of women in law and practice. This study is not intended to disprove their arguments; in a sense it cannot. Books such as *On Being a Jewish Feminist*, by Susannah Heschel, and *On Women and Judaism*, by Blu Greenberg, are comprehensive.

They deal with the rights of women in all spheres of the culture, including divorce, voting rights, and rabbinical authority.

I disagree with the interpretations of these authors in some cases because I believe they do not delineate between what is the law and what has been affected by prevailing social conditions. For example, the *shtetl*, or village, of eighteenth-century Europe was considered by most religious Jews as an upright Torah-observant community. Jewish feminists such as Charlotte Baum (1976:95), however, look with disdain at that way of life, pointing to the educational restrictions placed on women. Was this an aspect derived from the Torah or was it a reflection of the larger surrounding culture?

My intention is not to compete with the literature of the feminists. My aims are different from theirs. Because this is a fairly restricted study, I intend to look at the married woman's role only within the Lubavitcher marriage.

When I needed to introduce myself and reveal my intentions to potential Lubavitcher informants, most were quick to ask me what I had already read about them. Many books have been written about Hasidism, and, if there is any one thing that all the various sects agree upon, it is that they are not accurately represented. When an investigator quoted in Harris (1985:30) asked a Lubavitcher man if there were any books about Hasidism that might be helpful, he replied that none existed. I was surprised to find in my own interviewing that works produced by such people as Martin Buber (1955) and others, who are often considered by "the public" to be the foremost authors on Hasidic life, are not well respected by Lubavitchers. Harris (1985:30) quotes the reply given to another investigator: "Books about Hasidic matters always misrepresent things. They twist and change the truth in casual ways. . . . I trust scholars that I know who I can talk to face-to-face. But most books tell lies even if it's unintentional. . . . You want to know who we are? Read what we read. Read the Torah. Read Hasidic texts."

In 1985, however, a book was published that the Lubavitchers have approved of. Not one informant specifically stated that he or she "liked" it, but actions in this case speak louder than words. While visiting the Lubavitcher neighborhood of Brooklyn known as Crown Heights, I found the book being sold in every Lubavitcher-owned bookstore that I entered—eight in all. This is not to say that the book is flawless because my informants were quick to point out its weaknesses, but it is certainly worth reading. It is titled *Holy Days* and was written by Lis Harris, a secular Jew, as she terms herself, who lives in Manhattan.

Cultural Background of the Investigator

"Each man is like all other men, some other men, and like no other man" (Kluckhohn in Agar 1980:42). This quote from Clyde Kluckhohn summarizes the position of the ethnographer with the people whom he or she is studying. I feel that it is important to let the reader be aware of my position in relation to the Lubavitchers because "the personality and cultural background of the ethnographer becomes critical when you consider that the ethnographer's background is the initial framework against which similarities and differences in the studies group are assessed" (Agar 1980:42).

It is impossible for investigators to be aware of all the biases that they may carry from their own culture into that one being studied, so by learning personal background information the reader may gain a further sense of the investigator. In my particular case, I believe my background is conducive to presenting a subjectively informed —as much as humanly possible—study.

I was born a Conservative Jew and attended afternoon Hebrew school twice a week until the age of thirteen, when I was barmitzvahed. I never enjoyed this school. I would have rather played with my friends from secular school and have my father save his money. But he felt that it was his obligation that I learn Hebrew and gain a Jewish education. This may have been partly because my mother had little knowledge of Judaism and my father only became "religious" on Yom Kippur, the holiest day of the Jewish year, when Jews all over the world fast and repent for their sins. It is a day of remembering Jewish history and, for me, it was mandatory that I stay inside the house the whole day and read a Jewish book —I seldom did. Although my family does not keep kosher, no products containing pork are eaten in the house. At restaurants, exceptions are sometimes made, such as pepperoni pizza. I attended the synagogue with my parents only on High Holy Days, which consist of three holidays during the year. In summary, my interaction with Judaism is limited, but I have an identity of feeling Jewish.

Anthropologist Raymond Gorden has stated that the outsider "is more trusted than the insider who is suspected of taking sides if the group has been polarized, or who is considered too close to the problem to have the required perspective" (1969:43). There is little question that polarization has occurred within Judaism because four different affiliations exist today, each with a different philosophy. As a Conservative Jew, I would be considered an insider in my study of the Lubavitchers according to Gorden's argument. But do investigators who are insiders really lose the proper perspective? As Agar has pointed out, they may well be aware of the subtle details of the habits of a group (1980:22) that would give them an advantage over outsiders. The arguments by each author appear to be true, but I believe they must be put into context so that they relate to the particular culture being investigated.

In this instance, the Lubavitchers are very much involved in educating Jews who are interested in learning more about their heritage and culture. This is done through publishing literature and sponsoring events, such as weekend lectures in Crown Heights (Brooklyn, N.Y.), so that it is possible for other less-religious Jews to capture a feeling of what Judaism and specifically Lubavitcher Hasidism is all about. After considerable study of Hasidic texts and adopting the commandments found in the Torah, one may decide to become a Lubavitcher through adherence to the rebbe—this is a voluntary choice.

When I first made contact with the Lubavitchers at the Lubavitcher House, I knew nothing about the House nor did I know any of the fifty men and women who were present to celebrate the Jewish holiday of Sukkoth, the festival of harvest. Upon being introduced as "Phil, the anthropologist," I quickly had more friends than I could have imagined.

The informal interview became my central form of data-gathering during the first two months of research. It is important to realize that these interviews were not isolated events but rather were part of my participant-observation process, "which can be viewed as an encounter with an individual whom one has observed in a variety of contexts" (Becker and Geer 1957:30). Thus, often my informants were chosen by participant observation. During the Sukkoth meal, for instance, I was participating in the singing and observing to see who else was doing so with enthusiasm. When I say "with enthusiasm," I refer to the body motions that many of the men use. The enthusiastic individuals were the ones who were stamping their hands on the table and rocking back and forth while they sang. It was my impression that these people were the ones who would be most involved in Lubavitcher activities and could provide accurate accounts of what was occurring. The women did very little singing during the meal, probably because of the prohibition in the Torah, which I later learned states that a woman's voice is beguiling to a man so that women should not sing in public. If men are singing as well then it is permissible for a woman to sing provided her voice does not overwhelm that of the men.

Before long, it became clear to me that I needed additional sources that would have to come from outside the Lubavitcher House, pri-

Exterior of one of the four Lubavitcher centers in Philadelphia. Each center serves as a religious, social, and educational resource for its immediate community. (Courtesy of Elizabeth Ameisen)

marily because women seldom entered the House except on Shabbos and those who did were usually Orthodox rather than Lubavitcher Jews. The Orthodox women often provided me with information on what they felt was the difference between themselves and Lubavitchers, but without any Lubavitcher women present I could not compare their answers. I mentioned to Rabbi Moishe, one of my key informants, that it was critical that I have informants who were female Lubavitchers if I were to investigate the woman's role fully. He provided me with the name of a married Lubavitcher woman, whom I shall call Rachel, a resident of northeast Philadelphia.

She soon became my main female informant, though through her contacts with the rest of the Lubavitcher community I was introduced to two other married women. During the next four months, I remained in constant contact with Rachel, by interviewing her at her house, talking with her on the phone, and attending Jewish events with her. During my first two interviews at her home, I was introduced to a different girl friend of hers each time. They were all Lubavitchers so it provided me with two sets of data. The interviews were informal the first few times because I was still unsure of the focus for my questions.

Although the data collected from the men at the Lubavitcher House and from women informants such as Rachel were useful in providing a substantial amount of information, I was limited in the number of potential Lubavitcher informants because Philadelphia has only about ten Lubavitcher families. Moreover, those with whom I was able to talk were all "returnees" who showed a correlation in religious experiences. "Returnees" are Jewish people who adopt Lubavitcher affiliations and life whereas "lifers" are born in the Lubavitcher movement. As a result, I felt it necessary to spend some time (five days as it turned out) in Crown Heights (Brooklyn), the largest Lubavitcher community in the world (10,000 people), where a greater variety of data could be obtained.

While there, I stayed in the home of a Lubavitcher lifer couple, the P——s, and their five children. The trip was arranged through the courtesy of the Lubavitcher House. While there, I had the opportunity to further understand the woman's role and its importance within the marriage. I held formal and informal taped interviews with Mrs. P——. Additionally, I had the opportunity to observe her involvement in numerous Jewish rituals, some of which I elaborate upon below.

Especially through the data collected from Mrs. P—— and a few other women lifer informants, I was able to obtain a cross-section of data which could be compared to that collected in Philadelphia. Specifically, it was now possible to compare the responses of women lifers to the responses of women returnees.

The Origins of Hasidism

To understand the rise of Hasidism in the eighteenth century, it is necessary to trace even further back some three hundred years to the Middle Ages to realize the situations that allowed for its growth.

Simon Dubnow, author of *History of the Jews in Russia and Poland* (1916), has bluntly but accurately described that the only constants in the secular life of the Polish Jew in the Middle Ages were danger and despair. But this description could have been applied to Jews almost anywhere and at nearly anytime in their 5,700-year history. This history could be summarized as repetitive cycles of dispersion, resettling, integration, and persecution. Although life was usually difficult, there were times of general prosperity. For nearly three centuries, the Jews lived in relative peace in Spain. Cities such as Toledo and Madrid boasted Jewish populations of nearly half a million people, and Spain was looked upon as the glory of the Jewish civilization.

But this all changed with the new monarchy of Ferdinand and Isabella. Quickly after coming to power in 1492, they established the Inquisition, which forced Jews to convert to Catholicism or leave the country. It was the time of the Diaspora, the wandering, when Jews throughout Western Europe were being forced to migrate toward Eastern Europe, where many would settle on the shores of the Black Sea and in modern southern Russia (Dubnow 1916:39). But this was only the beginning, for in the next two centuries the wave of persecutions were to leave "the ground of Europe drenched with Jewish blood" (Eban 1968:233).

For example, a Russian historian of the time reported:

> Killing was accompanied by barbarous tortures; the victims were flayed alive, split asunder, clubbed to death, roasted on coals, or scalded with boiling water. Even infants at the breast were not spared. The most terrible cruelty however was shown towards the Jews. They were destined to utter annihilation, and the slightest pity shown to them was looked upon as treason. Scrolls of the Law were taken out of the synagogues by the Cossacks, who danced on them while drinking whiskey. After this Jews were laid down upon them and butchered without mercy. (Dubnow 1916:154)

During the latter half of the seventeenth century, many Jews in Poland were placed on religious trial for malevolent acts against the Church. Accusations ranged from desecration of Church statements to the ritual murder of children. The opportunity for a fair trial was almost nil because the Polish Diets were still under the control of the virulently anti-Semitic Catholic clergy. It has been estimated that within a ten-year period from 1648 to 1658 upward of nearly half a million Polish Jews lost their lives (Dubnow 1916:156; Harris 1985:37).

After reading of such calamity, one is forced to question how the Jews endured. They had no political homeland of their own and they were dispersed all over the world. Nevertheless, they carried with them a "priceless cultural and religious heritage which ensured a community of spirit and a unity of purpose that were to sustain them despite the loss of their sovereignty. Their loyalty went forth not to temporal rulers, but to an idea, a way of life, a Book [the Torah]" (Eban 1968:231).

The countless tragedies that the Jews endured throughout Europe for nearly two centuries provided the foundation in which the idea of the Messiah was grounded, but it was Isaac Luria, "the *theologica mystica*," who provided the reasoning that produced the start of what would later be termed the Age of Messianism and the rise of Hasidism (Eban 1968:235).

Born in Smyrna, Turkey, Sabbatai Zevi was versed in the Oral Law known as the Talmud. His ability to reel off passages word for word suggests that he was a brilliant man because this work comprises sixty-three tractates, or volumes, none of which is the work of one author. At some time in his youth, he decided to devote all his time to the study of Kabbalah (mystic texts), and before the age of twenty is believed to have derived from it the belief that he was the destined Messiah. Although Sabbatai Zevi had already won the confidence of a small following, the local rabbis were outraged by his claim and excommunicated him for his blasphemy. He thereupon left Smyrna and traveled throughout the Middle East, supported by his few ardent followers.

In 1665 Sabbatai's life changed forever when a rabbi of unquestionable character named Nathan of Gaza announced his ecstatic vision in which he saw Sabbatai as the true Messiah. The latter raced to Gaza on horseback in regal attire. To underscore his seriousness, he appointed some of his followers as his apostles (Harris 1985:45). "It was the awakening of Nathan of Gaza to his [own] prophetic mission which set the whole train of events in motion. The role of this brilliant and ardent youth, who at the time of the inception of the movement was only twenty years old [and a rabbi] has scarcely been understood. . . . he was at once the John the Baptist and the Paul of the new Messiah. He had all the qualities which one misses in Sabbatai Zevi: tireless activity, originality of theological thought, and abundant productive power. . . . he is by far the most influential theologian of the movement" (Scholem 1954:297).

News of the event in Gaza spread rapidly throughout Eastern Europe. *Encyclopedia Judaica* describes it as a mass hysteria where the weary, downtrodden masses joined with Jews of all classes from all countries to prepare for their long-awaited redemption. Jews from everywhere wrote to Sabbatai Zevi to ask him to restore their soul. Periods of fasting and ascetic exercises became an everyday matter and rituals of various sorts were practiced.

Many people in small hamlets and larger towns as well sold their homes and prepared for their journey to the Holy Land. But not everyone was won over; the rabbis of Jerusalem warned Sabbatai Zevi of the dire consequences he would suffer for raising the false hopes of his people. So he avoided Jerusalem and returned to his native home of Smyrna, where he was greeted by raucous crowds of admirers. Little did he know that the Turkish sultan's guards would be there as well to arrest "this charlatan" (Eban 1968:237).

Sabbatai was causing too great an upheaval to be tolerated by the ruler of Turkey: the former's choice was to convert to Islam or be put to death: "On September 16, 1666, with the greatest alacrity and in full pomp and ceremony, Sabbatai Zevi became Mohammed Effendi and vanished behind the walls of a seraglio" (Eban 1968:237). This supposed Messiah, in converting to Islam, added insult to injury. It goes without saying that he had a devastating effect on Jews throughout the Diaspora region.

All this emotional, religious confusion resulted in Jewish community leaders who had become deeply suspicious of any innovation or deviation of the Law. The majority of Jews—basically laborers, artisans, and farmers—were to obey the commandments and leave deeper, mystical matters to the scholars, who had the training to understand them. As a result, a schism was produced within Jewish Eastern Europe between the "ignorant" working class and the well-to-do rabbis and scholars of the upper class. The scene was set for the introduction of Hasidism, which would grow in numbers like a wild fire out of control and attain millions of followers within a fifty-year period (Harris 1985:47; Sharot 1980:325).

The Rise of Hasidism

The Hasidic movement began, it seems then, as a revolt of the "unlearned" against the strict rule of the rabbis. The founder, Israel ben Eliezer (better known as the Baal Shem Tov or by the acronym

Besht), was born in Podolia in 1698, and from the time of his youth was reputedly more interested in nature and the outdoors than he was in talmudic study.

When the Besht reached his mid-thirties, he decided to leave his studies and preach the message that is believed to have been blessed with the sparks of a heavenly force. Unlike the rabbis of his day, he believed that a simple, unlearned man could approach God directly through prayer and worship, and in coming closer to God, a man could bring Divine Influence through himself into the world. It was called "Being led into G-d" (Eban 215:1986), a joyous and ecstatic experience that could be attained through a number of experiences, such as through prayer, by the keeping of any commandment, and even by so simple an action as the tying of one's shoelaces. God was everywhere.

Most of the early followers of Hasidism lived in Lithuania and Poland among the poor, who felt that the traditional community had failed them. In the years following the death of the Baal Shem Tov, Hasidism became a way of life for tens of thousands of Jews. But many traditional rabbis saw the movement as a threat to their authority.

In its emphasis on the emotions rather than the intellect, Hasidism did not reject the tenets of traditional, or more aptly called today, Orthodox Judaism. Rather, it added innovations to the present Law by permitting the hours of prayer to vary so that people could pray in less of a hurry and, it was hoped, with more feeling. Additionally, Hasidism eliminated the need for a cantor during the religious service; any man could lead in the singing. Dancing and singing were also considered appropriate if not prescribed ways of expressing religious enthusiasm. Unlike the followers of Sabbatai Zevi, whose spiritual energy was directed outward, the Besht's followers were continuously urged to focus inward; the emotional gestures that now characterize Hasidism are only the overflow of the internal religious passion (Harris 1985:52). By the turn of the eighteenth century, more than a million Jews were Hasids. The movement broke into different groups throughout Europe, with each group containing a dynastic court and their own leader, called the "rebbe." The Lubavitchers acquired their name from the province in present-day Russia called Lubavitch (City of Love), where their first rebbe established his court. He was Schneur Zalman, who through his writing of the *Tanya* made the Lubavitchers recognized for their rationalistic inclinations. This work is basically the written form of Lubavitcher philosophy. The crux of its meaning is that, by searching the depths of one's soul, any Jew may learn to understand all the dimensions of the world and become a better person.

Since the death of Zalman, there have been six Lubavitcher rebbes, who were all related to one another. Four times the position was handed down to a son, and twice it was awarded to a son-in-law. Each rebbe has added a new dimension to the movement with his own ideas.

The current rebbe, Rabbi Menachem Schneerson, though almost eighty-five years old and having served thirty years in the position, instills a vibrant energy in Lubavitcher Hasidism. He has declared that the Lubavitcher motto be "*Uforatzto*"—"And you shall spread out . . ." (Genesis 28:14). He has opened more than two hundred Lubavitcher Houses on five different continents: South America, Europe, Africa, and Asia, and on many college campuses throughout the United States. He has established the Lubavitcher Women's Organization, the Lubavitcher Youth Organization, and the Jewish Peace Corps. He has created "Mitzvah Tanks" to "arm" children with knowledge through books and has been instrumental in establishing twenty-four-hour crisis hot lines from his headquarters in Crown Heights.

To understand the Lubavitcher woman and her role in married life, one must first understand the source of the rules by which she lives: the Torah. It has several methods of instruction. There are narratives, history, exhortation, and even poetry that attempt to establish and inculcate ideas (L.C. of G.B. 1970:217). Most importantly, there are duties and prohibitions that are comprised in the 613 commandments known as *mitzvahs*. The majority of these laws are prohibitive (1970:365)—"Thou shall not . . ."—and apply to both men and women. The positive laws (1970:248), which must be performed at certain times, were given only to men. Does this unequal distribution mean the gender roles are unequal? A Lubavitcher text suggests: ". . . this may well be an indication of the natural superiority of the Jewish woman over her male counterpart in some respects . . . to the extent that the mitzvahs constitute an exercise in self-discipline for moral advancement it would seem that the Creator has endowed the Jewish woman with a greater measure of such natural mitzvah characteristics" (1970:220).

Rabbi Moishe, one of my main informants, explained that, by exempting the woman from observing time-controlled mitzvahs (those that must be done at a specific hour of the day), the Torah has defined the Lubavitcher woman's role in life. He says, "The Torah has encouraged the woman's life-giving instincts and recognizes that her primary role is the foundation of the home and family." The fact that the woman's responsibility within the home takes precedence over the mitzvahs suggests the magnitude of her role.

The three mitzvahs especially entrusted to the Lubavitcher woman that play a vital role in perpetuating the tradition are the laws of family purity, observing the Sabbath, and following dietary laws. I will now discuss each of these rituals in the context of their importance in supporting the equality of the man and woman in the Lubavitcher marriage.

The Ritual Baths: The Mikvah

"The rabbis of Biblical times knew a lot more about what is really sexy than Masters and Johnson will ever know" (Sarah, a married informant).

Why did the Torah say that a menstruating woman is forbidden for seven days to her husband? . . . Since the husband is accustomed to his wife, he may begin to find her unpleasing. Therefore . . . let her be forbidden so she will be as dear to him as the day of her marriage (Meiselman 1978:127 from the Talmud).

Mikvah means "a collection of water." A mikvah is a natural body of water in which immersion renders someone ritually pure. Rachel informed me that the mikvah was in use nearly twenty centuries ago at Masada, in present Israel, where the Jews had built a fortress while the Romans destroyed the First Temple at Jerusalem in A.D. 79. Even in those desperate times, Jewish women were using the mikvah. The modern one does not look much different from the ancient one at the Masada because throughout time all are constructed according to the same requirements of Jewish law. However, the reasons for the use of the mikvah today are more restricted. In the early years of the mikvah, all Jews who contracted any of numerous sorts of "impurities" were forbidden to eat the sacrificial meat or enter the Temple of David. In order to clean themselves of the impurity, they were required to immerse themselves in the mikvah.

During their first year of marriage, Rachel and her husband lived at the Lubavitcher House near the University of Pennsylvania campus. Once every month, they would travel to northeast Philadelphia to make an unusual and private visit. While her husband waited in the car, Rachel entered a small, inconspicuous building. She sat in a waiting room, together with other Lubavitcher and Orthodox women whom she often did not know, until she was led by a woman attendant to a private, white-tiled room with sink, shower, and bathtub. There she bathed and showered for at least thirty minutes and meticulously removed any objects that she may still have been wearing, such as contact lenses or her wedding ring. She would then slip on a plain, white robe and press a buzzer to summon the attendant.

Together, they would walk down a small corridor to what appears to be a miniature, tiled, indoor swimming pool. Rachel would then remove the robe in the presence of the attendant and descend seven steps into the lukewarm water. It contained a minimum amount of fresh rainwater, collected from a funnel and purifier located above the building. Slowly she would crouch with her feet apart and her eyes open until her entire body was immersed. Then, standing, she would reach for a small towel to cover her head while she recited a prayer in Hebrew: "Blessed art Thou, O Lord our God, King of the universe who hast sanctified us by His Commandments and has commanded us to observe the Ritual Immersion." Rachel would then immerse herself once again the same way, and then a final time.

The attendant would help her out of the water and Rachel would return to her private bathing room, where she would dress, apply makeup and blow-dry her hair. On the way out, she paid the attendant six dollars and walked to her husband's car, parked "at least a block away." The entire procedure, beginning when she entered the building, took one hour. The couple made that trip faithfully every month rain or shine, typhoon or tornado, until they moved to northeast Philadelphia two years ago, which enabled her to walk to the same mikvah.

On the first day of her period each month, Rachel, like all Lubavitcher women, is rendered "Niddah," or impure. During this time and for an additional seven "clean" days (a minimum total of twelve days is required), she is forbidden to have sexual relations with her husband. At the end of this time, she must go to the mikvah for her ritual cleansing, which removes her "impure" state.

Today, some Jewish men still use a mikvah to purify themselves before certain holidays, but it is not a commandment. Brides, however, are supposed to perform the ritual before their wedding as one of the only three commandments reserved exclusively for women.

For the woman, preparing to use the mikvah is an elaborate process. She must ready herself so that the waters of the mikvah touch every part of her body. Even minute matter such as dirt that has collected under a finger nail or a false tooth has to be removed before the ritual can proceed.

I had the opportunity to visit the mikvah Rachel attends while it was closed, courtesy of the fire-extinguisher inspector who made his yearly safety inspection. Besides the interior of the building being impeccably clean, at the sink where Rachel removes anything forbidden, there is a whole array of products to assist her—from Kosher toothpaste to Q-tips to nail-polish remover.

The immersion additionally involves careful procedures. Rachel cannot immerse herself during the day, but rather must wait until forty-five minutes after dark while the stars are out. Her entire body must be immersed, including her hair. Neither her hands, eyes, nor lips should be closed. The attendant supervises everything to ensure that the ritual is done properly.

Although most Jewish women are not familiar with the Laws of Niddah, Rachel feels that it is the backbone of a successful marriage for those who practice it. When I mentioned to her that no Jewish women that I know observes the mitzvah or the mikvah, she replied: "They don't know what they are missing." Why did all my women informants feel so strongly about the significance of the mikvah? Most other Jewish woman believe that to be obligated by religious law to have to immerse themselves in water following the time of menstruation is something sexist. But, as Sarah, a lifelong Lubavitcher who has been married eighteen years, said: "The mikvah [Laws of Niddah] raises my life from the everyday to the spiritual and at specific times I am forbidden fruit to my very own husband."

To understand better what Sarah meant by "spiritual," it is important to look at the Lubavitcher philosophy. It places a great deal of emphasis on introducing the presence of God in everyday activities and reaching the highest spiritual level Jews can attain. By performing a mitzvah (commandment) that is a physical action, such as giving charity, those persons are elevating themselves to a higher spiritual level. The more mitzvahs they perform, the more spiritual they become. Figuratively speaking, Jews ascend in spirituality through fulfilling as many of the 613 commandments as they can. Surely, that is a large number of commandments, but not every Jew is required to perform each one. It must be looked upon as an ideal, something to strive for, to elevate oneself. In essence, a person cannot separate the physical from the spiritual because they are inseparably bound. Thus, physical intimacy between husband and wife is holy and spiritual when the Torah guidelines are followed, particularly because the potential to create another life is inherently holy in Judaism.

However, physical intimacy between the husband and wife during her menstruation is not a means of reaching a higher spiritual level. According to Friedfertig and Schapiro (1981:41), if a husband and wife are to share the physical intimacy that may be considered the exuberance of life itself at the same moment when the woman is losing the unfertilized ovum—a potential for life—then this demonstrates a certain insensitivity. To some degree, this is analogous to the kosher dietary laws: a cheeseburger is not eaten because the very same kind of animal that provided the cheese has been slaughtered to provide the meat for one sandwich. It shows more sensitivity if the ingredients are eaten separately.

Although the mikvah ritual may seem burdensome, if not destructive to the marriage, for those Jews who do not practice it, the Lubavitchers, men as well as women, feel that it leads to a healthier, happier life. This, however, is not the reason for adhering to the law; it is a divine commandment and therefore has a higher purpose.

Rachel says it was the hardest in the beginning of the marriage when she and her husband, who were both "returnees" to the Lubavitcher faith, had to practice the Laws of Niddah. "There has to be a solid foundation of trust between both of you [husband and wife] and you have to be committed to the Torah," states Rachel. "With time it gets easier and you really begin to appreciate the chance to communicate with your husband on a nonphysical basis."

Inevitably, the Laws of Niddah force the man to see his wife as more than a sexual object. It causes a couple "to develop parts of their relationship that never were noticed before." Additionally, declares Sarah, "it breaks up the static and keeps things moving. . . . it gives me an opportunity for privacy which sometimes I do not realize I really need." When I asked her husband, a computer programmer who works ten-hour days because he takes Friday off for the Sabbath, his feelings on the law, he responded: "It really gives an opportunity for privacy."

The abstinence phase is not a time of total exclusion between husband and wife. They sleep in separate beds but are still in the same room. Many of the activities that a couple may enjoy, such as biking for Sarah and her husband, are still done during her state of impurity. However, they avoid activities that may lead to physical contact.

It seems appropriate that the ritual of the mikvah would begin at as holy a time as the wedding. In fact, the very word for marriage in Hebrew is "kiddushin" from the root word meaning sanctified and separated. As Rachel explained, where there is *kiddushin*—sanctification—the relationship itself is sacred. Likewise in *kiddushin*—separation—there is a time when the husband and wife are separated physically from each other's touch. During a Lubavitcher wedding, one of the seven blessings that is recited deals with the two forms of love that are present in the marriage: the love of physical fulfillment and brotherly/sisterly love. Through the Laws of Niddah, it is hoped that a balance within the marriage can be struck between these two forms of love.

This balance is essential in a marriage not only because it affects the way a couple relates to one another, but also because it may affect the mental and physical abilities of an unborn child. As Sarah said: "Judaism builds on the idea of sexuality in a positive way. It says that sex is good; it is holy when the two people adhere to Niddah and treat each other with due respect. But if there is not a mutual pleasure then it could have serious repercussions on your unborn child. . . . I know a couple whose child is retarded; this has raised suspicions in the community before." When Sarah speaks of mutual pleasure, she is referring to the marriage contract, which states explicitly that the husband is obligated to provide sexual satisfaction to his wife, just as he must provide food and clothing (Meiselman 1978:121).

The positive attitude between men and women in adhering to the Laws of Niddah probably has a considerable influence in keeping the Lubavitcher divorce rate at what Rachel believes "is somewhere between 5 and 10 percent." "When you get married" declared Rachel, "think of your marriage like a garden, . . . like the Garden of Eden. Like any garden there will be times when it needs to be watered and times when it needs sunshine—it will have to go through cycles." She continued by saying that the Laws of Niddah are the ingredients that keep the marriage fresh and vibrant.

It is an interesting analogy that water, which is indispensable for a garden, is also an essential ingredient of the mikvah. But this is no coincidence. In the *Modern Jewish Woman*, published by the Lubavitcher Youth Organization, water has long been the symbol of life in numerous cultures; and the Torah, in Judaism, has been termed as the Tree of Life. Water has a strong identification with birth; a human fetus is 97-percent water by weight, and by adulthood it has decreased to 60 percent. By immersing in water at the mikvah "I feel young and refreshed," Rachel declares. The mikvah is also used by converts to Judaism; by immersing themselves in the water, they are "made to feel as if they were newly born" (Fried-fertig and Schapiro 1981:64).

The Essence of the Lubavitcher Home

While the man has always been the family's public representative,
the woman has been its soul.
(Meiselman 1978:16)

If love is the foundation of Lubavitcher marriage, the home is the foundation of Lubavitcher existence. It is there that the family is created, that children gain their values and eventually grow into respectable Lubavitcher Jews. To deem the Lubavitcher mother a "homemaker" is far insufficient for her role because she does more than just "make the home." The woman is the molder, the creator, and the one who instills Jewish values in her children. The way in which she presents the physical as well as spiritual setting expresses her uniqueness and individuality.

To capture the essence of the Lubavitcher home, I chose to study the events leading up to the beginning of the Sabbath as celebrated in Sarah's home in Crown Heights. It would probably be more beneficial if I could examine those that occur on the Sabbath, but this was not possible because I had other obligations with the Lubavitchers in attending prayer at the local synagogue. However, by providing a visual picture of the surroundings and the atmosphere before the start of the Sabbath, I hope that my account will help the reader gain a feeling for the Lubavitcher home and the role the mother plays in its creation. In Hebrew, the word "Sabbath" is called "Shabbos." In the pages that follow, I will use that term to designate the Sabbath because it conveys to Jews a stronger identification with the day it represents.

Shabbos is a special day for Sarah's family as well as other Lubavitcher families. Besides being one of the few occasions when the entire family is together, it is a time described by Jewish scholars when a person possesses an additional soul (L.C. of G.B. 1970:270). Although not to be taken literally, this description helps one understand that Shabbos is different from other days because Jews, and specifically Lubavitchers, on this occasion elevate themselves to a higher plane through performance of the commandments that strengthen the bond with God.

Sarah and her husband Richard live in a two-story townhouse in the center of Crown Heights. There is nothing special about the exterior of the building except for the chipped paint and broken window that seem characteristic of many of the townhouses in Crown Heights as well as the two doors one after the other that guard the entrance for added protection. On the upper third of the doorpost of the second door was a *mezuzah* enclosed in a metal case. This is a tiny scroll of parchment with a handwritten prayer affirming the presence of God. It has spiritual value in protecting the home and the family (Friedfertig and Schapiro 1981:173).

Once inside the home, I was welcomed to a spacious, carpeted living room with a plush sofa and chair near the front bay window. Near the back wall was a large oak dining table with a candelabra on top of it. Along the left wall were bookshelves filled with Jewish books, predominantly in Hebrew, a ram's horn known as a *shofar*, and a photograph of the current rebbe taken while he was praying at his synagogue, known as "770," just around the corner from the home. On a bookshelf as one enters is a picture of the entire family, including four sons ranging in age from four to twelve and a daughter, eleven. Additional pictures in a photo album on the coffee table show the youngest boy, Reuben, with hair down to his shoulders. I was certain that "he" was actually a "she" until Richard informed me of the Lubavitcher custom in some families to let boys' hair grow until they are three years of age.

Alongside the photo album is Reuben's comic book, "The Coming of the Moshiach [Messiah]," which Reuben's brother says "has more action any day than Superman ever will." Within each bedroom is a picture of the current rebbe and an intercom so Sarah can keep track of all her children. There are no posters of rock stars or Rambo, but rather pictures of Jerusalem and computer printouts of Hebrew letters in different geometrical designs.

No television is present because the parents feel it is a negative influence especially on the children. So, instead, the children play with the computer in the game room, which is programmed for games like "hangman" and "dungeons and dragons."

One of the things that caught my attention was the size of the living/dining room. There was much more room than was presently occupied by the furniture because a wall had been knocked out to make room for people to congregate. Sarah explained that every Shabbos she would have as many as twenty guests over to share the meal with her family. She told me that it is a mitzvah, a good deed, to invite others into one's home to partake of the Shabbos meal. Often these guests are yeshiva students or elderly in the community who do not have much to live on. Other times, the guests are fellow Jews like myself, who have arrived in Crown Heights simply out of interest.

Sarah starts her Friday mornings by preparing breakfast for her children and writing out the shopping list for the items she wishes to include for the Shabbos meal. Richard, a computer programmer, leaves for work before the rest of the family is awake, and therefore cooks his own breakfast. After seeing the children off to school, Sarah walks down Kingston Avenue, only a block from her home, where the Lubavitchers do most of their marketing. On a Friday during the morning hours and into the early afternoon, the avenue is dominated by Lubavitcher women pushing their baby strollers while shopping for the Shabbos meal. Nearly every drugstore front window features a large display of various kinds of diapers. Sarah told me that she is relieved that Reuben, the youngest, no longer needs to wear them.

As we walk into Weiss' Strictly Kosher Seafood, Sarah recognizes some of her "girl friends," as she calls them. They are discussing the *Fabrengan* that is scheduled to occur on Saturday afternoon. This is a gathering of the Lubavitchers at their world headquarters at 770 Eastern Parkway. This event occurs at least once a month, but it is important because the rebbe makes an address in person. For about four hours, he speaks in Yiddish about an issue relevant to Judaism. Subsequently, tapes in numerous languages are made and disseminated to Lubavitchers all over the world. Sarah interrupted the women's conversation to introduce me as "someone studying the community." They nodded their heads in response to my presence (no handshake) and continued talking. However, now the conversation turned to the wigs they each had purchased last week. This indicated to me that all these women were married because nonmarried females are not required to cover their hair.

As Sarah waves goodbye to her friends, she directs her attention to the whitefish that are lying on ice along the counter. Sarah visually inspects and smells one for a moment before gesturing to the Lubavitcher employee with her hand that she will take five of them. She has to be sure that the food she is purchasing is kosher in addition to maintaining her own standards of freshness. "Some foods are more kosher than others—it depends a lot upon how it's prepared." Sarah repeated this feeling of responsibility to me numerous times. "My family doesn't know what ingredients I've used or how I have prepared them but I am depended on to make a *kosher* meal." Unlike certain Catholic holidays, once prohibiting the eating of meat, Judaism has no restrictions upon the sort of food that is eaten on Shabbos provided that it is kosher. There were no lobsters, crabs, or shrimp to be found in Weiss's fish market because these creatures do not have both fins and scales, which are required to be considered kosher. Sarah could have bought some red meat provided the animal it came from chewed its cud and had cloven hooves. Some other animals that are considered kosher are chickens, ducks, geese, and turkeys.

Maintaining the dietary laws to a strict degree is of fundamental importance to the Lubavitchers. One of their monthly magazines (*Wellsprings* 1986:V2:4:21) points out that the dietary laws are considered to be one of the three most important commitments by Jews that have allowed for their survival. The other two "secrets" were deemed to be the commandment of keeping the Sabbath and observing the laws of family purity. It is significant to note that the woman has the fundamental role in each of these three commandments.

Sarah returned home by 1:00 p.m. in time to greet Reuben as he was stepping off the school bus. She tries to be home at this time everyday so she can welcome him back home and fix him a snack. Sarah, as well as numerous other Lubavitcher couples with children, emphasized to me that they will not send their child to a day-care program when they are busy unless it is Lubavitcher. Even then, as one woman informant told me: "I have no idea what they are teaching my child. . . . I want to instill our values [wife's and husband's] in my own child and know that he is the product of our time and effort so he will observe God's commandments and understand his purpose."

By mid-afternoon on Friday, the sidewalks in Crown Heights are filled with determined pedestrians: women rushing with their shopping bags to prepare the Shabbos meal and men in their black suits and hats zipping the other direction to attend prayer at 770. Because driving any vehicle is prohibited on Shabbos, and by this time it is only about an hour away, few cars crowd the streets. As the men pass Sarah, often one will stop walking and say, "Good Shabbos, Mrs. P——" and continue walking to the synagogue. However, as the introductory prayer service at 770 grows nearer, the men will most often just tip their hats to the woman as they pass in stride.

Meanwhile, at Sarah's home, every individual has a role in preparing for Shabbos. Leah is busy setting the dining-room table, and the boys are cleaning the kitchen table of the debris that remain from the salad Sarah prepared. Richard is at the men's mikvah as a symbolic way to make himself "cleaner" in welcoming the Sabbath. Although it is not a commandment for men to immerse before the Sabbath, many Lubavitcher men desire to do so.

Reuben has already done his part by taping all the light switches. One of the many prohibitions on Shabbos is turning anything on or off. So, to ensure that nobody touches the switches, Reuben tapes the bathroom lights on as well as the kitchen light. All the others in the house are taped off and must remain that way until Shabbos ends twenty-four hours and thirty-six minutes later. (With the introduction of electric timers, bedroom lights can be scheduled to be on or off without touching the light switch.) Shabbos begins eighteen minutes before sundown and ends eighteen minutes after that time. I am uncertain how the number eighteen was determined for this day, but the extra thirty-six minutes is specified to ensure that the entire period of Shabbos is observed.

The many restrictions on Shabbos that have been passed through tradition and through law are overwhelming to an outsider. During the entire Shabbos while I was at the University of Pennsylvania Lubavitcher House, I was on guard because of my uncertainty as to whether or not I was performing a prohibition. It is easy enough to watch or observe Jewish customs, but to participate in them requires a different way of thinking. Among the many prohibitions on Shabbos are cooking, baking, washing, cutting, writing, sewing, typing, building, gardening, buying, selling, pushing or carrying anything farther than six feet, turning on an electrical device, and probably a great deal more.

The prohibitions felt burdensome to me because I failed to capture the essence of Shabbos. It is designed to elevate Jews from their everyday existence. As Sarah explains: "In today's society, we are forced to run, run, push, push. In America many people do not slow down even on the weekend. Ah, but Shabbos teaches us that we are often slaves to the very same machines which are designed to make our life easier." It became evident to me after observing Shabbos a few times that the prohibitions in essence allow Jews of today to create a link with past as well as future generations by observing the occasion in a manner basically independent of technological innovation. By the prohibition of many of the things that are done during the workweek, family members are encouraged to interact with one another and discuss issues, almost always Jewish in nature, that they otherwise may not be able to discuss owing to their individual responsibilities.

To initiate Shabbos and create a connection with other Jews, timeless and spaceless in dimension, a minimum of two candles are lit (corresponding to two passages in the Torah regarding the observance of Shabbos) eighteen minutes before sundown. The prime obligation to light candles is on the woman of the house, but once a daughter is old enough she is given her own candle to carry on the tradition (Blau 1979:43). Sarah's daughter, Leah, has been lighting her own candle since she was three years old. One of the customs that Sarah follows, as passed down from her mother, is to add an additional candle with the birth of each child; each additional one is lit weekly until that child marries. Thus, Sarah, who has five children, lights seven candles.

Although this task may appear somewhat meaningless to an outsider, Sarah and Leah are very proud of this responsibility. I was asked to leave the dining room table as they prepared to light the candles, but, as an anthropologist, I felt the need to watch from the kitchen door. Once the candles were lit with matches, Sarah and Leah spread their hands out above and in front of the candles, moving their hands in a circular motion three times. Each then covered her eyes with her hands and repeated the Hebrew blessings to welcome the start of Shabbos. A moment of silence, probably a private prayer, then followed. When their eyes were uncovered, Sarah and Leah each said, "Good Shabbos." I noticed that Leah did her lighting and prayer independently from her mother. Although they began at the same time, Leah ended her prayer perhaps a minute after Sarah.

The lighting of the candles introduces an array of significant themes: the end of the week and the start of Shabbos; the literal and figurative brightening of what is often called a gloomy world; an opportunity to speak with God; and, most pertinent, the exclusive role of the woman, through the matrilineal link with future and past ancestors.

The next morning, Saturday, when I asked Leah to tell me about her experiences with lighting the candles, she was eager to speak. She personified the Sabbath by naming it the "Shabbos Queen," which she says "is a time to thank Hashem [another word to signify God] and pray for Jews in Iran and Russia who cannot light their candles." I continued talking to her for about half an hour on candle-lighting, and not once did she mention any prayers that focused upon herself. She felt it was more important to think of others, specifically her family and Jews who are oppressed around the world because "when the other [Jews] are happy, I am happy."

The Lubavitcher home captures its essence from the permanent physical surroundings, such things as furnishings, decorations, and food, as well as from the atmosphere created by visitors and the lighting of the Shabbos candles. The woman plays a vital role in meshing all of these elements to produce a religious home.

Rachel has not always been a Lubavitcher Jew. When she was fifteen years old, she had never seen a Hasid before. Although she was born Jewish, her parents were not religious and she felt little if any Jewish identity. But this all changed when she decided to take a course in Jewish philosophy in college at the University of Texas. The professor asked a lot of questions but provided few answers. Rachel wanted answers to such basic questions as: "Why am I alive?" and "What is my purpose?" She soon joined a Jewish youth group that hosted a number of functions organized by the Lubavitchers. Because their emphasis on understanding and explanation appealed to her, after one year she left college to study at a women's yeshiva university, dominated by Lubavitchers, in Minneapolis. There she learned the principles of Hasidism and the Lubavitchers. But she emphasizes that it was a slow transition from secular to Lubavitcher life.

The Lubavitcher concept of dating was foreign to Rachel. Not only was she encouraged to date only Lubavitchers (devout Orthodox who are not Lubavitchers are sometimes accepted as being appropriate dates), but also no physical contact between sexes was allowed. Any dating that occurred was done with the intention of marriage and often this would require the need of a chaperone. Any contact between the sexes outside the marriage was forbidden because "to touch" is something sacred that is reserved for the permanency that can only be found in marriage. "All of this was hard for me to swallow," reflects Rachel. "But you learn to realize what is really important to you is knowing who you are and Torah provides that for me. Before I became observant [following the 613 commandments], I was directionless like most adolescents in today's society."

Rachel says it took her five years to feel comfortable with the customs of the Lubavitchers. But now she is happily married to a returnee Lubavitcher rabbi living in Philadelphia and fully satisfied with her role as a Lubavitcher woman.

Sarah was one of nine children in a Lubavitcher family in Crown Heights. Her religious experience as a Jew and role as a woman has never been a question for herself. Lighting the candles on the Sabbath is first nature to her as learning to walk is for an infant. She informed me that she has never had a "Big Mac" and probably never will. She explained her situation to me: "When I was little I wondered what it would be like not to be observant or of a different religion. I made a mental picture of such a situation, but I felt it would be for what? I like what I have. . . . there is no need for me to have something else. If I have never had anything else, what is there to miss?"

This statement is precisely why Rachel feels that being a returnee is more advantageous than being a lifer. She has had a real taste of secular life, is better educated in most secular subjects, and therefore feels that she has a better perspective on the world outside the Lubavitcher community. "I've seen the darkness and the confusion of the other side," she points out. At a women's symposium I attended while in Crown Heights, a woman returnee talked about her experiences as a stockbroker. She first became interested in the Lubavitchers after feeling confused about her role at work "as one of the boys." After becoming a Lubavitcher, she remarried, to a returnee, but she still works in Wall Street, has nine children, and is now a well-respected member of the Crown Heights community. Although such a woman is more of the exception than the norm with Lubavitchers, she demonstrates that this type does exist—she just has to know her priorities as a Lubavitcher. This means creating a Jewish home, raising the children to be observant, and following the commandments herself, that is, family purity. Indeed, this is tough to manage, but a Lubavitcher man would rather have his wife "keep the Jewish heritage alive" than bring in money from a job that takes her away from her real duties.

There is no question that the stockbroker was able to handle the demands of work and religion only because her youngest child was fifteen years old. If a Lubavitcher woman has an infant or preschooler, as Rachel has, then it is impossible to have a job as well. This is not much different than it would be for any woman in the United States with a child. However, the secular woman could cope by day care or babysitter; the Lubavitcher woman on religious principles would rather give up the job.

Lifer as well as returnee women work in the job market, but it is usually restricted to the Lubavitcher or Jewish community. During the first year of her marriage, Rachel supported her husband and herself while he studied daily in a yeshiva. Because she lived in Philadelphia at the time, and still does, she worked at the University of Pennsylvania Lubavitcher House creating new slogans to attract other Jews, answering the phone, and working as a secretary. Sarah was a medical assistant to a Lubavitcher doctor within the Lubavitcher community. Where did she receive the training? "I'm a fast learner," she says. A Lubavitcher employer is willing to take the time to teach a skill to a member of the community. There is a network of interdependence.

After a year of study of Hasidus, the Lubavitcher man will embark on his job (the men are in all sorts of fields but tend to stay within Jewish sectors), and the woman will become strictly a homemaker. It is often at this point that the couple begin a family. Because no birth control is allowed, families will often be very large. Sarah told me that her cousin, a Lubavitcher living in Israel, has twenty children. Although this is a bit extreme, it is not uncommon for a couple to have twelve. "If Hashem wants you to have 'x' amount of children, so be it," declares Moishe, my informant from the Penn Lubavitcher House.

Another aspect of Lubavitcher life that Rachel had to grapple with, but was never really a concern of Sarah's, was a segment from the Written Law. Within the Talmud is a passage that when translated into English reads: "Women are temperamentally light-headed." Rachel explained this phrase to me by looking at the words that comprise the acronym of "Chabad," the other term for Lubavitcher. Chabad is made up of the words "chokhmah," "binah," and da'as. They comprise the intellectual powers that a human is endowed with. *Chokhmah* embodies an idea that a person creates; *binah* embodies the developing of that idea; and *da'as* is that idea which is written or communicated to others. Not everybody has these abilities to the same degree. As Rachel explains: "Both men and women have the power of *chokhma* [create an idea], but women to a greater degree than men have the God gifted power of *beena* [developing the idea]; however, women could not get to the next stage, that of developing the idea into action. . . . men have more *da'as*."

Thus, women are described in the Talmud as light-headed because "a woman will continually develop an idea without putting it into action." This is where the male is needed because he is more action-oriented in terms of "conquering new areas." "Throughout world history, how many women have started a war?" quipped Rachel. In her words: "The ability that women possess of developing an idea is what makes a woman more spiritual or inherently closer to God." Sarah agreed with this idea of the woman being more spiritual, as did Moishe. He states that a woman has unique powers of insight and can generally recognize the character of a person better than a man can. As one rabbi has stated, the woman possesses "a spiritual radar" (Miller 1984:60).

The spiritual radar is well exemplified in Sarah. Three years ago, when her husband was working with a large computer company, he was offered a promotion provided that he could move to the company's headquarters in Georgia. He was very excited because it was a substantial pay increase and a new position. However, Sarah told him she would refuse to move. "There would be little Jewish identity for the children. . . . it would be a fishbowl existence," she exclaims. The family did not move and soon afterward her husband went into private business. *In Search of the Jewish Woman* clearly elaborates on this spiritual aspect of the woman: "Woman serves to guard Man's humanity; but she can do so only if she herself is not exposed to the identical temptations. . . . out of the limelight, away from the roar of the crowd, uncorrupted by the power structure, Woman has an unclouded view with which to see the truth as it really is" (Miller 1984:62).

Rachel and Sarah have different perspectives associated with being Lubavitcher Jews. For Rachel, there was a period of searching and trying to understand. For Sarah, there was never such a need. She has always thought Lubavitcher. Despite their personal historical differences, each woman understands her essentialness within the marriage as a Lubavitcher Jew.

Conclusion

It is possible to comprehend the equality of the woman to the man in the Lubavitcher marriage when one realizes that each has different but complementary roles. The woman is felt to be blessed with different inherent abilities than those of the man; and, even though she has fewer mitzvahs to perform than the man, her role in fulfilling them is equal, if not "more" equal, to that of the man.

Although arguments can be raised about this nature/nurture approach to roles, it should be realized that the Lubavitchers refuse to believe that any change in the status of man or woman is necessary. There is only one reason why the two perform different roles; it is because God has commanded them to do so. Along those same lines, as one informant noted, "If God intended for us to have identical roles in life, he would not have made a male and female—one would suffice."

Perhaps one of the strongest arguments in support of the woman's status in Lubavitcher Hasidism is that more secular Jewish women in the United States than ever before are "returning" to the Torah-observant life-style of the Lubavitchers. This may very well be a reaction to present sociocultural conditions in the larger American society, where divorce is occurring at an alarming rate, as suggested by an unmarried twenty-five-year-old returnee whom I met in a Crown Heights bookstore: "I know I can find a husband who will be totally dedicated to the marriage."

9

Strategies for Strength
Women and Personal Empowerment in Lubavitcher Hasidism

Gita Srinivasan

The contemporary Lubavitcher sect is descended from the Hasidic community that first developed in eighteenth-century Eastern Europe. In an introduction to the first English translation of the *Tanya*, the sacred text of Lubavitcher Hasidism, published in 1962, the rebbe ("spiritual center") gives a general but comprehensive orientation to Hasidic thought. He describes it as

> an all-embracing world outlook and way of life which sees the Jew's central purpose as the unifying link between Creator and Creation. The Jew is a creature . . . whose purpose is to realize the transcendency and unity of his nature, and of the world in which he lives, within the absolute Unity of G-d. The realization of this purpose entails a two-way correlation: one in the direction from above downward to earth; the other, from the earth upward. In fulfillment of the first, man draws holiness from the Divinely-given Torah and commandments *to permeate therewith every phase of his daily life and his environment* . . . in fulfillment of the second, *man draws upon all the resources at his disposal*, both created and man-made, *as vehicles for his personal ascendancy and, with him, that of the surrounding world*. One of these basic resources is the vehicle of human language and communication. . . . Rabbi Israel Ba'al Shem Tov [envisaged] Chassidus as a stream of "living waters," growing deeper and wider, until it should reach every segment of the Jewish people and bring new inspiration and vitality into their daily lives [my emphasis]. (Zalman 1962:vii–viii)

This introduction summarizes the most significant features of Lubavitcher Hasidism. It introduces the Torah as the primary sacred text, which consists of the Five Books of Moses (the Written Law) and is believed to have been revealed to Moses on Mt. Sinai by God. The Torah specifies 613 possible commandments, or *mitzvahs*, for Jews to fulfill toward realization of "the unifying link between Creator and Creation" that the rebbe mentions above. Fulfillment of these commandments (comprised of "negative" prohibitions and "positive" duties) constitutes a major goal of an observant Hasid's life. Each commandment correctly performed helps to "elevate" the individual to a higher spiritual level, builds on the personal link one cultivates with the Divine, and strengthens one's Jewish soul.

The swift connection the rebbe makes between individuals achieving "personal spiritual ascendancy" and its effect on the achievement of spiritual ascendancy in "the surrounding world" links the microcosmic efforts of individuals with the macrocosmic world that surrounds them. The idea that an individual's private activities can have a significant impact on the world at large is a central theme that must be kept in mind throughout the course of this chapter. The fact that the rebbe emphasizes man drawing upon "all resources at his disposal," especially stressing language and communication, underscores the Lubavitcher practice of incorporating modern mass media and technology in their outreach mission. Lastly, the way in which the rebbe refers to Hasidic thought as "an all-embracing world view and way of life" is important. Lubavitcher Hasidism encompasses all aspects of life—it is not a source of spirituality that is categorized and set apart from the rest of living. In this vein, it is interesting to note that the word "Torah" means simply "path."

The Lubavitcher world headquarters is 770 Eastern Parkway, the Lubavitcher synagogue located in Crown Heights, Brooklyn. This community, which consists of approximately a thousand families (Sharot 1982:190), shares a deeply felt set of religious beliefs and values. In his book entitled *Messianism, Mysticism, and Magic*, Stephen Sharot describes the Lubavitchers as an introversionist group that clearly distinguishes between their members and outsiders (1982:191). Although the Lubavitchers do draw definite boundaries between themselves and other Jews, the true "outsiders" are non-Jews because Jews who are not Lubavitchers may still be drawn into the community through outreach programs. Nonresidents who wander into Crown Heights may feel as if they are entering another world: the shops that line the streets all cater to the needs of Hasidic Jews (kosher food stores and the like), the people dress differently, and the rhythms of life reflect those of the Jewish calendar. Yiddish is spoken in the streets.

The Lubavitchers sponsor many programs for religious instruction in Crown Heights and in greater New York City, organizing released-time religious classes for Jewish elementary school children, for example, to encourage them to greater religious awareness and observance. The Lubavitcher children I encountered did not attend public school. If they lived in an area where no Lubavitcher institute was available, they often boarded with families in Crown Heights in order to attend school there. In one family I came to know, the parents plan to start their own home school for their children. Young people, especially boys, are encouraged to travel to foreign countries, from Europe to South Africa, to do outreach work. Young couples may also decide to begin and run a new Chabad House in areas that are suggested by the rebbe.

Some of the more widely known features of Lubavitcher Hasidism distinguish the group in the eyes of outsiders. For example, many outsiders know that the women cut their hair at marriage and from then on wear wigs in public, that they participate in an immersion ritual called *mikvah* each month in correspondence with their menstrual cycle, and that the men grow beards and commonly wear black (or dark) long coats and hats. Of the various Hasidic groups, these people are perhaps most often in the public eye because they actively seek interaction with non-Lubavitchers in their outreach program. They are a visible presence in Brooklyn and in other large communities throughout the world because they lecture at public institutions, distribute literature and ritual equipment such as Hanukkah candles in public places, and hold weekend workshops and conventions to introduce outsiders to their faith. Perhaps the most visible technique of street proselytizing is the "synagogue on wheels"—also known as "tanks against assimilation"—and mitzvah mobiles, [these] small trucks adorned with religious slogans travel all over New York frequently . . . with Lubavitcher students eager to explain the use of sacred religious objects to any Jew who would listen" (Raphael 1984:174). I was continually amazed at the vast scope and efficiency of the Lubavitcher outreach mission. These people also form a formidable political presence in local New York politics because they often vote in a solid bloc.

I shall mention the concept of *Shabbos* (Hebrew for "Sabbath"), which is a major Jewish ritual referred to later. One of the Ten Commandments requires Jews to keep the seventh day holy. On this day, they "raise the dignity of the human personality" by paying tribute to the Creator, who created the world in six days and rested on the seventh; the occasion is also a memorial of the deliverance of the Jews from the Pharaoh's enslavement in Egypt (Millgram 1944:4). "Rest" on Shabbos entails a cessation of all physical labor and an emphasis instead on the spiritual and intellectual activities of prayer and Torah study. Candles are lit to usher in the "Sabbath Queen" on Friday evenings, and Shabbos lasts until the next evening.

Shabbos is a weekly reminder of the holy convenant between God and the Jews and is thus ideally a day of "joy and gladness" and "mystic sweetness and spirituality" (Millgram 1944:5). On Shabbos, Jews are believed to have a small taste of the future bliss that awaits them in the next world. They are believed to undergo a "miraculous transformation" on Shabbos: they possess a *neshamah yeterah*, an additional soul, during that time. A Jew is believed to be escorted home from Friday evening services by two angels, who bless the home if they find "the Sabbath lights kindled and the home radiant with the joyous Sabbath atmosphere" and curse it if Sabbath preparations have not taken place (Millgram 1944:1). Shabbos is an eagerly anticipated weekly holiday among the Lubavitchers and is considered to be a precious gift that God presented to the Jews.

✳✳

I am at home over winter school break, and I have made contact with the sole Lubavitcher family in northern Virginia. In a stroke of luck, they live within a five-minute drive from my house. I visited last night for the first time, to listen to a talk by the rebbe that was transmitted live on television from Crown Heights. About ten of us gathered to hear it—I was the only woman who had come alone. We listened to the rebbe's strong Yiddish; and the man of the house, a rabbi, translated during the breaks, when all we could hear was the lusty singing of the men in the synagogue.

As the night wore on, people began to quietly excuse themselves. As a zealous anthropology student, I was taking notes, and was the only guest to stay until the talk ended at 1:30 a.m. As I was getting ready to leave, I commented that, though I did not understand everything, it had been interesting to listen. The rabbi looked at me and said, "You may not have *consciously* understood, but sometimes it's good to just listen. . . . When a Jewish baby is in its mother's womb, it learns Torah. As it is being born into the world, an angel gives it a tap right here [he touched the small, curved cleft between his nose and his mouth]—that's why we have this mark—and the baby forgets everything."

I loved the story, and it followed me all the way home as I drove through the deserted suburban streets. The rabbi had ended the story by saying, "We spend our lifetime remembering."

****

Research Goals and Techniques

This study describes and analyzes the way in which "returnee" Lubavitcher women perceive the experience of their womanhood through Lubavitcher Hasidic religious precepts and individual inter- pretation. Specifically, the research focuses around the personal sense of empowerment that the women achieve through their reli- gion, and the cultural dynamics that allow this process to take place. In this context, the terms "empowerment" and "strength" are not meant in the political or utilitarian sense. Rather, they refer to the more psychological process that positively alters women's conceptions of themselves and each other. Among the Lubavitchers, these conceptions include faith in oneself on several levels and a feeling of being central to the teachings and practice of Judaism.

I begin my presentation and discussion of findings with a consid- eration of several theoretical positions pertinent to the study, con- cerning ethnicity and gender. To introduce this and the following sections, I quote from my field notes. These passages communicate the fieldwork experience in a different way than can the main dis- cussion of methodology employed, which follows the theoretical background.

****
It is almost 11:00 a.m. and several other girls from the *Pegishu* ("Wo- men's Weekend") and I are walking with eager anticipation toward 770 Eastern Parkway, where the rebbe will begin his *Farbrengan* (talk) in a few minutes. As I walk, I feel very conscious of whether my eyes, even if only for an instant, meet those of the black-hatted men traveling in the other direction. We enter through the crowded women's entrance. I watch those before me touch a hand to the small prayer scroll (*mezuzah*) on the door frame as they enter, and kiss the hand. I am last to enter of my group—I pause, touch, and kiss.

Inside, we climb upstairs to the women's section, a rectangular area with bleacher-like seats that looks down on the main arena below. It's smaller than I expected—or maybe it only feels that way because of the massed humanity of women and children in the close, stuffy area. "Are you for the pegisha?" A large woman in the front row decides to "adopt" me, and I manage to squeeze in next to her. I literally cannot move. But I'm in front, face up against the tinted plastic that encloses us. There is a strip of space about three inches in width where the tinted pane meets the low wall in front of me—just wide enough for a pair of eyes. I peer down.

A mass of black-coated, black-hatted, bearded men move together as a murmuring, living organism below. As far as the eye can see! No one looks up. The human sea divides to let a small, elderly, white-bearded man mount the central dais: the rebbe. He begins to speak in Yiddish, without a microphone—hundreds of women collectively crane. "Do you understand Yiddish?" I ask the kerchiefed woman standing next to me. "No," she replies, gazing down intently. I decide to follow suit, and fill my eyes. Later, during a break, the sight and sound of the men below singing joyously— and jumping! Clapping their hands!—wash over me with a power that startles.

✳✳

Theoretical Background

Lubavitcher women conceptualize the experience of their womanhood through Hasidic ideology and individual interpretation. I argue that this process contributes positively to their images of self within the context of Lubavitcher Hasidism. In studying the community, in which the primary focus is spiritual, I have recognized the inadequacy of certain paradigms commonly utilized in the anthropological study of gender. The conventionally defined dichotomies of "public realm" and "private realm," "universal/social good" and "private/particularistic interest" beg reevaluation in light of the gender dynamic that exists between Lubavitcher men and women. The cultural groundwork that informs conceptions of power and authority are primarily spiritual, not economic or political. Thus, although the Lubavitcher communities in Philadelphia and New York are subcultures within the larger industrial capitalist state, it is not appropriate to assume the encompassing culture's values regarding the social loci of status and value. In this section, I shall briefly review the anthropological literature pertinent to these issues and thus formulate the theoretical underpinnings of the ensuing study.

Studies concerning the cultural construction of gender often focus on the organization of prestige (or "social honor" or "social value"), defined by Ortner and Whitehead as follows: "Command of material resources (including human labor power), political might, personal skill, and/or connectedness through kinship or other reliable bonds to the wealthy, the mighty, and the skilled . . . conjoined with effective use of these factors in dealing with others or the environment and a modicum of largesse and concern for the social good" (1981:14). But what is considered to be the "social good"? As a general feature of gender ideology, the opposition between what Strathern calls "self-interest" and "social good" "involves the view that women . . . [tend] toward more involvement with (often divisive) private and particularistic concerns, benefitting themselves, and perhaps their children, without regard for larger social consequences, whereas men are seen as having a more universalistic orientation, as being concerned with the welfare of the social whole" (1981:7).

Furthermore, it is asserted by Ortner and Whitehead that men nearly universally control the public domain, where "universalistic" interests are expressed and managed. Women inhabit the domestic domain and see to the welfare of their own families. The male domain of public, social activity is seen as encompassing the smaller female sphere. Thus, the male domain is culturally accorded higher value (1981:7–8).

The categories of "public," "private," "social good," and "private interest" are useful ordering principles that I will rely on in framing the experience of Lubavitcher women. However, I find it misleading to construe them as pairs of opposites and to link necessarily private interest to the domestic sphere and social good to the public realm. The Lubavitcher world view features a highly elaborated set of distinctions and valuations concerning public and private domains. I found that these meanings were not always in consonance with those that inform the gender terminology. The terminological meanings describe the domestic sphere as particularistic in nature and "governed by informal and personal knowledge of individuals"; the public domain subsumes mother-child groups and "is concerned with formal norms of relations and publicly recognized characteristics of roles" (Rosaldo 1974:24).

I found that in Lubavitcher culture these distinctions are not always applicable; the domestic sphere, though it is linked to women, is perceived as the locus of "universalistic" activity for the social good. The private domain *is* concerned with formal relations and roles, and thus the culturally accorded higher value does not always inhere in the public domain. This basic shift effects a massive re-evaluation of women's work, domesticity, and status, which I believe form the core of women's sources of strength within the Lubavitcher community. This shift also forces a reconsideration of the idea that, to upgrade the status of women, they either must enter the public domain or men must begin to have a place in the home: "An egalitarian ethos seems possible to the extent that men take on a domestic role. . . . Women gain power and a sense of value when they are able to transcend domestic limits" (Rosaldo 1974:41). This analysis may not be functional in the Lubavitcher context because the domestic sphere itself is ideally a locus of cultural value and a source of power.

A society in which separation of the sexes is in effect often spawns two gender-specific cultures. Each may maintain distinct structures of authority and value, through mutual nonintervention or through keeping to separate but mutually dependent spheres of influence. The latter seems to be the Lubavitcher ideal in terms of gender relations.

Each of the two worlds has "a separate system of meanings and a program for behavior. . . . Sexual inequality becomes relevant when one world expands and the other fades away" (Sanday 1981:110). The Lubavitcher women I spoke with feel that sexual inequality is a non-issue; they do not compare their roles to those of men in this way, and they do not perceive their domain as being "subsumed" by that of men. A central purpose of this discussion will be the explication of women's informal and personal (or perceived) influence and power.

In the tradition of Mary Douglas's analysis of pollution and purity, I shall approach beliefs concerning the female body and its sexuality as symbols and analogies of the social order: "Beliefs about the virulence of the power inherent in female bodily or sexual functioning is neither a reflection of castration anxiety nor of sexual inequality. Rather, the presence of such beliefs provides us with a clue to the presence of critical human concerns. By projecting the concerns onto women, people provide themselves with a stage on which to control the dangerous forces they face" (Sanday 1981:92). Lubavitcher women's understanding of their physical connection to such "critical human concerns" contributes to their sense of personal empowerment within the religion because the connection is given positive valuation in the Lubavitcher context. Pollution beliefs give clues as to the maintenance of boundaries among crucial social groups.

In terms of the Modesty Laws in dress that Lubavitcher women observe, my study incorporates a perspective inspired by Fatima Mernissi's idea of the "active female sexuality" that she shows prevails in the Muslim context (Mernissi 1975:1). Rather than relying on literary textual support, I questioned informants on how their feelings about their bodies changed as a result of observing the Modesty Laws. My interpretation of an "active female sexuality" in the Lubavitcher context emphasizes how a woman realizes the power and value that are perceived to inhere in her body, and thus gains a new sense of respect (and empowerment) concerning her sexual desirability. In this study, I wish not to legitimate one form of Jewish practice over another or even deal in terms of objective cultural truths, but rather deal with women's perceptions of themselves and each other through Lubavitcher Hasidism. This research is presented in the spirit of Carol Gilligan's *In a Different Voice*: "My interest lies in the interaction of experience and thought, in different voices and the dialogs to which they give rise, in the way we listen to ourselves and to others, in the stories we tell about our lives" (Gilligan 1982:2).

****

We are upstairs in the large study room at the Machon Chana Institute for Jewish Women, and I am talking with Mrs. J——, a director of the Day Yeshiva. It is lunch hour, and around us students are leaving class, studying, and chatting over brown-bag lunches. I hear snatches of foreign languages. Mrs. J——, a middle-aged woman, is an Israeli, and speaks forcefully in heavily accented English. New York police sirens shrill outside; my tape recorder hums. We are talking about trust.

"In Israel there is trust between people. People *talk* with each other—by the end of a bus ride you could already be friends with someone. . . . I remember the first time I came [to New York]; I was riding in the subway and I saw people sitting there . . . [holds body rigidly and stares fixedly ahead]. If somebody minds somebody else's business, they would think they were up to trouble. It was like . . . [heavily, deliberately, and pausing between each word]—IT—WAS—HELL. I thought, this is a little bit of what Hell looks like. No contact between souls."

****

Methodology

The methodology employed was in many ways determined by the background of the researcher: the product of intermarriage (German Jewish and Indian Hindu) and a sketchy Reform Jewish education, I am what the Lubavitchers would term a "secular Jew." I do not keep kosher or observe an orthodox Shabbos, yet I do identify myself as a Jew. As I mentioned in the introductory section, it is the Lubavitcher outreach mission to bring nonobservant Jews back to what they perceive to be the heart of Judaism, observance of the Torah Laws. They also teach the Lubavitcher Hasidic philosophy. All Jews, whether they know it or not, are believed to have a spark of godliness within that may always be kindled out of dormancy.

The issue that this belief raised in doing fieldwork is that I was often perceived as a potential "returnee" to religion. This had benefits in terms of the data I gathered, but I felt the need to redefine my position continually. I did not choose this project purely out of intellectual interest—the choice *did* stem from personal interest in Judaism—and this fact seemed to satisfy both the Lubavitchers and myself. I felt considerable ambiguity, however, when informants told me to "use the data in good ways" or to use what they had said "if you think it will help anyone to become more religious." I was asked numerous times, rather conspiratorially, how my parents felt about the fact that I was engaged in this project and received surprised responses when I replied that it did not pose a problem for them.

Many *ba'alot teshuvah* women ("returnees" to Yiddishkeit, or Jewishness) are young women such as myself: college-educated in secular knowledge but eager to learn about Judaism. The Lubavitchers are probably more used to giving interviews and explaining themselves to outsiders than any other Hasidic group because they actively seek this type of interaction with other Jews. They are also often approached by non-Jewish reporters and other outsiders. Lubavitchers often feel chronically misrepresented by the press, but, rather than withdrawing, they seek to present the correct story. The fact of my own Jewishness and their general openness to outsiders (within certain parameters, to be discussed later) together set the tone for my participant-observation methodology.

My fieldwork began with a Friday night Shabbos visit to the Lubavitcher House at the University of Pennsylvania. This institution sponsors Jewish activities for students and other Jews in the community. Services were held in the House itself, followed by a communal Shabbos meal for the thirty-odd guests and residents. I intended to leave after the services, but circumstances and mild coercion led me to stay for the entire Shabbos, until Saturday evening. Since then, I have found that the most effective way to do fieldwork on this holy day is to experience the entire cycle. This left ample time for casual questioning and conversations, included the major weekly rituals, and gave me a sense of household rhythms and social dynamic that would not have been apparent in more formal, shorter visits.

After I decided to focus on the women's community, I spent Shabbos with Lubavitcher families, away from the more institutional Lubavitcher House. The House rabbi introduced me to a network of Lubavitcher families in Philadelphia, and made the arrangements for my first trip to Crown Heights, in New York. These initial contacts branched out, and at this point I decided to conduct fieldwork in Virginia, New York, and Philadelphia. I spent Shabboses with four different families in these areas, and participated in the rituals as fully as I was able. I lit my own Shabbos candle, said the blessings, went to services, and so on. The only areas in which I could not participate fully involved the singing of songs I did not know, and certain prayers I had not memorized (in these cases, I repeated them after someone else). However, these factors did not cause feelings of discomfort because the families were used to having non-Lubavitcher guests.

On Shabbos visits I tried to spend as much time as possible with the woman of the family, helping her prepare the meals if possible, setting the table, playing with the children, answering the door, and performing other small household duties. This narrowed the gap between myself and my informants and helped maintain a relaxed rapport. Also, whenever I did fieldwork, I observed the Modesty Laws for women, which means that I wore skirts together with high-necked shirts with long sleeves. I did not sing in the presence of men unless it was an appropriate occasion. On Shabbos, I followed all the prohibitions that those around me did, for example, not writing or turning lights on or off, carrying anything outside the house, and traveling except by foot.

Because writing is prohibited, data-gathering was accomplished through casual conversations with my hosts and guests and through reading Lubavitcher literature in family libraries. Shabbos is a time for "learning," the Lubavitcher term for Torah study, so I participated in formal and informal study groups. I felt that as a Jew I was often taken as an insider—a point that became clear once when a non-Jewish reporter and I were both Shabbos guests. Shabbos visits were an integral part of my fieldwork. One drawback was that, after spending a twenty-four hour period with the Lubavitchers and not recording observations, I often felt so saturated with cultural data and experiences that it was more difficult to frame my thoughts in order to write them down.

Shabbos-visiting was one field technique. To obtain more detailed, specific information from as wide a range of perspectives as possible, I also conducted interviews. They were usually fairly informal— I found it most effective to work loosely around a set of central issues rather than pinpointing questions. Often the issues I was addressing were intimate, such as body image and sexuality, and point-blank questions would have been intimidating. Questions had to be tailored so as not to create a large insider/outsider gulf, to minimize the fact that the value system I lived by was in clear contradiction with that of the Lubavitchers. For example, if I had asked a mother how often she gets out of the house as an indicator of her happiness and independence, she may have become defensive and said that those differences were not the important ones. Interviews were either tape-recorded or written, depending on the wishes of the informant and took place in a variety of settings (ranging from alone at home to a crowded school or dormitory). Some "interviews" were more like discussions between two or more informants, in which I was a marginal member. Such data were especially valuable because of the naturalness of the conversation. Some questioning was also done over the telephone.

Some of my informants were very eloquent and excellent story-tellers; others were more reticent or had not thought about the issues I was raising in the same way as I had. The single most pervasive problem I encountered in conversing and in interviewing was getting past the certain stock phrases and explanations common to Lubavitcher outreach discourse. I became aware of the fact that there were several layers of possible data, among them outreach language, the different perspectives of *ba'alot teshuvah* and those who were born Lubavitchers, and criticisms or dissatisfactions with Lubavitcher life. From an anthropological perspective, all the layers are significant; I only wish that I had a more evenly distributed sampling.

My informant pool was hardly representative of the entire Lubavitcher community—for example, nearly none of them had been Lubavitcher from birth. I spoke much less with men than with women and thus cannot include the masculine perspective on the issues I raise. However, I did achieve a good balance in married women informants, between those managing Chabad Houses (and thus very accustomed to dealing with outsiders) and those who are less active in outreach work and in the women's community. In Machon Chana, the Institute for Jewish Women I visited, I also spoke with a balanced mix of both marginal and completely committed members.

The most intensive fieldwork was accomplished during two separate trips I made to Crown Heights, Brooklyn. The first time, I attended Women's Weekend (*Hanuka Pegisha*) in December 1986 and stayed for four days. This was a program of lectures, social events, and workshops for women who were interested in learning about the Lubavitcher faith, but not necessarily Lubavitchers or even religiously observant themselves. I attended this program as a participant: only the Lubavitcher family who hosted me and a few other individuals knew I was writing a "report." The first visit was an experience in cultural immersion: I listened to panels, attended services, heard the rebbe speak, and participated in Hanukkah rituals with "my" family, among other things. Most of all, I talked endlessly with other participants from surprisingly diverse backgrounds, many of whom were in the process of returning to religion. I made the three-hour drive home with a Lubavitcher family, which afforded an opportunity for sustained conversation. I did not conduct interviews at this stage because the project did not yet have a focus. I was still developing a more general grasp of the culture. However, notes and written recollections from that first trip formed the basis for the future direction of the study.

My second trip to Crown Heights was in March 1987, for two and a half days. I stayed with the same family, but this time there was no program of events: I went back primarily to do follow-up interviewing. By now, specific issues had developed, and there were certain individuals I had met before or to whom I had been referred. For example, I had kept in touch with a friendly dorm counselor at Machon Chana Women's Jewish Institute. Via telephone, she acted as a liaison between myself and other students, arranging an appropriate time for my visit. My fieldwork centered around this institute, where I attended two classes; dined in the dormitory; went on walks with students; and interviewed a teacher, an administrator, two counselors, and numerous students. I also interviewed two married women in their homes during this trip.

Another source I used in gathering field data was Lubavitcher media publications. Various Lubavitcher organizations are prolific producers of pamphlets, advertisements, books, films, taped lectures, and monthly magazines. During the course of my research, I made use of all these types of data, borrowing from the homes of informants or receiving my own as a participant in the Women's Weekend. I listened to a three-hour talk by the rebbe that was transmitted live on television from New York to Virginia via telephone/stereo connection, for example, and heard lectures by the popular lecturer Rabbi Friedman on a taped series provocatively entitled *"Not* for Women Only." Lastly, I also consulted prayer books that the Lubavitchers hold sacred.

✳✳

I lie down to sleep in the guest room at the Y——s, the home where I am staying in Crown Heights. Tired but filled with the day, I feel very, very alone. Premonitions, mystical encounters, and rebbe miracles whirl inside—all day I've been taping and speaking with young women at Machon Chana. Today, Esther ransacked her room to find a particular book with a famous Jewish mystic pictured on the frontispiece—it was important to her that I see it. She thrust the picture of the bearded man with seer's eyes before me with breathless enthusiasm and waited for my response, as if to say "Look! Gaze deeply . . . and *see!"*

And there was another, that young woman with anguished eyes —three of us took a walk this evening, and because we never found the wedding we had set out for, simply walked and talked. She spoke of being alone before God and searching, always searching. "It's hard being on a spiritual search," she said. I nodded. Cars whizzed by. "Have you seen the rebbe? What did you think?" she asked. I murmured words like "respect" and "admiration"—she seemed unimpressed. The first time she saw the rebbe, at a distance, in synagogue, his face came up out of the crowd close to her and smiled. She'll never forget it. (How can I ever understand? How?) I stopped on the steps of Machon Chana to linger a moment in the night air. She turned abruptly, facing me, eyes wide. And then she said almost angrily, "You know, I'm playing this game for high stakes. I'm playing for my *life."*

✳✳

Data Analysis:
On Becoming a Lubavitcher Woman

I

"First, we teach a girl who she is ..."
> —Mrs. J——, an administrator at Machon
> Chana Jewish Women's Institute

A *ba'alat teshuvah* woman's sense of personal empowerment begins to form through a process that I will term "affirmation and reevaluation." Through the taking of partial life histories and attendance at a Women's Weekend, especially geared for those just entering Lubavitcher life, patterns began to emerge. The cultural system that these women were being exposed to is one that advocates absolutist beliefs, in contrast to what is perceived as the modern world of relativism. The Lubavitcher outreach appeal stresses "Getting back to who you really are." This process involves: the establishment of an absolute, positively valued Feminine Nature; becoming a "mythic figure," that is, a vital part of the mission to bring Moshiach; and gaining a new sense of respect for the power and value that inhere in one's physical body. The process also involves gaining a new understanding for all aspects of one's life through belief in an all-pervasive Divine Providence.

The process entails affirmation of a woman's sense of self as well as her life experience and positive evaluation thereof, which may have been lacking in the secular world. Often, and this is the crux of the affirmation/reevaluation process, traits that are perceived as undesirable in secular society are given legitimation and positive value because they correspond to the Lubavitcher concept of Feminine Nature.

This concept, constructed in the process of "Getting back to who you really are," involves certain fixed principles concerning relationships, marriage, and family. Marriage and having children are not only established as valued goals, but as responses to natural feminine needs. They are necessary parts of life in order to be a woman in the fullest sense. Rabbi Manis Friedman, in his taped lecture entitled "The Feminine Mystique," states: "When ... a woman decides not to have children when she can, that's not normal. ... it's denying one's capacity to be a woman" (February 1980). This approach may appeal to modern young women who struggle with the fact that secular society presents several (often conflicting) scripts concerning what it means to be a woman and what women should value in life. Home and children or career and independence? Both? These questions are solved when one believes, as one Machon Chana administrator put it, that "Women are different—the way their minds work, their emotions . . . and the physical needs and abilities are different. And we don't relate to it as a biological or spiritual accident or misfortune as many people in the secular world do . . . women especially." The conception of an absolute Feminine Nature provides women with a script for action and a means by which to legitimate that action as justified and worthwhile.

To illustrate the particular point concerning a revalued ideal of marriage, family life, and specific gender roles, let us examine the case histories of several young women who are students at Machon Chana, the Lubavitcher college in Crown Heights for *ba'alot teshuvah* women that is named in honor of the mother of the present Lubavitcher rebbe. It was founded about fifteen years ago for women with little or no previous education in Judaism. Mrs. J——, an administrator, said that they come from countries such as Brazil, Argentina, and Chile, South Africa, Europe, Iran, and Canada. There is a full-time, two-year live-in program that culminates in a Teacher's Certificate for Jewish Education or a Certificate of Higher Jewish Studies. There are also part-time, one-semester, and evening-study options. The program offers study of Torah and Chassidus (the mystical teachings of the Torah); Hebrew; Jewish history, philosophy, and law; and the Yiddish language. Classes are bilingual in Yiddish and English.

One afternoon during my second trip to Machon Chana, I had a lengthy discussion/interview with two students. All of us were sitting around one of the long, institutional dining tables in the dormitory general-purpose room. Sarah (a pseudonym), a pretty, vivacious young woman in her twenties, and Diane, a tall stylish woman about the same age, and I were having a spirited conversation concerning some of the benefits both women have found in Lubavitcher life. Sarah gesticulated and spoke animatedly, but Diane appeared to be troubled and a bit withdrawn. Around us, other young women chatted, ate, and wove colored ribbons through small plastic baskets, preparing them for Purim festivities, during which they would be filled with delicacies and given as gifts to members of the community. Other students were at work constructing the set for a Purim play they were going to put on, enacting the story of Queen Esther. Amidst ribbons, chatter, and pseudo-Persian styrofoam columns, several young women were praying, facing an eastern wall. Others sat at tables with prayerbooks, going through the prayer after a meal (it was just after lunch). The Lubavitchers believe that Jews can pray anywhere, not just in a synagogue. Most prayer rituals I witnessed occurred in domestic settings. One faces a wall because, inasmuch as one is in the presence of God, people should not walk past.

I learned that Sarah is Brazilian and that she had only been in the United States for five months. In Brazil, she had trained in the law and studied computing. She has held jobs as a lawyer and in publishing. She was an Olympic pistol shooter on the Brazilian team; had participated in the Olympics; and was courted by the Russian team, who wanted her to go to Russia and train there. She wrote to the rebbe to decide what to do and received the response: "Go where you can find a good husband." She came to Crown Heights, and, when I spoke to her in March 1987, was to be married in three weeks. She and her husband, another *ba'al teshuvah*, plan to open a macrobiotics business with another Lubavitcher couple. She will initially stop her shooting when she marries but resume it later. "I could shoot in a skirt, now I'll shoot in a *shaytl* (wig)!" she chuckled.

She described her life in Brazil as a career woman as one in which she felt continually assaulted by the sexual harassment she experienced on the job and in which she had to be fiercely competitive to succeed. She described her dilemma in responding to male lawyers who would ask her out, knowing that winning or losing a case would depend on her answer. She felt as if she were "selling her soul." She wanted respect from men, and attributed her treatment to the Brazilian "macho mentality." (At this point Diane interjected, "It's not only in Brazil! Go to Miami—you'll see the macho mentality!") Sarah described the way in which men would always touch her, hug her, or kiss her on a date or even casually. "They are *invading you; they are invading your privacy.*" She attributes the widespread frustration, depression, suicide, and cults in the secular world to the fact that young people are searching for respect, but "people don't know how to treat each other." Sarah described her relations with men in Crown Heights as wonderful: "Men here respect you a lot, they treat you like a *person*. They are interested in you, not what you do."

Dating among the Lubavitchers is arranged by a matchmaker or interested third party. When a woman feels she is ready to marry, she begins to go out on dates arranged in this manner. The man and woman do not touch each other, but, as one unmarried woman put it, a woman should feel free to "let the chemistry flow" and be attractive. The date usually centers around getting to know each other through conversation. Only if *both* are interested in seeing each other again (they report back to the third party, thus no one's feelings are hurt) will another date be set up. If not, the woman may begin seeing someone else. This process continues until the match is hit upon, and the marriage usually takes place rapidly thereafter. Marriage is believed to be the coming together of two halves of a soul—it completes both the man and the woman. For every Jewish man and woman there is believed to be a particular spouse whom God has chosen.

Diane joined the conversation that Sarah and I had been having. She does not live at Machon Chana, but takes classes there and had just moved to an apartment near Crown Heights. She is not committed to a Lubavitcher life-style and had actually experimented with other types of spirituality before returning to Judaism. She bitterly described the sexual revolution as "a big lie." She believes that "it just lets men exploit women more" and that, in spite of all the openness about sex in the secular world, the attitudes of men are "just as chauvinistic as ever." She feels that, today, a woman is expected to be many things at the same time and cited examples where men feel it's "a status thing" to have a well-educated wife but don't really encourage her to follow up with a career. She finds that in her age group there are a lot of highly successful women who are lonely and unhappy because, she states, "It's going *against your nature* as a woman not to have a husband and children."

Later that evening, I had dinner with all the Machon Chana students living in the dormitory. Everyone eats together, serving themselves onto paper plates from communal dishes of plain but hearty institutional fare. On my left sat a young woman who had been a television actress before she became a Lubavitcher. Now, because TV acting would conflict with Shabbos observance, she is looking into voice-dubbing for radio and cartoons. She plans to settle in Los Angeles someday and start a Lubavitcher community there.

On my right sat an (Anglo) woman from South Africa, Rachel. She had come to Machon Chana only very recently. She was slightly older than most of the women there—in her thirties—and had been previously married and divorced. When I met her, she was not committed to becoming a Lubavitcher or even to studying for a considerable period of time at Machon Chana. She wanted to become "frum" (religiously observant) but feared becoming too dependent upon the rebbe if she settled in Crown Heights. Then, she felt, she might not be able to leave there and settle in Israel, a fond wish of hers.

She is college-educated and in South Africa handled public relations for a large firm. She also told about "cultivating her masculine side" (the "hard business approach") to climb the ladder of success and becoming increasingly alienated from her "feminine side." This was a conflict within her. She spoke of "the complete degradation that a woman experiences in the business world." Before she returned to Judaism, she was interested in Eastern religions and felt that Judaism was horribly oppressive to women because it denied them the same roles as men. "I was the biggest anti-Semite ever!" she exclaimed. In a rather experimental yeshiva she attended in Israel, she wore pants "to make a statement," she laughingly related.

She has made a complete turnaround in terms of her attitude toward Judaism, saying "Now I see that women have *clear roles* and aren't torn. Now I know what I've got to do. And that's very freeing. Now I can get on with actually *doing* things." She feels that Judaism "reaffirms the feminine principle" and bridges the mind-body dichotomy so that she feels "much more in touch with what's going on inside . . . in a very deep way." She cited as an example the period of separation between a Lubavitcher husband and wife during a woman's menstrual cycle. This helped her not feel "out of control—I'm not at the mercy of all the chemical changes going on in my body. . . . I *do* feel angry and destructive during those times, and wouldn't want to hurt the man I love. So, this is a natural way of dealing with those feelings."

Rachel and I spoke several times during my two-and-a-half-day visit, after that initial connection over dinner. The last time I saw her was when I dashed downstairs to say goodbye. She was seated at a table with several other students. When I came in, she looked up, smiled at me, and said, "I've decided I'm going to stay."

These three women have entered a world where they feel more respected and valued as women. Although better male-female relationships are a "side effect," they claim, of leading a Jewish religious life, the bottom line is coming closer to God.

Further components of the Lubavitcher conception of Feminine Nature became apparent during the Women's Weekend and through interviews with *ba'alot teshuvah* women. Women are believed to be naturally more spiritual than men. They are spoken of as being on "a higher spiritual level" than men. It is easier for them, it is believed, to act, on unconditional faith; women do not always have to be convinced through intellectual understanding of God's word. An oft-cited Torah passage is the story of the parting of the Red Sea, in which the women, led by Miriam, were the ones who truly believed in God's deliverance. Rabbi Friedman's recorded lecture on

"The Feminine Mystique" contends that "The truth is sometimes intuitively felt, and doesn't need to be explained. . . . the feminine mystique means being open to godliness *beyond* rational reason."

It is appropriate here to note the difference between two kinds of Jewish *mitzvot* (a good deed or a Torah commandment and duty): *chukim* and *mishpotim*. The chukim are mitzvot that one could not derive from the human intellect alone. Mishpotim are mitzvot such as not killing and not stealing, which a moral society would dictate on its own, even if the laws were not explicitly stated in the Torah. The Ten Commandments are a mixture of these two types of mitzvot. The class discussion focused on the idea of doing mishpotim "because of kabbalah soul," and not "because you understand it." The process of intellectual understanding and rationalization, the woman teacher said, *disconnects* the doing of the commandment from Hashem. Doing something out of "kabbalah soul" means, one rabbi told me, "to receive upon yourself the yoke of heaven, [and] to do something just because God said so, and to *put aside your intellect.*" The purpose of doing mitzvot in general, the teacher said, is "to make you a better human being. . . . it is elevating our souls, refining our selves."

An instructor at Machon Chana explained: "The ultimate reason we do things is not because we understand them intellectually but because God told us so. . . . intellect is changeable." Intellect *alone* is described as "lifeless, cold and dead" on Rabbi Friedman's "The Feminine Mystique" tape, but he adds that "the Alter Rebbe breathed *life* into intellect and made it so that you could study Torah with intellect." The "heart" and the "intellect" ideally come together in the study of Torah, each fulfilling a necessary and complementary role.

Women are also believed to possess *binah* (a woman's sixth sense), variously described by informants as "the source of understanding" (*binah yisod*) or "an extra measure of wisdom or understanding." There are three philosophical levels of a person's thought, speech, and action: wisdom (*chokhmah*), understanding (*binah*), and knowledge (*da'as*). *Chokhmah* is more masculine, described as the spark of an idea or the inspiration. *Binah* involves developing the *chokhmah*, taking an idea and following through until it becomes part of you (this is the stage of *da'as*), and you are able to give it over to another person. I found that women often developed rather personalized definitions of *binah* that may fit with the way they view themselves. The overall definition of *binah* may encompass all of these views; in that case, each woman chose to stress a different aspect:

"Binah means working things out, logically. Women are seen to be more logical in some ways than men . . . more analytical. Maybe [women] aren't as *linear*." (Mrs. L——, forties, Crown Heights)

"Women have this innate sensitivity to God that men don't have. . . . I know in the goyishe [non-Jewish] world they call it women's intuition. . . . You take [*chochma*] and draw it down [moves hand from throat to stomach] so that it becomes knowledge. To know is . . . not even having to think about it, but feeling and internalizing and being aware of the fact, constantly and forever, that this thing exists. That's the woman's kind of knowledge." (Mrs. Y——, late thirties, Crown Heights)

"Women are very accepting, ready to understand, and have high ideals. . . . a woman perceives correctly what needs to be done." (Chana, mid-twenties, Machon Chana)

Perceptions of self are enhanced by belief in a Feminine Nature, which includes great spirituality and *binah*. Women I spoke with uniformly characterized themselves as very perceptive people and thus may be more likely to trust their ideas and instincts. One Machon Chana dorm counselor stated, "If we don't speak up . . . in a way of commenting and encouraging, it's everyone's loss . . . because we have that responsibility to the Jewish people and future." Internalization and identification with positively valued characteristics attributable to Feminine Nature contribute to the empowering idea that each woman has "a potential within . . . that is absolutely infinite," as one rabbi stated to the women assembled at the Women's Weekend.

Another component in the process of affirmation and reevaluation involves instilling a new sense of respect for the power and value that inhere in a woman's body. Fatima Mernissi describes, through textual analysis, the concept of "active female sexuality," which underlines the Muslim practice of covering women's bodies in public (1975:1). Although Lubavitcher culture poses a different set of data, Mernissi's analysis led me to examine, in a slightly different vein, the transformative process that alters a woman's perceptions of her own body once she begins to observe the Modesty Laws. Lubavitcher women dress modestly, cover their hair after marriage, and generally strive toward modesty in thought, speech, and action. Their clothing has high necklines and covers the knees and elbows; pants are not worn.

Despite the fact that they must always observe modesty rules in public, *ba'alot teshuvah* women did not express feelings of psychological discomfort or shame concerning their physical selves. Rather, they often experience a new recognition of the "preciousness" of their bodies: terms such as "jewel" are used in describing the body. Leah, a Machon Chana dorm counselor, said, "You finally realize what you have, and that it *is* precious." When she first began to obey the Modesty Laws, she experienced shyness and vulnerability ("I just couldn't look a man in the eye"). Now, however, she feels "freer than before when you had to work so much at attracting attention." Underlining the central concept of "Getting back to who you really are," Channa, the other dorm counselor, said that the Modesty Laws "help me to be *me*" and "protect who you really are."

Mrs. Y——, who is in her late thirties and resides in Crown Heights, told me:

> "The hair of a woman is her most beautiful asset. Once she *becomes* a woman—in other words, once she marries and can do everything that a married woman does *that* is when her hair becomes her most crowning glory. . . . It's beautiful as a girl . . . but once she marries it becomes even more beautiful. That's when she has to cover it for everyone but her husband."

> **Gita:** "If a woman's hair is her most beautiful asset, why must she cover it? And why are there no expressions of affection visible between husband and wife?"

> **Mrs. Y——:** "Just as the relationship between man and God is a personal relationship, *not* something that can be shared with outsiders, the relationship between husband and wife, because it is so precious, has to be hidden. . . . And that's the same thing with the woman's body—why she only shows it in the mikvah [ritual bath, which is a very private affair] and with her husband, which is also very private!"

Feminists, I was told, feel "free" to bare *more* of their bodies and be "proud" of them but are mistaken in never expecting men to react to their exposed bodies. It is a Lubavitcher belief that men and women possess different types of sexual desire: men are more pleasure-oriented, and women seek intimacy and closeness more. Therefore, my informant said, men *will* react to an immodest woman.

Lastly, a significant factor in the affirmation reevaluation process is that women are given the opportunity to become "mythic figures," or to play a vital role in bringing Moshiach. Lubavitchers exhibit a very strong personal identification with heroes and heroines from the Torah. They often draw analogies with their own lives by citing a Torah figure or telling his or her story. They refer to these characters with a certain familiarity, as known role models, not distant archetypes. A young married man I met after Saturday morning services at the Lubavitcher Center in northeast Philadelphia told me how he traveled to New York from his hometown to first meet his wife. When I asked him if such travel was common practice among the Lubavitchers, he replied by citing a Torah story about a man who was sent out from his homeland to find a wife. "That's how it started," he explained.

This strong sense that one's life participates in a great tradition of mythic proportions is typical. An exhibit entitled "Women Who Change the World" was part of the March 1987 Week of the Jewish Woman conference in Virginia. It featured pictures of Torah matriarchs, each matched with a photograph of a living, modern woman. For example, Sarah's Shabbos candles are believed to have burned extraordinarily brightly because of her righteousness and gift of prophecy, so the modern woman next to Sarah is shown lighting Shabbos candles. The fact that women are believed to be innately more spiritual than men is referred to as "a special *inheritance* of every Jewish woman," stressing a genealogical link with women in the Torah. Women perceive themselves as being infused with a collective inheritance from the Torah matriarchs and as having a vital role in the mission to which these powers that accrue to them are applied. This perception contributes toward dimensions of female psychological empowerment that have been stressed in this section, such as increased self-respect, reliance on one's own ideas, and awareness of a strength that is unique to women.

A rabbi who is well known as a speaker gave the closing remarks at the December Women's Weekend I attended. About fifty women ranging in age from the early twenties on up were assembled in a Crown Heights home, where we had all had brunch. The lecture, entitled "Can We Talk?" (presumably a play on comedienne Joan Rivers's celebrated phrase) was the wrap-up of the weekend's events and experiences. The rabbi stressed several of the points that I have touched upon in this section as ideas for women to take away with them into the outside world. He emphasized self-acceptance with phrases such as "Beautiful is what you *are*." Among his closing comments, he made this statement, which is also an effective closing to this section of analysis: "Now that you've discovered the secret, it's not a secret—*teach* somebody. Don't feel inadequate. In what you know, *you* are the authority."

"It's time. The battles have been fought and won. The buttons are polished to a shine. Now nothing stands between us and the *guela* [redemption], but one final push for MOSHIACH NOW. What worked for our ancestors must work for us. And what was that? When it came down to the wire, when the darkness became so thick that even the memory of the light faded, the woman always came through. Strong, hopeful, uncompromising, they led us out of exile into the light.

"Now it's up to the woman again. We must make our cries heard —we must entreat for the sake of our children and the unborn generations that deserve to live lives of freedom and glory . . .

"We are holding a raffle to send a group of Jewish women to Kever Rachel in Eretz Yisroel [Israel] to pray for MOSHIACH NOW. While there, they will also visit the Cave of Machpeila and other holy sites, as representatives of Jewish women the world over. Any women or girl over the age of 12 may enter."

—From a flier published by the AD MOSAI Committee of Crown Heights, distributed at Machon Chana (AD MOSAI means literally "Until when?" meaning "How long do the Jews have to wait before Moshiach comes?")

II

"The next question is: 'Why am I different?' . . . What does it mean to be a Jew?' To be a Jew means you have certain responsibilities . . ."

> —Mrs. J——, an administrator at Machon Chana, describing the second phase of a young woman's education

As we have noted earlier, a main purpose of living a Jewish life is to "elevate," through Torah commandments, all that is physical to a higher spiritual level. Performance of those commandments strengthens one's bond with God. For every physical phenomenon in the world, there is believed to be a spiritual counterpart. Through this elevation by observation of Torah commandments, an individual becomes part of a larger goal of helping to bring Moshiach. This is the central belief around which this chapter pivots. In this section, I will examine how the elevation of every aspect of life, even the most personal or mundane, transforms activities deemed as "particularistic" or for "personal interest" into activities that contribute to the *social good*. Not only are they for the immediate social good, but many such activities, which may take place within the domestic domain, are perceived as having some incremental input toward the *cosmic* good because through them comes the arrival of the Messiah.

In a December talk delivered at 770 in Crown Heights, the rebbe stated that every mitzvah (good deed, Torah commandment) done adds to a Jew's physical strength. I also learned from numerous informants that every mitzvah done "strengthens the voice of the neshama" (Jewish soul). This strengthening of soul and body through mitzvahs may take place, to a large extent, within the domestic domain. Lubavitchers, in fact, perceive the home as more important in terms of religious observance than the synagogue. "A Jew can pray anywhere" is the belief, and in Virginia for example (where there is no Lubavitcher synagogue) I witnessed an entire Shabbos ceremony take place at home. At many of the Friday-night ceremonial dinners I have attended, my hosts have informed me that during the meal the dining table serves as an altar, in place of the altar which was taken down in the destruction of the ancient Second Temple in Israel. In one of the rebbe's most recent "campaigns" to hasten Moshiach's arrival, he encouraged each family to make their home into a "little temple" by keeping a *siddur* (prayer book), *tzedakah* box (for charity), and the Five Books of Moses (the Torah, for learning).

Furthermore, it is a Lubavitcher ideal to keep one's home relatively open to other Jews, in keeping with the central tenet of "Ahavas Yisroel," loving one's fellow Jew. For example, the majority of families I encountered practiced a policy of often inviting guests for Shabbos on Friday night, some of whom would stay on through Saturday evening, when the holy day ended. Such guests need not be close friends or even other Lubavitchers; I, for example, was invited to many homes after establishing only a passing acquaintance.

I spent Shabbos with two families in which the husband and wife team were each starting and running a new Chabad House. In both cases, because sufficient funding was not yet available to build a separate religious center, the majority of Chabad community activities took place in their homes. Such activities included a "Dial-A-

Jewish-Story" telephone line, a "Permanent Possibilities" Jewish dating service, several weekly classes, programs for children, community social gatherings on religious holidays, and literally about a dozen other functions, all run by the husband-wife team.

The domestic spaces are pivots for the dissemination of Jewish ideals with those outside the immediate community. The distinction between public and private is thus blurred, though the sanctity of the interior space is preserved. In addition, women perceive some of their "private" activities (including both domestic and specifically *personal* activities) as affecting the outside social world in very real ways. For example, the strengthening of one's *neshama* (soul) through teaching the practice of Jewish principles may have the ultimate effect of hastening the arrival of Moshiach.

Let us examine how women perceive "personal interest" activities as having concrete ramifications for the good of the Lubavitcher community and beyond, to the larger Jewish community. Mrs. Y———, with whom I spent Shabbos in Crown Heights, told me that "being frum [religiously observant] is like being an ambassador" to the outside world. She explained that everything she does (including the way she dresses, talks, keeps her house, and carries herself) is *setting an example to others*. She feels at all times like a representative of observant Lubavitcher Jews and knows that she is in a position to make or break outsiders' stereotypes of Hasidism. "If you smell bad, people will immediately jump to the conclusion 'Oh —dirty Jews!'" she quipped.

Sarah, from Machon Chana, told me a story in the same vein, this time about how a "personal interest" activity, keeping to her diet, has an effect not on outsiders but on the development of her *neshama*. She explained that a Jew has two souls, an animal soul that must be tamed and a godly soul that must be encouraged to grow. When Jews "take on" tasks that are difficult for them to perform, it is said to "create an arousal from above" and contribute toward taming the animal soul. Both these examples show how women claim experiences from the realm of "personal interest" into the realm of larger religious significance. I do not assert that such processes do not take place for men; I refer only to women here because they are the focus of my research.

Mrs. Y———, while describing women's innate sensitivity to spirituality, once commented: "[Men] don't have that *long sight*. . . . we can see the greatness in changing the diaper on this baby [she smiles]—because of the import of taking care of this baby, because of what this baby represents: a guarantor of the Torah, the future of the Jewish generation." This quote highlights a crucial cultural factor pulling together several of the issues previously mentioned (marriage, women spurring the coming of the Messiah, and others): the attitude toward children. Lubavitcher men and women have variously described Judaism to me as "child-centered" or as "based on children." Children are perceived as having a major role in spreading Judaism, and their innocence is seen as sincerity to do the will of God. With all the social and religious changes that will take place when Moshiach comes, one rabbi told me, "the only thing which will not be disturbed is the [Torah] learning of small children." In homes and at social/religious gatherings, I have observed children being treated with loving attention and respect.

Most significantly, for the purposes of my argument, having children is one of the major ways in which women are believed to help bring Moshiach. The Lubavitchers believe that there are a finite number of Jewish souls that go through cycles of reincarnation. For Moshiach to come, all the Jewish souls that exist should be brought into physical being. To this end, Lubavitcher women do not practice birth control. Mrs. J——, the Machon Chana administrator, says: "The soul has certain things to accomplish in this world. Sometimes, it cannot accomplish everything in one life. Therefore, it has to come again. Moshiach can come after every soul has accomplished everything it had to accomplish. So one of the ways to help this process is by giving birth. ... if you don't let the soul come again and finish its job, then you are holding back Moshiach. So ... one of the campaigns we have is talking to women who are either limiting the amount of children they can have, or—God forbid —[having] abortions. ... our women fight this."

A woman, as the "foundation of the home," is charged with creating an *atmosphere* there that is conducive to the study and practice of Judaism. She is instrumental in teaching her children the first basic prayers and blessings as well as many of the practical aspects of living an observant Lubavitcher life. The entire process of having and raising children must be seen in a new light once it becomes desirable not only for personal satisfaction and fulfillment but also as a contribution toward the deliverance of the Jewish people as a social whole.

"Come, my Beloved, to meet the Bride; let us welcome the Shabbat."
"My God, guard my tongue from evil and my lips from speaking deceitfully. Let my soul be silent to those who curse me; let my

*soul be as dust to all. Open my heart to Your Torah, and let my
soul eagerly pursue . . ."*
—From "Prayers for Welcoming the Shabbat,"
a selection from *Maariv for Shabbat* (evening
prayer), from *Siddur Tehillat Hashem, Nusach
Ha-Ari Zal* in English translation.

The fourth Shabbos I spent with a family was in Philadelphia,
with a Lubavitcher family (three small children) who had recently
started a new Chabad House in the center city. Mrs. T—— and her
husband run the operation together. The office is a room upstairs
in their home, and many Chabad activities, such as teaching classes,
serving Shabbos meals, and reading Jewish stories to children, take
place at home. As I helped her set the table with plastic cutlery
for the thirteen or so guests who were to share Shabbos with the
family that evening, Mrs. T—— jokingly remarked that when she
got married she did not realize she would be setting up "an institution!" This institutionalization of the domestic sphere was something I observed to a greater or lesser degree in many settings: Lubavitcher homes nearly always featured Jewish art and pictures or
photographs of the rebbe and other Lubavitcher figures placed in
prominent positions. Folding chairs, extra tables, and paper plates
always seemed available to accommodate new guests or a large gathering.

I arrived at the house on Friday afternoon, during the typical pre-
Shabbos flurry of activity. All food for the next twenty-four hour
period that needs to be cooked must be prepared because cooking
and turning a stove on or off are prohibited during Shabbos. Light-
timers, which turn lights on and off automatically, must be set,
if the family uses them, because the light switches cannot be used
either. A middle-aged woman (non-Jewish) who takes care of the
young children was playing with them in the dining area when I
arrived. I followed Mrs. T—— to the kitchen, where we talked about
Shabbos as we prepared a salad for the evening's dinner. When I
asked her more specifically how the prohibitions against doing work
or "changing the form" of anything during Shabbos pertained to
making a salad on Saturday, she explained that this was not considered to be cooking, but that tomorrow she would chop the cucum-
bers in a slightly different manner "to remind me that it's Shabbos."
The spaces that the Lubavitchers move in always seem invested
with continual "reminders" of the sacredness of the world—the elevation of the everyday.

People were arriving steadily as we chatted. Soon it was time to light the Shabbos candles eighteen minutes before sundown and usher in the "Sabbath Bride." Shabbos ends eighteen minutes after sundown on the following day. Mrs. T—— and I each lit candles in their gleaming holders, saying a prayer welcoming the Shabbos. Females above the age of three are eligible to light candles, and some mothers, like Mrs. T——, do so for each child of theirs. A minimum of two candles are lit by the woman of the household. Lighting the candles is a mitzvah for women; it is specifically their commandment, and, as one informant put it, "each candle lit is bringing Moshiach a little closer." After the flame was lit, Mrs. T—— passed her hands, palms down, over the candles three times and then covered her eyes with both hands and said a private prayer. This is a special prayer time for women alone, when they can communicate very personally with God their prayers and wishes.

Then it was time for Friday-night services: I walked with Rabbi T—— and several guests to the large institutional Jewish center, where Lubavitcher services are held on an upper floor, and sat on one side of the *mechitza*, the fold-out wooden divider that separates the men from the women during prayer. Mixing of the sexes during worship is felt to be distracting, especially for men. I was one of only three women present at the services, compared to about twenty men. Most women, having obligations at home, pray there instead of going to the synagogue. Women are exempted from all mitzvahs that are time-bound because activities in the home and with children may interfere. Duties in the home are given a higher priority than presence at certain religious rituals. However, as I have previously mentioned, it is believed that a Jew can pray anywhere. It is required that a man pray three times a day, but the commandments pertaining to women are more flexible.

Shabbos dinner was a festive affair, with Mrs. T—— on one end of the table, her husband at the head, and over a dozen guests seated in between. Among the guests (the majority of whom were not Lubavitchers, but Jewish) were an elderly male schoolteacher; a young Moroccan cantor (singer of Jewish prayers and melodies during worship services) who studies at Yeshiva University, in New York; a male dentist and a woman lawyer (both unmarried young people); and a reporter from a Philadelphia newspaper who was writing an article on "Baby Boomers Return to Religion."

The meal began with Rabbi T—— putting on his long black coat and hat to say the *kiddush*, or prayer of sanctification, over the wine. (This donning of ritual garb for a domestic ceremony, which I often observed, was another way in which the private realm grew to have that "public air.") He filled a silver wine cup to overflowing, held it in one hand while he recited the prayer, and then drank the wine. A ritual hand-washing takes place before the meal, in which one pours water from a small container or cup three times in succession onto each hand, and prayer is said: "Blessed art Thou, Lord our God, King of the Universe, who has sanctified us with His commandments and commanded us concerning the washing of hands."

After this hand-washing, not a word is spoken until the prayer has been made over the *challah* bread and pieces of it have been touched to salt, distributed to everyone at the table, and eaten. The two loaves covered by an embroidered cloth represent the extra manna that God gave the Israelites on the first Shabbos eve of the Exodus. The salt is symbolic of salt used in ritual sacrifices in the days before the Second Temple in Jerusalem was destroyed.

The dinner progressed with course after course of traditional food such as gefilte fish, chicken soup, baked chicken, noodle kugel, and cake for dessert. Eating was interspersed with singing of Jewish songs (the Lubavitchers have their own songs, or *niqunim*, which are composed by their rebbe), toasts with Scotch and cordials, and storytelling. All of the talk, I realized when someone brought up the latest Woody Allen movie later on, centered around topics in some way related to Judaism.

After dinner the guests retired to the living room, which was set up for Shabbos with extra chairs and Jewish books set out on a small table. This is a time for study, talk, and rest, which is what we proceeded to do for the rest of the evening. Much of Jewish learning seems to be done through conversation and argumentation: "There is not room for passivity in Judaism," said Rabbi T——. "One who is bashful will never learn." By this time, the journalist had left, and I heard a fascinating discussion concerning the representation of Lubavitcher Hasidism in the media.

Saturday began with a morning service at the Jewish center. There were about six women present this time in addition to myself, and the day progressed with large, ceremonial meals, talk, prayer, and socializing. There was a continual flux of guests coming and going during the day. Although having many guests demands work and preparation, Lubavitchers I spoke with unanimously agreed that Shabbos was an occasion they looked forward to. They consider it a time when they are freed from the pressures of the weekday world and have time to put into relationships with family, other Jews, and God.

Each Shabbos I attended was stamped with the individual mark of the particular family. There were times when I was the sole guest or one of very few. On one occasion, I attended a women's study group on Saturday afternoon: neighborhood men's and women's groups meet to learn about the weekly "Torah portion." At the group I attended, one woman (out of the twenty-five I observed who were present) volunteers each week to prepare a discussion of the Torah selection and present it before the group. The meeting took place in a family living room, and afterward there was a tea with dainties, gossip, and discussion of the "Torah portion."

Another variable feature was that sometimes the man of the family, at the start of Shabbos, would sing songs paying homage to the two angels who are believed to follow each Jew home from synagogue on Friday night. He would also sing songs from the first chapter of the Book of Proverbs in praise of his wife ("A woman of valor who can find, for her price is far above rubies"). This song was interpreted by early Kabbalists as praise for the *Shekhina*, the female aspect of God (Harris 1985:66). Shabbos ends with a *havdalah* ("separation" in Hebrew), that is, a ceremony separating Shabbos from the weekdays. This includes the lighting of a plaited candle and a blessing over wine similar to that performed at the Friday-night dinner. A sweet-smelling spice box is passed around for all to sniff, "to raise spirits that might be saddened by the passing of the Sabbath" (Harris 1985:76).

A tour of the newly built Crown Heights mikvah ritual baths was part of the Women's Weekend. The Lubavitchers emphasize that the mikvah ritual bath [described by Baldinger in the preceding essay] is not some form of "primitive menstrual taboo" [from a Lubavitcher pamphlet, "The Purifying Waters"]: it does not deal with "clean" and "dirty" but with purely spiritual concepts of "purity" and "impurity." Blood, it is said, is a "touch of death," which confers spiritual impurity on a menstruating woman. The attendant (and tour guide) told us that "pots and pans and ladies" use the mikvah: kitchenware manufactured by non-Jews is dipped into the mikvah to purify it for use in a kosher kitchen. Although it is not a specific commandment for men, they have their own separate mikvah, in which they purify themselves before Shabbos.

Lubavitcher women's attitudes toward the ritual of mikvah seemed strongly positive: in addition to keeping one's children Jewish, the physical separation associated with the ritual is often said to allow a woman some privacy "at a time when she may need it" ("Purifying Waters" brochure), allowing her an exclusively woman's space. Women spoke of the positive "side-effect" benefits the separation has on married life: that it keeps a continual spark of romance alive, and that it encourages different kinds of deep communication between husband and wife that do not depend on touch.

The metaphors I heard used over and over again to describe the experience of mikvah are significant in that they evoke some of the most important rites of passage of life-cycle events for women: birth and marriage. Not only do women describe feeling "like a new bride" after immersion, but also the mikvah waters are often compared to the amniotic fluids of the womb. A woman is spiritually *reborn* each month. The mikvah is in fact closely linked with birth and marriage: a woman performs this ritual for the first time the day before her marriage. The marriage is not only usually scheduled around the woman's cycle, but also the mikvah is in fact the basic, most essential institutional component of a Jewish community. A community low on resources can always pray at home, but the mikvah is essential: "It is the experience of mikvah which makes Jews holy. . . . without mikvah there is no Jewish life," declared a woman lecturer at the Women's Weekend who spoke on marriage.

Furthermore, the time of ritual abstinence coincides with a woman's least fertile time of the month; the time she is sexually active with her husband is when she is most likely to conceive. Each month, in effect, a significant spiritual purpose of marriage is refulfilled. There is a symbolic identification of purity with fertility and impurity with infertility. These are crucial orienting concepts of the culture. One reason that the mikvah is the most necessary institution is perhaps that it establishes the rhythm of these categories for each family unit and mediates the operation of spiritual power within the states of purity and impurity. The simple fact that critical categories are inextricably linked with women's biological cycle does not necessarily imply that they find the ritual of mikvah affirming—after all, the symbolic meanings of the categories could have strongly negative connotations for them. From the rather limited information I could gather on this topic, however, I did not find this to be the case among Lubavitcher women. Rather, their intimate connection with the flux in spiritual states seemed to imbue them with a sense of connectedness to the central core of what Judaism is, what "makes Jews holy," as the marriage lecturer stated.

It is an ideal for all Lubavitchers, men and women, to be continually "working on themselves" to attain ever higher levels of personal spiritual growth. Superlative achievement in spiritual growth and wisdom is recognized, for women, through titles of respect such as "morah," or teacher, but this is only true in exceptional cases. By and large, women are recognized informally by their peers and by personal realization of success.

The Lubavitcher women's community seems always to be striving to improve itself spiritually. Crown Heights epitomizes the continuous whirl of activity: workshops, lectures, community services, and more. The rebbe even emphasized in a recent campaign the institution of the *mashpia*, or spiritual adviser, for both men and women. Individuals choose a person (usually of the same sex, though several Machon Chana students pick male teachers) to play this role and meet with this person for "spiritual checkups," to make sure that their spiritual growth is progressing well. The *mashpia* may give the individual spiritual projects to work on. As one informant explained, "It's just so we don't slack off—we're all lazy!"

Not only are the work and rituals of women valued within the domestic sphere, but also the cultural conception of "expertness" allows them to feel and be treated like authorities, of a sort, on the basis of their achievements in "personal interest" activities. They *do* have significant contact with the outside world, and because of their perceptiveness and ability to relate to people they are often thought to be better at doing outreach work than men. Within the community, women organize themselves for action in areas such as helping out neighbors who give birth; advising other women (concerning such topics as child-rearing, money management, and family life) via specialized phone listings for women; and helping women to convert kitchens into kosher. This is a miniscule set of examples from the extremely active women's network, but from even this partial listing one may sense the way in which "private, personal interest" activities are recognized by the extra-domestic Lubavitcher community as important and how women performing them perceive them to be valuable social skills.

****
And there were the Lubavitcher children. The endless tapes of "Uncle Moishe and his Mitzvah Men," accompanied by gleeful hand-clapping. There was seven-year-old Debbie, whose mother had put a copy of the *Tanya* (the alter rebbe's mystical works) in her crib every night. No nursery rhymes, but "Love your fellow Jew as yourself" and "Make the world a dwelling-place for God."

Chani is a bright, inquisitive eight-year-old. "Do you know what we do on Shabbos?" she queries, eying me boldly. "You'll see. I sit on daddy's lap and he tickles me!" It's time for juice and crackers, so I carry out the cups and begin pouring. Chani prances around the table, giggling, singing, and clapping her hands, "We're going to thank Hashem! We're going to thank Hashem!" She says the *bracha* (prayer) quickly (to impress me?). Her little brother, almost two, is just learning the prayer before eating—he's just learning to speak. He says the "ba-ruch-a-to-adonai" in soft baby sounds, repeating his mother's slow but insistent voice. These are some of the first words he has ever spoken, I realize. How many times will he repeat them in his life?

In my mind's eye, I imagine the scene Mrs. G—— described to me: when a newborn child first comes home from the hospital to Crown Heights, all the young neighborhood children gather around the crib to say the *Shema* with the new baby: "Hear, O Israel, Our Lord is our God, the Lord is One."

✳✳✳

III

"The rebbe once said, 'If a man knew what a woman has to know, he'd be happy.'"

—Mrs. J——, an administrator at Machon Chana, on the difference in men's and women's religious education

We have seen how Lubavitcher Judaism personally empowers women with a positive sense of identity within the parameters of a well-defined Feminine Nature, and how the religiously informed valuation of public and private realms confers new meaning on the potential for power through domestic activity. Although women perceive themselves as special and different—one might say that they are "otherized"—the cultural system maintains the validity of both gender-specific worlds in such a way that women do not feel marginalized within the religion. This section captures perhaps most vividly the effectiveness of the previous two points concerning women's sense of empowerment. In it, I shall explore the ways in which women's interpretations and "translations" of religious precepts serve to legitimate their nonmarginalized position in Lubavitcher Hasidism. The creation of personalized definitions of *binah*, mentioned earlier, is an example of this phenomenon.

Some of these constructions are not explicitly shared with the world of men; others are recognized and encouraged by men. They seem not to be formally articulated or written down, but, true to typical Hasidic practice, are often told in story form.

Let us examine the issue of household decision-making authority and the domestic dynamic that exists between husband and wife. A woman is perceived as being able to influence and "make the will of her husband," sometimes while maintaining the appearance of male dominance. On the other hand, she may be deferred to in making certain decisions even if she does not know a great deal about the facts because her powers of intuitive understanding and perceptiveness must be respected. It is widely reported that the husband is charged with earning the money for the household, but that the wife manages and spends it. A woman is considered to be "the foundation of the home," where, ideally, she *creates an atmosphere* conducive to good Jewish living. She is responsible for "guiding" her husband in Torah learning (words such as "encouraging" and "enabling" are also used in this context).

However, I found that some women believe that the husband should have the final say at home and that "the wife is under the husband." During my second visit to Crown Heights, I related such an exegesis to Mrs. Y——, a young *ba'alot teshuvah* woman, and she reacted with great surprise and indignation. She explained hotly to me that the woman who had made the statement *must* be a *ba'alot teshuvah*, that she probably has a submissive personality, and that "There are some people who feel resentful and bitter [toward the religion] for having changed their life-style so much." Whether or not this was true in that particular case, there are clearly divergences in practice concerning household authority.

Let us examine the way in which women conceptualize this experience in a manner that is empowering to them. The following is an extract from an interview with Leah, an unmarried Machon Chana dormitory counselor, in which she relates a lesson learned from Machon Chana teachers that reflects her expectations for married life:

> **Leah:** "There's a man who's not smart at all and his wife figures 'OK, so he's not smart, but I'm going to make him feel like he *is*.' So, every so often she'd do something like say, 'You know what would look good here? Blue curtains.' And then later on, in front of people to make him feel good, she'd ask him: 'What color curtains do you think we should have in this kitchen?' and he goes, 'Blue.' And she goes, 'Wow! That's such a good idea! . . . it's all subtle and he won't even remember that she is doing this. . . . It's *very* subtle. You're dealing with a male ego. A male ego is incredibly sensitive, you know."

Gita: Do you think women have an ego (like that)?"

Leah: "No, it's not the same way."

Gita: "What's the difference?"

Leah: "A man has to know he's boss."

Gita: "But you were just saying that the man really *isn't* the boss!"

Leah: "He isn't, but he doesn't *know* he's not! . . . Mrs. J—— tells everyone this story. . . . But the whole thing shows that the woman makes the will of her husband—she does! The power of a woman is incredible. It's incredible for unholiness and it's incredible for holiness. . . . a woman can really . . . direct her husband, and let him go to his limits."

Gita: "And he doesn't have control of her in the same way?"

Leah: "It's not the same way. A man is a lot more simple. They're less complicated."

Gita: "A man's mind?"

Leah: "Yeah. Women are . . . totally different. [Men] are also not as —cunning is not a good word, because it would be negative. They're [pause] more direct, straightforward."

Gita: "Hmmm."

Leah: "It's not even a *will* of theirs to make the will of their wives. They just *think* they do, you know! [vehemently] Every man has to feel like that on some level—*every* man, as liberated as he says he is. There's a level at which he's going to have to be the man."

Gita: "Do you think it's a compromise for the woman to make him feel that way?"

Leah: "No! No! Because she's really being the most of a woman also. She's getting what she feels is correct, . . . and she's making the man she loves feel good as well. . . . It takes a lot of strength and a lot of selflessness, but . . ."

Gita: "It sounds like it takes more strength than the man [man's role] does, actually!"

Leah: "Sure. Sure it does . . . because there's so much control involved . . . and patience."

This part of a longer interview demonstrates a mystification of domestic-power relations that legitimizes women's own ways of being authoritative. Overtones of "Getting back to who you really are" and the positive conception of Feminine Nature, which we have touched on earlier, resurface again.

Another facet of the household authority dynamic that exists between husband and wife was revealed to me by Mrs. Y——, a *ba'alot teshuvah* in her thirties who lives in Crown Heights. Over breakfast in her house, she related a story describing the almost oracular way in which she is consulted by her husband. He had an opportunity to make a job change that was financially appealing, but which had some drawbacks. He asked his wife (in her words) "What should I do?" and she encouraged him without a doubt to take the offer. The decision turned out to be a huge success. Mrs. Y explained to me, "I said 'Move, definitely. You'll be much happier.' I just *felt* very strongly—don't ask me why!" Later in the conversation, she told me that Jewish men are very aware of women's intuitive and perceptive abilities. They "really appreciate their wives. They're taught that their wives are on a pedestal and should be treated as such. . . . Religious men are very sensitive to the blessings that come to them through their wives."

Women and men are believed to have different ways of thinking as well as acting upon their thoughts. Torah commandments for women tell them to *do* something, rather than to *abstain* from something, as is the case for men. A woman's three main responsibilities in the home are keeping kosher, lighting the Shabbos candles, and following the Laws of Family Purity. The fact that some of women's commandments are different and that women are perceived to think and take action in different ways from men has an effect manifested in the different types of Jewish education the two sexes receive. Men's education involves more textual analysis of works such as the Talmud and the Code of Jewish Law. It is a positive commandment for a man to learn Torah. Women concentrate more on the writings of the prophets and philosophers and philosophical aspects of the Torah but focus more than men on learning the practical aspects of daily life. Differences in education that could be considered by outsiders as "unequal" are elaborated upon by women, for example, in the following ways that were pointed out by Mrs. N——, a Machon Chana administrator:

"The man does extra studying which is not . . . necessarily applicable, not that *practical*. In terms of the philosophical, internal aspects of Torah, that everyone needs to know. But in terms of studying the oral Torah that has more to do with Halachic [Jewish Law] implications, the woman has to know *what she has to do*. Men study it in the way of a lawyer—all the opinions that different sages brought up, back and forth, back and forth . . . this the woman doesn't have time to do. She has other important things to take care of."

"Men need something that women don't need. . . . Women have this innate sensitivity to God that men don't have. Men have to impose it from the outside. Which is why men have to [pray] three times a day, they have to do all those mitzvot we don't have to do—they *have* to learn, in a way that women don't have to learn, trying to impose on themselves this sensitivity to God that we have innately."

"Although men, through learning, can intellectually understand the purpose and ramifications of a mitzvah, a woman innately senses it. Which is why it's so much *easier* for a woman to do her mitzvot. A man cannot do a woman's mitzvot. A woman can do hers *and* a man's . . . if she makes the time . . . A man is not—*emotionally* is the wrong word—he's not *physically* equipped for it. And he's not *spiritually* equipped for it. Not that he doesn't have his role [laughs], don't think . . . I'm not demeaning man, believe me! I'm really not [laughs], I'm just trying to explain the difference. . . . It's easier for [a woman] to cook and keep kosher, for example. If it was a man he'd lose sight of it. He would see it only as, 'I'm standing here chopping this onion, you know' . . . because *they don't have that long sight*. We can see the greatness in changing the diaper on this baby."

Throughout the majority of conversations I had on this subject, I noted (as evident above) the recurring types of word choice which say that men *need something that women do not*, that women *possess abilities that men do not*. Women, Mrs. Y—— told me, have all the traits and capabilities that men have *plus* special abilities for compassion and nurturing. The word usage itself is indicative of the fact that the informants perceive the spiritual preserves of the women as prime sources of religious value, and do not view themselves on the margins of Jewish learning because their curriculum differs from that of men. Sarah, a young woman student at Machon Chana, said, "The men, they sit down and study *why* this rabbi answered like this and *why* that rabbi answered like that, and *finally*, they come to a conclusion. *We* [triumphantly] go *straight to the fact!*" Mrs. K——, whose teenage daughter attends a Lubavitch school, told me that the girls think the Talmud is "boring" and that they are glad not to have to study it! It is men who are seen as being left out of certain godlinesses in the world, for, as Mrs. Y—— states: "Hashem created us . . . to share the very pinnacle of His success with us, which is creation. And that he shared with women. Not only that, but he created His entire world in cycles. Everything in the world has a cycle [pause, for effect]—except a *man*. A man has no cycles. He has to impose cycles on himself from the outside. . . . Women have this innate understanding because our very *nature* is cyclical. Men don't have that at *all!*"

Previous quotes have brought up the comparison of intellect and heart, rational understanding and feeling. Lubavitcher Hasidism stresses the primacy of the mystical connection with God, but posits that mind and heart complement each other in prayer and learning. As mentioned earlier, the ultimate reason to obey commandments is not because of intellectual grasp but because "God said so." A non-Lubavitcher Bryn Mawr student who participated in a six-week Lubavitcher-sponsored Ivy League Torah Study program told me: "I think the men [in Crown Heights] might be a little envious" of the women. She loved the "specialness" she felt as a woman in Crown Heights, saying "I don't *have* to sit there and pray to get a spiritual high [as men do]—I can get it just by entering the synagogue and hearing a song." The central point I have made here is that the beliefs of gender difference in education and prayer are elaborated upon by women and become sources of strength in their collective consciousness. This is not a completely hidden or subversive consciousness. Men would agree that women are more spiritual than they are, for example, but some of the ways in which women conceptualize their abilities in comparison with those of men seem uniquely their own.

The collective consciousness among Lubavitcher women (which includes the shared perspectives on men) has a significant effect on the relationships they form among themselves, how they perceive each other, and how they view themselves *through* other women. Both Machon Chana students and older, married women agreed that they had experienced much closer, more meaningful relationships with other women since becoming Lubavitchers. It is important to note that this is not simply a correlate of there being two separate gender-specific worlds. In *Women United, Women Divided* (Caplan and Bujra 1979), for example, cross-cultural case studies that exhibit how "social relations may be structured in such a way as to inhibit the development of a collective [primarily economic] consciousness among women" are cited. Even with a separate-worlds society, relations among women may be divisive. The fact of close relationships by itself is not greatly significant, but learning how and why they differ from those experienced before becoming a Lubavitcher shed light on the women's sense of individual autonomy within a collective mission.

Young girls and students in Crown Heights have ample opportunity to participate in activities with other women, but a married woman's life may center more around her family. In Brooklyn, women may become involved in the active Lubavitcher Women's Organization or other more informal all-female groups. For women living outside of the close-knit Crown Heights network, though, there may be fewer opportunities for such large-scale gatherings. The married women I spoke with had vastly differing degrees of contact with other women. However, Mrs. K—— voiced some common sentiments when she stated: "Women can respect each other more because they're not taking their cues from a society that says men are doing something more interesting and more profitable. . . . You're not looking to men all the time for reinforcement. Ultimately, reinforcement comes from the Torah." Referring to Lubavitcher women's conventions, which take place yearly and feature the types of activities I participated in at the Women's Weekend, a Machon Chana administrator said, "Women are identified and attached by what they want to accomplish, and when they gather they strengthen and inspire each other to do it in a better way."

This sense of being spiritually reinforced and inspired by other women, which was palpable at the Women's Weekend I attended, seems similar to the sense of "sisterhood" experienced by Western feminists: both stem from a solidarity and strength based on gender alone. Leah, a Machon Chana counselor, described the way she feels in a large group of women at a Lubavitcher convention: "You feel proud that you're a Jewish woman. . . . I feel [she looks around her, as if in amazement] . . . all these women! We're all going to bring Moschiach!" Other women, both married ones and students, felt that their friendships with women in the secular world were plagued by the "cattiness" that comes with competition for male attention. It would be wrong to give the impression, however, that this is a completely idyllic women's community. As in any human group, some more marginal members of Machon Chana felt excluded by their peers and believed that there were different kinds of competition present among women. This type of data was more difficult to obtain because of the several "layers" of data I mentioned earlier in the Methodology section.

****
"We have to live with our babies from the moment of conception.
. . . Pregnancy is just the initial stage in a life of seventy years or
more—every child holds in his hand the message of the future.
Every newborn child arrives on this earth with a message to be
delivered to mankind. Clenched in his little fist is some particle
of yet unrevealed truth, some missing clue which may solve the
enigma of man's destiny. He has a limited amount of time to fulfill
his mission and he may be our last hope."
—From *Motherhood: A New Philosophy*, adapted by Karen Leeds from a
speech given at the 1979 Lubavitcher women's convention in South Africa
by Dr. Van der Vaat, a gynecologist.
****

Suggestions for Further Research

My fieldwork revealed several facets of Lubavitcher life that I
was unable to pursue, either because of circumstantial constraints
or because the issues were not immediately within the parameters
of my chosen topic. One such area, as I mentioned earlier, was the
perceptions of Lubavitcher *men* on the issue that I have approached
here from the perspective of women. Because the men's and women's communities each inform the other, ultimately, an understanding of the position of women in the religious community is
lacking without knowledge of the masculine perspective. This
would be a fascinating topic for further study, though a male anthropologist would probably be best suited for the fieldwork. Are there
analogous "affirmation/reevaluation" processes involved in the experience of male *ba'al teshuvah*, or are different cultural mechanisms at work? What degree of agreement is there concerning the
roles of women between the two gender-specific worlds?

Non-Lubavitcher Jews usually had very strong (usually negative)
reactions to the Lubavitchers when I mentioned my project in casual conversation. Many perceived them as a sort of cult that brain-
washed its members. Concerned friends warned me to "be careful."
Other Jews were typically familiar with some of the more obvious
of the special elements of Lubavitcher life but failed to make the
perceptual "leap," or shift, in value systems necessary to appreciate
another culture, perhaps because they themselves would be too
closely implicated in that shift. Rather, they tend to see the incon-
gruities between Lubavitcher values and their own way of practicing
Judaism and reject Lubavitcher life wholesale. This "otherizing"

phenomenon (which goes on increasingly among Jews in the modern world who wish to legitimate their own form of worship, often at the expense of others) is another fruitful topic for further study. What are the parameters of the "otherizing" process, and upon which variables does it depend? Among the Jewish groups from Reform through Hasidic, what are the variables that determine the degree of solidarity? Does the use of distancing techniques go both ways, from more traditionally observant to less, and/or vice versa?

Another area that invites anthropological investigation is the role of the rebbe, and the nature of the relationship that exists between him and "his Hasids" as the Lubavitchers affectionately describe it. Mystical powers are attributed to him: "A rebbe's look heals," says Rabbi Friedman in a taped lecture, adding that "not much is said or written [about the relationship between rebbe and Hasid] . . . because it is a very personal relationship" ("Chassidic Thoughts at Baid Chana: Rebbe and Chosid" tape). The rebbe occupies a position at the heart of the vast Lubavitcher international network yet maintains extensive correspondence with specific individuals. He is a public role model for both men and women, yet his personal life seems to be kept private. He is called upon to advise in life's major decisions, yet the Lubavitchers do not seem to feel that they lack free will. One informant noted, "The rebbe knows me better than I know myself . . . but he never takes away free choice. I wish he'd make *more* decisions for me! . . . He leaves a lot up to you." It would also be interesting to learn exactly what is involved in "deciphering" a letter from the rebbe. One informant, who has been a Lubavitcher from birth, said, "They are subtle. You have to know how to read them, and if you don't you should take it to someone who *does* know how."

A final intriguing point is the relationship between the secular and Lubavitcher worlds. The ideological boundaries dividing the world into the "outside" secular society and the "inside" religious community are, I believe, repeatedly blurred and reinstated in maintenance of the "inside" cultural system. On the one hand, the Lubavitchers truly do see themselves as a chosen people and an example to others, and they flatly reject many secular values. On the other hand, in the effort to teach Jewish ideas at the level of their audience, the Lubavitchers incorporate many aspects of modern secularism into their outreach appeal, and into their lives. "We take what is good from the secular world," one Machon Chana counselor explained. For the Lubavitchers, incorporation of some aspects of secular culture is consonant with the idea that the Torah is a text that is constantly being reborn—it is as relevant today as it was when Moses received it on Mount Sinai.

In outreach, Lubavitchers stress the idea that Hasidism is not ancient and out-of-date, but up-to-the-minute and relevant. They perceive the idea that their religion is old-fashioned as a pervasive popular myth that they work to dispel. I noted, especially at the Women's Weekend (a time when more "secular Jews" are present), that many words, phrases, phenomena, and the like from secular culture were included in the program. Rather spectacular conversion testimonials were given: one woman was a television celebrity interviewer and jet-setter who had first read the *Tanya* in a bikini while sunbathing in Europe. Lectures were frequently peppered with colloquial phrases and allusions to current issues such as AIDS, pornography, and nuclear disaster. Names from Bill Cosby to Bertrand Russell and Steven Jay Gould were mentioned. In one lecture entitled "A Taste of Honey in a Sugar-Free World," the existence of the soul was supported through examples of "indirect experimentation." Scientific disclaimers were viewed as examples of the way in which science acts as a "garment," allowing people who want to be in complete control of their lives to live comfortably.

Lubavitchers in general seemed to take a certain delight in publicly breaking the stereotypes that society sets for them. A rabbi who lectured at the Women's Weekend told the story, chuckling, of how he went to a high school religious debate wearing a leather bomber jacket. Another rabbi, who runs an outreach center with his wife, told how he often baked the *challah* bread for Shabbos, which guests would discover when they paid the conventional compliment to his wife. In outreach programs especially, aspects of secular culture are incorporated and in some sense tokenized in an effort to refute the popular conception of Hasidism as ancient and out-of-date. This appeal seems to be enormously effective. The point here is not that there is an explicit contradiction in the Lubavitcher position vis-à-vis the outside world, but that the religion is validated by reference to secular society for those to whom this approach is meaningful. It would be interesting to study this phenomenon to appreciate better the relationship between central "core" cultural characteristics and the flexible nature of outreach strategies.

Part IV

Ethnicity and Religion
The Persistence of Collective
Representations

It is not surprising that religious experience is intimately connected with ethnic cultural life. This is partly so because the "holistic" cultural formations that are the historical precursors to modern American segmented ethnic cultures included religion as part of a total life "design for living." That religion is still important in American ethnic life no doubt is accounted for in no small degree by the deep primordial cords that are evoked by both ethnic *and* religious experience (cf. Geertz 1973). When these are combined, powerful emotional commitments and symbolic elaboration can be anticipated. American assimilation processes have also contributed to the persistence of ethnic religion. Where language, dress, family forms, and other aspects of ethnic cultural diversity have been discouraged, this has not been so for religion. In fact, many sociologists have observed that never is America so segregated as on Sunday (or even Friday or Saturday!).

It is clear that a strong association between ethnicity and religion serves to confirm the great sociological insights of Durkheim (1961). He pointed out that the experience of religion is essentially *social* and *communal* (for example, the sense of religion as "church") so that group affiliation is at the heart of religious understanding. For this reason, symbols seen as "collective representations" are richly represented in church music, iconography, art, and religious persons themselves.

The following essays specifically examine the ethnic cultural dimension as represented in ethnic religious experience. Some of the chapters in previous sections also consider religion so that overall these studies show that ethnicity and religion are strongly interrelated into a mutually reinforcing symbol system. This association will be the focus of attention in the following pages.

No doubt religious experience is universally similar in, for example, its evocation of powerful affective states (e.g., Geertz 1973; James 1958) or in religion's function, which serves to, among other things, account for "misfortune" (Spiro 1967). Nevertheless, at the cultural level, religion is the key institutional setting for the expression of behaviors that are *simultaneously* sacred (religion) and ethnic (secular but perhaps primordial). It would appear that for this reason also a significant portion of ethnic experience in America persists and is experienced through the medium of church in the context of sacred symbols. The following essays demonstrate the symbolic significance of language in the Greek Orthodox experience; of the ceremonial calendar for Jews; of geographic place (North Carolina) for Indian Protestants; and of the church, seen as "home" by Catholic Puerto Ricans. In each case, symbol and ethnic identity are mediated by church or religious school.

10

Our Lives Revolve around the Holidays
Holidays in the Transmission of Jewish Ethnicity

Anna Dahlem

Methodology and Research Goals

Approximately once or twice per week in the mornings I sat in as an observer in the prenursery and nursery grades of a Jewish day school, which was operated under Orthodox auspices, from October 1985 until March 1986. Within the classroom context, I functioned partially as a neutral observer, partially as an assistant. Trying to gain an understanding of the educational enterprise, I talked to parents and teachers, visited one of the synagogues with which the people in the preschool community were affiliated, and reflected throughout the year on Jewish cultural transmission.

In examining the content and process of instruction in the school, this study seeks to shed light on the enculturation into Orthodox Jewry, in particular the transmission of the historical consciousness at the center of Jewish ethnicity as it is expressed specifically in the holidays: "For the Jews the sacred holidays commemorate historical occurrences that reaffirm reasons for continuity" (DeVos 1975:375).

The Community

The families whose children attend the school belong to three main synagogues that represent Orthodoxy in the western suburbs of Philadelphia. One synagogue attracts primarily professionals and thus has a population of at least 60—rumors speak of 80—medical doctors in a congregation of approximately 230 families. This congregation is referred to both by members and by outsiders as a "modern Orthodox" group. This means, for example, that many women in the community are professionals themselves, such as doctors and lawyers; that they wear pants; that they will work throughout their children's preschool years; and that they and their husbands generally favor an integrationist position with regard to participation in American society. They were described to me by one mother as people who "worried about their education in their twenties, are having their children in their thirties, and might strive for the attainment of status and position in their forties." Their primary consideration in moving into the area in order to establish their families in a suburban environment was the existence of this *shul* (school).

Those parents of the children at the school who belong to the traditional segment of Jewry are affiliated with two congregations closer to the city. These are generally families with greater numbers of children (the two nursery teachers, for example, come from homes with eight and fifteen children) who are linked with the *yeshivot* (intensive religious studies for boys) in the area through the males who are rabbis. The women of this part of the Orthodox community highly value motherhood as a form of self-actualization and often voice criticism of the working mothers and their elaborate child-care arrangements.

The school was a meeting ground for the various aspects of Orthodoxy. When we talked about the shifting values within the community because of women's increasing participation in the professional world, one prenursery teacher told me that the "old yeshiva-type families" were decreasing and the modern families, in which the mothers relied on the school's preschool program as well as other forms of day-care support in raising their children, were increasing. All teachers in the program spoke of their ambivalence toward this development, and especially those who themselves come from a traditional background believe that the children are deprived in many respects because of their mother's professional life.

On the whole, the Orthodox community (three synagogues) in the western suburbs of Philadelphia, though small (approximately 2,000 to 3,000 people), appears to be thriving. For example, new families are constantly moving into the area. Residents pointed out with great enthusiasm that there were currently seventeen pregnant women in their midst—a large number of pregnancies always being a healthy sign for any Jewish community. Among other things, this means that the school's future is secure. The community includes people who have adopted an observant life-style and those raised in traditional homes who have developed a more laissez-faire attitude toward religious behavior and stress the ethnical and spiritual values of their Judaism, as well as a handful of Israelis, some of whom have American spouses.

The Institution

The school was begun by a group of parents in 1964 with a kindergarten class. In its official handbook, the main objectives of the school's educational efforts are stated as being "the transmission of the principles of Torah and its moral and ethical values. Strong emphasis is placed on instilling in students the observance of the basic tenets of behavior for a Torah Jew—Mitzvos between the individual and God and between the individual and his fellow man. . . . The aim of the school's curriculum is to impart knowledge and skills while inspiring within its students an intrinsic desire and love of learning."

Since 1979 the school, which at the time of my research had 235 children enrolled, has been located in a fairly spacious former public school building. It offers classes from prenursery through eighth grade. Because most of the parents dread the idea of sending their sons off to Baltimore or New York to attend a religious high school there, plans are currently underway to create a high school. Many of the parents labeled "modern" are highly educated, and one of the fathers I talked to as well as the principal stated that as many as 30 percent of all the parents had an advanced degree.

There are many cases of families enrolling all their children at the school, which enables siblings to be in contact with each other during the school day as they meet in the gym or in the lunchroom or walk through the hallways. Some of the staff also have their children at the school. An interesting example of these cross-generational ties is the case of the nursery teacher, whose mother currently works as the kindergarten assistant. The teacher attended the school herself, and her sisters and brothers are scattered across the various grades. Many of the parents maintain close personal relationships with other parents, including visiting each other at home, particularly when their children are playmates; participating together in school-related events such as working for the annual Passover-Foods cooperative; providing the refreshments for the weekly Shabbos party; and visiting the school throughout the year on several scheduled occasions.

A phrase that often comes up in talking to parents and teachers about the school is: "It's a very parent-run school." It appears that the modern parents in particular are strongly involved in shaping the institution's future direction. The existence of a prenursery grade that caters to working mothers and the expressed desire by some parents to adopt spoken Hebrew (preferably with the Sephardic pronunciation in use in Israel) as a worthy goal next to the mastery of liturgical and Biblical Hebrew attest to the striving toward an integration of observant Judaism with modernity.

Although individual community members may perhaps view this integration with reservation, the school has essentially taken a stance on this issue. The principal, for example, proudly showed me the school's computer room on my first visit. In general, there is considerable effort toward introducing the children to science. The upper grades had recently participated in a Science Fair, for which various groups prepared projects illustrating scientific inventions, and one of the prenursery's class trips was to the Benjamin Franklin Science Museum, in Philadelphia.

Visitors to the school for the first time would find themselves in an environment where American cultural items are intricately linked with Jewish historical and philosophical concepts as well as artifacts. American non-Jews would probably interpret what they saw as exemplary of extremely traditionalist Judaism, but to my German eye the American components of the school—the flags (American and Israeli) next to the stage in the auditorium, the many flashy displays decorating the hallways, the children's and adults' general cultural reference system (such as "coffee shop," "school bus," "The White House," "Geo Magazine," and "toy guns")—were equally striking.

The Preschool

There were thirty-two children in the preschool: in the prenursery eight boys and eight girls, and in the nursery ten boys and six girls. Each grade has two women taking care of and teaching the children, one functioning in the role of general planner and implementer of the curriculum and the other as her assistant. The two main teachers coordinate many of their activities and often teach similar subjects, especially in preparation for a holiday. On the whole, there did not seem to be much difference in content of the curriculum in the two classes, but rather in style of presentation, which had to be appropriate for the children's level of functioning. For example, the nursery children can maintain their attention longer and can memorize more of the liturgy for the morning prayer.

The teachers are addressed by the children by the term *morah*, which is the Hebrew word for a female teacher. They in turn call the children *yeladim*. The two assistants and the nursery teacher are themselves graduates of the school and returned to teach there after high school and a year at a teacher's seminary in Jerusalem, where they studied religious subjects together with educational theory. The prenursery teacher was hired by the school after she had married a man from the "modern" community whose parents had been among the founders of the school.

The two teachers view themselves as professional educators specializing in early childhood. They create an elaborate environment of toys, materials, constantly changing theme-displays on bulletin boards and doors, musical stimulation (the prenursery has a radio-recorder, the nursery a record player), arts and crafts projects, and key symbols from American and Jewish culture. Mickey Mouse, Winnie the Pooh, Big Bird, The Pink Panther, Humpty-Dumpty, Superman, and the Care Bears populate the walls and shelves together with miniature Torah scrolls, holiday displays, the Hebrew calendar, a poster on Israel, and illustrated boards with blessings and commandments on them.

The time is structured by the teachers for the children. There are set routines, such as going to the playground, free play inside, having a snack, listening to a story being told or read, performing the morning prayer, going to the bathroom, eating lunch, doing physical exercise, engaging in "Show and Tell," accomplishing an art activity, or going on a class trip. Discipline is fairly rigid, and the children are expected to clean the room after play periods and dispose of their cups and napkins after each snack.

When talking about her goals in teaching the prenursery children, the teacher stressed that she wanted them to have a "good first school experience" and that she thought being in the program was an important aspect of their socialization. Her goals for Jewish education during this first year were to convey the holidays as something tangible, which the children could actually experience; to celebrate *shabbat* together on Friday mornings; to teach the students "anything moral" like sharing, not hitting, not fighting, and giving charity; and providing in general a sense "that there is a book called the Torah which is a way of life." She pointed out to me that by eating together, which entailed saying the blessings as a group, or by her answering their questions about, for example, *kashrut* (dietary laws), the children would be able to acquire a basic foundation and that she wanted them to understand in particular that they were part of a community.

When I asked the nursery teacher how she viewed her role, she also conveyed to me the same sense of love of the religious tradition. As a result, she seeks to make the children as knowledgeable as possible about it as well as to stress the social relations facilitated by the nursery environment. She told me that, by upholding a fairly strict standard of observance, those students who came from homes that were not fully observant—where the children were not led to say the blessings before eating—would have a chance to learn more and sometimes even be able to teach their parents some of these things. When I asked her why she thought it was important for the children to be in the program at this age, even though some of them had the option of staying at home with their mothers, she said that "a child is like a twig" and that "whatever they take into their heads now will be their foundation for later education."

For their parents—at least those to whom I spoke—enrolling their child at the preschool seemed to be a result of their membership at the three main synagogues. They intend their children to attend the school through the seventh grade, perhaps even until high school graduation, and are eager to have them start out with their "age cohorts" rather than remain at home. For those mothers who stay at home, there exist, besides their desire to have their children start as early as possible with Jewish education and education in general, pragmatic reasons such as "getting the kids out of the house" and to have them through participation in the program be well connected socially within the community.

Obviously, not all Orthodox families in the area feel the necessity to enroll their children in the program. Within the segment that does support the educational philosophy of the school on the whole, the motivations may range from the firm decision to have the children attend the school through their later school years in fulfillment of the commandment "And thou shalt teach thy children diligently . . ." (Deuteronomy 6:4–9) to the need for a full day nursery because both parents who also happen to be Orthodox Jews are working full time.

The prenursery teacher explained to me that the way in which she viewed her role was that at home the children should simply be exposed to the living tradition and learn from their parents' everyday behavior the rudimentary ethical principles, and in the classroom she would "lecture" them on the tradition in a more detached, abstract manner.

On the whole, the school's preschool program can best be understood as fulfilling two crucial functions: (1) the community's need to impart its way of life, which is based on a complex system of beliefs, concepts, and behavior to new members; and (2) enabling those families in the community who have chosen a professional dual-career life-style in American society to have access to a form of day care that lives up to the best standards of the larger society, namely *educational* day care, versus a mere babysitting service.

The established pattern of American middle-class and upper middle-class children receiving status and access to resources in society by following an educational program that consists of an early childhood program, nursery, kindergarten, elementary school, high school, college, and graduate or professional school can be seen in operation in these parents' support of the two preschool grades.

From a child's point of view, attending the preschool is one aspect of growing up among observant Jews. The children are taken at ages two and three to services on Saturday mornings at the synagogue, and they learn the songs that are sung by their parents during the Friday-night dinner. Some of them are more eager than others to display their ability in the most valued activities and behaviors of the community. Often there is a significant difference in the ease with which a child functions in the classroom context and at home. Although conformity is expected of them all to a high degree (obedience and respect for one's teacher are important values at the school), they often introduce spontaneous self-expression into the cultural system they are acquiring. Some point the rules out to their peers, and others ignore the teacher's commands or carry them out in idiosyncratic ways.

The Concept of Observance

Orthodox Jewry represents that segment of the religion that continues to regard the teachings contained in the Five Books of Moses (Torah) and the Talmud as binding for the conduct of their lives. Although observance begins with in my view an irrational premise, namely that these texts represent God's will for the Jews as transmitted to their prophets and sages, the community's methodology for basing behavior on scriptural verses represents a consistent rational system in its own right. Hence, non-Jews noticing observant Jews today could ask questions about every seemingly irrational behavior they observed—for example, not speaking after washing their hands before blessing their food or touching the doorpost upon entering a room—and would receive a reference to some religious source with its irrational explanation 99 percent of the time.

The 613 commandments are divided into positive and negative ones. They regulate the behavior between an individual and God, and between an individual and his fellow man. Women are exempted from the positive commandments, which should be performed at specific times, because they are viewed as being already obligated to their children. The phrase "It's a mitzvah [commandment]" accompanies the constant appraisal of behavior by the standards of the tradition. One should always be eager to fulfill a commandment. The sense of obligation and loyalty toward tradition on the basis of an inherited covenant that God made with the Jews when they accepted the Torah supports the acceptance of the commandments on the part of the individual.

Jewish children learn observant behavior mainly through imitation. Technically, observance is not binding for them until they are thirteen years old in the case of boys or twelve years old for girls and formally declare themselves to be "bar" or "bas" mitzvah in a public ceremony in the synagogue. But they live in an environment of observance throughout their childhood and so are constantly inspired to imitate it through their parents' and their teachers' praise for "observant" behavior. The most visible aspects of observance in the Orthodox communities of today are the keeping of the Sabbath, the dietary laws, the holidays, saying grace after meals, the men covering their heads, and the orientation of communal life around the synagogue. By affirming their loyalty to the way of life of Rabbinical Judaism, Orthodox Jews, despite a myriad of individual differences in their actual practice of observance, essentially surrender personal "free" will to what to them represents God's will: the Torah.

Observance in the Preschool

The commandments that are practiced in the preschool are basically:

kipah: covering the head with skullcap (boys)
tzitzit: wearing a *tallit* (garment worn under outer garment) (boys)
netilat yadaim: washing hands before eating (nursery)
Berachot: reciting the appropriate blessings (Berachot) before eating
bentching: saying grace after meals

daavening: shacharit (morning prayer) as one of three daily prayers
tzedaka: collection of charity
kashrut: the food consumed in school is all dairy and not meat

The level of observance is more strict with the four- and five-year-old children in the nursery than with the three- and four-year-old ones in the prenursery. This is particularly evident in two areas: mastery of liturgy for the *daavening* and the wearing of *kipah* and *tzitzit* for boys. In the prenursery, there were always a few who came to class wearing neither a *kipah* nor the *tzitzit*. Remarks were made about this by the teachers and by other adults who came into the classroom. The prenursery's morning service is very short and those of the children who stay for lunch are not expected to wash their hands before eating. In the nursery, however, all boys wear their *kipah* and *tzitzit* and perform the ritual hand-washing before eating, if they stay on into the afternoon.

In general, the teachers seek to uphold a standard of observance by introducing the students to the elementary concepts of blessings, prayer, holidays, giving charity, and exposure to the Torah. They guide the children in their behavior, but some of them are more willing and responsive than others. For example, the children should recite a blessing before they start eating, but at various times they start eating without waiting for their teacher to recite the blessing. Likewise, during the daavening, some of them might remain silent or just hum along without saying the words. That this is not due to lack of ability was evident from the moments when these same children would spontaneously join in the singing loudly and clearly.

The Jewish Holidays

The Jewish holidays usually consist of the three agricultural festivals Pesach, Shavuot, and Sukkoth; the New Year with Rosh Hashanah and Yom Kippur; and the minor holidays of Purim, Hanukkah, Tu B'Shevat, and Simhat Torah. All these occur within the framework of the Jewish calendar, which commences with Rosh Hashanah usually falling on a date in September or October: "The Jewish year is reckoned not by the sun but by the moon and consists of 353 or 354 days. For civil purposes the year begins in spring; for religious purposes in autumn" (Gaster 1952:26).

In addition to the above major and minor holidays, there are a number of fasts observed by religious Jews in commemoration of martyrs or the destruction of the Jewish Temple in Jerusalem in 586 B.C. as well as a number of modern commemorative days such as Yom HaShoa (Holocaust Remembrance Day), Yom HaAtzmaut (Israel Independence Day), and Yom Yerushalayim (Jerusalem Reunification Day).

Each of the holidays, except for Tu B'Shevat, has a historical or philosophical theme, derived from Scripture:

Rosh Hashanah: Beginning of the year, first day of an intensive ten-day period of *tshuva* (repentance) and reconciliation with those one has wronged; a small "judgment day"; God is imagined as the judge of the world who decides the fate of each person in the coming year; the *shofar* (ram's horn) is blown.

Yom Kippur: Day of atonement for all transgressions between the individual and God, as well as between the entire House of Israel and God.

Sukkoth: In remembrance of the Jews who left Egypt and dwelt in booths in the desert, one should erect a booth and dwell (today: eat) in it.

Simhat Torah: Celebration of the completion of the annual cycle of reading the Torah in the synagogue.

Hanukkah: Commemorates the victory of Judah the Maccabee (Jewish resistance fighter) over Antiochus IV (Syrian king) in 165 B.C. and rededication of the defiled Temple in Jerusalem; according to legend a miracle occurred when the oil burned for eight days in the Temple's *menorah* (candleholder) (Gaster 1952:233).

Tu B'Shevat: "On the fifteenth day of Shebat, so it is said, the sap begins to rise in the fruit trees in the Holy Land. It is therefore customary on that day to partake of such fruits as grow in the Holy Land. . . . In modern Holy Land the New Year for trees has taken on a new complexion. Largely under the influence of the familiar American Arbor Day, it has become the custom to go out into the fields, on the fifteenth of Shebat, and plant saplings . . ." (1952:255, 259).

Purim: "Purim, or the Feast of Lots, is celebrated on the fourteenth of Adar in memory of the triumph of Esther and Mordecai over the machinations of Haman, vizier of King Ahasvuerus (Xerxes) of Persia, who had selected that day by lot for the extermination of the Jews" (1952:215).

Pesach: In remembrance of the Exodus of Jews from Egypt, for seven days unleavened bread (*matzoh*) is eaten and a festive meal (*Seder*) is held at which the story is recounted.

Shavuot: Harvest festival in biblical times, now celebrated as the day on which the children of Israel received the Torah at Mount Sinai.

Next to language, food, and dress, a distinctive calendar represents one of the most powerful mechanisms of boundary maintenance. The Jewish holidays and commemorative dates all contain formulations of Jewish historical consciousness. Because collective history is that part of transmitted cultural knowledge which justifies ultimately the existence of an ethnic group, the holidays are impressed upon children in the most vivid way possible because they contain the historical interpretation that binds Jewry together.

Holidays create a sense of community both in the present by uniting the people observing them and also across time by linking the generations in historical transcendence. Although all the holidays grow out of historical or mythohistorical events, they are celebrated by people in an affirmation of the present. Even though every system of holidays and commemorative dates is highly particularistic to a given ethnic group (which may succeed, however, in impressing it upon other peoples), the drawing of meaning through ethnic identification with a particular people's annual cycle serves a universal function of a cultural structuring of natural time. For a people to develop and then perpetuate an entire calendar of seasons, holidays, and memorial days may be one of their great cultural inventions and at the same time the most effective way of boundary maintenance. The transmission of the Jewish calendar may thus be one of the crucial goals in the process of "initiating" new members into an ethnic group.

Holidays in the Preschool

The yearlong preschool curriculum, besides exposing the children to basic concepts of Western culture such as "time," "weather," "duty," "science," "the body," and "sharing," is essentially structured and constrained by the occurrence of holidays. A holiday usually starts in the classroom anytime from one to four weeks before the official date. The more important and conceptually complex it is, the earlier the preparations for it begin. For instance, although the prenursery teacher started four weeks before Passover to tell the story of the Jews in Egypt to the children, Thanksgiving displays were up on the bulletin boards only about ten days before the holiday.

The Jewish holidays are dealt with in the preschool: for example, Rosh Hashanah, Yom Kippur, Sukkoth, Simhat Torah, Hanukkah, Purim, Passover, and Shavuot. Of the Jewish commemorative days, only Israel Independence Day is taught to the children. Although the school officially recognizes Thanksgiving and Memorial Day by holding a general assembly and giving the days off, not all the parents celebrate these holidays. The preschool position on American secular holidays is that the children will be taught about Thanksgiving, the presidents' birthdays, and Mother's Day. Although not all of the three traditionally oriented teachers view these holidays as their "own" (when I asked the nursery assistant, for example, if she would have a Thanksgiving party at her home, she said "No, we have enough holidays of our own"), they nonetheless make the same efforts and use the same strategies in teaching them to the children as they do with the Jewish holidays. The only difference lies in the time devoted to the preparations and instructions: less time for the American holidays.

For the children who obtain experiential knowledge of the holidays both at home and at their parents' synagogue, learning about them in the preschool facilitates their acquisition of definitional and symbolic knowledge. Following are the two main questions around which the teachings of the holidays are organized: "What do we do on . . . ?" [behavior] and "What happens/happened on . . . ? [philosophy/history]. The behavior associated with a holiday is related to the philosophical and historical content. For example, in the case of Purim, the story is the narrative in the Book of Esther about how the Jews of Shusan in Persia were saved from the extermination planned by Haman (the Wicked). The prenursery teacher told this tale to the children with the aid of four finger puppets depicting the main characters of the story. Before beginning the story, she reviewed the main activities of Purim:

1. Go to the synagogue and listen to the reading of the Book of Esther.
2. Make noise with a *gragger* (noise maker) every time Haman's name is read.

3. Prepare *lishloach manot* ("sending portions") baskets with fruit, wine, and pastry, and give them to friends.
4. Eat *hamantashen*.
5. Dress up in costume.
6. Give charity to the needy.

In order for the children to be able to relate to the concept of a holiday, the teachers employ five main techniques: visual representations in the form of picture-displays on bulletin boards and classroom decorations; arts and crafts projects: creating a symbol in/on paper or as food; reading, telling, and reviewing a story; celebrating in the classroom; and acting.

The detail that goes into creating visual representations and the labor it represents was commented upon jokingly by the nursery teachers themselves when they teased each other about their "drivenness" in making the symbols look not only identifiable but also beautiful. Initially, I wondered if the children were attuned to this constant flow of visual information. In the course of my observations, however, I often had the opportunity to see a child walk over to a display and gaze at it for a few seconds before moving on. When I questioned a girl on a symbol on the bulletin board whose meaning was obscure to me (a pot wearing an apron), she gave me a surprisingly definite answer: "mommy." To me, this was evidence of the congruity of the visual representations in the classrooms with the actual life experience of the children and therefore their sensitivity to them.

Aside from recreating symbols in or on paper, the second major manual activity is their expression in food. Essentially the preschool is limited to baking cookies. Sometimes the food medium serves to express a symbol in a more tangible manner; at other times, the food itself symbolizes the holiday. For example, the custom of dipping apples into honey is associated with the New Year. Also Hanukkah and Purim, which both loom large in the preschool, though they are usually classified as the "minor holidays," are characterized by special foods, namely the *latkes* (potato pancakes) and the *hamantashen*. The *menorah* (candleholder) of Hanukkah, on the other hand, was used as one of the cookie shapes during a baking activity for this holiday. The symbolic foods are also often expressed in or on paper.

Aside from the birthday parties that are celebrated in the preschool for each child, the students also have holiday parties with special foods, songs, and sometimes costumes. The teachers take pictures that are then posted on the hallway outside the classroom next to other pictures that show the children's activities.

I only observed the Thanksgiving party, where the children reenacted with their "Indian headdresses" the historic meal of peace. With sixteen birthday parties and a weekly Shabbos party on Friday, the added celebration of the holidays in the classroom makes for an impressive number of celebrations. One should keep in mind, furthermore, that the children also celebrate all these events with their parents at home.

In order to arrange for this mass of festivities in an efficient way, the teachers use all the amenities of American party culture, such as paper tablecloths, plates, and cups. For the children, the main aspect of the classroom celebration is the sweet food and the sense of significant distinction when they see the teacher making special preparations.

A final major element of holiday transmission in the preschool are the plays the children prepare for the parents, specifically for the Hanukkah and Purim celebrations. By acting out in a historical scene a behavior associated with the holiday with their whole bodies, the children can experience on yet another plane an abstract concept in a more tangible manner. Although I did not have a chance to see a Purim play at the school, I learned from an informant with a Jewish day-school background that this play is a vital part of the holiday for the children and that they aspire to be given the key roles. With their parents as the audience, the objective of such plays becomes the demonstration that the new generation has been exposed to this particular aspect of history and has formed a personal link with it.

Given the fact that the children are considered too young to start learning to read and to write, the holiday-oriented preschool curriculum represents an elegant compromise between the cognitive limitations of the preschool child and the imperative to transmit Judaism. To children the Jewish holidays are their first exposure to the history and beliefs of their people. The general attitude toward holidays in Orthodoxy is expressed through the following nursery assistant's statement: "Our lives revolve around the holidays." Given that this orientation to a distinct ritual calendar will have far-reaching influences in an adult's life, the significance of being enculturated at this early age into the cycle cannot be overestimated.

Aside from the learned content that could essentially be transmitted at any age, the *attitude* toward holidays and the emotional states associated with them are acquired by the children. In this process of forming a positive emotional attachment to symbols and concepts, the early age is crucial. It appears evident to me from seeing the students' reactions to the teaching about the holidays that indeed at this age a conceptual foundation is erected that eventually through annual repetition becomes strongly ingrained. This foundation is the Jewish calendar cycle.

In a way, these children, who grow up in observant homes, might not need to be taught formally about what they experience at home, but the continuous focusing on the holidays in both school and home strengthens their identification with the cycle. The teachers can take for granted the children's experiential memory and thus concentrate their efforts on the more complex aspects of the holidays, such as the history behind them. In this manner, the transmission of one of the most basic and yet most consequential aspects of Jewish ethnicity, namely the Jewish calendar, is ensured.

11

Fayetteville or Raleigh?
An Analysis of an American Indian Baptist Church

Beth Batten

Between late November 1986 and mid-April 1987, I visited a Baptist church in Philadelphia whose congregation is mostly American Indian, the term church members use to denote Native Americans. My fieldwork and associations with the people of this church produced the data that are presented in this paper.

One Sunday evening a group of church members were in the church, waiting to begin the evening service. Two others had gone to run an errand and were taking a long time. When they finally returned, the preacher said to them, "So, did you go to Fayetteville or Raleigh?" and everyone laughed.

None of the people who were in that room has lived in North Carolina for over thirty years, yet it remains central in their minds. The state is the origin of their religion and of their Indian identity, the two defining factors that make them a community in spite of the fact that they are scattered over the Philadelphia area, both in terms of residence and work.

The core of the congregation is composed of three middle-aged couples, their female children, and their grandchildren. These three couples are all originally from North Carolina, though they came to Philadelphia as long as thirty-four years ago. Two of the couples are from the Lumbee tribe, located in Robeson County, North Carolina, and the third couple is Haliwa-Saponi, another east North Carolina tribe. Each of the men, whom I shall call Brother A, Brother B, and Brother C, plays a visible role in the church service: Brother A is the preacher; Brother B is a secondary sort of preacher, making announcements and organizing church functions, as well as filling in when the regular preacher is absent and playing the piano; and Brother C plays the electric guitar.

The general focus of church services is on salvation rendered by God through Jesus Christ. This salvation brings peace of mind, which manifests itself in healing; in respite from worry about the stresses of daily life; and in the promise of a life (after death) far more beautiful and pleasant than this one, in a place where a person will be reunited with all dead or lost relatives and friends. The main theme reiterated in various forms each Sunday morning is the use of the church as a tool and salvation as an inspiration to rise above the trivialities and tribulations of inner-city life.

The church has a strong evangelical tradition of trying to help others avoid and recover from the pitfalls of alcoholism, drug abuse, domestic violence, crime, and other common reactions to economic hardship. Church members have many stories of encounters with these problems, in friends, neighbors, relatives, or even their former selves. Older church members, particularly, often recount stories of their salvation in what are called "testimonials." These are high-spirited recitations of a person's former sins, followed by a description of the happiness they have received from Jesus; interjected are short phrases of praise for Jesus and God or affirmation of Their goodness.

The evangelical tradition is strongest in those who have "sinned" and subsequently been saved because they know the isolation they felt before their salvation, as well as the strength of the church community and its support network. Thus, they wish to extend the network through the incorporation of new members, offering a helping hand to those whose situation they have experienced previously. This network is as much material as it is spiritual, as I shall demonstrate in the course of the paper, and extends to evangelistic actions.

One Sunday, Brother B, Sister L, and I were driving to visit another church, and we stopped to get gas. A man at the gas station who was drunk and had no money, asked Brother B for some cash to purchase gas and drive home. Brother B complied and said, "I'll give you the money, but let me give you a little direction, brother; what you need is Jesus Christ; you need to go to church." The man then responded, "Yes, I know; you're right; I'll try."

This story illustrates at least two points. One concerns Brother B's reaction to the man's situation. Although he is unable to challenge or to change the economic conditions that have created the inner city, he is nonetheless able to take some responsibility, to change or try to change a part of what the environment there has wrought. Brother B explained his actions by saying that you never know who it is you feed or clothe or help on the street. But there is always the possibility that the beggar you look out for is God. That is, you never know how far your actions will reach. Religion of this type gives a reason to act, even in the face of the possibility that action is useless and insignificant.

The other point that the story illustrates concerns the man's reaction: He did not brush off Brother B's suggestion as ridiculous but instead viewed it as an acceptable ideal if not an achievable one. The idea of salvation (in this case, as a method of being cured of alcoholism) was a valid one in his cultural vocabulary, as it would *not* be for most members of the academic intelligentsia or business leaders, both of whom might choose a rehabilitation program that focused exclusively on the problem of alcoholism and was based on scientific principles. It is likely that the drunken man at the gas station had gone to church every Sunday as a child and that his continued exposure to the supportive function of the church community accounts for the validation of the idea of salvation in his cultural vocabulary.

Churches are very common in the inner city because they provide a symbolic (or real) kin group that serves as a source of economic and (just as important) emotional support, thus helping to alleviate the causes of such problems as alcoholism. These church groups are similar to the support networks of the "non-kin-regarded-as-kin groups" type described by Carol Stack in her study of below-subsistence-level black urban families in *All Our Kin* (1974).

In *Urban Renegades* (1975), a study of the Boston Micmac Indians, Jeanne Guillemin discusses the "urban tribal network." This network disseminates "information on jobs and transportation [that has] to be shared" (1975:211). Such information about jobs, sales, and how to operate within the city's bureaucracy is one kind of key economic support provided by the tribal or the "kin" network. The Philadelphia church functions in many instances in the same way as the tribe does for the Micmac, providing networks of kin and kin-friend relationships (sources of economic support), a common and familiar cultural background, and a sort of emotional refuge from the inner city, much like the Micmac reservation.

It is pertinent to note that much of the preacher's community work is involved with Indians. There is often talk in the church about saving all the Indians in Philadelphia, though "then we'd need a bigger church than this; we'd have to build a whole new one." In other words, they would have a stronger community, one capable of finding the resources to build a new church. The idea of evangelism is seen as an extension of the community network: extending the "common and familiar" community is the primary goal of evangelism, and in this case that community potentially consists of any and all the Indians in the Delaware Valley.

The four most common subjects of conversation among the people of the Philadelphia church are religion; North Carolina; the "warmth" and "family" atmosphere of the church community; and references to Indian friends, relatives, activities, and characteristics. For the people of the church, the "common and familiar cultural background" is North Carolina, as manifested in their church services, which resemble almost exactly those of similar churches in North Carolina (which I have seen on videotape). For their relatives in North Carolina, the "common and familiar cultural background" is Indian. Both the Indian and the North Carolina identities are maintained in Philadelphia, largely through religious practices and through the functions of the church community.

History

Only one of the people who regularly attend the church is not Indian: a white woman who lives close to the church and who converted four years ago. She is now the church secretary and has been described by the group as "almost Indian." All other regular members are Indian and are either from North Carolina or are related to someone who is.

As indicated above, the current church membership is drawn mainly from three families, all originally from that state. Two of the families belong to the Lumbee tribe, of Robeson County; and the third, which is related to an officer of the Philadelphia-area Native American support center, the United American Indians of the Delaware Valley (UAIDV), is of the Haliwa-Saponi tribe. In addition, there is a Cherokee woman, also from North Carolina, who comes to church regularly with her children.

Neither the Lumbees nor the Haliwa-Saponis retain any aboriginal language or technology. The Lumbees live in an area that during colonial times was very swampy and inaccessible. They are apparently descended from a mixture of white colonists, runaway slaves (both Indian and black), and a wide mixture of Indians of various tribes, including Cherokee and Tuscarora, who were trying to escape various Indian wars. The swamps provided a perfect hiding place as well as the freedom of isolation. Through this sort of backwoods mixing, the Lumbees learned to speak English and eventually took on white frontier life-styles: "When first 'discovered' in the eighteenth century, all the Lumbees spoke English and lived like white frontiersmen in regard to their dress, their housing, and their drinking habits" (Hudson 1976:493). The Lumbees did, however, retain Indian racial characteristics. This is true of the Philadelphia church's congregation as well: most people have some Indian racial characteristics, though to a greater or lesser degree. Variation is great, even among siblings.

Many Lumbees as well as other people, especially some nineteenth-century historians, believe that they are descendants of members of the "Lost Colony" of Roanoke Island, North Carolina. In 1587 a colony was commissioned by Sir Walter Raleigh and settled on the island, off the coast of North Carolina, under the governorship of John White. The colony experienced a food shortage, and White returned to England for supplies, leaving about ninety-five colonists on the island. When he was finally able to return in 1590, White found the colony abandoned and the site in disarray. He also discovered the word "CROATOAN" carved in a tree near the front gate, as per his instructions to leave a message describing any change of the colonists' location. "Croatoan" is an Indian word referring to another island occupied by the Hatteras Indians, with whom the colonists were friendly. White attempted to go to Croatoan Island to search for the colonists but was prevented from doing so by bad weather.

None of the colonists was ever found, but Stephen Weeks, a nineteenth-century historian, suggests that they and the Indians they were with ended up on the mainland and eventually were pushed back into the Robeson County swamps (these are surrounded by the fertile farmland on which many of the older Philadelphia church members and their relatives have worked, picking cotton and tobacco) by encroaching colonization. Weeks says that the "other end of the [Lost Colony] chain is to be found in a tribe of Indians now living in Robeson County and the adjacent sections of North Carolina, and recognized officially by the State in 1885 as the Croatan Indians. These Indians are believed to be the lineal descendants of the colonists left by John White on Roanoke Island in 1587" (1891:463).

Weeks follows this statement with a fairly convincing argument for its validity, which includes an examination of the similarity of Lumbee names to those of the colonists, as well as a short comparison of Lumbee speech to fourteenth-century English. However, Weeks's argument does not hold up under closer scrutiny. His linguistic analysis is superficial, and the name connection is tenuous at best because most of the colonists' names were so common as to be numerous in any phone book today. (Incidentally, none of the Philadelphia church members has any of the colonists' surnames.)

Modern historian David Durant evaluated Weeks's argument: "In the late nineteenth century, romantic attempts were made to show that the Lumbee Indians of North Carolina were descendants of the lost colonists: in 1891 Stephen Weeks ingeniously interpreted their quaint pronunciation of the language as being Old English. . . . But . . . few colonists, certainly no more than a dozen at most —may have avoided the massacre" (1981:164). The massacre of which Durant speaks is the one that he feels was responsible for the state of disarray in which White found the site of the settlement. Although this condition could have just as easily been caused while the colonists were living at another location, Durant does make a good point. There were hostile Indians in the vicinity, and this factor, combined with other difficulties of New World living, made it rather unlikely that more than a few colonists survived to travel into the interior and reproduce. Even though there may be a grain of truth to the "Lost Colony" speculations, it is most likely that these colonists are not a major ancestral element of the Lumbees; as I stated earlier, they are of primary Indian stock. One woman from the church probably explained the situation best when she told me: "I think it's pretty much impossible to find my heritage; we'll never know."

There are over 30,000 Lumbees in the Robeson County area today, which makes them one of the largest Indian groups in the United States and the largest one in the Southeast: "Until recently most of the Lumbees were farmers, some owning substantial farms. But as farming has become mechanized, small farming has become eco nomically unfeasible, and they have been forced to take jobs else-where. During World War II they began going north in search of work. It was at this time that they began settling in East Baltimore, where today some 2,500 Lumbees live and work. Few of them are permanent émigrés. Some stay for a while and then return to North Carolina. And even those who do become permanent residents re-turn to North Carolina for frequent visits" (Hudson 1976:493). The church members who were born in North Carolina used to work on the cotton and tobacco farms there and have often spoken about practices before machines came along, about how hard the work was compared to the jobs their children have, and about the long hours they used to work. But people generally speak fondly of these things and remind you of how strong and alive they were, so much so that they went to revivals after working all day in the fields and stayed at times until two or three o'clock in the morning. In North Carolina, going to church was, as it is in Philadelphia, an escape from daily drudgeries.

Part of the reason for the postwar northward migration was the extremely low wage scale, and part was probably because of a decrease in jobs as people returned from the war and the population increased, and possibly as agriculture began to mechanize. I have visited the Lumbee section of Baltimore, when the Philadelphia church attended a "homecoming" there. The church where the celebration was held was quite large, with lots of people, most of them Lumbees. Some of the Philadelphia church members have friends or relatives in Baltimore, though they have many more relatives in North Carolina. They make a habit of visiting the state on special occasions—such as weddings, illnesses, and special revivals—even after living in Philadelphia for more than thirty years.

There is very little literature on the Haliwa-Saponis, and in a general sense their history is similar to that of the Lumbees. The only direct reference to them that I found said that in "addition to groups in the Southeast who have a clear claim to Indian ancestry, there are a large number of groups whose claim is only partial. . . . Some of these people, such as the Haliwas of eastern North Carolina, are in the process of establishing for themselves an Indian identity" (Hudson 1976:497). However, the Lumbees in the Philadelphia church are no more nor less Indian, either racially or culturally, than the Haliwa-Saponis there, and both groups are accepted by other Philadelphia-area Indians as Indian people.

Living Conditions

The church members whose homes I visited live in older wooden row houses in various sections of the city; I have no idea if this is true of other church members. I was in one home several times, staying there on Sunday afternoons between the morning and the evening services; the one other home that I visited was similar in decor.

The home I often visited is a row house located on a small street. It has a basement and an upper story in addition to the main floor, and a very small concreted backyard, about ten by twelve feet in size. The backyard is one in two continuous rows of them, each fenced with a chain-link fence so that other people's yards and dogs are visible, but not reachable. Thus, a complete block of row houses surrounds a kind of sectioned-off courtyard. Visible at the end of the block are some houses in disrepair, which look as if they may have been involved in a fire. In the backyard of this house there is a large, shy black dog and his house, and a clothesline, along with various other household items.

In the front of the house I visited there is no yard, only concrete steps and the sidewalk. The grandchildren who come over for Sunday dinner often go outside and play with children who live in other houses on the block. Many of the row-house occupants are either black or Puerto Rican. The street in front of the house is the only place to park, and sometimes people will save parking spaces for those who come home from work late by putting chairs in the street.

Inside the house, most of the activity takes place on the main floor; the upstairs consists of bedrooms; and the basement is not very accessible, with the staircase doorway being behind the dining table. The main floor contains the living room, the dining room, the kitchen, and a bathroom. The kitchen is very small, but there are usually at least two people in there preparing the Sunday dinner. The cabinets are stacked high with dishes owing to lack of space, and the same could be said of the entire house; it is small but full of things—and people.

The dining room has a table with assorted styles of chairs, another cabinet stacked with dishes and glasses, a long buffet table against one wall, and a couple of other pieces of furniture. The dining table seats only six, so people usually eat in shifts, and the children do not eat at the table at all. Above the buffet table is a long rectangular mirror; the buffet table is covered with a white cloth on which are all sorts of knickknacks such as pictures of family members and relatives, dishes, and the funeral service program for a thirty-three-year-old nephew who had been in trouble with alcohol.

Alcoholism is a common problem among the Indians and one that the church tries hard to combat. The preacher once said, "I've never seen an Indian that could drink"; he himself is a reformed alcoholic and frequently mentions the role his conversion played in his rehabilitation. Sister B commented on her nephew's death, saying, "It like to kill me when I heard of it. Didn't bother me my father died; didn't bother me my brother died, but . . . [someone finishes the sentence: 'this young one'] . . . yeah." Children are considered to be very valuable, and young people are the focus of much attention and worry because they are the most susceptible to the vices of city life, especially those relating to alcohol and drugs.

The living room contains two well-worn couches and an easy

chair, a low rectangular coffee table, an upright piano, and a floor-based television with a VCR that is used mainly to record religious programs and to view videos of churches in North Carolina. The TV is almost always on in the background, and its use reminded me strongly of that of the Micmac, as described by Guillemin: "The person who turned the set on wanders away; children sit down in front of it and begin to play . . . ; a grandmother shifts her chair and inadvertently blocks out the screen from the view of most others in the room. After some time, the baby of the family will switch the channel, perhaps find something familiar or amusing such as cartoons, and fall asleep on the floor in front of the T.V. Later still, an adult will reach past the grandmother and turn off the set" (1975:86).

There is a closet that is almost always overflowing with coats as well as a set of shelves and a table crammed with more knick-knacks: pictures of children and grandchildren and marriages and graduations in addition to piles of things that will not fit anywhere else. There is a lamp with a base that is shaped in the figure of an Indian, painted red and wearing a feather headdress; and across the room there is a picture of an Indian and a tepee. On one wall, there is a figurine of Jesus, and there are other religious symbols or sayings hung about.

The "artwork" in the house seems to fall basically into three categories: pictures of children, renditions of Indians or Indian scenes, and religious symbols or sayings. This was also true in the other house I visited. Each of these categories is of special importance to these people: the helping hand of Jesus acting through the church, their Indian identity, and their children.

Children are another great topic of conversation and are one of Indian peoples' greatest resources because they ensure the survival of the culture. They are highly valued in Indian societies—from the Boston Micmac, to a Mohawk man who was interviewed in a Philadelphia public-television program called "Credo" about Native American religion. According to this Mohawk: "In the Mohawk culture . . . when the creator made us the number one rule was family . . . to have children, a lot of children and raise them up in our—in our what you might call *our* teachings" ("Credo" with Dr. David Reed, 1983).

There is another lamp, on the floor by the television set, that is made out of a large piece of driftwood. It was given to Sister B by her brother-in-law in North Carolina, who had been offered over $200 for it. As she commented, he could easily have found another piece of driftwood, but he did not want to sell the lamp.

This illustrates two things: the continued strength of relationships with relatives in North Carolina; and the importance of friends and relations over money, even though money is scarce and therefore valuable.

Indianness

One time, as Sister A introduced an Indian friend to a white visitor in the church, she said, "This is Sister B. She's from the same tribe as I am, back in North Carolina." When I first began my fieldwork, Sister A introduced me to everyone in the church and indicated their tribal affiliation. One woman asked me if I was an Indian (this is not so odd as it may sound; there are a number of people in the United States with a quarter or half Indian blood who do not have any apparent Indian characteristics). In non-Indian society, people are usually introduced with names and professions; students usually want to know what a person's major is. The Indian identity is the primary identifying factor among the members of the Philadelphia church, along with the older people's North Carolina origins. Many members of the church wear such items as Indian jewelry, silver and turquoise watchbands, bracelets, rings, belts buckles, and earrings as another way of identifying themselves as Indian. The preacher makes and sells this kind of jewelry.

The church has many members who are in one way or another associated with the United American Indians of the Delaware Valley (UAIDV). The preacher has been an alternate on its advisory board, and a church member's brother is currently the organization's president. The daughter of two other church members was a princess at one of the UAIDV's annual Pow Wows, held every August. The UAIDV also holds open houses several times a year, and sometimes church members will attend them if they are not too busy that day.

In religious matters, the church's identity is maintained in its evangelistic tradition, which deals in a large part with Indians in the Delaware Valley. Another aspect of these people's religion that strikes me as being very Indian is their perception of Jesus; their relationship to Him seems to be very close to that of other Indians' relationship to their spirit animals—that is, personal guardian spirits that are discovered on a vision quest.

This similarity was brought up by a Creek Indian, Phillip Deere, during the television program "Credo": "And so in early times, real early times, the Indian ministers couldn't read or write English, so they couldn't read the Bible. But they were sought out through visions or through dreams. The church people would go out into the woods and they would pray in the woods, and somebody would have a vision, or somebody would have a dream, of one of the mens [*sic*] . . . becoming a pastor" ("Credo" 1983).

Many of the church members' descriptions of salvation are personalized descriptions of dreams or visions of Jesus, of a sudden awakening after much praying or reflection (as in the vision quest, when Indians would suddenly receive a vision of their guardian spirits after spending several days fasting and praying in the wilderness). Some illustrative comments of informants are: "I read it [the Bible] a million times and I never understood it, but when the light comes, you suddenly understand"; "Jesus is my and everybody's *personal* savior"; "We know He's real because we feel Him"; "When I was first in the church, I picked Peter, Paul, and others like them as my role models. But later I suppressed my desire to be like them in order to be like Jesus. Jesus wants *you* to be like Him"; and "I'll [Jesus] be with you in the Spirit."

The preacher spoke several times of how he could *feel* the thorn crown in Jesus's head before crucifixion, as if he had been there, and the church was remodeling according to a vision he had. And visions are usually the way people are called to preach; a guest minister from North Carolina said, "God penetrated the glass and steel of a '54 Chevy [truck]"—and that vision was his inspiration to preach.

Conclusion

The people of this church have succeeded in creating and maintaining a strong kin and kin-friend based community within the inner-city area of Philadelphia. This community perpetuates an Indian identity that helps to maintain a sense of self in the cultural conglomerates of both Philadelphia and North Carolina. The community members' sense of self is also maintained by their identity as North Carolinians in the Philadelphia context; this identity is maintained through continued relationships with relatives in the state; through retaining its food habits; and through re-creating a North Carolina-style service in the Philadelphia church.

The church maintains its solidarity through serving to perpetuate common symbolic and experientially based ethnic identities and through maintaining a trade and support network among its members. This network involves the distribution of food and clothes;

information on jobs, sales, and transportation; child care; emotional support and assistance in the form of money, labor, and expertise. Both an Indian identity and the material support function to sustain these people in the face of the stresses of inner-city life. The church is a vital element in its members' lives, and from them it elicits a deep, continuous faith.

12

Issues in Greek Orthodoxy That Define and Maintain Greek-American Ethnicity

Karen L. Belsley

A Historical Perspective

The history of Greek-Americans in the Philadelphia area dates back to the early 1900s, the "era of mass migration" of Greeks to America (Moskos 1980:11). In the decade between 1900 and 1910, some 167,519 people emigrated to the United States; in the next decade, the number rose to 184,201 (Moskos 1980:11). The Greek homeland at the time was characterized by severe poverty among the peasant class. According to Moskos: "It cannot be overstated that the overriding motive for Greek migration to the United States was economic gain. The intent of the overwhelming majority of immigrants was to return to Greece with sufficient capital to enjoy a comfortable life in their home villages" (1980:9).

Saloutos also notes that the wave of immigration in the early 1900s was encouraged by the depressed economy in Greece during the 1890s (1964:29). Currants, then the principal export crop, had experienced a severe decline in price because of trading complications with France and Russia. The Greeks had destroyed many of their olive trees in order to grow currants—now they were left with a severe blow to their export crops (1964:29). Saloutos writes: "The response of many Greeks to this depressed state of affairs was immigration. . . . If the depressed state of the currant trade was the immediate cause of the immigrant wave of the 1890s the unhealthy state of the Greek economy and the natural disasters that struck Greece over these years were the underlying reasons for the continuing out-flow" (1964:29).

In any event, the Greeks who came to America in the early 1900s were largely peasants. They preferred to work in the larger cities, where they were attracted by quick returns on their work in the form of a weekly paycheck and social interaction with other Greeks in the area (1964:46).

In 1905 the Greek population in Philadelphia numbered roughly one hundred (*The Hellenic Chronicle* 1985:unpaged). These people had a single house of worship, Annunciation, which was a rented hall on Fourth and Pine streets; before that time, they had attended a nearby Ukrainian church. Annunciation moved to a church building on Ninth Street in 1907; again in 1960 it was relocated, to Elkins Park, where a Byzantine style Greek Orthodox church stands today. The second Greek Orthodox church in the area, St. George, was established on South Street in 1921. It was followed by St. Demetrios in 1942 (rebuilt in 1967), St. George in Chester in 1943, and St. Luke in 1959 (the church building actually opened in 1963). I do not have statistics as to where St. Luke's present parishioners attended church before it was built; however, my data indicate that the majority of them attended St. George in Philadelphia.

Outside of the establishment and growth of Greek Orthodox churches in the area over the years, the history of the Greek community in Philadelphia appears to largely parallel developments of Greek-American communities in other large cities—though the extent of the population in Philadelphia in no way matched those of Chicago and New York. Moskos estimates that "several thousand" Greek-Americans each were living in cities such as Philadelphia, Pittsburgh, Buffalo, Cleveland, Toledo, Detroit, Gary, and Milwaukee (1980:21).

Most important in the establishment of the Greek-American community in cities such as Philadelphia was entrepreneurship. Saloutos points out that

> Business appealed to the Greeks for a wide variety of reasons. The desire to acquire wealth and status, and perhaps return to their native villages and flaunt this in the faces of detractors, motivated some. Many entered business with the belief that this was the surest way to wealth and success, and certainly preferable to working for wages. In the old country the more discerning observed that the commercial and financial classes were emerging into prominence and the United States was living proof of what could be accomplished. Wherever one turned, the admonition was to work hard, save, invest, succeed, become independent, and "be your own boss." (1964:258)

Emphasis on entrepreneurship has been passed down through generations. In a random sample of fifteen men in the community of St. Luke's, 40 percent were self-employed businessmen, and another 26 percent in business administration (none of the women questioned was self-employed). Although clearly this sample is not large enough to give an accurate figure for St. Luke's parish as a whole, it does indicate an emphasis on entrepreneurship and the adage "Be your own boss."

In the early 1900s, the Greeks who emigrated to Philadelphia were concentrated in the city proper, specifically Gaskill Street. Later, "Greektown" was moved to its present location on Locust Street. The few hundred Greek-Americans in the early 1900s largely made their living working for other Greeks in restaurants and shops as well as managing their own food stands. Often a young man from Greece would be sent over to live with and work for his more established relatives. Moskos notes that "Greek business . . . tended to concentrate in certain areas: confectioneries or sweet shops, food service, retail and shoeshine parlors" (1980:23). Based on life histories I have gathered, it appears that many of the Greeks moved out toward the suburbs as their businesses gained ground and they were able to afford a grander living style. This is an economic trend that is apparently still at work today.

The origins of Greek Orthodoxy in America can be attributed to the Greek-Americans themselves (Moskos 1980). An area that held a significant number of immigrants would form a community council, or *kinotis*. The primary function of the kinotis was to arrange for the creation of a local Greek Orthodox church. In these early times, the church was a crucial center for the Greek-Americans because there they could keep in touch with their ethnic and religious heritage. In present times, the archdiocesan administration of North and South America, under the Ecumenical Patriarch of Constantinople, is situated in New York. The United States has been divided into eight districts, each of which constitutes a Greek Orthodox diocese. The Greek Orthodox Church of St. Luke is in the diocese of New Jersey but located in Broomall, a suburb of Philadelphia.

In my research, I discovered that, though Greek Orthodoxy plays the primary role in the expression of Greek-American ethnicity, it is by no means its only one. Hellenic clubs, such as AHEPA (American Hellenic Educational Progressive Association) and the Hellenic Universities Club, as well represented among Greek-Americans. The Hellenic Universities Club plays a specific role among the Greek-Americans on the St. Luke's community. Greek-Americans also express interesting facets of their identity through their attitudes toward American and Greek politics. There is a small, but significant, amount of "business networking" in the Greek-American community. Younger Greek-Americans are often sent to Greece to learn about areas of their ethnicity and religion that do not seem to be provided through the Greek Orthodox church in America.

Considering these factors as well as sensitive issues in Orthodoxy, I formulated a lengthy list of questions for informants that yielded a broad range of data. It was not too difficult to discover some of the sensitive issues expressed in the Orthodox church because they kept being raised in conversations. Yet, others, such as the social versus the religious nature of the Orthodox service, were issues with which many informants were clearly uncomfortable. Other fieldwork areas, such as participant observation, indicated to me that they were, however, important issues, and I continued to press for information. The three particular broad issues that I deem to be the most significant are, in no particular order: (1) the transmission of the Greek language among Greek-Americans over the generations, and how it has affected the use of the language in the Orthodox services; (2) the social versus the religious nature of church attendance over the generations; and (3) rites of passage: the closing of the old St. Luke's Greek Orthodox Church and opening of the new one. Before analyzing the data yielded by these questions, I will discuss my fieldwork methodology.

Fieldwork

I chose to study the Greek-American community associated with St. Luke's after hearing from a friend that the people were in the process of building a new church. Apparently the whole community was involved in this effort to create a Greek Orthodox church in Byzantine style. I found the address and made an exploratory visit to the church one afternoon. At that time, the new building was still far from complete. Behind it stood the old one, originally a gymnasium. Connecting the new to the old was a structure I later learned was the Education Building.

My reasons for choosing the church as a means of studying the Greek-American community at the time were twofold. An acquaintance who had mentioned the church to me had identified the community as a specific group of Greek-Americans and had related to them in terms of their concerted efforts to raise a church. For that reason, I felt that, of all the various ways in which this community maintained a boundary between itself and the rest of the area, the church was obviously the most important. For purely practical reasons, I also thought that the church would be a good means of beginning study of the community. My initial meeting with the priest of St. Luke's proved my hunch to be correct; he was extremely helpful, even going so far as to give me a list of names of people whom he recommended I interview.

During the months of October, November, and December 1984, I observed the community by attending church on Sundays as well as the Greek Language School, on several week nights—both the children and adult classes. My background reading was largely concentrated on theories of ethnicity, the historical view of Greek-Americans, and information on Greek Orthodoxy. The Orthodox church publishes a number of books and pamphlets that were invaluable in providing an emic view of Orthodoxy and Greek-American ethnicity with which to begin.

Without exception, the Greek-Americans I interviewed felt that they differed from other "types" of Americans in that they believed in and were baptized in the Greek Orthodox Church and they were of Greek descent or married to someone of Greek descent. Other aspects noted by most of these people were that they upheld Greek traditions (mostly Orthodox), ate Greek food (at least on occasion), and spoke the Greek language (in varying degrees). Others added club membership, specifically the Hellenic Universities Club.

I asked informants if, as children, being Greek-American had made them feel different in any way. A typical answer was that given to me by a first-generation woman in her thirties or forties [paraphrased]:

As a child, the first words I spoke were Greek. When I was old enough to go outside and play with the other kids, I ran inside crying because I couldn't understand what they were saying. I learned enough English to converse quickly, however. My mother took me and my brother into St. George's Greek Orthodox Church in Philadelphia each Sunday. My father didn't go because he worked the night shift at the restaurant and was too exhausted by Sunday morning to do anything but sleep. ["Did this make you feel different from other kids?"] I was different because I went to a Greek Orthodox Church and because I went to Greek School, and because my parents spoke Greek and ate Greek foods. I don't remember having an overwhelming sense of being out of things because of it, however. I was happy to get the different foods, because they are so good! My brother reacted more strongly to it, I think, because Greek School was held on Saturdays, and he couldn't go play ball with his friends.

The completed, Byzantine-style, gold dome of St. Luke's Church in Philadelphia. (Courtesy of Elizabeth Ameisen)

Another first-generation woman recalled not being allowed to speak English at home because her parents were afraid she would forget Greek. Yet another first-generation woman recalled not being allowed to speak Greek at home, so that everyone could learn English! One first-generation woman with whom I spoke noted that she did not have a problem with feeling "different" because she was Greek-American inasmuch as she had grown up in the Greek section of New York City. Many of her friends were Greek, her neighbors were Greek, and there was an Orthodox church every four blocks. There were enough others around like her that she did not feel out of place.

This account contrasts directly with that of a second-generation, American-born male, who noted that there were hardly any other Greeks around where he lived or went to school. The nearest Greek Orthodox church was fifty miles away. Yet, this informant noted that, when he left home and went into the service, one of the first things he did at his new base was to attend the nearby Greek Orthodox church and become acquainted with the Greek-American community in the area.

The way in which Greek-Americans perceive themselves as different from other Americans is largely dependent upon the generation, though all generations gave some similar responses, citing Greek Orthodoxy and the Greek language as the principal factors. For earlier generations, the degree to which cultural aspects such as Greek language and traditions influenced or were imposed upon them is much more significant. Many first-generation informants noted that, during their social lives as teenagers, their parents strongly influenced them to date other Greek-Americans. Based on the preliminary data, we can conclude that the most important factors that separate Greek-Americans from other Americans are Greek Orthodoxy and church-related activities. The cultural aspects of tradition, values, food, and language are present to varying degrees in the community, according to individual situation and preference.

Language in Greek Orthodoxy: A Controversial Issue

In November 1984 the parish priest of the Greek Orthodox Church of St. Luke announced to the community that "due to the requests of members" the Liturgy would be conducted in English once each month. Previously, largely Greek had been employed. In a later interview, the priest noted that the use of English in the services was a "highly sensitive issue." Pressure in this regard came from a younger group of Greek-Americans, members of the second

American-born generation. Very few of the members of this generation speak enough Greek to understand the services, and their children even less. In order to attend services they understood, many younger members were going to other churches that featured more English.

Problems with the issue of language in the church went back well over a decade. In 1970 a meeting had been held among the clergy-laity congress in New York on the language issue. The result of this congress was that the use of English in the Liturgy was allowed at the discretion of the parish priest (Moskos 1980:71; field notes). The fact that the English Liturgy at St. Luke's was not introduced on a regular basis until thirteen years later suggests a relatively conservative parish. However, Moskos notes: "The progression to English would have been inevitable and relatively smooth had it not been for the large influx of immigrants from Greece since 1966. Older traditionalists could now join forces with a new constituency committed to the Greek language. The Greek Orthodox Church was more ready, in effect, for English in 1960 than it is today" (1980:61).

Despite the local recent decision to include an English Liturgy once each month, language is still a touchy issue in the parish. There is a small but vocal group of older immigrant women (known by many as the *yiayiá:* "yaya's," or grandmothers) who are adamant on the use of Greek. Although they are a small group, they are the elders, and therefore respected. Interestingly enough, only one of the elderly Greek immigrants I spoke with appeared to mind the English strongly. Most of them felt that a once-a-month English Liturgy was a good balance. In that way, they could understand it, and so could their children and grandchildren.

Out of the fifteen first American-born generation Greeks I questioned, twelve claimed to speak fluent Greek, two noted that they understood some, and only one responded "none at all." Among nine second American-born generation Greeks, four claimed knowledge of the language, and five indicated none. Are these figures an accurate representation of this particular community? The impressions given to me by informants indicated that there were not as many proficient Greek speakers as my data indicated. One possible explanation for this is that there are many degrees of language capability, and perhaps several informants who answered that they did speak the language in fact were less than fluent. If I had thought of it at the time, a more telling line of questioning might have been to ask them to rank their language abilities on a scale from 1 to 10.

I questioned several informants on how their Greek language abilities were acquired. All ten of the first American-born generation informants learned Greek primarily from their parents. Of the second American-born generation informants I questioned, visits to Greece had proved to be a major factor in learning to speak the language fluently, as well as the instruction of their parents and at language school.

Considering that there are well over 400 families who are members of the St. Luke's community, it is natural to question whether results from such a small group of people are sufficiently valid. Those questioned were picked at random, but, with so few responses, it is difficult to say how significant the results actually are. Background literature indicates that a good number of first American-born generation Greeks were familiar with the language. Moskos contends that, "even though most second generation (same as first American-born generation) Greek-Americans were familiar with the Greek language, and many could speak it quite well, English became the language of American-born Greeks in their own homes as well as on the outside" (1980:92).

This statement supports the indications I received that second generation Greek-Americans who knew Greek learned it from other sources as well as their parents, such as trips to Greece and at Greek school. It was the general opinion of those with whom I spoke that the second generation did not have a significant competency in Greek and were therefore somewhat lost during the Liturgy of the Greek Orthodox service. However, the attendance in the children's classes at the language school run by the church is impressive. It appears that many of the third American-born generation Greek-Americans will have at least a rudimentary knowledge of Greek.

The topic of the use of English in the service was one I discussed in detail with many of the informants I interviewed. I began the subject by questioning them as to how they felt about the use of English in the service. Did they feel it was necessary? Was once-a-month a good balance? To illustrate the variation and nature of the responses, I have summarized the responses of several informants:

Female (first American-born generation, in forties, Greek is "atrocious"): The service should be conducted entirely in English every week. It doesn't do any good to have services in a language that no one can understand. Religion is terribly important in the family, and very few of the younger people understand Greek. The services should therefore be conducted in English.

Male (Greek immigrant, in sixties, Greek is first language): Services should all be in Greek. It is a Greek Orthodox Church, and the language should conform to the nationality of the services. If people wish to be Greek Orthodox, they should learn the language.

Female (first American-born generation, in forties, Greek is fluent): The once-a-month plan is a good balance. It doesn't do any good to go to services if no one understands what is going on. On the other hand, I don't like the fact that no one seems to follow the book anymore and try to understand the Liturgy. By having both languages, we can understand what is going on without letting completely go of the Orthodox language.

Female (first American-born generation, in fifties, Greek is fluent): You need English in the services for those who don't understand the Greek. The problem with both languages being used is that an interminable amount of time is spent making announcements in one language and then the other, and that is just silly. The service is long enough.

Female (second American-born generation, in twenties, Greek is fluent): The ratio of Greek and English in the service should be 50–50. Parts of the Liturgy simply do not translate well into English; they are much better left in their own language. On the other hand, the church is family oriented. It doesn't do any good if not all generations of the family understand what is going on.

It is evident from these excerpts that there is a significant range of variation in the responses.

In general, according to my impressions, it is interesting to note that, though members of the second American-born generation do not show considerable fluency in Greek, their children are well represented in the language school run by the church. There appears to be a concerted effort among Greek-Americans to preserve at least some aspects of their linguistic heritage.

The language question is still a sensitive issue, characterized by varying viewpoints. The priest explained that he must "gauge" his use of English and Greek on each occasion, depending on the backgrounds of those involved. For instance, during funerals or weddings, he must take into consideration the extent of the ethnic and religious identity as well as the language capabilities of the participating families.

There are those in the parish, specifically in the second American-born generation, who believe that the priest is too conservative on the language issue. Yet, he must listen to the protests of all groups, including the older "yaya's" of the parish. Most of the first American-born generation feel that the priest has done a laudable job of balancing the needs of the entire community. It will be very interesting as the years go by to see how many of the third generation learn Greek and how the balance of English and Greek in the church services evolves.

The Social Versus the Religious in Church Attendance

Gauging how much of a person's attention and thought are directed toward the religious aspect of church membership and how much are directed toward the social aspect is a virtual impossibility. Many Greek-Americans are uncomfortable with facing the question, and there is certainly no accurate way of measuring the importance of each aspect. However, it occurred to me early in participant observation that there was a social aspect of Greek Orthodoxy in this particular community that was strong enough to warrant attention. My intuition on this matter was borne out repeatedly over the first few weeks of participant observation.

I was told several times that there was a group of younger members of the church who felt that the Greek Orthodoxy of their parents was far too social in nature and that a return to the religion itself was in order. In *The Greek Affair*, an article written by the younger members of the community articulates the problem: "Many Greek-American young people feel that the church is far too 'social' and that a greater emphasis must be placed on spiritual activities. We want to ensure that ethnicity is not an impediment to Orthodox spirituality, and we want to learn how to truly experience a personal relationship with Christ" (Gregory 1984:65).

It is in the activities of the younger adult members of the church that we see an indication of the way it is heading. The Young Adult League (YAL) is a group of Greek-Americans, whose organization is founded on four principles of Orthodox Christianity: Liturgia, their relationship with God through worship and sacramental life; Martyria, witnessing of the faith; Kiakonia, service; and Koinonia, fellowship (1984:65). Ideally, these four principles are balanced evenly to provide a well-rounded organization. It has been noted that it is a little less than balanced these days and was characterized by one informant outside of the group as "Bible study" and little else. From within the group comes the argument that, with its present membership of seven, it is difficult to create a perfect balance of activities. From what I have seen and heard, the spirit of upholding all four principles appears to be genuine.

I asked informants how much of their church attendance they felt was "religious" in nature and how much was "social." It was a difficult question to answer (in great part the two issues are not separable) and one that required follow-ups to clarify the responses. A typical response I received to this question was that the informant felt that his or her church attendance was either "more religious" or "more social" than it had been at another time in his or her life. One woman gave a history of more or less religious times in her life that seemed to have less to do with Orthodoxy than with basic rites of passage in a person's lifetime. She noted that she went to church as a child because her parents took her with them; she did not think to rebel against them and refuse to go. When she left home to go to college, however, she stopped attending church because she saw no reason to do so. When she married, suddenly religion and ethnicity became important again for the sake of raising children. So she and her husband began going to church again and raised their children in the Greek Orthodox faith.

These data suggest a phenomenon having to do not with being Greek-American or Greek Orthodox so much as simply identifying with religion and ethnicity in different degrees during one's lifetime. Although this sort of situation might prove to be a key part of a discussion of Greek Orthodoxy and Greek-American ethnicity in its own right, I am more interested in the trends experienced by the church community as a group than by individuals. The stronger religious bent and attitudes I have observed among several of the younger informants are unusual in face of the attitudes of their elders and suggests a strong reaction of the younger against something of which they do not approve. The nature of their disapproval was articulated in the previous quote from *The Greek Affair*, as well as in a speech given on National Youth Sunday recently by a second American-born generation woman. She stressed that churchgoing at St. Luke's had become too social in nature and that a return to the religious was needed. This "social" nature is well known in the history of Greek-Americans. Saloutos states: "To some youths, the church was a building where their parents and other older people gathered on Sundays to extend their greeting and exchange gossip" (1964:318).

Indications of the highly social nature of Greek-American church attendance are evident from participant observation in the Sunday services. They are scheduled to begin at 10:00 a.m. If you enter the church at this hour, you can expect to be relatively alone for a good half an hour. Around 10:30 people start filtering in, lighting candles and exchanging greetings. By 11:00 the church is filled and the children are in Sunday school. The coffee hour held after services is well attended by the congregation. Clearly, church attendance offers social as well as religious value.

Not many informants were willing to admit that their reasons for going to church were more social than religious. All those who thought that their attendance had passed through more social or more religious periods in their lives believed that they were presently in their more religious phase! A defensive remark often heard was that the practice of Greek Orthodoxy in Greek villages was almost entirely social in nature but that Greek-Americans took a much more serious approach. Nevertheless, my conclusion on this subject is that there is a significant social aspect to Greek Orthodox church attendance. I think that this can largely be explained by the fact that the religion is also a primary expression of Greek-American ethnicity.

Rites of Passage: The Closing of the Old St. Luke's and the Opening of the New

The importance of the Greek Orthodox church in the lives of Greek-Americans in the western suburbs of Philadelphia is well illustrated by the attention and detail lavished on the building of their new church. Since its opening in September 1963, the Greek Orthodox Church of St. Luke had been temporarily housed in a building that had been designed as a gymnasium. Care was taken to transform the surroundings into an atmosphere befitting a church. A rich, red carpet blankets the floor of the main area of worship. Upon the walls hang a plethora of holy icon paintings. The altar is separated from the rest of the church by a screen, known as the *iconostasis*. During the Liturgy, the priest remains behind it, facing the spiritual world. Campbell and Sherrard note the importance of the building itself in Orthodoxy: "The church is regarded as a sacred space, the mirror of the Kingdom of God, or the House of God, and each architectural member has its place in a coordinated symbolic structure. Thus the sanctuary is the image of the spiritual world, of which the altar is the heart. It is separated from the main body of the church—the nave—by a screen or iconostasis—[which]

has a symbolic meaning, being regarded as the dividing line between two worlds, the divine and the human, or the spiritual and the sensible worlds" (1968:200).

The spiritual world behind the screen encloses the "mysteries," or sacraments, that are basic to Greek Othodoxy. The iconography is a central feature of the religion: "Matter and sensible existence may participate in the life of the spirit, they may be spirit bearing; and indeed the whole emphasis of Orthodox spirituality is on the transfiguration of human existence and all other created forms through this participation in divine life. Icons are regarded as testimonies to this process of transfiguration, for in them is felt to be present something of the deified reality of the prototypes—Christ, the Mother of God, angels and saints—that they represent and make visible" (1968:201). Although the old St. Luke's may have been located in a gymnasium, on a Sunday morning the lit candles, the smell of incense, the sounds of the changers (*psaltis*), and the iconography decorating the walls provided a richly aesthetic portrayal of Greek Orthodoxy.

In 1982 procedures to begin construction of a formal Greek Orthodox church in Broomall were set in motion. It was to be built in the Byzantine style, located on a lot adjoining the present church and Education Building. Along with the various activities associated with the architectural plans and fund-raising, ceremonies were held to bless the laying of the foundations of the new church and the placing of the first cornerstone. On February 24, 1985, a ceremony was conducted marking the official closing of the old church. The new one would be opened in a ceremony known as Thyranixia (The Opening of the Doors).

On March 17 the Thyranixia service was held. It began at about 10:00 a.m. with the reading of the blessing of the holy water. Holy water was sprinkled on the doors and some of the congregation standing outside. After the sanctification of the church and parish community, an unwritten tradition of bidding for the gold key to the church took place. By 10:30 a.m., it had gone to a bidder for $16,000. There were at this time an estimated 1,500 people standing outside the church, waiting to enter. The archbishop and priest, two other priests, and a candidate for the deaconate entered the church. The crowd followed, lighting candles. The choir sang the doxology as they entered the church. Many people had to stand at the back for lack of room.

The Liturgy was performed in Greek by the archbishop. Then the ordination ceremony took place. As the archbishop presented the deacon with each vestment, he asked the congregation to shout that the deacon was "worthy" of the vestment. After the ordination ceremony, the ceremony of the adoration of the Holy Cross took place. The Thyranixia service was then officially over. Later there was a banquet at the Mark Hotel, attended by 850 to 900 people.

The Thyranixia ceremony celebrated the creation of the new church in religious, social, and economic forms. The sprinkling of the holy water upon the doors and the parish standing outside served as a religious incorporation into the church. The golden key itself was symbolic as the means of entering the holy place, but the bidding for it had an economic function of raising money for the further beautification of the new church. The key also served as a status symbol for the highest bidder. The involvement of the whole community in some of the singing and in the responses also served to incorporate the audience into the new building because it served to make everyone present feel religiously and socially a part of the whole affair. The attendance of the archbishop added importance and prestige to the occasion, as well as a spiritual presence. In conclusion, the Thyranixia service and banquet served religious, social, and economic functions. They resulted in a drawing together of the local Greek-American community and a separation from other Greek-American communities.

Conclusion

I have examined major issues affecting the Greek Orthodox Church of St. Luke in order to obtain a concept of Greek-American ethnicity. Looking at the people who attend that church, I define them as an ethnic group at the most inclusive level based on the factors of church baptism, Greek descent, a field of communication and interaction in St. Luke's, and certain economic and geographic boundaries. The economic and geographic boundaries are important because they reflect a measure of success in the lives of the Greek-American families since their emigration to the United States. These boundaries also represent an aspect of the American side of the community's dual ethnicity. The Greek side of that dual ethnicity is strongly represented by the Greek Orthodox church. As an institution, it allows Greek-Americans broad-based opportunities to fulfill their personal religious, social, and ethnic needs.

Bennett defines the phenomenon of the "new ethnicity" as "the proclivity of people to seize on traditional cultural symbols as a definition of their own identity" (1975:3). This definition explains ethnicity as a matter of one's personal identity. In the Greek-

American community of St. Luke's there are a number of ways in which people maintain their ethnic and religious identity. The reasons *why* they maintain these identities are best explained by the fact that through varying degrees of involvement in the Greek-American community they are expressing their personal identities. Although the young are influenced to remain active in their ethnic and religious groups, it is eventually up to all individuals to decide for themselves how and in what ways it is important for them to define themselves as Greek-Americans.

In general, the Greek Orthodox Church is the main institution through which members of this community make this definition. They all have the option of maintaining the religion for themselves and their children through services and Sunday school; furthering the culture through language school and assorted church groups; and bolstering economic ties with other Greek-Americans and support of the new church. The church thus houses a well-rounded body of cultural, religious, and economic institutions that serve to allow Greek-Americans to subscribe to their own personal blends of ethnic heritage.

13

Es como si fuera la casa de uno
The Role of the Community Church in Maintaining Puerto Rican Ethnicity

Monica Schoch-Spana

After tracking down the address of La Milagrosa Chapel, I took the Highspeed line and subway to Spring Garden Street. Being as much of a participant observer on the sidewalk as I could, I scanned the faces of people who passed by me as well as the storefronts. I was looking for a Hispanic community. A "Farmacia" (pharmacy) sign was the one Hispanic element I found on my five-block walk to the church. The chapel itself was very small; in fact if I had not looked up once I arrived at the corner of 19th Street and noticed a statue of Mary, I would have passed it by.

> *"La capilla chiquita es tan grande!"*
> "The tiny chapel is so large!"
> —Aurea

> *"Hay amor en Milagrosa."*
> "There is love in Milagrosa."
> —Margarita

The warmth expressed by these two informants' remarks more appropriately captures the role of this church in the Hispanic community than the proposition that, in its ritual and its socioreligious functions, it provides a forum for the expression and maintenance of ethnic identity.

I began my fieldwork thinking that the church would be merely a means of meeting "community" members, from whom I could determine a focus. After attending my first Mass at Milagrosa, however, I was struck by a formula of ritual that did not exist in Anglo Catholic churches with which I was familiar. Early in my field notes I committed myself to sorting out "that which is Catholic from that which is Puerto Rican or Hispanic."

Transcending a mere trait list of Puerto Rican embellishments to "formal Liturgy," I hoped to see how the church served as a means of cultivating a sense of identity. In the sacred realm (ritual and symbol), it provides an arena for the regular display of a "style" of worship that has historical antecedents on the island of Puerto Rico and that reflects greater cultural themes. To best minister to the people, the Anglo priest at Milagrosa has attempted to enculturate himself in Puerto Rican values and facilitate worship that is customary to his congregation.

In addition to a form of worship that serves as a diacritic marker, the sacred realm calls people together. They pray in their mother tongue, and they share expectations of behavior. Comparing Masses they have attended among "Americans" to those at their own chapel, members of Milagrosa feel that the former are "empty" and "cold."

The church also serves to mobilize congregation members in the form of "cofradias" (religious organizations). These not only carry out ecclesiastical responsibilities, such as preparing Liturgies and checking up on the greater community's participation in church activities, but also act as an embodiment of a key cultural feature: the extended support network.

Although active participation in formal activities and adherence to mandates of the church do not characterize the overall form of Catholicism among Puerto Ricans, the church functions as a major mechanism in maintaining ethnic identity. I did not find "a community" at Milagrosa but instead discovered the process of identity that is community.

Sociocultural Background

"*Una tarde partí hacia extraña nación,*
"One afternoon I departed for a strange nation
Pues lo quiso el destino
Well then, destiny had chosen it
Pero mi corazón se quedó frente al mar
But my heart remained facing the sea

Es como si fuera la casa de uno   269

En mi viejo San Juan"
In my old San Juan"

—*En mi viejo San Juan*

"Puerto Rico is a beautiful place, but there is no work . . . so people come to the mainland. Many return, some stay, and others just move back and forth."
—Margarita, an informant

There is great traveling back and forth to Puerto Rico. According to my priest-informant, "They say the Puerto Rican population is divided in three: a third at the Island, a third in the mainland, and a third in motion between the two. The flux is constant." Klose (1985:9) remarks on this pattern of return migration, which is facilitated by unrestricted travel as a result of citizenship and relatively inexpensive air transport.

Christensen (1979:270–271) sketches two groups of Puerto Ricans who reside in the United States. The island-born Puerto Rican, who first established residence and brought up a family on the mainland, contrasts in many ways with the "Neo-Rican," a member of the second or third generation growing up in the urban environment and adapting to its demands. "Having been brought up in another climate, with another language, with different fears and aspirations," this second Puerto Rican is different from his or her parents' generation, though retaining "a strong influence from and linkage to a primarily Latin American setting." The pool of informants for this study, however, were all island-born and came to Philadelphia during the 1950s and 1960s.

Philadelphia's Puerto Rican population has been concentrated in an area north of the center city whose "boundaries" in 1965 were "Spring Garden Street on the south, Lehigh Street on the north, Front Street on the east, and Tenth Street to Wallace from Lehigh and 23rd Street to Spring Garden on the west" (Klose 1985:10). This community was composed of four neighborhoods. The one significant for this study is that known as the "Spring Garden area," which in 1979 included the region marked by "Spring Garden on the south, Fairmont Avenue on the north, Broad Street on the east, and 21st Street on the west" (1985:11). Although Spring Garden is characterized as a Puerto Rican neighborhood, it lies "outside *the* Puerto Rican community," which is composed of northern census tracts with the "heaviest concentration of Puerto Ricans" (1985:11).

A significant institution for the Spring Garden neighborhood and the city's greater Puerto Rican community is "La Capilla Hispana de Nuestra Señora de la Medalla Milagrosa." The priest now assigned to the church reports that, geographically, Milagrosa "used to be at the heart of the Puerto Rican community," which has since burgeoned northward.

This Catholic chapel was founded in 1912 by Vincentians from Barcelona, in response to the needs of Philadelphia's Hispanic population. It is referred to as the *cuna* (cradle) by the Hispanic community because it was the first Spanish-speaking church in the city. Many Puerto Ricans, since the time of their concentrated migrations to Philadelphia in the 1950s, have adopted the church as their own (Klose 1985:12; Koss 1965:91; field notes, November 1985).

During the mid-1970s, the present priest recounted, the administration of the chapel passed from the Spanish order to the Philadelphia archdiocese. The chapel now functions as an appendage of the cathedral and does not have parish status, employing only a part-time priest. It serves approximately 400 families in the immediate area, in addition to dedicated members who have moved away but still attend.

The church, the priest explained, consists of a variety of Hispanic groups, including Cubans, Argentinians, Colombians, people from the Dominican Republic, and Mexicans—though Puerto Ricans make up the majority of the parishioners. Puerto Ricans, the priest remarked, are the most geographically close "knit" community in comparison to the other dispersed Latin American groups. This process of insulation is facilitated by a sense of a Hispanic neighborhood: "The community created is self-sufficient. One need not leave the area for food, clothing, medical attention, or entertainment" (Klose 1985:11) because there are "bodegas" (grocery stores), bars, variety stores, and churches that cater to a Puerto Rican clientele (Koss 1965:86–93). According to one of my informants, several blocks from Milagrosa a city run clinic with Spanish-speaking personnel is operated.

The chapel not only plays a significant role in the community's religious life, but also its church hall participates in the social realm. The hall is the site of church-related activities such as missions and baptisms and weddings. Rented out at a low rate, the hall also provides a place for funerals held by those families who cannot afford other arrangements.

Recently, the hall has become a symbol for the neighborhood to rally around. In 1984–85 the hall, used exclusively by Puerto Ricans, was closed by a court order, solicited by Anglos within the neighborhood. Complaints related to parking problems, noise, and trash resulted in the closing. In February 1986 the church reopened the hall after challenging the decision. The hall will operate under conditions set for a probational year to prove the responsibility of the people who use it. The court victory has evoked community pride in that Hispanic needs are no longer subordinated to some of the racist Anglos who have entered the neighborhood through gentrification efforts (see Klose 1985).

Ethos

Leavitt (1974:46–48) proposes that out of the New World's Spanish heritage evolved a Latin American ethos. The emphasis on individuality, which derives from the Spanish Catholic's acknowledgment of a person's value due to his or her soul, is a very salient feature. Social interaction is governed by the principle of *respeto* (respect), which serves to preserve the *dignidad* (dignity) of the individual. Tied to this emphasis on the individual is the concept of *personalismo*, expressed through a network of interpersonal relationships maintained by reciprocity, the strongest of which are kin ties, both blood and ascribed.

A strong sense of responsibility to others is demonstrated by this account: "I remember when we were growing up, my mother would send us out into the neighborhood to help people. She told us 'Don't come home with any money!'" (Ramonita, an informant).

Compadrazgo, a socioreligious system operating throughout Latin America, "is an artificial kinship complex based on various Catholic rituals and the subsequently formed relationship between a child's parents and his godparents" (Clark 1979:133). Although godparents sponsor the child during the conferring of a sacrament, namely baptism, social and economic obligations are established between sets of co-parents. This institution serves to expand the support network of all the parties involved.

The norm of *respeto* implies responsibility in social interaction to demonstrate "consideration for the self-image" of others; the guideline "respect and be respected" manifests itself in deferential acts (Lauria 1972:38). This behavior or attitude is but one aspect of the complexity of Puerto Rican interaction, rather than a dominant theme of "standoffishness." "Impersonal relationships between human beings are anathema to Latin Americans" (Leavitt 1974:47); this accounts for their propensity to maintain a support network and cultivate *confianza*, an expression of "pure friendship, based on mutual understanding and appreciation, without the obligations of kinship, either real or fictive."

Puerto Rican culture is noted for its gregariousness: "Puerto Ricans love to talk, discuss, gossip, speculate, and relate. No one needs an excuse to have a fiesta. Music, food, and drink appear instantly if someone comes to visit. Group meetings, even those of the most serious nature often take on some aspect of a social activity" (Christensen 1979:270–271).

The concept of family is also central to the culture. According to Ramonita, an informant: "The Hispanic family is 'tighter' than the American family. We help each other out. I take in the laundry that my oldest son brings home, because I can help him out this way. . . . We have a rule; every child who goes to college must help the next one afford it also. . . . I feel sorry for American eighteen- or nineteen-year-olds who are packed up and out of the house and expected to make it on their own. No wonder kids never visit their parents in the rest homes. It's very sad." Children are loved and appreciated; a baby receives much attention when taken out in public (Christensen 1979:272).

Traditional male-female relations are governed by differential sex statuses and roles, as Stycos (1972:77–79) points out. A man proves his *machismo* by his virility, masculinity, and the respect of his peers. The female's role of *Marianismo* requires her to be submissive, modest, and chaste. "She is not expected to provide for the family—double standard places her firmly in the home as wife and mother . . ." (1972:79).

As the island of Puerto Rico undergoes a process of "Americanization" and as immigrants encounter mainstream culture on the mainland, a conflict of core values can occur. Migration disrupts extended family ties; personalistic values come into question during "the slow and steady substitution of impersonal norms, norms of the system rather than norms of personal relationships" (Fitzpatrick 1971:97). The premises of *machismo* and *Marianismo* are looked down upon. "Respect is gained through prosperity and material accomplishment" (Ghali 1979:232). The economic situation may require the woman to participate in the labor force. The value placed on "getting ahead," achieved through aggressiveness, in American culture, contrasts with "submissiveness, deference to others, and passivity [that] are encouraged as the ultimate in civilized behavior" (1979:233).

Puerto Rican Catholicism

The brand of Catholicism evolving on the island was characterized not only by ethos but also by a cultural theme of the *pueblo*,

as well as by varying degrees of "orthodoxy" and emphasis on organized activity. This last aspect was a consequence of the limited
incorporation of the majority into the formal church (Koss
1965:401) and of the greater de-emphasis on lay/clergy interaction.
Churches and their priests were concentrated in the towns, far from
scattered rural settlements. Because the clergy wielded significant
secular power and associated with the ruling elite, "the lower
classes, conspicuously isolated from the dominant groups, retained
the medieval Spanish cult of the virgin and the saints, mixed with
Indian and Negro beliefs in magic, and the majority attended church
only for a christening, a wedding, or a funeral" (Leavitt 1974:44).
Orthodoxy existed among the urban upper classes and syncretism
of Catholicism and folk beliefs and practices among the rural population (Koss 1965:400–401; Stevens-Arrogo 1974:119).

This historical Catholic/colonial legacy—including town
churches, great distances from rural communities, discrepancy between the concerns of the priests and the parishioners, and the existence of three pools or belief systems (Indian, African, and Spanish)
—helped shape a peculiar form of Catholicism on the island that
persists today: "One paradox in Puerto Rican culture is the disparity
between formal affiliation with the Roman Catholic church and
the meager concern for its dogmas. According to various estimates,
approximately 85% of the Puerto Rican community is Roman Catholic, but only 15% are sufficiently devout to follow church mandates and rituals with any regularity" (Deigado 1979:217).

Rather than conclude with "negative" allusions to the religiosity
of the Puerto Rican Catholics (in terms of North American standards), we can consider the system of Catholicism that characterizes
Puerto Rico and other Hispanic regions. Latin American Catholicism demonstrates potent community as well as personal dimensions. To be Catholic is not only to be associated with an institutionalized structure; it is an intrinsic part of identity: "Identity as
a Catholic was conceived mainly as identity with a community,
a *pueblo* which was Catholic, rather than in terms of personal responsibility as a member of the Church or parish" (Fitzpatrick
1971:50).

Religious practice demonstrates a significant degree of "personalismo," the pattern of close personal relationships characteristic of
Spanish cultures everywhere. "A person's spiritual life is intimately
tied to the Saints, Mary, or various manifestations of the Lord"
(1971:117). This reciprocal spiritual network manifests itself in
one's devotion to these sources of support: "He looks on these as
his compadres, his close friends. He prays to them, lights candles

to them, carries them in processions, builds shrines to them in his house, makes promises to them, and expects them to deliver the favors, help or protection he needs" (1971:117).

The style of Catholicism operating in Puerto Rico is a product of historical processes and is characterized by: (1) the prevailing theme of community; (2) de-emphasis on the organized church; (3) manifestations of ethos, particularly *personalismo*; and (4) syncretism with folk practices and spiritism. The "paradox" of Puerto Rican Catholicism appears as something of an etic evaluation, particularly when reading the following remarks made by an American priest on the island: " 'They may be Catholics by culture,' the priest said, but they were not 'Catholics by religion' as he knew it. 'I don't think they know what Catholicism is, or what Christianity is,' he said. 'They love God, but not the Church'" (Steiner 1974:471).

Fieldwork

The objective of my first trip into the Spring Garden area was to locate the church and familiarize myself with the neighborhood. Because I was there, I rang the rectory's doorbell and was greeted by the priest, an Anglo. So, I explained my interest in the parish and my focus on ethnicity. He was familiar with my purpose inasmuch as he had been contacted previously by a Bryn Mawr student/anthropologist. In my field notes after our first meetings, I remarked on the priest as an informant: "Advantages of having him as an informant include: 1) he has worked extensively and lived within Puerto Rican communities . . . 2) he has collected his own set of 'cultural' observances and seems very happy to share these; 3) because he has had to enter the community on his own, any anecdotes of 'socialization' may be valuable; 4) he can provide me with information about Puerto Rican 'deviations' from the standard church procedure; 5) he can act as a 'respectable' means of meeting people of the community." After our initial encounter, the priest was a valuable informant in subsequent interviews, during the fall 1985 and spring 1986 semesters, as well as a valuable means of meeting members of the parish.

In addition to interviews with the priest, my fall fieldwork activities included attendance at Sunday services and informal introductions facilitated by the priest after Mass to some members of the community. Besides these interviews of ancillary and key informants, my fieldwork included regular attendance at Mass on Sundays, Holy Days, and some weekdays, as well as participation in the closing services of the Lenten Mission, held at St. Edward's parish. Approximately twenty Puerto Rican delegations from parishes in the metropolitan and surrounding areas attended this event.

The techniques I relied on most heavily were the traditional participant observation and informant interviews. As my data will show, my foci of concern were the ritual realm and the sociostructural realm of the church, so that my main techniques accommodated these two emphases.

The Mass was important for me in two respects. First, as I once commented in my field notes, "I think regular attendance at Mass insures that I am a familiar face"; people I had already met would hopefully notice my continued presence and interest, and those I had not met would wonder why I had suddenly taken up the habit of attending their services. I was concerned with maintaining acceptability and a certain level of curiosity. Second, the details about ritual behavior that I derived from my regular attendance at Mass were a major source of data.

Identifying the Mass as the primary social situation (Spradley 1980:39) with which I was concerned, I became a participant observer sensitive to the place, actors, and activities associated with the ritual. My field notes reflect collection of these three basic areas of data. The church service provided an ideal arena for participant observation: it was accessible and a free-entry situation, for which I did not need permission to participate; it occurred regularly so that I could cross-check my observations and construct a pattern; I speak Spanish and am familiar with Catholicism so that I was able to participate, thus reducing the degree of my obtrusiveness (Spradley 1980:46–52). These same characteristics were true for the Lenten Mission.

A Composite: Mass and Socioreligious Activity

Walking down Spring Garden early Sunday morning, one is struck by the lack of cars and street noise that characterize the center city at any other time. After arriving at the corner of Spring Garden and 19th, one only has to pass the first apartment section on this block of row houses to look up and see a three-foot statue—with chipping blue paint—of the Virgin Mary. This statue and the glass with gold lettering that reads "La Capilla Hispana de Nuestra Señora de la Medalla Milagrosa" over the heavy wooden doors are the only two indications of the existence of a church, which resembles a house.

Climbing the concrete steps that lead to the chapel, one enters through the first set of doors. To the right is a bulletin board. Tacked to it is a copy of the Sunday church bulletin, which gives the theme of the day's sermon; a list of Masses and on whose behalf they are being said; the amount of last week's collection; special announcements such as the youth group's next meeting); and a request for prayers on behalf of the sick and the recently deceased.

In addition to church news, there is an announcement of the amount of blood donated during the recent parish drive. This notice hangs next to an invitation to attend a photo-essay exhibit on Puerto Rican diaspora, held at the *Galería del Taller Puertoriqeña* (Gallery of the Puerto Rican Artisan Workshop) in northern Philadelphia. A woman enters through the first wooden doors, passing by the wooden crucifix to the left of the foyer. She gently touches the foot and nail and then brings her hand to her forehead, completing the sign of the cross. Leaving the vestibule, she dips her fingers in the font of holy water, crossing herself once again.

Walking down the middle aisle, one chooses a seat in one of the eight pews on either side of the church. Three smaller ones are tucked away at both sides as well, those on the right situated next to an unused organ. Commemorative relief sculptures of the stations of the cross line the sides of the church. Statues of Mary in her various manifestations are positioned throughout the church, each image holding special meaning for the variety of Hispanic nationalities: Our Lady of Providence for Puerto Rico, Our Lady of Guadalupe for Mexico, for example. The flags of these countries and others surround the base of the statue of the chapel's patroness —Our Lady of the Miraculous Medal—which is to the right of the altar. Metal frames holding votive candles stand in front of this image. To the left of the metal frames is a small wooden box for donations: a dollar for the large candles and fifty cents for the small. Large votive candles also stand before a statue of Jesus that is located to the left of the altar.

The woman I had observed entering the church, who has knelt in the middle of the rail for a minute or so, moves to the right, beneath the chapel's patroness statue. She removes a small change purse, takes out a dollar, and slides it into the donation box. She makes the sign of the cross from forehead to heart and shoulder to shoulder, bringing her thumb and fist to her lips. After a few minutes, she then moves to the statue of Jesus on the left side, kneeling once again. After completing her devotional prayer, she takes a seat in one of the pews. A friend of hers, who has entered the church, walks up to greet her friend with a smile, first clasping her hand and then giving her a kiss on the cheek.

The second woman is dressed in a white skirt and blouse; around her neck is a red ribbon holding a medal with the image of the Sacred Heart of Jesus. Leaving her friend, this woman walks behind the altar to return with two vases holding red and white carnations. Removing the two candles that stand at the side of the statue of Jesus, she places the vases. A third woman appears from behind the altar carrying a box and a stack of papers, each sheet covered in plastic. Out of the box she takes four bows made of red and white ribbon, each bearing gold-glitter letters that read "Sacred Heart of Jesus Society." She hangs one on the inside of the first four pews on the left. She distributes the papers by placing a stock of them in each of the four rows. The two women retreat behind the altar.

More people arrive. Some of them genuflect immediately after passing through the doors or quickly do so as they reach their pew. Most of these individuals go up to the front rail to pray. A woman has taken out her rosary beads, as have others throughout the church. The red and white uniform appears again as more women begin to gather at the front pews reserved by the ribbons, kneeling down to pray after exchanges of greeting.

As 9:00 a.m. nears, a woman's voice, sharp and confident, begins the series of prayers that constitute the Rosary. Guiding the congregation and announcing the "mystery" (the particular New Testament scenario associated with that segment of the rosary), she leads the prayer. The parishioners, also with clear and positive voices, respond with the second, or response, portion of the prayer (Hail Mary, Lord's Prayer) introduced by the woman.

As the time for Mass draws nearer, the women in uniform move to the back of the altar, gradually disappearing. A few minutes later, a song, led by a member of the group and sung by the congregation, begins, and the procession starts to form as the members of the Sacred Heart Society file out from behind the sacristy, walking in not-so-perfect pairs down the left-side aisle and up through the middle. A member carrying a 1½-life-size image of Jesus with the Sacred Heart leads them; as she goes up to the altar to place it, the members fill up the reserved pews. Although the general pattern is from front to back, some of them choose other seats. Two of the members of the sodality follow the priest to the altar, where they stand next to their seats, waiting for him to deliver the initial rites. The song finishes as the priest takes his position behind the altar.

He wishes the congregation a good morning, and everyone responds with a warm *"buenos días, Padre."* He then recites the salutation of *en el nombre del Padre, y del Hijo, y del Espíritu Santo;* the parishioners make the sign of the cross. All of them, except for the handful of "Americans" who are present, complete this sign by drawing their thumb and fist to their lips.

After the initial prayers, parishioners and priest retire to their seats as the readings from Scripture begin—in Spanish. One lector comes forward to the microphone to deliver the first readings; she concludes with "Brothers and sisters, this is the word of the Lord," to which the congregation responds: "We praise the Lord." The same woman delivers the reading of the Psalms, followed by the second lectorat. Once the two readings are completed, the priest walks to the microphone to present the gospel, the high point of this portion of the Mass.

While he reads, a woman enters the church through the front wooden doors, making her way to the front rail, where she kneels. The priest continues with the gospel, never noticing the late arrival, who is only eight feet from the podium. After a few minutes, the woman rises, moving to that portion of the rail facing Our Lady of the Miraculous Medal, and she kneels to pray. Nearing the end of the gospel, the priest encounters a word difficult to pronounce; he stumbles over it several times and members of the congregation begin to chuckle. Completing the reading, he waits at the microphone as the congregation sits down so that he may begin the sermon.

Hands resting on the Bible that is opened across the lectern, the priest starts to preach. He refers to the Scripture that recounts Jesus's confrontation with Satan in the desert. The woman who has been praying at the base of the patroness statue gets up and goes to the front pew on the right to sit while the delivery of the homily continues. The priest challenges the parishioners to confront the troubles that they have in life. He says that parents who try to break up a daughter's serious relationship with the wrong boy, by packing her off to Puerto Rico, are avoiding the root of the problem. He urges more communication and understanding between parents and children and a different way of dealing with adolescents' sexuality. He recounts the time that a daughter was sent back to Puerto Rico by her parents to live with relatives to cool off her relationship with a boyfriend. The young man, however, followed her to the island, estranging the girl even further from her parents. As the priest tries to communicate his message, he walks to the middle of the sacristy and closer to the parishioners. His animated style is marked by a variety of inflection and much gesticulating. Upon finishing, he returns to the microphone to lead the profession of faith.

Following this prayer, one of the lectors returns to the podium to deliver a series of petitions, beginning with the needs of church and political officials and ending with the needs of the congregation members: for the sick . . . Ramona Guevera, José Luis Santiago . . . for the recently deceased, Don Gregorio Fontánez . . . Two men leave their pew seats to find the wooden-handled collection baskets, and several members of the Sacred Heart Society go to the back of the church to participate in the offertory procession, at which time the wine, water, and host are brought to the priest. A woman's loud and clear voice leads a song that is accompanied only by the congregation.

In the silence immediately preceding the hymn, the clinking sound of change can be heard as everyone prepares to drop an offering into the baskets. The monetary offertory gifts are presented, and the ushers file down the aisles collecting money: everyone drops in something. An older women, modestly dressed, takes out her coin purse and removes a dollar bill to offer. An adolescent girl rummages in her pockets to find some change; a mother puts some coins into the hands of her young daughter, who eagerly drops it into the basket as it comes by, while the mother drops in a bill herself. After passing the baskets through each of the pews, the ushers deposit the money in the main collection basket. A woman who is about sixty years of age leaves her seat and walks up the middle aisle to where the two ushers stand. With the voice of the priest in the background as he blesses the offertory gifts, the woman hands the usher a dollar bill, smiles, and returns to her seat.

The priest proceeds with the consecration of the host. The congregation kneels except for one woman who continues standing, as she will for the remainder of the Mass. When the priest recites the same words used by Jesus at the Last Supper and when the altar boy sounds a bell at their conclusion, a woman lowers her head and says a small personal prayer as a means of preparing herself to receive Communion—to receive *El Señor*, (the Lord) in her heart, because "It is our Catholic faith" (field notes: informant). After the consecration of the host, the people rise and stand as they prepare to recite the Lord's Prayer.

Following this prayer, the priest recalls that Jesus gave his apostles a blessing of peace. The priest then invites the congregation to share in a demonstration of peace. At that, he descends from the altar and sacristy to circulate through the church shaking hands and kissing the cheeks of the women closest to the edge of the pews. The congregation has begun to sing in enthusiastic voices "La Paz Esté con Nosotros" ("The Peace Be with All of Us") or at other Masses "Dame la Mano" ("Give Me Your Hand"). The congregation breaks out into song, clasping of hands, and an exchange of kisses. People reach as far down their pews as they can, so as to wish everyone "peace." Although the middle aisle divides the church, women and men wave their hands, which are in the shape of a "peace sign," and smile to those on the other side. As the song draws to a close and the priest is only through half of the main aisle, as he slowly makes his way back to the altar, the nun, who works within the community, leads the congregation singing the "Lamb of God" verse so as to continue the Liturgy. She has jokingly chastised the priest in the past for getting so carried away with this portion of the Mass (field notes: informant).

The priest concludes with the series of prayers that immediately precede the distribution of the Communion. Taking the chalice, he is joined by the nun, as the two move to the split in the front rail to offer the congregation hosts. As the members of the Sacred Heart Society file out of their pews, one of them starts a song with members of the congregation joining in. A woman who has just received the host does not return to her pew but kneels in front of the statue of Mary, where she will remain until everyone has received communion and the church announcements are made. The majority return to their pews to kneel, and the priest retreats to the altar. After preparing the chalice and other instruments for storage he returns to his seat and joins the congregation in a moment of silence.

He then walks up to the microphone to give announcements. He thanks the community for their donation of blood. Reading out the sum of last week's collection, he expresses sincere gratitude for their generosity. His Spanish is only broken by his announcement, in English, that the youth group will meet next Monday night. Returning to Spanish, he states that today is the birthday of José Navarro and Luz Sanchez; after he congratulates them, the congregation responds with applause. During the concluding prayers, he invites the congregation to join in a devotional "Hail Mary" to the chapel's patroness. As the priest and altar boys prepare to leave, the members of the Sacred Heart Society lead the congregation in a recessional hymn.

The altar boys and priest pass up the middle aisle, out the front door, and down the steps. One of the boys carries a stack of church bulletins, handing them out as the building empties. The members of the Sacred Heart Society remain in their pews as the rest of the congregation slowly move toward the door. A crowd begins to form in the foyer of the church. While people slowly move by the fonts of holy water, anonymous hands poke through in eager attempts to make the sign of the cross with the water. Other hands reach for the large wooden crucifix that is located just before the main entrance. Two women touch the nails and foot and then make the sign of the cross. After touching the painted blood at the site of the nail, a woman draws her fingers to her lips. A man's hand also goes from the nail to his forehead as he completes a sign of the cross just before putting on his hat.

The priest waits at the bottom of the steps greeting people as they come down with a handshake or a kiss. Smiling and joking with those who come to see him, he inquires about work, the family, or life in general. Small groups of people have formed on the sidewalk. Laughter and conversational noise fill the air outside the chapel, while inside one hears the low prayers of those who have gone to the front rail to pray. Some of them have purchased votive candles to either Jesus or Mary. The number of flames burning, however, is greatest in front of the patroness statue.

After finishing the recessional song, members of the Sacred Heart Society prepare to attend their meeting, which takes place immediately following the Mass. Someone picks up the papers, another removes and stores the ribbons, and the red and white flowers hanging at the side of the statue of Jesus are taken down. Most of the group walk behind the altar and through the vestment room to descend a narrow set of stairs leading to the lower half of the building, which contains the meeting room and the priest's office.

Inside the crowded meeting room stand five tables. The front collapsible one holds a wooden lectern and a statue of Jesus with the Sacred Heart surrounded by an artificial flower arrangement. Parallel to this table at the back of the room stands another one holding the food supplies for the meeting: a coffee machine; pitchers of coffee, milk, and orange juice; bread; and butter. Three other tables are set in the middle of the room, each surrounded by folding chairs and covered with place settings. Some members take their slots at these tables while others help prepare the modest breakfast.

At the direction of the president, the members stand and recite a series of prayers to begin the meeting ("Our Father, Hail Mary, Glory Be . . ."). Sitting down once again, members strike up conversations, punctuated with laughter, and several women begin to circulate through the room offering coffee and juice as well as placing plates of buttered bread on the tables. No formal business is addressed for several minutes until the president rings a bell, calling for everyone's attention to roll call. The secretary, in a quiet voice, goes down the list; some women jokingly answer, others just respond with a simple "I'm here." When a voice does not answer, someone offers an explanation or a speculation as to the member's absence. Throughout the roll call, the heavy flow of conversation continues.

The priest comes into the room, greeting the women at the back, and then takes a seat at one of the tables. He has just returned from his office, where he had spoken with a young couple about baptizing their baby. He had noticed these new faces since they had first appeared in church about a month ago. He arranged a time with them for instruction on the responsibilities of parents and godparents of the child. The priest hopes that the parents will continue to participate in the church, but is afraid they may be *Católicos de boca* (Catholics by word alone). The priest remembers another couple who had recently approached him, asking for holy water so that they might have a customary baptism at home (*echar agua*), at which time the godparents sprinkle water on the baby. In the past, he tried to discourage this but soon gave up his efforts to a "tradition that has been going on so long" (field notes: informant).

Leaving his "dogmatic responsibilities" in his office, he joins the Sacred Heart Society's meeting and breakfast. He goes to the front, standing at the side of the president, who announces that the priest would like to "have a word" with them. The priest approaches the podium, says "Hola!" (Hello) and then steps back. The room bursts out in laughter. After his joke has taken its full effect, he continues by thanking the group for their marvelous organization of the procession on the evening of Holy Friday. While the priest moves to take his seat, the president also contributes her praise for the members who helped stage this walk from the church through the neighborhood and the Mass, held in the church hall.

Following these few minutes of "business," the members return to increased socializing, as the level of conversational noise steadily rises. A woman with a brown paper bag and a roll of red tickets circulates through the room selling chances for the *rifa* (raffle) at a dollar a ticket. The winner from last month's drawing provides the door prize. By buying a ticket, each member pays her membership dues. Once the purchases are completed, a child of one of the members picks the winning number and reads it aloud. The talking subsides for a moment as everyone looks around for the winner, but the pause becomes too long and members turn their attention to their conversations. The winner announces herself and receives her prize, something practical for her home.

Ringing the bell again, the president tries to attract everyone's attention; concluding that the minimal drop in noise is enough for her to proceed, she begins to speak. She announces that, because the membership of the Sacred Heart Society and the Rosarianas (Rosary Circle) overlap, the latter group, a smaller one, should be formally recognized because of her concern about the unequal distribution of women in both groups. She suggests that this "subgroup" have one uniform to designate its dual membership, so that its members need not worry about maintaining two uniforms. The Rosarianas wear a white blouse and a black or navy skirt, as well as a black ribbon with a medal. The group consensus about the proposal is positive, and the members within the two groups identify themselves. The formal agenda disappears once again as socializing recurs.

A woman with a styrofoam cup goes around the room collecting fifty cents from each member to help subsidize the group's next breakfast. People finish eating and the meeting appears to come to an end. One by one, members prepare to leave, but the president remarks that it is not time to leave. The secretary announces several times that they need a volunteer to bring the orange juice for the next meeting. Another officer announces that the group is preparing a basket of household items to be raffled off on Mother's Day: each member is responsible for contributing "something useful for the home" and for selling tickets. Chairs are pushed in; several women with trash bags go around picking up the used place settings. The president announces once again that it is not time to leave, though several members have already begun to depart. General business slowly concludes and the room stands clean, ready to be used for catechism class during the week.

Dominant Themes in Ritual Activity at Milagrosa

Now, after providing the reader with a description of a "typical" Mass at Milagrosa, I would like to address the process by which an ethnic group claims a generic Liturgy. I will address this focus on the "personalization" of a symbolic system by discussing what themes characterize Puerto Rican activities in the sacred realm.

From my observation, I first propose that a theme dominating the participation of congregation members is the primacy of the informality over a structured ritual behavior. Adhering to the script, the rules of the Mass, is a secondary consideration. Formality acquiesces to the participants. Several instances suggest this emphasis. The sign of peace is a particularly rich moment for Milagrosa. In an interview, however, the priest told me that the scale of this portion of Mass at Milagrosa is "liturgically incorrect."

This element, occurring on a regular basis, is complemented by isolated occurrences that reinforce the idea of the flexible Mass, subject to departures from formal proceedings. In the composite Mass, described earlier, we found that one woman arrived late and went to the front of the rail for devotional prayer, although she "interrupted" the gospel and homily. The Mass format dictates that she should join members of the congregation, who were seated at their pews. After receiving the host, a woman knelt at the front rail, beneath the patroness statue, while the congregation retires to the pews. At another Mass, a woman knelt during the entire service, neither sitting nor standing in time with the rest of the congregation.

One can also recall from the composite Mass that a woman left her pew to give her dollar donation to the ushers once the priest had begun blessing the offertory gifts. Another example is the time (related to me by the priest) that a child left his pew to join the priest at the altar for the remainder of the Mass. No "embarrassed" mother or "distracted" parishioner moved him. One of the more outstanding occurrences "out of sync" with the formal proceedings was the time an intoxicated young man wandered into the church during the reading of the scriptures and sat with members of the *Hijas de Maria* (Daughters of Mary) in the first two rows. He later went to the rail, knelt down for a while, made an exaggerated signing of the cross (in typical Hispanic fashion), and then wandered to the back. Later returning to the front, he spoke loudly, sat down once more, and then left abruptly. The response of the congregation to him included a woman close to me shaking her head, though most of the people did an incredible job of ignoring him, and a girl in the *Hijas de Maria* trying to "contain" his behavior by showing him a Mass book.

I later recounted the event to two of my informants and asked what they thought of such behavior. One woman said that she remembered the time and explained that no one acted against him because *whoever* comes to the church (particularly someone with his problems) needs to be there: "Why should they throw him out?" Another woman concurred with this attitude, saying that the church is open to all and "it is wonderful if people such as the drunk would even think of coming to the church." This second informant also recalled that at one procession, she saw an intoxicated man join in—she knew him and understood the cause of his drinking. She worried, however, if he would be a distraction. She was pleased, then, when he sat down without "a scandal."

I believe that the acceptance of the drunk as well as deviations from ritual protocol indicate more than Christian tolerance. Rather, the style of Mass suggests that the governing directives are subordinated to the expressive/worship needs of the collective. This is not to suggest, however, that disregard for the liturgical structure exists. There is concern for the flow of events. At one Mass, the priest had delivered the homily and proceeded with prayers for preparation of the offertory gifts—but someone had forgotten to bring up the water and wine. The error was eventually noticed. Rather than having someone at the back bring up the glass containers, which would have been the most expedient method, two members of the Sacred Heart Society went to the back and brought them up. Their role was not denied.

I believe that the style which elevates the needs of the individual participants over rigid directives derives from the "comfortableness" that Milagrosa provides. The implicit feeling of "community" of family contributes to the relaxed style of ritual behavior. This atmosphere of Milagrosa will be discussed later.

In addition to this implicit feeling of community are those times the typical Mass provides for a celebration of the lives of its members. One sees in the composite Mass the announcement of birthdays. At another Mass, a couple who had been married twenty-four years joined the priest at the front of the altar to receive a blessing. After the benediction, a yell came from the congregation for the two to kiss. After they did so, the priest congratulated them with embraces, and the parishioners gave them a round of applause. At another Mass, which the Sacred Heart Society members had prepared, a new member was initiated. Just before the recessional, the woman and a sponsoring member of the group joined the priest in the sacristy. He blessed the medal and put the red ribbon on the woman. The woman who accompanied her then gave her an embrace and kisses of congratulations.

In addition to this theme of community and the concomitant primacy of individuals in the ritual, I believe that the element of "personalismo" also manifests itself at Milagrosa. The demonstration of a high degree of devotion is recognizably Puerto Rican/Hispanic in nature. Whether or not a person subscribes to this manner of worship, however, is not as significant as the fact that public demonstrations preserve a style of worship at Milagrosa. The importance of one's spiritual network with the saints, the Lord, and most importantly, Mary, varies from person to person. For example, one informant, in discussing "superstition" among Puerto Rican Catholics, said that someone may pray to a particular saint saying, "If you grant me X, I will light three candles in church." This woman, who teaches catechism class and is a little "dogmatic," states that she tells people that it is not the saint granting the favor but God, through that saint.

The most recurring expression of commitment to one's spiritual network is the lighting of votive candles, with the greatest attention to Mary. When I mentioned to two of my informants that I had noticed the purchase of candles before and after Mass, one responded: "Es costumbre" ("It's just customary"); and another attached no particular significance to the activity "for a person just lights candles; it is a personal decision." According to my notes, however, there is a definite trend toward the purchase of more candles at the patroness statue and more saying of prayers at this portion of the rail. Perhaps at the completion of a private promise for a favor granted, one member of the Holy Name Society purchased five one-dollar votive candles at the patroness statue before a Mass.

Trying to discover how one informant perceived her spiritual network, I asked if she had a favorite saint and she responded "No," but that she was very committed to Mary. I feel that this devotion to Mary is the most frequently expressed publicly within Milagrosa. Five different images/manifestations of Mary adorn this small church, which has only twenty-two pews; each Hispanic group has its particular patroness displayed. At an archdiocese-sponsored mission, attended by twenty Puerto Rican delegations, from a variety of parishes, a large picture of Mary (2½' X 4') draped in a blue cloth and surrounded by greenery, adorned the sacristy.

The importance of the Rosary to Milagrosa best exemplifies this commitment to Mary. A congregational recitation of the Rosary precedes *every* service; it is usually led by a member of the "Rosarianas" (Rosary Circle) or another of *las doñas*, the committed women who attend Mass everyday. This organizational activity also supplements the personal recitations occurring before, during, and after Mass. One woman next to me took out her rosary beads and began to recite the prayers, throughout the reading of the Scripture. In addition to the recitation of the Rosary with every Mass, special activities occur during May, the month of Mary. An informant said that, on each Monday within this month, a street procession leading into the church occurs; participants may carry flowers and recite the Rosary. In addition to these public, church-related Rosaries, this devotional prayer has extreme importance for worship in the homes of parishioners.

Worship at Milagrosa, then, is characterized by the theme of community and by expressions of "personalismo," most recurrent in adoration of Mary. Another aspect that I feel distinguishes ritual behavior at the church is "stylistics": knowledge of and participation in a manner of doing things. In one interview, the Anglo priest said that, when he had first served a Puerto Rican congregation, he had been leading the Rosary and was stopped and instructed in the "correct" way to say it. He led by introducing the first verse of the prayer, to which the congregation should respond with the second. He learned that one should alternate this pattern at each set of "Hail Mary's" and use the password "Gloria Santa Maria" to indicate the place of the congregation. He soon became familiar with the "inverted" delivery of the "Hail Mary," as well as the other "embellishments" (added phrases and prayers) to the "formal" prayer he had learned.

In addition to this unique form of the Rosary, characteristics of ritual behavior at Milagrosa that were significantly different from my own Catholic experiences include the following. Members make the sign of the cross and end by putting the hand (thumb forward) to the lips—a form used by some of my friends at home who are Mexican-American. One woman praying the Rosary at the front rail began by making a sign of the cross and then touched the crucifix (of the rosary set) to her forehead, making small crosses there as well as at her lips and heart. She concluded by crossing herself once again and began the Rosary. This repeated crossing also occurred during Holy Week services, when the priest swung burning myrrh and sprinkled holy water on the congregation. Members responded by a series of crossing themselves.

Differential "potency" of symbols complements these mechanical considerations in my discussion of dominant themes in a Hispanic style of worship. Fernandez (1965:911) suggests that "symbols which are elaborately expressive for some, conjuring up conceptions basic to the cult world-view, are simple *situation referential* for others"; symbols with a depth of meaning for one person may be just "ritual paraphernalia" for another. The statues at Milagrosa have greater meaning for participants than the same images at Anglo parishes with which I am familiar.

In the composite Mass, one sees the veneration of the crucifix at the front door; upon entering the church, a man once kissed the nails and blood-covered feet of the wooden image. At Good Friday services, a wooden bust of Jesus bearing a crown of thorns was placed at the front rail. I saw one woman touch the shoulder of the bust and then cross herself two times with the same hand. Two other women did the same, crossing themselves only once. The priest says that he has entered the church when the women have been cleaning and found one of them kissing the various statues.

Ritual activity at Milagrosa is marked, then, by the degree of veneration for representations of Catholic "deities," demonstrations of commitment to a spiritual network (particularly in adoration of Mary), and the sense of community "comfortableness" that tolerates idiosyncratic forms of worship.

"Es como si fuera la casa de uno"

This attitude toward the chapel was expressed to me again and again in conversations with my informants. In response to the question, if she had to move away from Milagrosa and attend Mass at which she was the only Hispanic, Margarita lamented, "I would feel very sad and alone." She called Milagrosa "el corazón de los Hispanos" ("the heart of the Hispanics"); she feels that there is more love within the Hispanic church than within the "American" church. Although she has attended other churches, it is at Milagrosa that she feels "most comfortable . . . as if it were the *house* of someone."

Margarita recounted that people who have moved away from the Spring Garden area and into other parishes still return to Milagrosa for Mass; people have mentioned to her that other Masses are *vacia* (empty). They come back to Milagrosa because *tiene algo* ("it has something"). Margarita feels Hispanic congregations offer a warmth and openness not found in other churches, particularly "American." Bringing up the sign of peace, she said that Hispanics offer their hands with much warmth. She feels a distinct lack of this when she has encountered *Americanos* in church services. They do not offer a "sincere" expression of peace.

Ramonita also expressed a similar sentiment: "Americans are so cold." She encounters a number of them at St. Francis parish, her own, a few blocks from Milagrosa: some are warm and sincere but others are "stuck up." The same "coldness" exists at a church she attends in the center city where "people wear their mink coats and diamonds." The worst crowd, however, she remarked, is at the cathedral. At Milagrosa it is *tremendously* different; in fact, she contended: "They go a bit overboard; going from corner to corner and all over the church. Even the priest goes up and down the aisles kissing everybody."

The Anglo Priest Becomes Padre Muñez

The priest's fervor during the sign of peace was commented upon by his colleague Sra. Josephine, who also works with the Spring Garden community. She believes that he gets "a little carried away." The Anglo priest has undergone a process of enculturation in his attempts to minister to Milagrosa in the most appropriate fashion. He has recounted to me his own learning process. To the members of Milagrosa, according to informant Aurea, *el es número uno* ("he is number one"); he is the best priest that they have had at the chapel. His sensitivity to expressions of culture has, in fact, accorded him an honorary Hispanic status, as some anecdotes of informants suggest.

Upon joining Milagrosa, the priest was readily and enthusiastically incorporated into the community, he feels, by virtue of his being the "padre." To the community, the "padre" is a respected and loved personality. He feels that "a priest could rob them blind and the community *would still* hold him in esteem, not saying anything bad of him." The congregation is very protective of their priest, and he knows that wearing the collar in the street assures his ability to move safely throughout the neighborhood.

Although he has capitalized on the value placed on his position by the community, he has had to readjust his "Anglo" training as a priest and discover how to appeal to and understand his congregation. As a seminarian first serving at a Puerto Rican church, he was "instructed" in the Rosary most familiar to the participants, as previously mentioned. His style of preaching has been modified to a delivery characterized by gestures, forceful and pointed words, and phrases familiar to the congregation. The ability to preach is highly respected, remarked my informant; the standards are set by "hermanocheos." These are not laymen, but professional preachers who serve a revivalist function. A "mission" from Puerto Rico with these laymen had come to Milagrosa in the fall of 1985.

The priest attempts to pick up key phrases that serve to move the people while delivering a homily. He watches the response of the congregation and can sense when he is giving an "Anglo" sermon. Jokes are one means he uses to gain rapport with the congregation, but he recalls the "flopping" of Anglo jokes as well as his own "misdelivery" of Hispanic ones.

In addition to learning modified prayer forms and adopting an animated and articulate preaching style, the priest has redefined "block visits." His job description, prescribed by the archdiocese, includes dropping in on members of the community. Within an Anglo parish, a priest can accomplish a "block" pattern of visitation. This methodical way, however, is inappropriate within the Puerto Rican community. The priest said that, when he first made "block visits," many people wondered why he would "just show up." Visits from the priest play a very important social role; they do not serve as merely "a spiritual checkup." Members who know him well expect more than a "visit"; often a meal is involved. The "quick chit-chat visit from the priest might work in an Anglo community but is almost insulting within the Hispanic community." He is under pressure, however, from the diocese, which demonstrates a quota mentality.

My informant Luisa recognizes the cultural sensitivity displayed by the priest. She thinks that he not only tries to understand the customs of Hispanics, but also helps to facilitate their traditions. The priest, as mentioned before, is approached by people wanting holy water for "home baptisms" by godparents; although he tried to discourage the practice, he eventually gave in to its historical and contemporary significance for his parishioners.

Laughing a great deal, informant Ramonita recounted some anecdotes of the priest's attempts to master Spanish appropriate to the community of Milagrosa. He may pick up an expression in conversation familiar to people from a particular region and later use it while at the altar—"that is why some of the older people will smile upon their hearing of it." Ramonita also recalled times in which her priest has used expressions with a double meaning unknown to him while speaking to the people during Mass. After she has pointed out some of his gravest errors, the two of them have laughed about it together.

The priest's attempts to accommodate the needs of his community and adopt a personal Hispanic life-style may be dangerous for him, Ramonita suggested. She referred to his propensity to please his hostess by "eating greasy or questionable food that even she cannot eat." Aurea also attested to his gratitude for hospitality shown to him through traditional food; "After eating a home-cooked meal, he never complains if he happens to get sick."

When questioned about an Anglo priest serving in a Hispanic

community, informants Tomasita and Aurea responded: "He is practically one of us!" Aurea commented upon his trustworthiness, his openness, and his commitment to the church. She used the word *dulce* (sweet) to describe his character; his deep concern for the members of the church manifests itself in the "times he has cried over young people in trouble."

In addition to the internal community bonding that Milagrosa facilitates, the chapel also cultivates a feeling of "continuity" with the island of Puerto Rico. By its sponsorship of "missions" from there, for example, the church promotes a sense of Puerto Rican nationalism. At the archdioceses mission that I attended, the agenda included a Rosary, a sermon from an *hermanocheo*, and a Mass. The services concluded with a waving of the Puerto Rican flag while the entire congregation sang "En mi viejo San Juan." By its contribution to preserving continuity with the island, by its public and sacred arena for expression, and by its capacity to mobilize a community support network, the church contributes to the maintenance of a Puerto Rican identity. Milagrosa's role in the Hispanic community is so rich that one member refers to it warmly as "someone's home."

Part V

Dislocation and Ethnicity

Demographic dislocation has significant consequences for the modification and creation of ethnic cultural systems. Involuntary relocation, altogether too common, usually has serious consequences for populations that are forced to move. Dam construction, atomic-weapon testing, reservation policy, and the like have serious consequences for human populations. A more common type of dislocation is evident in the process of immigration. In America, for example, ethnic cultural experience is, as the previous sections have illustrated, a matter of cultural change and persistence. This dynamic process necessitates a significant theoretical concern within immigration study with such questions in mind as: How long has an ethnic group been in the United States? Why and who immigrated from some particular place to this country? What is (or was) the prevailing socioeconomic context in this country at the time of arrival?

We are all familiar with the flow of European immigrants into the United States and the gradual "assimilation" of successive "waves" of populations into the "melting pot." The popular image exists of the "poor" and "illiterate" Irish, Italian, and other immigrants who once passed through Ellis Island and by subsequent hard work and initiative became successful either directly or later through the success of their children. Asians, Hispanics, Caribbean Islanders, and other immigrants nowadays evoke similar imagery as did their counterparts of previous generations. But certain cultural practices among the Irish and Italians, for example, of the earlier group were "adaptive" for continued existence here in the New World, particularly in the face of discrimination and exploitation. The Catholic church was a source of "charity" for each group; and for the Irish, the local political system through its ward bosses often provided jobs, loans, and other forms of legal and illegal "assistance." The Italian Mafia, a family-based institution, sometimes furnished jobs and even a form of justice when official agencies failed to assist immigrants.

Concerning domestic migration, the last section demonstrates that religious affiliation is a particularly potent social response to the frequent problems posed by such movement. Indian identity with historical roots in North Carolina and Puerto Rican identity with Caribbean antecedents are now maintained in Philadelphia as a function of religious experience.

The term "new ethnicity" is particularly suitable for the American scene because the process of "Americanization" (assimilation) occurs simultaneously with a process of pluralism. American ethnicity cannot be understood apart from the *context* of national religious, economic, and political experience (cf. Gleason 1982). Pettigrew, for example, states: "In a nation of immigrants, assimilation is not the opposite of but part of the same process as pluralism. The two conceptually separate processes are in reality inseparable parts of the same ball of wax called American Society. For such a society, any claims of complete pluralism are even more absurd than the melting pot metaphor" (1976:15).

The first chapter in this section considers the persistence of arranged marriages from the perspective of Cambodian ethnic consciousness. Popenoe clearly demonstrates a cultural tension arising from arranged marriages as a pluralistic tendency against the backdrop of opposing assimilation tendencies in the wider society.

Dislocation of an extreme form occurs in the process of "homelessness" that is seen nowadays in most urban and even suburban communities. Millstein, author of the second chapter in this section, set out to discover if any ethnic pattern could be found to characterize the adaptive strategies of homeless residents of Philadelphia. He did discover that such a question is quite a broad one, given the limitations of time and resources. Nevertheless, he did locate one good key informant, a Jewess, who provided much information relevant to ethnicity theory. She seems to have lost much of her opportunity for an ethnic Jewish experience while on the streets, and therefore little ethnic cultural context is evident in her life. But, even in her extremely dislocated environment, apart from community and symbolic reinforcement, some small measure of ethnic behavior is present. Overall, however, Millstein's research shows that, at least for his informant, ethnicity is not some "primordial need," but is, rather, best understood in terms of context and occasion for its expression, either real or inferred by others. In general, his empirical data support Jean-Paul Sartre's classic but extreme "interactionist" opinion that "the Jew is one whom other men consider a Jew" (in Dashefsky 1976:93–94).

Both chapters in this section directly address the question of dislocation and its consequences for ethnic cultural experience. Popenoe shows how she systematically worked to acquire access to Cambodian informants. Her interview materials are nicely framed around the subject of marriage, though she set out to study another subject, a quite common experience of students. Millstein closely followed the pioneering research of Spradley (1972) on urban nomads. He interviewed extensively one informant in terms provided by Spradley with some innovations of his own. He collected his data with a view to a *life history*, a chronological method other students find quite useful in their research as well (see Langness and Frank 1981).

14

Cambodian Marriage
Marriage and How It Is Changing among Cambodian Refugees in Philadelphia

Rebecca C. Popenoe

Refugees from Cambodia are mostly Khmer, the ethnic group to which 85 percent of Cambodians belong; Chinese; or some mixture of these groups with occasionally Laotian or Thai relatives as well. In addition to the Cambodian refugees in the United States, there are Southeast Asians from Vietnam (as many as 500,000) and from Laos. The government supports all these refugees through various social service agencies, providing orientation programs, English classes, health care, job placement and counseling services, housing, and welfare funding. Each refugee or refugee family has a sponsor —an individual, church, or agency—that helps them to become established and assists with such tasks as shopping, enrolling children in school, and generally adjusting to American life.

In Philadelphia, four volunteer agencies are now assisting Indo-Chinese refugees: the Nationality Service Center, Jewish Vocational Services, the Lutheran Children and Family Service, and Catholic Social Services. Over 95 percent of the sponsorships are by organizations rather than individuals. The Cambodians of more recent arrival are clustered in three neighborhoods: west Philadelphia in the forties, south Philadelphia, and the Logan area of north Philadelphia. All school-age children are enrolled in public schools; and the adults are either in English programs, attending training school or community college, working, or unemployed. The majority of all Southeast Asian refugees are young; in 1983 about 90 percent were under the age of forty-five (Muecke 1983:431). According to the leader of the Cambodian Mutual Assistance Association, anywhere between 50 and 80 percent are on welfare.

Of the first-wave immigrants, many are living in the suburbs and have become quite assimilated into American life. Among those who came later, however, many are living in scantily furnished, dilapidated apartments, speak little English, and live their daily lives within the circle of their families and other refugees. Although some orphans came to the United States as adoptees of foster families, most Cambodian refugees could only be accepted to come here if they were part of a family, and, as time went on, they had to have some relatives or connections in the United States. Most of the refugees in Philadelphia live in extended family households, and most of their social interaction takes place among relatives or other Cambodian friends. There is one Cambodian organization in the city: the Cambodian Mutual Assistance Association, known simply as the Cambodian Association.

When I began interviewing these refugees, the subject of my research was concepts of health. In three early interviews, however, the topic of marriage and marital conflict came up when the conversation turned to emotional health. Suspecting that marriages were under great stress in the refugee community and sensing that this subject was something people wanted to talk about, I switched my topic of study to marriage. In the end, I discovered that marriages seem to be one of the most stable and unaffected social ties for Cambodian refugees. Although my initial expectations that they were a stressful aspect of life were mistaken, the subject turned out to be interesting and fruitful.

Besides the interest of the subject in and of itself, and much of the following study is descriptive, an understanding of Cambodian marriage is important in understanding the wider issue of refugee adjustment. I originally planned to examine marriage synchronically, but soon discovered that any element of refugee life must be looked at in a diachronic framework because the initial years of resettlement and adjustment are a time of rapid change. As these people adapt and assimilate into American culture, one element of their traditional culture that is undergoing change is marriage customs and the nature of the marriage relationship. Attitudes and practices surrounding marriage are one salient way in which Cambodians differ from Americans, and they are becoming very conscious of this. The manner in which Cambodians give up or retain traditional marriage customs is a reflection of how American they are becoming as well as an indicator of their sense of Cambodianness. Thus, one context of this study is the subject area of intercul-

Oriental art is integrated into the urban landscape in Philadelphia's well-established Chinese community. Cambodians, Laotians, and other Asian immigrants are endeavoring to form communities. (Courtesy of Elizabeth Ameisen)

tural contact, assimilation, and the development of ethnic consciousness.

Theoretical Background:
Ethnicity and Marriage

As a recently arrived group, Cambodians as well as other Southeast Asians have not yet settled into a niche in American society. Indeed, native Philadelphians I know were surprised to learn that over 10,000 Indo-Chinese were living in their midst; they were not yet conscious of this new and relatively large ethnic presence. Conversely, Cambodians themselves have not yet developed a consciousness of their own status and identity as an ethnic group. Just how they will assimilate into American culture over time and how they will retain their Cambodian-ness are still open questions.

Some anthropologists treat ethnicity as a concept of identity or a self-concept, and in this sense Cambodians do perceive themselves as an ethnic group. M. G. Smith's definition of ethnicity expresses this notion: an ethnic group consists of those who "conceive of themselves as being alike, by virtue of their common ancestry and . . . are so regarded by others" (1982:4). The Cambodians in Philadelphia recognize their shared cultural heritage, their shared experience of traumatic escape from their homeland, and their biological interrelationship. They also identify, though to a lesser degree, with the wider group of all Southeast Asian refugees. Ronald Cohen's notion of "nesting dichotomizations" (1978:387) describes this bilevel sense of ethnicity that Cambodians have. According to him, ethnicity can be broadened or narrowed, depending on the context of the situation. Although the Cambodians and the Vietnamese have different histories, in the United States, all Southeast Asians, including the lowland Laotians and to some extent the Hmong, also from Laos, recognize the cultural elements they share and are often regarded as one group by Americans. My informants often grouped themselves together with other Southeast Asians, and even with other Asians in general, with reference to food, parent-child relationships, and many other aspects of their culture.

The formal organization of Cambodians in Philadelphia is weak at this time, but from talking with leaders in the community I sense that the people are starting to find that they have common economic and political aims, and that they can act collectively to achieve them. For example, they are setting up a job club, and they recently held a rally at Independence Mall to protest the treatment of Cambodians in Thai refugee camps. As the immigrants achieve economic stability, learn English, and leave their refugee status behind to become citizens of the American "melting pot," their sense of Cambodian-ness will no doubt go through many transformations.

A study by George Scott (1982) of the Hmong refugees in San Diego may point the direction that a Cambodian sense of ethnicity will take. The Hmong are a Laotian mountain people who have to make the biggest cultural adjustment of all Southeast Asian groups in their transition to America. Scott discovered that their sense of ethnicity has been increasing and that they are setting up more boundaries to outsiders while building a more self-contained community. As he describes this emerging ethnic consciousness: "What before had been accepted unhesitatingly as the 'natural' ways of thinking and behaving became recognized as distinctive cultural elements that must be consciously and emphatically embraced so as to provide the security of a familiar identity in an alien environment" (1982:152).

The Cambodians have come to recognize the differences between their own culture and American ways and expressed this to me over and over as they described arranged marriages, bride-wealth, and their attitudes toward premarital sex, among other things. I do not think these people, who have quite a diffuse community, will become as self-contained as the Hmong in San Diego have, but they will start to understand and assert their ethnicity in new ways. Just what significance Cambodian-ness will take on as the immigrants become more assimilated into the American social and cultural context has yet to be seen.

As the Cambodian refugees become "Americanized" and at the same time develop a sense of their own ethnicity, one element of the culture that will surely affect and be affected by the adaptive process is marriage. Marriage is an element of culture in many forms: It is an institution within the social structure, it is a culturally patterned relationship, and its creation constitutes a cultural ritual as well as a rite of passage. Every time a marriage is arranged, a wedding occurs, and a new marriage relationship is formed, Cambodians are expressing their culture—their ethnicity—at each step of the way.

The relationship between marriage and ethnicity also occurs at another level. Not only does marriage as a culturally patterned entity express traditional beliefs and practices, but it is also one of the main loci through which culture is perpetuated. Whether members of a culture marry within their group or outside of it is a crucial determinant of how the group's boundaries and the strength of its cultural consciousness will be maintained. Marriage also perpetuates culture because it is the basic tie that creates the nuclear family, where socialization takes place and culture is passed from one generation to the next. Thus, marriage is a relationship and an institution that can both reflect and lead change in a society. The data I present in this paper are largely descriptive of how marriage was and is for Cambodians, but I also examine the manner in which it is changing and how this relates to a developing Cambodian sense of ethnicity.

Fieldwork

I entered the Cambodian community through two separate avenues. This is significant, I believe, because it opened up two separate networks of people and gave my study more breadth. My first introduction to Cambodians was through a teacher in the English (ESL) program for refugees, who happened to be an anthropologist and whose name was given to me by one of my professors. This anthropologist/ESL teacher both introduced me to the Cambodians who became my first informants and guided me to the network of agencies that deal with refugees in Philadelphia. About six weeks after making this contact, I was invited by a fellow anthropology major who was studying Laotians to attend a meeting of the leaders of the different Southeast Asian refugee groups. There I met the president of the Cambodian Association, who led me into a different section of the Cambodian community than that which I had met in the English class. Through the class, I met refugees who had arrived within the last year; and, through the president of the Cambodian Association, I met leaders in the community, some of whom were highly educated and had been in the United States for four years or more.

The research on which this study is based was primarily informant interviewing, carried out over a period of about six months between November 1984 and April 1985. During this time, I conducted seventeen structured interviews with fifteen different informants in nine different households. The questions I asked varied from interview to interview but usually included asking about parents' and relatives' marriages as well as the marriages of informants and how they came about. I also asked specific questions about emotion, roles, and conflict in marriages; and I talked with informants about coming to this country and life in general here. Besides the interviews where I sat notebook in hand and led the conversation around preplanned topics, I also had a certain amount of informal contact with my informants and other Cambodians. This included chatting before and after interviews and on the phone; sharing meals; learning how to cook Cambodian food; and helping two informants deal with school, welfare, and job agencies. My contact with the community for the purposes of this paper ended with the Cambodian New Year on April 13, a gala celebration that I attended with several refugee families.

Although my initial expectations about Cambodian marriage—that it was under great stress in the United States and that the incidence of conflict was high—turned out to be wrong, the topic proved to be a felicitous choice. I was able to observe marriage relationships directly in almost every household I visited; the subject was relatively easy to discuss; and, because it does not involve a particularly specialized vocabulary, language problems were minimized. Certain aspects of marriage, such as sexual relations, were too delicate for me to investigate, especially as an unmarried person, but generally people talked openly about many aspects of marriage.

Twelve of my informants were married, including three couples with whom I talked to both the wife and husband. In addition to hearing direct accounts of nine marriages and observing interaction in three, I heard about the marriages of parents, relatives, and friends of these informants. Of the nine couples among my informants, seven were married in Cambodia, one man in a Thai refugee camp, and one woman for a second time in this country after leaving a husband she was forced to marry under the Pol Pot regime in Cambodia. Six informants were married before the Communist takeover in 1975, three were married under Pol Pot, and one couple married after the Vietnamese takeover and before escaping to Thailand. All the married informants had at least one child, and the children ranged in age from one to seventeen years old.

Of the three unmarried informants, two were college-age, one woman and one man, and one was in high school. The two single informants of marriageable age talked to me about other people's marriages and various general subjects; when it came to the possibility of their own marriage, both became shy. With the high school-age informant, a girl, I explored the parent-child relationship and the adjustment of young refugees in America.

Marriages in Cambodia are arranged by the parents or older relatives of the woman and man to be married. A man may pick out a woman he would like to marry and suggest her to his parents, but in many cases parents do all the arranging themselves; and, even with a son's input, they have the final say. Once a man's parents have settled on a potential bride, they meet with the woman's parents in order to make a formal engagement, pay bride-wealth to the bride's family, and set up a wedding. The woman's parents consult their daughter for her opinion, but she may not seek out a husband for herself. Parents look for certain qualities in a daughter- or son-in-law, which will be elaborated below.

All my informants' marriages were arranged according to this general scheme, with some variations caused by the war. In the United States, marriages are still being arranged according to the traditional customs, though there are some signs of change. The description and analysis that follow of how marriages are arranged were composed from my fieldwork, though I have mentioned previous ethnographic research on Cambodia where it was pertinent or where it was in some way at variance with what I discovered. For further information on how marriages are traditionally arranged in Cambodia, see Ebihara (1971:96–105, 466–473), Leclere (1916:531–555), and Martel (1975:89, 206, 218).

When my informants were questioned about the topic of marriage, generally the first thing they said was that in Cambodia marriages were arranged by parents. Indeed, all the married informants had their marriages arranged by parents or older relatives if their parents had died. As Bun So, a thirty-three-year old male informant, stated: "My parents engaged her parents." According to the literature (Leclere 1916:535; Martel 1975:206; Ebihara 1971:466), ideally a son makes a choice of a bride and then suggests her to his parents, who will approve or reject the choice after investigating the woman and her family.

Of my informants, two out of eight clearly chose their own bride, and I heard of several other cases where men had found fiancées on their own. Ron, one of the two informants who found a young woman he wanted to marry on his own, said that his parents had at first rejected his decision and had accepted it only after he made a case for the woman again a few months later. This man had not been living with his parents for some years because his father had remarried and he was not on the best of terms with them. The other young man, Cham, had married in a refugee camp in Thailand, largely in order to emigrate to America. His parents had not been happy with his decision to marry, perhaps because it meant leaving them, and he looked away with some embarrassment, even shame, when he told me of his parents' disapproval. Both these men were rather outgoing and sure of themselves, and this personality factor, along with their slightly unusual circumstances, may account for why they chose their own wives while the other six married men I spoke to had not.

A third informant, Haing, had had his eye on a pretty young girl, but, when his older sister (his parents were dead) suggested another woman, he agreed to marry her without, it seemed, a second thought. Bun So, a fourth informant, said that his parents had consulted him when arranging his marriage, stating that some parents simply tell their son or daughter whom he or she must marry.

In summary, it seems that, though the stated custom is that a man may pick his own bride and then leave the formal arranging to his parents, in fact they often find the spouse; and, though sons may be consulted, they yield readily to fiancées of their parents' choosing.

A woman has very little say in the arranging of her marriage. If she looks at other men before then, she is considered a "bad girl," but, though she may not choose a husband, she can influence her parents as to when and whom she marries. Sok, a forty-five-year-old female informant, did not wed until she was twenty-five because she was going to medical school. Her mother kept asking her, "What are you waiting for?"; and, though this nagging shows parental concern, it also indicates that at least the timing of the marriage was up to her. It is customary for parents to consult with their daughter once they receive a proposal of marriage, but, as in one thirty-two-year-old informant's story, this may often be more of a formality. Roeun hid and eavesdropped when her future husband's relatives came and made a proposal of marriage to her parents. When her parents later asked Roeun for her opinion, she "didn't say anything. It's up to them. . . . It's my custom in Cambodia." Another informant answered her mother's queries by saying "If you think he's nice," and told me, "I plan[ned] to obey my parents."

Bun summed up the role of parents well when he told me: "We marry according to our parents." Their relationship with their marriage-age children is not an autocratic one; in most cases I saw, a loving concern for their children's future on the part of the parents is reciprocated by a loving respect for the parents. Ebihara notes that "forcing a child into marriage was thought to incur the wrath of ancestral spirits" (1971:467). Although I never heard this, I did learn that a child's preferences and circumstances are taken into account when a marriage is in the offing, especially of a son. Parents and older relatives exert a strong influence on their children, however, and in the majority of cases they do all the arranging of a young person's marriage, and their judgment is not questioned.

The arranging of a traditional marriage involves three steps (see

Ebihara 1971:470–472; Martel 1975:206), but, though informants told me this, among the stories of their own engagements there were some variations from this norm. Before any formal proposal is made to a woman's family, the man's family investigates her and her family to find out if she is a suitable match. This is done by inquiring among relatives and friends. If parents arrange a marriage themselves, it is often set up by related women, such as cousins, for their children, their own nephews, or nieces to marry each other. In other cases, a network of friends and relatives is used to set up a match between a woman and a man from nearby villages or from adjacent neighborhoods in a town or city (cf. Ebihara 1971:468).

The first traditional step in an engagement is for the groom's family to send an intermediary to "sound out" the woman's family. After they subtly indicate their feelings toward the proposed marriage, if they are interested they will investigate the potential son-in-law and his family (Steinberg 1959:84). This intermediary procedure, though described by informants, was only followed by the parents of one man. In the other cases, the arrangers of the marriage were relatives and thus did not need to send an intermediary and investigate each other's families, or the marriage took place during wartime, when such formalities had to be dispensed with.

According to the literature and to informants' accounts, the next two steps are a meeting between the two families, where gifts are given to the fiancée and her family; and an official betrothal ceremony, where relatives and close friends attend, the engagement is sealed, and the groom's family gives more gifts. Details of these procedures can be found in Steinberg (1959:84), Ebihara (1971: 470–71), and Martel (1975:206); informants' descriptions were not elaborate. Six of them were married during or after the Pol Pot period, when the customary engagement stages were usually cut short, and the other six informants did not give full descriptions. The key aspects of this engagement sequence, however, seem to be the meeting of the families to legitimize the marriage agreement; and the giving of gifts, including bride-wealth, by the groom's family to the bride and her family. The bride-wealth is decided on between the two families, with the bride's family trying to obtain as much as possible. According to informants, it can be a hefty sum, depending on how wealthy the two families are.

The qualities looked for in a spouse were quite uniform among my informants. Parents want a son-in-law who will respect them, who will work hard and support the family, and who will not drink, play cards, or go out often. Young women, according to Loeun, a twenty-eight-year-old female informant, "always wish for a handsome man, and a man who is a doctor, lawyer, or teacher." But, she added, "it doesn't depend on the daughter, it depends on the parents." In a daughter-in-law, parents look for a woman who is modest and who will respect and obey them, and who works hard and is not lazy. Both the young men and women seem to be attracted mostly by a pretty face.

No informants cited a particular age that is appropriate for marriage. In the past, age at marriage was younger than in recent years; one informant's mother married at fourteen. The youngest bride I encountered was the wife of an informant, who wed at eighteen. The woman who had been a medical student considered herself an old bride at twenty-five, but two female informants had married at twenty-two and another at twenty-four. It seems that, as education for women increased in Cambodia, so did the acceptable marriage age for them. For men, the average age at marriage was somewhat higher: the youngest age I heard of was twenty, the age of Cham when he married his eighteen-year-old bride in the Thai refugee camp; and the oldest age I heard of was an informant's brother who had married at thirty. The informant did remark that this was old, and his mother had been glad to arrange the marriage with the daughter of a close friend. The ages at which my informants had married corresponded with what Ebihara gives as the average ages for marriage: late teens and early twenties for women and early to mid-twenties for men (1971:488). As with women, it seems that men who obtain higher educations wed later; and, for both men and women, marriage in towns and cities seems to have been at slightly higher ages than in the villages.

There are no clans or lineages in Cambodia, nor rules of marital preference (Ebihara 1971:96). First cousins may marry, but it is uncommon according to one informant and the literature (Martel 1975:219). The informants stated that some families favored the union of cousins or second cousins because it kept property in the family. One female informant said that it was not a good idea, however, because the offspring of such a match would have "no good mind." One couple I spoke with were second cousins, and I heard of other matches where relatives had married one another. There are no rules of exogamy or endogamy (Ebihara 1971:96), but people tend to find spouses from nearby villages (among my informants were three such matches) or from neighboring areas in a town or city (one couple I spoke with met in this way).

There is one important factor to consider when evaluating someone as a potential spouse: the person's family. When parents investigate potential partners for their children, whether or not these individuals come from good families is a prime concern. What constitutes a "good family" was not made explicitly clear to me, but it seems to include one that has not been involved in any sort of scandal and one in which the parents work hard and are respectable members of the community. The importance of a potential fiancé(e)'s family to his or her desirability highlights the nature of Cambodian marriage as a relationship set up within a web of kin and social ties and not merely as a match of two isolated individuals.

Cambodian marriages take place for the benefit of the families of the bride and groom and for the sake of the wider social structure rather than for reasons of personal attachment between the couple. Thus, it is understandable that the bride and groom do not know each other in many cases before they marry, and in no case should they have had any physical contact. Eight of the twelve married informants had known their future mates in some capacity before the engagement and wedding, two had not, and for two I do not know. Several informants mentioned that their parents had never seen each other before the wedding day. Informants whom I asked said they felt nervous and scared before their weddings. Roeun, married in 1975, said she felt "scared and shy, because I didn't know about him [her fiancé]." Her parents told her that he was nice and not to worry, but, when asked if she believed them, she laughed and said "No." Even in cases where the couple to be married knew each other before the match was arranged, or when they met a few times between the engagement and wedding, people told me they did not feel they knew their spouses-to-be before the wedding.

In addition to the role of parents in arranging marriages, the fact that the bride and groom did not know each other before marriage was a point informants dwelt upon. This is a major difference between their own marriages and the American marriages they see around them. Personal sentiments are not the key factor in the planning of a marriage for Cambodians; instead, the focus is on parental judgment and the social context of the family and the community.

How a Marriage Comes About: Changes in the United States

I spoke directly with only three unmarried Cambodians, two aged twenty-two and one aged seventeen, and with one woman who was married in the United States. Consequently my information on how the arranging of marriages is changing, or staying the same, in this country is less complete than the preceding account of how marriages came about in Cambodia. On the basis of what the above informants told me and the comments of married informants about changes they perceived, I will make some tentative statements about the present and future status of Cambodian marriage arrangements in the United States.

Change of various kinds occurs at different rates among different sectors of the Cambodian population. My field notes describe an incident that seems to indicate the beginning stages of change in the marriage pattern:

> At the end [of the interview] Vantha, a twenty-eight year old male friend of Haing, and Buthy and Sitha [Haing's college-age male relatives] all came downstairs. Somehow Vantha started talking about how his wife's sister, who it turns out is sixteen, has had a marriage arranged with a guy who is twenty-five or so and is a student in Virginia somewhere. Vantha went on rather boisterously about how this all got arranged, and Buthy and Sitha were really hysterical with laughter at times. Finally I asked them why they were laughing so hard. Sitha answered my question: "Because what he [Vantha] say is very hard, but he speak easy."
> What I make of that answer is that Vantha was talking about a very serious subject—arranging a marriage—and something that is done according to custom and not talked about in the distanced, almost mocking manner. Perhaps now after being in the States a few years they do have more of a perspective on their own culture and that's why Vantha could talk about it in this way. The way Sitha and Buthy were laughing, I felt almost as if it were a kind of "taboo" thing to talk about, at least in this way, and that's why their laughter was almost hysterical.

The Cambodians I spoke with are very aware that arranging marriages is something that is not done in this country, and, though in these first years here Cambodians follow their traditions, knowing no other way, I take the incident above to be a first stage of change. By comparing their ways with American ways, these Cambodians have developed a consciousness that somehow their traditional arranging of a marriage is something old-fashioned, and something that can be made fun of.

Buthy and Sitha, who were both of marriage age, expressed their uneasiness over the close-to-home subject of arranging marriages by turning to laughter, but two other young adult informants expressed shyness or embarrassment when the subject was brought up. One of these was Prea, a twenty-two-year-old woman from Phnom Penh who is now in college here. When, after discussing other people's marriages for a while, I mentioned the subject of marriage for Prea herself, she very quickly dismissed the issue with an answer like "I don't know." I definitely gained the impression that this could not be a topic of conversation, whether because of her own nervousness or shyness about the subject or because of something else. Even when I asked about her twenty-eight-year-old aunt, who is still single, she laughed a little and said she did not know: "That's her private, I cannot say."

In these early years of resettlement, it seems that marriages are still arranged, as in Vantha's case, using whatever relatives have come to this country, or through new Cambodian friends made here. For people like Prea, who has been here for about three and a half years, her family may still be uncertain of where husbands for her aunt and for her will come from, and thus there may be an extra amount of nervousness and embarrassment over what is a sensitive topic anyway.

In another case, Bitha, a thoughtful and mature twenty-two-year-old, had spoken to me very openly and insightfully about how he thought Cambodians regarded marriage. After the interview with Prea, where I felt I had stepped out of bounds asking her about her own potential marriage, I was somewhat hesitant to ask Bitha how he might get married. I mustered some ethnographer's tact, however, and asked the question. He did become somewhat shy and looked away, but he told me very frankly: "For me, I think I will follow the old people." I asked if this bothered him and he said "No"; it seemed that, though he recognized that this was odd to a young American woman, this was the way it would be done.

One informant mentioned that, in the years before the coup in Cambodia, customs surrounding arranging marriages were already beginning to change. Especially in the cities, young men increasingly chose their own wives, and couples even did some low-key dating before their marriages. Although I heard of no dating among Cambodians in the United States, and despite Bitha's attitude, these trends are no doubt continuing in this country, particularly the increasing independence of men.

One example of this trend is the case of Sopha, the woman who was forced into marriage under Pol Pot and who recently remarried in this country. She had known the man vaguely through relatives, and a year before they married he declared his love to her. She was not at all impressed or surprised by this and said such a declaration had been made to her before. Although she did not make any reciprocal statement of love, she did not turn him away. The man then went to her older brother and sister, and a marriage was arranged. It is in some ways special because Sopha is twenty-seven, quite "old," and has a four-year-old son; and her husband is, at thirty, also quite "old." But in other ways, such as the absence of parents (all dead except Sopha's mother) and the initiative of the man, this marriage arrangement may be typical of the way some Cambodian marriages are being arranged in the United States. Although formal arrangements were still made through the woman's older relatives, the man not only chose his wife but also arranged the marriage; and the couple knew each other beforehand.

There is one other measure of how changes are taking place, and that is informants' current value judgments of their own and American customs. Several informants said that they like the way Americans knew each other before marriage, though for most of the Cambodians this does not include any physical contact beyond hand-holding. I did not hear anyone criticize the fact that parents arrange marriages, but this was probably out of respect for parents and not because the young people do not want to choose their own spouses. Most Cambodians look favorably on the idea of more personal choice in the decision about when and whom to marry. Among the women of marriage age, however, this may be more of an ideal than a real change. Both men and women told me they liked the fact that women have more freedom in this country, but I did not see any evidence of women taking a more active role in deciding their own marriages. Even Sopha, who is a strong and intelligent woman and who has been married once already, left her second marriage up to her older brother and sister.

Where change will come, I believe, is in the generation of Cambodians who are now going through American primary and secondary schools, and then the change may be dramatic. Although the Cambodians I met were proud of their country and their customs, none expressed a particularly avid desire to maintain all the engagement and marriage customs of their culture. In fact, several men complained about the expense of bride-wealth; and, as I said above, most informants liked the idea of more personal choice in marriage arrangements.

Bride-wealth itself may already be becoming more a way of paying for the wedding than a gift to a woman's family to compensate them for her labor. Some informants did say that in the years right before 1975, bride-wealth was not paid in the same way and both sides sometimes chipped in to pay for the wedding. Two married male informants said that they wanted to keep the traditional wedding ceremony but that they thought it was a good idea to let young people get to know each other and decide for themselves, and then they (the older people) would "follow up." Perhaps only the formalities of the traditional parental arrangements will be retained as young adults conform more and more to American ways of dating and planning marriages. When I asked a few parents of young children if they wanted them to marry Cambodians, none answered adamantly in the affirmative, and most said the person's behavior was more important.

Conclusion

I have discussed the ways in which marriage customs are changing. Marriage is a cultural and social institution and an expression of cultural meanings and values. In addition, it is the relationship through which the nuclear family is created and through which culture is passed on from generation to generation. The ways in which marriage practices and the nature of the marriage relationship change among an ethnic group over time reflect changes in the culture and effect changes in it. I think that marriage customs, such as the traditional wedding ceremony and the formalities of parent involvement in an engagement, will continue among Cambodians and may become, in time, symbols and as such maintainers of ethnicity. The wedding, especially, seems to be one of the culture's happiest and proudest ceremonies, and I believe that Cambodians will try to maintain its quality. However, bride-wealth, already on the wane, will probably die out in favor of a more cooperative arrangement between the two families to pay for the wedding.

15

Ethnic Expression in a Jewish Street Person

Andrew Millstein

After approximately six weeks of studying ethnicity in Senior Conference, I was not quite sure about the nature of my projected research. However, on the night of October 26, 1983, when I was working as a volunteer for the Philadelphia Committee for the Homeless, I unknowingly met my would-be key informant, who would later reveal to me certain details about her life, both on and off the streets, as well as the meaning of Jewishness to her.

The Philadelphia Committee for the Homeless (PCH) is a relatively new organization (approximately two years old) that feeds and aids seemingly "needy" people four nights a week. Each night, several pairs of volunteers canvas center-city Philadelphia with food, clothing, and conversation as well as information about public and private shelters and medical care. On the night of October 26, a more experienced volunteer (whom I shall refer to as Carolyn) and I proceeded to a well-known gathering spot of PCH recipients, in the vicinity of Twelfth and Walnut streets. As on most warm and dry evenings, a large collection of regulars congregated near the northeast corner of Twelfth Street. Approximately ten to fifteen persons were gathered around two large circular benches. After dispensing sandwiches, drinks, and greetings, Carolyn motioned with her finger to me to move across the street.

Alone on a Jefferson Hospital Park bench sat Martha. Well-kempt and smelling faintly of perfume, at first she did not meet my expectations of a street person. However Carolyn was familiar with her. I was introduced as a "new volunteer" and then readily drifted back a few paces in order to observe the remaining interaction. In the course of their conversation, Carolyn mentioned "Jesus Christ" within a religious context. Immediately upon hearing this, Martha replied, "I don't believe in Jesus Christ; I'm Jewish." I listened attentively—more than slightly bemused.

Several questions immediately occurred to me. For example, what were the conditions of Martha's Jewishness? Does she consider herself a Jew by birth? Is she a recent convert to Judaism? Why did she identify herself as a Jew? If she was concerned with so identifying herself why not wear a religious medallion? Moreover, if, indeed, she were a Jewish "urban nomad" (see Spradley 1972), what effect would street life have had upon her Jewishness? These are just a portion of the questions I investigated, but a short, direct statement, such as "I don't believe in Jesus Christ; I'm Jewish," reveals that there are underlying complexities of the phenomenon of ethnicity.

In addition to the intrinsic worth of studying the effects of street life on a person's Jewishness, there lies a fundamental reason for the existence of this project. As a Jew, I was attracted to a project concerning my own ethnic group. For good or for bad, I cannot deny this attraction to the group that comprises a portion of my identity. However, I managed to combine an interest in the questions concerning Jewish ethnicity in conjunction with a phenomenon with which most people are only superficially familiar: homelessness.

In America today, nearly 2 million people are affected by homelessness (Hombs and Snyder 1982:XVI). At no time since the Great Depression have the homeless poor represented so broad a crosssection of American society (1982:83). In spite of this, I was extremely surprised to find any Jews among the swollen ranks of Philadelphia's homeless street dwellers. My chagrin, I believe, is due to the commonly held old belief that Jews are immune to poverty and would not allow one of their own to live without proper shelter. Wolfe (1977:137) writes: "For a reason that is not altogether clear, the Jewish community did not recognize the relevance of this phenomenon [poverty] to its own people." Furthermore, she states (1977:138): "Because the myth that the American Jew has conquered poverty has been generally accepted by the affluent Jewish minority, we do not even have reliable statistics on the extent of Jewish poverty." She goes on to say that "a large number of Jewish poor people exist, living below a certain level of income" (1977:135).

As Spradley illustrates in *You Owe Yourself a Drunk* (1970) and "Adaptive Strategies of Urban Nomads" (1972), urban streetdwellers are members of a definite and distinct subculture within the urban American scene. According to him, "The distance between most Americans and urban nomads cannot be measured in miles; they are separated from us by cultural distance. Their style of life is not only strange but also abhorrent to most Americans. They are socially alienated and culturally separated from us but still they are in our very midst" (1970:63). Thus, by focusing on Jewish street people through the eyes of one of their kind, I have selected for study a specific ethnic category within the larger subculture of urban nomads.

The ethnic formula used in this chapter is well defined by Herman (1977:9). He states: "Ethnic identity is an inherently social psychological concept in that it refers to a state of mind shared by the members of a collectivity, formed through social interaction, and anchored in historical and social structural processes." Furthermore, he contends: "Ethnic identity relates to that which the individual shares in common with some other men, along with whom he is set off from still others by the possession of certain attributes" (1977:29).

Thus, ethnicity is an idea that links members of a particular social group. This idea may function through space and time: a Jew in New York identifies with one living in Israel, and both of them identify with Jews who lived generations ago (1977:453). Ethnicity also depends upon normative behavior patterns, the nature of social organization, and basic value orientation. All the ingredients combine to form ethnicity. However, one cannot fail to recognize that it continues to exist despite the absence of one or more of these ingredients. Concerning Jewish ethnicity, Glazer and Moynahan (1963:164) write: "While at one time the problem of Jewish identity was no problem for the individual who lived a distinctively Jewish life in his home, his synagogue and the community, today there is little that marks the Jew as a Jew except Jewish self-consciousness and association with fellow Jews." Although this statement is not, in my opinion, entirely true, it emphasizes the importance of Jewish self-consciousness. Logically, it would seem that this self-consciousness is reinforced by the existence of other ingredients of ethnicity. Thus, Herman (1977:45) has found that the most self-conscious Jew is one who is the most religiously observant, who also lives in a predominantly Jewish community and identifies with all Jews everywhere at all points in time.

Approximately 3 million Jews immigrated into the United States in the three-hundred-year period between 1654 and 1954. However, about 90 to 95 percent of them arrived during the seventy-year period between 1880 and 1950 (Weinryb 1957:4). Most of them arrived between 1880 and 1920. They were mostly Eastern European Jews from Poland and Russia. As a result, the striking features that define the character of the American Jewish community evolved from these Jews who immigrated from Eastern Europe at the turn of the century (Wolfe 1977:130).

The Eastern European Jewish life from which these people emigrated was characterized by the impact of the *shtetl* culture from within and severe anti-Semitism from without. For Jews, life was nothing if it was not with their people, with their community while within the larger society. As Mandelbaum (1958:511) explains: "For each individual, the ideal center of gravity is not in himself, but in the whole of which he is an essential part. Every person is not only a part of the whole, but feels himself to be an essential part, so that if he severs himself from the social whole, he knows that both he and the group are the less of the severance." Furthermore, in *shtetl* culture, the individual maintained a strong sense of his or her worth as a member of the group and a responsibility to play the proper role in it. A significant underlying continuity found in Jewish culture is the importance of the in-community. In a tentative and somewhat hypothetical tone, Mandelbaum (1958:511) suggests that Jews, in particular, place an extremely high value on affiliation with and approval of the in-group.

Although a small group of Jews are believed to have lived in Philadelphia in the 1740s, the formal Jewish community began with the construction of the first synagogue in 1782. Throughout the rest of the eighteenth century, Jewish immigrants continued to come to Philadelphia. These were mostly Ashkenazi Jews from Western Europe. Thus, by the time large numbers of Eastern European Jews began to pour into the city in 1882, a well-established, tightly organized Jewish community obviously existed. During the next four decades, the central problem confronting this community was the assimilation of Eastern European immigrants. Many were poor and ignorant of American language and customs. Fortunately, the in-place members of the Philadelphia Jewish community were prosperous and charitable. German Jews donated thousands of dollars to these immigrants, and the more fortunate Russian Jews contributed a great deal of financial aid as well. For example, the Association of Jewish Immigrants, in which all the officers were Russian Jews, was formed in 1884 at 931 South 4th Street. During 1885, the association afforded shelter to 848 newly arrived immigrants, processed 900 applications for employment, and provided many other services, including protection from "sharpies" bent on taking advantage of ignorant immigrants.

Many of these Jews settled within a small area along 4th and

5th streets, south of Pine Street, which soon became known as Philadelphia's "East Side." The Jews who came into this south Philadelphia "ghetto" were a pious people with their own religious ritual, language, and traditions. They soon founded congregations and built their own synagogues. Of the eight synagogues in 1882, only one was south of Market Street. By 1900, the number of synagogues in the city had doubled; five of the eight new synagogues were located within an area of two city blocks in the Russian-Jewish ghetto (Baltzell 1957:274, 281).

Methodology

For all intents and purposes, the first night of my research began on October 21, 1983, and continued through mid-May. However, several weeks of preparation after first meeting Martha were needed in order to establish her as a key informant. One does not approach an almost complete stranger expecting to ask personal questions about potentially sensitive issues. As an initial research strategy (without yet advising my informant), I continued my volunteer work with the Philadelphia Committee of the Homeless, returning to 12th and Walnut at least once a week in order to establish a base of familiarity with Martha. Fortunately over the next several weeks, I met her on two occasions in the same context, as a PCH volunteer. In addition to these encounters, I happened to meet her accidentally within the same general vicinity during the day. However, these extra meetings were outside of a formal encounter. By this time she began to greet me by name with a good degree of familiarity.

During these formulative encounters, which I shall label the "rapport-developing stage," Martha and I chatted each time for ten to fifteen minutes. I spoke intentionally about mundane generalities in a very conversational manner. However, I did attempt to establish some continuity to our meetings by mentioning such topics as her dress, health, and the weather in relation to our previous meetings. Lastly, I utilized these first encounters to establish the validity of her "ethnic" and street states. This I accomplished with very subtle and indirect probes. Without such validation, this project would not have been worth continuing. However, with Martha's Jewish street person status confirmed, I could gear these initial encounters toward an upcoming meeting, when I would "pop the fateful question."

As I have already mentioned, I had always intended to seek Martha as a key informant concerning my research into the supposed ethnicity of Jewish street people, presuming that such individuals even exist. I wanted her as one of a few informants, representing data sources for my anthropological ruminations concerning "Ethnicity among Philadelphia's Jewish Street People." Fortunately, she consented. Unfortunately, I came to realize that several factors would prohibit me from pursuing my research with more than one informant. For instance, locating Martha was a constant problem and a source of irritation. On many occasions, she would simply forget that an appointment had been previously arranged. Very often she would refuse to meet at a specific time or place. When this occurred, I sometimes had to spend hours tracking her down within a wide range of locations, over a broad geographical territory. With an element of luck, I could find my informant. Or, perhaps not. This problem should be expected when conducting research among nomadic individuals, possessing a wide range of potential haunts. And it adds to the overall excitement of discovery while conducting fieldwork.

Because my particular research situation seemed increasingly to warrant a single key informant, the importance of selecting a "good" one was absolutely essential. While I was in the initial rapport-developing stage of research with Martha, I utilized the guidelines set out by Spradley (1979) to facilitate the selection process with a maximum amount of confidence. They enabled me to make what turned out to be the proper selection. First and foremost, in his words, "a good informant" will have undergone a thorough enculturation process of learning a particular culture. Potential informants vary in the extent of their enculturation: good ones know their culture well (1979:47). As I found out, my informant has lived on the streets of center-city Philadelphia for roughly fifteen years. In my estimation, she would not have survived that long unless she had fully mastered the necessary strategies for "street living." Thus, I felt that she satisfied at least this one minimum requirement.

The "ethnographic interview" label suggests a formal encounter in which the ethnographer and informant are part of an information exchange. When such an exchange exists, however, it is veiled in the wraps of a friendly conversation. As Spradley (1979:58) writes: "Skilled ethnographers often gather most of their data through participant observation and many casual friendly conversations. They may interview people without their awareness, merely carrying on a friendly conversation, while introducing a few ethnographic questions. It is but to think of the ethnographic interview as a series of friendly conversations into which the researcher slowly introduces new elements to assist informants to respond as informants." In this manner I probed Martha's understanding of such subjects as community, friends, and family and her feelings toward such topics as Israel, non-Jews, anti-Semitic remarks, churches, and alcoholism. At the same time, I confirmed information about her daily patterns on the street. I chose culture concepts because of their importance within the ethnic literature (Jewish ethnicity and history).

Ethnic Cultural Socialization

Martha was born in 1924 to Jews of Russian descent who had emigrated to Philadelphia in 1918. Upon arriving there, they established residence in a row house in Strawberry Mansion on 32d Street and Susquehanna Avenue. According to Martha, this neighborhood was "predominantly Jewish." As she recalls, all her neighbors and friends as well as her parents' friends and fellow workers were Yiddish-speaking Eastern European Jews. Furthermore, the economy of this neighborhood was controlled by Jews: the shopkeepers, store owners, and restaurateurs were Eastern European Jews and catered specifically to this group.

Martha's father, Chaim, was a tailor by trade. Originally he worked for another Russian Jew in a small tailor shop within Strawberry Mansion. However, in later years he became a shoe salesman for a large Philadelphia department store. Martha's mother, Rose, was a seamstress until she died at the early age of forty-two. Martha's only family were her mother and father. She had no siblings. Moreover, she has no relatives outside of her nuclear family. On repeated occasions, she reaffirmed the fact that she has no aunts, uncles, or cousins. Thus, she stated, "the only family I ever had were my mother and my father." I found this fact difficult to believe, but I had no evidence to suggest it was not true.

Rose and Chaim were nonpracticing and nonreligious Jews. According to Martha, they were "very much Jewish" but did not believe in the religious aspects of the culture. Their Judaism avoided the ritualized aspects of its religious life. They were atheists and socialists. The Judaism they embraced was a cultural one. They were very well versed in the history of the Jewish people, knowledge of the Old Testament, Jewish literature, and the place of religion in the lives of many Jews. However, they wanted a Jewish life without its ritual restrictions. They never went to synagogue, never celebrated the holidays or practiced the rituals in a formal sense, or even pretended to do so. They knew about many of the holidays, their significance and the ritualistic form they most often take. However, this was purely in the realm of knowledge—not of action.

As a result, certain rituals practiced by Jews at large were transformed within Martha's family context. The bond between Jews was expressed but not within a religious setting. For example, Martha recalls that on most Passovers her parents would entertain other Jews. Passover, in many Jewish homes, is recognized and enacted in the form of a Seder: a ritualized meal that celebrates the Jews' Exodus from Egypt. The form of the Seder is dictated by its accompanying prayer book, the Hagadah. Martha knows these facts, but she proudly noted the untraditional nature of her parents' Passover dinner. She stated: "Our Passover dinner was a time to celebrate, but in our own way. We ate, drank, spoke in Yiddish and argued. Passover was the time my parents and their closest friends forgot and had fun." In a sense, the Passover was celebrated within Martha's household, but it took a unique form in her parents' grip. She seemed to speak of this occasion with fondness and sentimentality.

In addition to this Passover meal, the Sabbath was celebrated, but the traditional ritualized formality was ignored. Martha's family had a special meal on Friday nights. What marked its significance was the food, the meal's length, and the nature of discussion during and after dinner. According to Martha, on Friday night they had an especially prepared beef stew with *kasha* (a form of grain). In addition, a friend or friends of the family would usually be invited for dinner. Unlike those on other nights of the week, the Friday-night meal was generally longer and more animated. Conversations were usually heated and political in nature. As Martha stated: "My parents loved to argue. On many occasions I would see my father nose to nose with someone else, locked in argumentative combat." Thus, in an extraordinarily eloquent manner, Martha captured a main ingredient of the Friday-night Passover meal in her home.

As you can see, the dinner table within the home was an important element in Martha's pre-street Jewish life. She spoke often of these occasions, when various people would eat and relax in her parents' home, while engaged in conversation in Yiddish. Interestingly enough, the occasions of which she speaks are adaptations of the Sabbath and Passover rituals, major events in the Jewish world. Moreover, the people invited to the "special occasions were always Yiddish-speaking Jews from the Strawberry Mansion community."

Ethnic Expression in a Jewish Street Person   319

Another holiday of prime importance is Yom Kippur. This is known as the Day of Atonement, and for many Jews it is the most sacred of holidays. They may fast for an entire twenty-four-hour period and spend many hours in solemn prayer. Once again, Martha's family altered this sacred holiday to fit their needs and expectations. As she recalls, her father and mother would not go to work on Yom Kippur, but they would not fast or attend synagogue. They were not members of any congregation because they did not believe in organized prayer. However, Yom Kippur for her and her parents was a "private day" set aside for self-reflection. She would not attend school in order to "spend time away from the rest of the world."

In summary, Passover, Yom Kippur, and the weekly Sabbath were the only occasions noticeably marked by her family. Martha also expressed knowledge of other holidays such as Rosh Hashanah, Purim, and Sukkoth, but these were not salient landmarks in her life.

The words "neighborhood" and "community" were used constantly by Martha when referring to Strawberry Mansion. I thought this was especially significant because the former word was used when referring to the general area she inhabits on the streets in center-city Philadelphia. The common denominator in both circumstances is the "comfortableness" that she experienced as a resident in Strawberry Mansion and the "comfortableness" she feels now in her self-prescribed neighborhood. For her, Strawberry Mansion was a neighborhood because she was "used to the people, the surroundings, and the feel of the place." Although she referred to her street environment as a neighborhood, the context of the label reflects differences in the meaning of the word. I will discuss these differences below in the context of Martha's street life.

The Street Period

At the center of her present "neighborhood" at 12th and Walnut streets is the Thomas Jefferson Hospital Park and Emergency Room. On cold mornings, she will emerge from the emergency-room lobby around 7:00 a.m. According to her, the people at the emergency room are very nice to her. She estimates that she spends at least some portion of every night, throughout the winter, "dozing" on a chair there. Usually, she stays throughout the night. However, at times she would rather spend a part of the night indoors and a part outdoors. Fortunately, the personnel allow her to come and go as she pleases. She usually arrives at the emergency room about 7:00 p.m. and remains there until the next morning, when the night shift leaves. The nights in the lobby are spent sitting on chairs, "where it is warm." Martha does not sleep in the emergency room; she sits and dozes off. This is an important distinction because in other situations she is able to sleep (these are described below). During the night, she is permitted to use the hospital rest room.

When the new shift arrives, Martha leaves the emergency room and "goes for coffee" at a luncheonette on 12th and Walnut. However, one must understand the full import of this phrase. In the first place, Martha is never without three white plastic shopping bags and her black pocketbook; in other words, her hands are always full. Moreover, she is arthritic and has extremely swollen feet. According to her, walking is a "painful" and "slow" process. As a result, the entire rhythm of her day is much slower than that of normal individuals. Perhaps this explains her comment: "People always seem to be in such a rush"—but she likes to "sit and watch" them. This is an especially attractive activity that can be done in various places. It is something she looks forward to as a time-filler. For this reason, a "cup of coffee" at the luncheonette is a significant event within her day. Martha walks slowly to a booth and sips coffee for at least an hour.

Martha then chooses from several possible options. Her choice depends only on what she is in the mood to do. Thus, for example, she may choose to walk to a thrift shop between 13th and 14th on Walnut Street. Once inside, she "shops" for scarves and jewelry. According to her, "new things come in every day," and she is never quite sure what she may find. On one occasion, I observed her in this thrift shop for two and one-half hours. Within this time, she handled numerous items, questioned the salespeople about prices, and appeared to be perfectly content as she browsed through the aisles. She did not see anyone she knew on this occasion. However, sometimes she encounters her friends and acquaintances at the shop. Generally speaking, she goes there about three days a week.

On other days, Martha may spend the morning and early afternoon in various combinations of activities. The possibilities appear to be fixed, though their particular arrangement on any given day may vary. For example, if Martha forgos the thrift shop in the morning, she may go later in the afternoon. If such is the case, she may window-shop along Chestnut between 9th and 14th. When this occurs, she may walk as far as Wanamaker's and use the ladies lounge on the second floor. Along the way in either direction, Martha may stop at a Rite Aid pharmacy to purchase "odds and ends," such as hand lotion, bobby pins, and a comb. Possibly she may stop at the Mercantile Library, on Chestnut between 11th and 12th streets. She enjoys reading, and the library is usually quiet and warm. If she wants some more coffee, she will usually stop at the McDonald's on Chestnut between 11th and 12th or the New World Pizza, right next door. If the sun is out and she feels warm, she may sit in the Jefferson Hospital Park for hours watching the people go by. This activity seems to be reserved for spring and summer or an unusually "nice winter day."

Around one o'clock, approximately four days a week, Martha has her "lunch-time meal" at the Pennsylvania Hospital cafeteria, on 8th and Spruce. It is open to the public, and no one is discouraged from eating there. Martha sometimes meets her "friend" at the cafeteria. These luncheons are never prearranged because, according to Martha, she is never quite sure what she will want to do. She does look forward to meeting her friend at the cafeteria and enjoys their luncheon meetings. On any given occasion when eating at the cafeteria, Martha will usually recognize people she has seen before and one or two acquaintances. But she will eat alone unless her friend is there. Furthermore, like other actions or events in her life, the meal is consumed slowly.

After lunch at the cafeteria, Martha usually walks north on 8th Street to Market Street. Stretching from 9th to 12th on Market is an indoor shopping mall called the Gallery. Martha passes significant amounts of time there during the cold winter days. On occasion, she will spend five to seven hours on the lowest levels of the mall. This level, like the others, has shops, restaurants, and fast-food establishments. However, unlike the two levels above, it has several different sitting areas that are reserved for the public. Moreover, it has public rest rooms that Martha uses. If she decides to skip lunch at the hospital cafeteria, she will usually eat at the McDonald's on the bottom level of the Gallery. Her friend sometimes eats here, and Martha may meet her.

When in the Gallery, Martha may sit for hours smoking cigarettes and "watching the people." If she gets bored sitting in one spot, she will window-shop as she moves to a new position. I must emphasize that the Gallery is three city blocks long, has hundreds of different shops, is usually crowded, and is dry and warm. As Martha once said, "It has everything I need." Thus, she can occupy hours in the place. After a long afternoon there, she usually walks up Market Street to 11th, where she turns toward 12th and usually purchases dinner at McDonald's or New World Pizza. Then, sometime after the night shift has arrived at the Jefferson Hospital emer-

The Gallery, a sprawling, urban mall, serves as a temporary sanctuary for many of Philadelphia's homeless. (Courtesy of Elizabeth Ameisen)

gency room, she returns for another night of "sitting and dozing" —only to begin the process once again in the morning.

This is a typical day in the life of Martha. However, some variation may occur. For example, she does not always go immediately to the emergency room in the early evening. She may sit across the street at the Jefferson Hospital Park if it is warm and dry outside. In fact, this is where I met her for the first time. Moreover, twice every month she will walk to the post office at 4th and Chestnut in order to pick up her social-security check. If the weather is exceptionally brutal and she wishes to sleep and avoid walking along the streets during the day, she will stay at the Mercy Hospice, at 344 South 13th Street. This is an interesting situation and warrants further discussion.

In the first place, other than the Jefferson Hospital emergency room, the Mercy Hospice is the only place Martha wishes to stay. According to a volunteer there, she has refused all permanent non-street placement she has been offered: "She lives on the street and will live nowhere else." But, approximately four times a month, she will walk to the hospice for a "night's sleep in a bed with blankets." On the following day, she will sit indoors watching television. She never remains at the hospice for more than a night at a time. Furthermore, she may only come once, twice, or three times a month, when the weather is unbearably bad and she wants a shower and/or clothing.

According to Martha, she goes to the Mercy Hospice for several reasons. It is within her self-prescribed neighborhood, not too far from the places she likes to go. The people who run it are always nice to her and do not ask questions. And they always give her what she needs and do not try to pressure her into staying there more than she wants to. For these reasons, it does not disturb her that the hospice is run by Catholic nuns and volunteers. She states: "They don't ask you what you are. . . . They don't preach or make you go to any religious sermons." It does not bother her if she is not surrounded by Jews. The people she knows who utilize the hospice may or may not be of that faith. According to her: "I really don't care." In fact, those whom she considers her friends at this period in her life are not Jewish (discussed further below).

In addition to the Mercy Hospice, the only other charitable organization Martha utilizes is the Jewish Family Services. Approximately once a month, or once every two months, her financial needs force her to use this charity, which is located on 23d and Arch streets, so she goes out of her way to walk there. According to her, she does not like the Jewish Family Services because she does not get along well with the women whom she sees. The social worker, Mrs. N——, always "lectures" her and makes her "feel guilty" for the money she receives. However, a different story is told by the social worker.

According to Mrs. N——, Martha comes to her more than once a month asking for substantial sums of money. When she does not receive what she demands, she often becomes hostile and violent. On one occasion, she had to be removed from the social worker's office. Mrs. N—— seemed to resent Martha's exorbitant requests, when so many other people are in need. Obviously the relationship between these two women is not good. I was unable to discover the reason.

Importantly, Martha utilizes the Jewish Family Services and the Mercy Hospice for charitable donations. I know of no other institutions besides these and the United States government that she uses. Furthermore, her activity and living space are largely confined to an area stretching from Pine Street to Market Street (south to north) and 3d Street and 14th Street (east and west). The focal point of the "neighborhood" is 12th and Walnut streets, the location of the

Thomas Jefferson Hospital Park and Emergency Room. In general, the abstracting and objectifying of Martha's movement through her mentally and spatially defined neighborhood reveal that very few of her behaviors express her Jewish ethnicity. Although some do, I will first focus on the large majority that do not.

Life-Stage Ethnic Dislocation: Assimilation to Street Life

In comparing the Strawberry Mansion neighborhood and Martha's street neighborhood (as defined above), some very apparent differences are evident. The former was largely residential and inhabited by Yiddish-speaking Eastern European Jews; the latter mostly comprises commercial businesses. Most of the people whom one sees during the day and night in the "street neighborhood" do not live there; generally, they are going to or from work, on lunch break, or come to this neighborhood to shop and eat. They are of mixed racial, religious, and ethnic origins. Moreover, they do not form a community, as defined earlier. The people who work and live within this neighborhood are not members of an ethnic enclave who speak a common minority language or possess a common cultural heritage. In spite of this, Martha considers this area to be her neighborhood. She is familiar with its surroundings and does not wish to move from them; she would rather live on the street in her neighborhood than find an apartment in a strange place.

Of the thousands of people passing through or living in this neighborhood, only a few are Martha's acquaintances. She sees them occasionally in her daily routine. According to her, they are her acquaintances because she knows them through repeated contact. For example, a man who often stops and says hello to her as he passes through Thomas Jefferson Park is an acquaintance. Their interaction is short, formal, and not very personal. Martha does not care one way or the other if these people are Jewish. Moreover, she does not know, so a record of the individuals with whom she speaks during the day will not reveal any significant "ethnic" trends. Their ethnicity is not a primary factor in their relationship to Martha as an acquaintance. The same would not have been true in Strawberry Mansion. There were a large portion of people to whom she spoke on any given day who were Jewish, and she used the Yiddish language. Today, she speaks to the people passing through her neighborhood in English.

Outside of this group of acquaintances, there is another acquaintance, one that does involve Martha's ethnicity. Living at 8th and Walnut streets is a woman named Ruth with whom Martha converses in Yiddish. She is aware of no others in her neighborhood who speak this language. Thus, when she "feels the need" to converse in Yiddish, she seeks out this woman, but Martha says that Ruth does not leave her apartment anymore. Therefore, Martha rarely has the opportunity to speak Yiddish. From our interviews, it appears that she does not feel the urge to speak the language very often. According to her, she does not think she would, even if presented more often with the opportunity. Interestingly enough, she never used a Yiddish expression in our many hours of conversation. She does not wish to "call attention to herself" with the use of the language. As the reader will see, this coincides with her current ideological stance. But, before exploring the realm of subjective thought, I will further elaborate upon observably etic phenomenon.

Of extreme importance is the fact that Martha's sole friend is a non-Jew. This is the woman named Mary whom she meets at the Pennsylvania Hospital cafeteria or the McDonald's in the Gallery. According to Martha, she enjoys being alone and does not mind the fact that she has fewer friends than acquaintances. This allows her the freedom she likes. Furthermore, she extremely dislikes the "holds" that many friends put on each other. Perhaps we should note the fact that all her friends were Jewish while living in Strawberry Mansion. Martha says that her present friendship is based on the fact that she and Mary get along very well together. They enjoy sitting and watching people. Nobody else she knows has the patience Mary has. Thus, the person with whom Martha spends most time (seven to ten hours a week) would not lead an investigator to any conclusions regarding Martha's ethnic expression, nor would other objective observations.

For example, unlike Hasidic American Jews, Martha does not express her ethnicity in terms of dress. The sound of her speech does not reveal her cultural background. The last time she celebrated a Sabbath or Passover with a special meal was "sometime in the late 1940s." Thus, to the observer, these two holidays would not appear to be different for her from any other days. The same is true for Yom Kippur. Martha knows the dates and times of these occasions, but they are no more objectively significant than any other day. Thus, the only observable activities that might mark her as a Jew are her Yiddish conversations and contact with Jewish Family Services. All the other observable behavior mentioned above possesses no inherent ethnic factor. We must conclude that observable characteristics of ethnicity were more apparent in Martha's Strawberry Mansion existence than they are now. In order to uncover a stronger expression of her ethnicity, we must turn toward her ideological stances.

Basically, Martha is an assimilationist who believes in interethnic relationship. In conversations about Israel, intermarriage, friendship, acquaintances, neighborhoods, and American citizenship, she voices her consistency. Yet, at the same time she believes and has demonstrated through action that Jews should affirm their identities when tested.

On at least one occasion in the last year, Martha has been involved in an anti-Semitic encounter. At that time, she expressed her Jewish identity. She believes that all Jews when put in a similar situation ought to state "proudly" their ties to the culture. As one would expect from her history, religiousness is not a factor in her definition of a Jew. She agrees with the Halachic definition that a Jew is defined by birth. "Jewishness," for her, is knowledge about the Jewish people.

She does not believe in any necessity to keep an exclusively Jewish social existence. Thus, she maintains that a Jew can continue to be one in spite of having non-Jewish friends. She does not distinguish between a Jew or a non-Jew as a potential friend or acquaintance. She takes this a step further by saying that interethnic marriage is not a bad phenomenon. According to her, these marriages "are not bad because they mix the blood. . . . Too much inbreeding is bad because both the good traits and the bad traits stay within the group." When two ethnic groups intermarry, Martha theorizes, "the good traits from each group will be enhanced." Consistent with this view is her belief that, over and above any religious or ethnic consideration, all the individuals from any type of group are Americans. Americanism is the linking agent between all people. Martha's ethnic identification is surpassed by her nationalistic allegiance. In other words, she professes to view marriage between an American Jew and a member of any other American ethnic group as a marriage between Americans. This bounding will cull the positive traits from each ethnic group.

Martha classifies herself as a Jew—not in some other group. She identifies with other Jews in the United States and the rest of the world. She uses her Jewishness—though it is mostly in the realm of cultural knowledge—when in need of money. At this point in her life, her Jewishness is not expressed in terms of predominantly Jewish social situations. Hypothetically, she does not consider ethnicity to be an important part in the articulation of this social structure. Her actions support her view.

Ethnic Expression in a Jewish Street Person   327

On occasion, she speaks Yiddish, and allows her need for money to override her disaffiliation with Jewish identification. An anti-Semitic remark is too fundamental a threat to ignore. On these occasions, she affirms and reaffirms her ethnicity. However, in contrast to the overpowering Jewishness of Strawberry Mansion, her ethnicity has clearly diminished.

What we observe in Martha's case is an overlapping and mixture of value systems. Each of them is useful to her, but primarily in its original context. Under the pressure of street life, though, the former system is gradually replaced. Yet the Strawberry Mansion system was so actively functioning, widely supported by, and successfully inculcated into Martha, that it continues to exist in the face of a street-life system of values. We must recognize that this is a necessary phenomenon if she wishes to maintain any semblance of a sane life.

Conclusion

Philip L. Kilbride
Jane C. Goodale

In the fall semester of 1985, the editors of this volume and Carolyn Friedman formed a graduate seminar on methodology. We decided to devote the seminar to a review and evaluation of sixty-
five Senior Conference papers for possible inclusion in a volume
on ethnicity. We invited Professor Emerita Frederica de Laguna, of
Bryn Mawr, and visiting Professor Michael Lieber, of the University of Illinois, Chicago Circle, to address our seminar in order to
advise us on conceptual issues to consider in our organizational
format for the projected book. The former had previously edited
a collection of papers selected by students on the history of anthropology (de Laguna 1960); and the latter, a past president of the
Association of Social Anthropology in Oceania (ASAO), had recently been concerned with the issue of cross-cultural comparison
in Oceania anthropology, particularly on how best to organize topical symposia for presentation within a comparative perspective.

Lieber cautioned us to be sensitive to the operational definition
of key terms, particularly in our grouping together of papers in a
section or even for inclusion in the volume. The study of ethnicity, for example, can emphasize, often to the exclusion of other
theoretical concerns, such aspects as class, power, and conflict or
the cultural (symbolic). Although all these (and other) aspects are
addressed in this book, the common, and therefore comparable,
aspect in all the studies is the cultural-symbolic dimension of description and interpretation.

In fact, de Laguna, after listening to descriptions of some of the studies that were being considered for inclusion in this collection, felt that the common theme she detected was at the level of "values." She was, of course, correct. It would not be difficult to construct a "value" inventory about "desired qualities of life" relevant to each ethnic group considered in this volume. For example, a number of "value" ethnic markers are discussed in the studies, such as African-American food, Greek language, Irish dance, Ukrainian Easter eggs, and the Jewish holiday calendar.

Lieber also mentioned some concerns that were epistemological. To what extent would the editors of this book select papers and then edit their content concerning cultural material in a manner that excluded other aspects of equal or even more import? To what extent did the Senior Conference students, trained by the professors in cultural analysis, overemphasize the significance of culture versus, say, social stratification? These are, of course, important concerns not only for this study but also for the entire discipline, which now recognizes that interpretation is always problematic (cf. Devereux 1967 for an early classic statement).

As a rule of thumb, in the Senior Conferences, an attempt is made to reduce bias by encouraging the students to let their informants, whenever possible, "speak for themselves." The professors believe that the "insider's" view of cultural experience is in fact richly used by all our students in comparison with other possible modes of data presentation. Thus, all the essays in this volume are grounded in life narrative interviews, participation with individuals, and other modes of personalized representation of informant experience. Therefore, a common conceptual and also methodological concern in the studies is that of personal "ethnic identity," or more broadly the "individual in culture." In sum, all of them emphasized more or less how the individual experiences ethnic symbols (for example, the culture).

There can be no doubt that the "new ethnicity," or contextual approach to ethnicity, is supported by the papers, particularly those in Part II, which covers "self-chosen" ethnicity. Nevertheless, some properties associated with the "old" tribal, holistic cultural formations are still analytically appropriate. This is especially true for the Lubavitchers. Also, as is shown in Parts III and IV, there does appear to be, for example, something primordial about ethnicity, particularly as seen in its modern persistence along with religion, perhaps itself another "primordial" experience. For this reason, a number of the students found a "naturalistic assumption" to be useful. Clearly, the ethnic group may be to some extent "natural"; and for this reason, perhaps, ethnic intermarriage is so problematic for many such groups. However, it is also true that intermarriage rates do vary over time and are dependent on the nature of the ethnic combinations (Yinger 1985). "Natural" is therefore always informed by culture and social context (Barth 1969). Importantly, we have also seen that class and economics are essential as part of social context. The former theme is illustrated in Part I and the latter in Part II.

We hope that in future anthropological research on American subcultures, including ethnic ones, more conscious steps will be made to constitute a data base in order to accelerate the discipline's attack on *stigma* associated with cultural differences (plenty of which still exist in the United States). As this Conclusion is being written, the city of Philadelphia, typical of urban America, continues to experience ethnic conflict. Black and racially mixed couples are harassed by hundreds of "whites" for attempting to move into "their" neighborhood. Or Korean street signs erected under English ones (so that elderly Koreans can safely cross the streets) evoke hostile reactions and public taunts of "go back to Korea." These are just two examples of the problem.

This volume has not attempted to address these conflict issues specifically, but such an omission is not to understate the significance of conflict in ethnic cultural study. The editors think, however, that this book can best be concluded by pointing out our collective hope that the cultural approach to ethnic diversity will in some small way contribute to a better appreciation of all ethnic groups in America and elsewhere, thereby perhaps reducing future conflict.

The main purpose of the Senior Conference Seminars is, of course, to provide an opportunity for undergraduate students to engage directly in ethnographic fieldwork. Perhaps even more important than "scientific" fieldwork is the "humanistic" opportunity for intensive interaction with the remarkable individuals that "off-campus" social research frequently involves. One necessarily thinks of people such as the Catholic priest in Schoch-Spana's paper, the street woman in Millstein's article, and other such personal field encounters experienced by Senior Conference students and reported in these and other papers not included in this collection. The Introduction of this volume directly addresses student perception of fieldwork.

We believe that the discipline of anthropology with its culture concept as significant, along with its emphasis on firsthand fieldwork, will increasingly prove relevant for application in the United States. This volume is published as testimony that anthropology *as practiced by undergraduate students* should receive more curriculum support in American colleges and universities.

Appendixes

Appendix 1. A Two-Semester Course: Bryn Mawr College

Anthropology 398/99   Professors Goodale and Kilbride

Date	Class Discussion (2 hrs/week)	Fieldwork
Sept.	Definition: Cultural group, ethnic group, culture concept, expressions of ethnicity, Class/ Category, Ethics of field-work. Reading: Last year's reports and selections from bibliography to be assigned (TBA).	Begin selection of an"ethnic"group—survey, mapping, census, boundaries, initial interviews. Entry.
Oct.	Discussion: collection of data, participant observation and note taking. Selected Readings TBA.	Observation and participation.

Nov.	Discussion: Research proposals	Select "focus." Continue informal interviews.
	Participant observation and formulation of focused problems.	

WRITTEN ASSIGNMENT # 1: Describe and analyze a single event drawing on your observations and informal interviewing. (4–8 pp.). DUE: Monday, November 11.

Dec.	Discussion: Research proposals continued. Theoretical and empirical background, methodology (field, and analytical), budget, time allocation.	

WRITTEN ASSIGNMENT # 2: A Research Proposal (limit 8 pp single space/ 16 pp double-space). Two (2) copies.
DUE: December 2nd. Discussion of proposals December 9th. (last class for semester).

Jan./Feb.	Discussion: devising strategic methods for data collection and analysis. SPSS (statistical package for social sciences).	Primary data collection. Interviews—formal and focused.

WRITTEN ASSIGNMENT # 3: Report on your analysis of some specific data relating to your focus (qualitative or quantitative) approx. 5 pp.
DUE: February 24th.

Mar./Apr.	Organization of written reports.	"Bowing Out"

WRITTEN REPORTS DUE: APRIL 21. ORAL REPORTS DUE ON APRIL 28.

Bibliography

Selected assignments will be made in these works. In addition many of these will be of use to you in formulating your theoretical models and fieldwork strategies. You should make yourself familiar with the contents of all of these sources in the first month or so.

Available in Bookstore and on Library reserve

Agar, M. (1980) *The Professional Stranger.* New York: Academic Press.

Barth, F. (1969) *Ethnic Groups and Boundaries.* Boston: Little, Brown.

Bennett, J. (1975) *The New Ethnicity.* St. Paul: West Publishing Co.

Berry, B., and H. L. Tishler (1951) *Race and Ethnic Relations.* Boston: Houghton Mifflin.

Cohen, A. (1974) *Urban Ethnicity.* New York: Tavistock.

Crane, Julia G., and Michael V. Angrosino (1984) *Field Projects in Anthropology.* Prospect Heights, Ill.: Waveland Press.

Epstein, A. L. (1967) *The Craft of Social Anthropology.* London: Tavistock.

Glazer, N. P., and D. P. Moynihan (1963) *Beyond The Melting Pot.* Cambridge: MIT Press.

Jacobs, Glen (ed.) (1970) *The Participant Observer.* New York: George Braziller.

Junker, Bufford H. (1960) *Fieldwork.* Chicago: Chicago University Press.

Keesing, Roger (1975) *Introduction to Social Organization.* New York: Holt, Rinehart & Winston.

Kottak, C. (ed) (1982) *Researching American Culture.* Ann Arbor: University of Michigan Press.

Kroeber, A. L., and C. Kluckhohn (1952) *Culture, A Critical Review.* New York: Vintage Books.

Langness, L. L., and G. Frank (1981) *Lives.* Novato, Calif: Chandler and Sharp.

Maranda, Pierre (1972) *Introduction to Anthropology.* Englewood Cliffs, N.J.: Prentice-Hall.

Pelto, P. J., and G. H. (1978) *Anthropological Research,* 2nd ed. Cambridge: Cambridge University Press.

Spradley, J. (1978) *The Ethnographic Interview.* New York: Holt, Rinehart & Winston.

(1980) *Participant Observation.* New York: Holt, Rinehart & Winston.

Spradley, J., and M. Rynkiewich (1975) *The Nacirema, Readings on American Culture.* Boston: Little, Brown.

Wax, R. H. (1971) *Doing Fieldwork: Warnings and Advice.* Chicago: University of Chicago Press.

NOTE: In addition to readings on ethnicity, fieldwork, etc. each of you must also search out any specific literature on your selected ethnic group *and* on the anthropological (social/cultural) topic you have selected for your focus.

PLAN TO DO MOST OF YOUR READING DURING THE FIRST SEMESTER, AND YOUR MORE INTENSIVE FIELDWORK DURING THE SECOND SEMESTER.

However. You must begin your fieldwork in September, have selected your research group in October, and your topic in November. While your more focused fieldwork will be in January and February, you will need to review pertinent reading, and do additional reading through March. Plan to spend *at least* 2 weeks in writing the *final* draft of your report. It will take at least twice as long as any "term" paper.

Suggested length: 50–100 pages.

Two (2) copies must be handed in—you will receive one back with comments—the second copy (without comments) is kept in department for next year's class to consult.

The final class meeting will be open to all members of the department (including next year's senior majors). For this meeting each of you will prepare and give a 10 minute oral report on the results of your nine months of research.

Appendix 2. A One-Semester Course: Darwin Institute of Technology

Ethnic Cultures in Australia   Professors Goodale and Healey

This unit is designed to familiarize students with the development of ethnic studies in the contemporary anthropological and sociological traditions and with methodological and analytic methods used in the anthropological study of culture in a multi-cultural industrial society. Through personal involvement in a field investigation and its analysis of a self-selected cultural group other than one's own, a greater understanding of the complex relations between ethnic group, class, and cultural values in contemporary Australian society will be achieved. In addition, students should achieve practice and experience in designing and carrying out a practical and feasible field investigation of a selected problem and in the analysis and reporting of results.

The unit will be heavily based on discussion concerning assigned readings, individual field/research strategies and problems and solutions in which a free exchange of experience between staff and students leads to a greater understanding of the particular nature of anthropological data collection through observation, participation, interviewing, and use of schedules and questionnaires.

Each student will select one defined "ethnic group" with which s/he will work throughout the semester. No one should select the group of which they are a member since it is extremely hard to be objective about one's own cultural identity. After a period of "preliminary observation" and rapport building, each student will select a specific "research topic" on which to focus throughout the remainder of the field period. The third section of the semester will be the "bowing out" of the field, the analysis and writing of the report, and the oral presentation of one's findings to the rest of the class.

The class will meet regularly (Wednesdays 12–3) for discussion and attendance at these meetings is mandatory.

Outline of Unit:

Part One: Weeks 1–5 Ethnic group selection and preliminary observations:

During these 5 weeks contact with selected ethnic group must begin, permission gained, and observation of general activities initiated.

In addition, much of the pertinent reading must be completed: Assignments and selections from the following:

READING: (on closed reserve)

Agar, M. (1980) *The Professional Stranger*. New York: Academic Press.

Pelto, P. (1970) *Anthropological Research*. Cambridge: Cambridge University Press.

Cohen, R. (1978) "Ethnicity: Problem and Focus in Anthropology." *Annual Reviews of Anthropology* 7:379–403.

Other READINGS:

Barth, F. (1969) *Ethnic Groups and Boundaries*. Boston: Little, Brown.

Bennett, J. (1975) *The New Ethnicity*. St. Paul: West Publishing Co.

Spradley, J. (1979) *Participant Observation* (alt. *Ethnographic Interview*). New York: Holt, Rinehart & Winston.

Crane & Angrosino (1984). *Field Projects in Anthropology*. Prospect Heights, Ill.: Waveland Press.

Epstein, A. L. (1967) *The Craft of Social Anthropology*. London: Tavistock.

Jacobs, Glen, ed. (1976) *The Participant Observer: Encounters with Social Reality*. New York: George Braziller.

Keesing, R. (1975) *Introduction to Social Organization*. New York: Holt, Rinehart & Winston.

ADDITIONAL READINGS will be pertinent for your selected ethnic group/culture, and selected topic.

Be sure as you do this reading that you take notes together with complete bibliographic information and page numbers as you will wish to consult these and other readings in the writing of your report and throughout the semester's work.

WRITTEN ASSIGNMENT # 1: Describe an "event" which you have observed in your initial encounters with your group. Include any incidental information/comments/explanations which informants have given you as well as any "insights" concerning the meaning of the event which you may have had. Length approximately 3 pages. Due at the end of 5 weeks.

Part Two—Weeks 6 through 9 (including break if feasible)

During this period of time you will choose the particular topic on which you wish to focus, conduct informal and formal interviews and continue your participant observation. This is your primary data collection time and you should spend at least 2–4 (or more) hours each week "in data collection in the field." Discussion in class hours will be on both general and specific problems of data collection, recording and analysis. Your readings should supplement your fieldwork being relevant to the culture and topic of your research.

WRITTEN ASSIGNMENT # 2: A proposal outline of Research Group and topic. 2–3 pages. This will also serve as a preliminary outline of your final report. DUE at the end of the 9th week, in class.

Part Three—Week 10–14 with additional week after classes end.

During this period you begin to "bow out" (Agar), using your field time for more formal methods designed to check and provide quantitative data to back up your general impressions, and begin to analyze and organize your data for your final report.

A FIRST DRAFT of the report must be completed before the final class meeting on November 12th. At that meeting a 20 minute oral summary of your FINDINGS AND CONCLUSIONS will be presented to the group for discussion and questioning. Information arising from this discussion and comments will be incorporated into the FINAL DRAFT.

Final paper—25–30 pages

[*Editors' note*: Groups studied in Darwin (Australia) included Sikh, Greek, Islamic, Filipino, and Urban Australian Aboriginal.]

Bibliography

Ablon, J.
  1982 "Field Method in Working with Middle Class Americans." In *Anthropology for the Eighties*, J. B. Cole, ed., pp. 28–43. New York: Free Press.
Adler, Morris
  1963 *The World of the Talmud*. New York: Schocken Books.
Agar, Michael H.
  1980 *The Professional Stranger: An Informal Introduction to Ethnography*. New York: Academic Press.
Allport, Gordon W.
  1954 *The Nature of Prejudice*. Reading, Mass.: Addison-Wesley Publishing Co.
Aschenbrenner, J.
  1976 "Humanism in Black Culture." In *Ethnicity in the Americas*, F. Henry, ed., pp. 333–346. The Hague: Mouton.
Ashton, Elwyn T.
  1984 *The Welsh in the United States*. Hove, England: Caldra House.
Bales, R. F.
  1962 "Attitudes Toward Drinking in the Irish Culture." In *Society, Culture and Drinking Patterns*, D. Pittman and C. Snyder, eds., pp. 157–187. New York: John Wiley & Sons.
Baltzell, Digby
  1957 "The Development of a Jewish Upper Class in Philadelphia, 1782–1940." In *The Jews: Social Patterns of an American Group*, Marshall Sklare, ed., pp. 271–287. New York: Free Press.
  1958 *Philadelphia Gentlemen: The Making of a National Upper Class*. Glencoe, Ill.: Free Press.

Barry, Philip
1939 *The Philadelphia Story.* New York: S. French Co.
Barth, F.
1969 *Ethnic Groups and Boundaries: The Social Organization of Culture Difference.* Boston: Little, Brown.
Bascom, W. R.
1951 "Yoruba Food; Yoruba Cooking." *Africa* 21:41–53, 125–137.
1977 "Some Yoruba Ways with Yams." In *The Anthropologists' Cookbook,* J. Kuper, ed., pp. 82–85. New York: Universe Books.
Bateson, Gregory
1973 "Style, Grace, and Information in Primitive Art." In *Primitive Art and Society,* Anthony Forge, ed., pp. 235–255. London: Oxford University Press.
Baum, Charlotte
1976 *The Jewish Woman in America.* New York: New American Library.
Becker, Howard S., and Blanche Geer
1957 "Participation-Observation and Interviewing." *Human Organization.* Vol. 16, No. 3:29–32.
Beckett, J. C.
1984 *A Short History of Ireland.* London: Hutchinson & Co.
Begrie, I. C.
1966 "Food Habits in Uganda." *Review of Nutrition and Food Science* 3 (April):8–11.
Benedict, Ruth
1963 *Thai Culture and Behavior.* Data Paper No. 4, Southeast Asian Studies. Ithaca, N.Y.: Cornell University Press.
Bennett, J. W.
1964 "An Interpretation of the Scope and Implications of Social Scientific Research in Human Subsistence." *American Anthropologist* 48:553–573.
1975 (ed.) *The New Ethnicity: Perspectives from Ethnology.* St. Paul: West Publishing Co.
Berry, Brewton
1951 *Race and Ethnic Relations.* Boston: Houghton Mifflin.
Biddle, Livingston, Jr.
1950 *Main Line: A Philadelphia Novel.* New York: Julian Messner.
Biddle, Nicholas (comp.)
1931 *Biddle Anniversary: Celebrating the 250th Anniversary of the Arrival in America of William and Sarah Kempe Biddle.* Philadelphia: Engle Press.
Birnbach, Lisa (ed.)
1980 *The Official Preppy Handbook.* New York: Workman Publishing Co.
Blau, Esther
1979 *A Candle of My Own.* New York: Lubavitcher Women's Organization.

Blauner, R.
1970 "Black Culture: Myth or Reality?" In *Afro-American Anthropology: Contemporary Perspectives*, N. E. Whitten and J. F. Szwed, eds., pp. 357–366. New York: Free Press.

Blessing, Patrick J.
1980 "The Irish." In *The Harvard Encyclopedia of American Ethnic Groups*, Stephen Thernstrom, ed., pp. 524–545. Cambridge, Mass.: Belknap Press.

Boas, Franz
1963 *The Mind of Primitive Man*. New York: Collier Books.

Boyd, Robert
1957 *Main Line Girl*. New York: Comet Press Books.

Bram, Joseph
1972 "The Lower Status Puerto Rican Family." In *The Puerto Rican Community and Its Children on the Mainland*, F. Cordasco and E. Bucchioni, eds., pp. 103–113. Metuchen, N.J.: Scarecrow Press.

Brameld, Theodore
1972 "Explicit and Implicit Culture in Puerto Rico: A Case Study in Educational Anthropology." In *The Puerto Rican Community and Its Children on the Mainland*, F. Cordasco and E. Bucchioni, eds., pp. 19–35. Metuchen, N.J.: Scarecrow Press.

Brigham, John C., and T. A. Weissbach (eds.)
1972 *Racial Attitudes in America: Analyses and Findings of Social Psychology*. New York: Harper & Row.

Brown, L. K., and K. Mussell
1984a (eds.) *Ethnic and Regional Foodways in the United States: The Performance of Identity*. Knoxville: University of Tennessee Press.
1984b "Introduction." In *Ethnic and Regional Foodways in the United States: The Performance of Identity*, pp. 3–15. Knoxville: University of Tennessee Press.

Brunvard, Jan
1968 *The Study of American Folklore*. New York: W. W. Norton.

Buber, Martin
1955 *The Legend of the Baal-Shem*. New York: Harper & Brothers.

Burger, P.
1977 *Facing up to Modernity*. New York: Basic Books.

Campbell, John, and Philip Sherrard
1968 *Modern Greece*. New York: Frederick A. Praeger.

Caplan, Patricia, and Janet M. Bujra (eds.)
1979 *Women United, Women Divided*. Bloomington: Indiana University Press.

Christensen, E. W.
1979 "Counseling Puerto Ricans: Some Cultural Considerations." In *Understanding and Counseling Ethnic Minorities*, G. Henderson, ed., pp. 269–280. Springfield, Ill.: Charles C. Thomas

Chyz, Yaroslav
1939 *Ukrainian Immigrants in the United States*. Scranton, Pa.: Ukrainian Workingman's Association.
Claiborne, C.
1984 "Old Linen, Fine China, and Carolina Soul." *New York Times*. Feb. 5, 1984, pp. C1 and C6.
Clark, Dennis J.
1973 *The Irish in Philadelphia*. Philadelphia: Temple University Press.
Clark, Margaret
1979 "Mexican-American Family Structure." In *Understanding and Counseling Ethnic Minorities*, G. Henderson, ed., pp. 123–137. Springfield, Ill.: Charles C. Thomas.
Cohen, Abner
1974 *Two-Dimensional Man*. Berkeley: University of California Press.
1981 *The Politics of Elite Culture*. Berkeley: University of California Press.
Cohen, Ronald
1978 "Ethnicity: Problem and Focus in Anthropology." *Annual Review of Anthropology* 7:379–403.
Cohen, Y. A.
1961 "Food and Its Vicissitudes: A Cross-Culture Study of Sharing and Nonsharing." In *Social Structure and Personality*, pp. 312–350. New York: Holt, Rinehart & Winston.
An Coimisiún le Rincí Gaelacha
1969 *Thirty Popular Figure Dances*. Freshford, County Kilkenny, Éire: Wellbrook Press.
Corkery, Daniel
1968 *The Fortunes of the Irish Language*. Cork, Ireland: Mercier Press.
Crane, Julia G., and Michael V. Angrosino
1984 *Field Projects in Anthropology*. Prospect Heights, Ill.: Waveland Press.
Cussler, M., and M. L. de Give
1942 "The Effect of Human Relations on Food Habits in the Rural Southeast." *Applied Anthropology* 1:13–18.
Dashefsky, Arnold, and Howard Shapiro
1974 *Ethnic Identification among American Jews: Socialization and Social Structure*. Lexington, Mass.: Lexington Books.
Davidson, Bill
1978 "Cymru Conquers the British." *TV Guide*. May 27, pp. 6–8.
de Fréine, Sean
1965 *The Great Silence*. Dublin, Ireland: Foilseacháin Náisiúnta Teoranta.
de Garine, I.
1972 "The Socio-Cultural Aspects of Nutrition." *Ecology of Food and Nutrition* 1:143–173.

Deigado, Melvin
 1979 "Puerto Rican Spiritualism and the Social Work Profession." In *Understanding and Counseling Ethnic Minorities*, G. Henderson, ed., pp. 216–231. Springfield, Ill.: Charles C. Thomas.
de Laguna, Frederica
 1960 *Selected Papers from the American Anthropologist, 1888–1920*. Washington, D.C.: American Anthropological Association.
den Hartog, A. P., and A. Bornstein-Johansson
 1976 "Social Science, Food, and Nutrition." In *Development from Below: Anthropologists and Development Situations*; David C. Pitt, ed., pp. 97–123. The Hague: Mouton.
Devereux, George
 1967 *From Anxiety to Method in the Behavioral Sciences*. Paris and the Hague: Mouton et Cie.
DeVos, George
 1975 "Ethnic Pluralism: Conflict and Accommodation." In *Ethnic Identity*, DeVos and L. Romanucci-Ross, eds., pp. 3–41. Palo Alto, Calif.: Mayfield.
DeVos, George, and L. Romanucci-Ross (eds.)
 1975 *Ethnic Identity: Cultural Continuities and Change*. Palo Alto, Calif.: Mayfield.
Dickens, Dorothy
 1945 "Some Effects of a White Cornmeal Shortage." *Journal of the American Dietetic Association* 21:287–288.
Douglas, M.
 1984a (ed.) *Food in the Social Order: Studies of Food and Festivities in Three American Communities*. New York: Russell Sage Foundation.
 1984b "Standard Social Uses of Food: Introduction." In *Food in Three American Communities*, M. Douglas, ed., pp. 1–39. New York: Russell Sage Foundation.
Downey, James
 1983 *Them & Us*. Dublin, Ireland: Ward River Press.
Draper, Susan Hayward
 1980 *Once upon the Main Line*. New York: A Hearthstone Book.
Dubnow, S. M.
 1916 *History of the Jews in Russia and Poland*, Vol. 1. Philadelphia: Jewish Publication Society of America.
Du Bois, William E. B.
 1903 *The Souls of Black Folk*. New York: Premier Edition.
Durant, David
 1981 *Raleigh's Lost Colony*. New York: Atheneum.
Durkheim, E.
 1961 *Elementary Forms of the Religious Life*. New York: Collier.
Eames, E., and J. Goode
 1977 *Anthropology of the City*. New Jersey: Prentice-Hall.

Eban, Abba

1968 *My People: The Story of the Jews*. New York: Behrman House.

Ebihara, May

1971 *Svay, A Khmer Village in Cambodia*. Ph.D. dissertation. Ann Arbor: University Microfilms.

Edwards, Owain T.

1972 "Music in Wales." In *Anatomy of Wales*, R. Brinley Jones, ed., pp. 207–266. Peterston-super-Ely, Wales: Gwerin Publications.

Elkins, S. M.

1968 *Slavery: A Problem in American Institutional and Intellectual Life*. Chicago: University of Chicago Press.

Ellison, R.

1964 *Shadow and Act*. New York: Random House.

Epstein, A. L.

1967 *The Craft of Social Anthropology*. London: Tavistock.

Farb, P., and G. Armelagos

1980 *Consuming Passions: The Anthropology of Eating*. Boston: Houghton Mifflin.

Far Eastern Economic Review

1983 Letter from Stockson. June 30, p. 44.

Fernandez, James

1965 "Symbolic Consensus in a Fang Reformation Cult." *American Anthropologist* 66:902–927.

Figgis, Allen (ed.)

1968 *Encyclopedia of Ireland*, pp. 170–175. Dublin, Ireland: Hely Thom.

Fischer, John L., and Ann Fischer

1966 *The New Englanders of Orchard Town, U.S.A.* New York: John Wiley & Sons.

Fitzpatrick, Joseph P.

1971 *Puerto Rican Americans: The Meaning of Migration to the Mainland*. Englewood Cliffs, N.J.: Prentice Hall.

Fogel, R. W., and S. L. Engerman

1974 *Time on the Cross: The Economics of American Negro Slavery*, Vol. 1. Boston: Little, Brown.

Frazier, E.

1966 *The Negro Family in the United States*. Chicago: University of Chicago Press.

1957a *The Negro in the United States*. New York: Macmillan Co.

1957b *Black Bourgeoisie*. New York: Collier Books.

Freeman, Derek

1983 *Margaret Mead and Samoa: The Making and Unmaking of an Anthropological Myth*. Cambridge, Mass.: Harvard University Press.

Fried, Marc

1963 "Grieving for Lost Home." In *The Urban Condition: People and Policy in the Metropolis*, L. J. Duhl, ed., pp. 151–171. New York: Basic Books.

Friedfertig, Raizel S., and Freyda Schapiro
  1981 *The Modern Jewish Woman: A Unique Perspective.* New York: Lubavitcher Education Foundation for Jewish Marriage Enrichment.
Gaster, Theodor H.
  1952 *Festivals of the Jewish Year: A Modern Interpretation and Guide.*
  New York: William Sloane Associates.
Geertz, Clifford
  1963 (ed.) *Old Societies and New States: The Quest for Modernity in
  Asia and Africa.* New York: Free Press.
  1973 *The Interpretation of Cultures.* New York: Basic Books.
Ghali, Sonia Badillo
  1979 "Cultural Sensitivity and the Puerto Rican Client." In *Understand-
  ing and Counseling Ethnic Minorities,* G. Henderson, ed., pp. 233–259.
  Springfield, Ill.: Charles C. Thomas.
Gilligan, Carol
  1982 *In a Different Voice.* Cambridge, Mass.: Harvard University Press.
Gladney, V. M.
  1972 "Food Practices of Some Black Americans in Los Angeles County."
  County of Los Angeles Department of Health Services, Community
  Health Services pamphlet.
Glazer, Nathan
  1957 *American Judaism.* Chicago: University of Chicago Press.
Glazer, Nathan, and Daniel P. Moynihan
  1963 *Beyond the Melting Pot.* Cambridge: MIT Press.
Goodale, Jane C.
  1971 *Tiwi Wives: A Study of the Women of North Australia.* Seattle:
  University of Washington Press.
  1988 "Plural Societies, Ethnic Minorities, and Tribal Aborigines: Where
  Are the Tiwi?" Paper read at the Fifth International Congress on
  Hunter and Gatherer Societies, Darwin, Australia.
Goode, J., J. Theophano, and K. Curtis
  1984 "A Framework for the Analysis of Continuity and Change in Shared
  Sociocultural Rules for Food Use: The Italian-American Pattern." In
  Ethnic and Regional Foodways in the United States, L. K. Brown and
  K. Mussell, eds., pp. 66–88. Knoxville: University of Tennessee Press.
Gorden, Raymond
  1969 *Interviewing: Strategy, Techniques, and Tactics.* Homewood, Ill.:
  Dorsey Press.
Gordon, Milton
  1964 *Acculturation in American Life.* New York: Oxford University
  Press.
Greeley, Andrew M.
  1977 *The American Catholic.* New York: Basic Books.
Greenberg, Blu
  1981 *On Women and Judaism.* Philadelphia: Jewish Publication Society
  of America.

Greenberg, Julie

1986 Unpublished remarks at Bryn Mawr College.

Gregory, George D. (ed.)

1984 *The Greek Affair*. Broomall, Pa.: St. Luke's Publications.

Griffin, William D.

1981 *A Portrait of the Irish in America*. New York: Charles Scribner's Sons.

Guillemin, Jeanne

1975 *Urban Renegades: The Cultural Strategies of American Indians*. New York: Columbia University Press.

Gutierrez, C. P.

1984 "The Social and Symbolic Uses of Ethnic/Regional Foodways: Cajuns and Crawfish in South Louisiana." In *Ethnic and Regional Foodways in the United States*, L. K. Brown and K. Mussell, eds., pp. 169–182. Knoxville: University of Tennessee Press.

Haag, W. G.

1955 "Aborigine Influence on the Southern Diet." *Public Health Report* 70:920–921.

Haines, David

1982 "Southeast Asian Refugees in the U.S.: The Interaction of Kinship and Public Policy." *Anthropological Quarterly* 55:170–181.

Halich, Wasyl

1937 *Ukrainians in the United States*. Chicago: University of Chicago Press.

Hannerz, U.

1973 "The Significance of Soul." In *Black Experience: Soul*, 2d ed., L. Rainwater, ed., pp. 15–30. New Brunswick, N.J.: Transaction Books.

Hansen, Art, and A. Oliver-Smith (eds.)

1982 *Involuntary Migration and Resettlement: The Problems and Responses of Dislocated People*. Boulder, Colo.: Westview Press.

Harris, Lis

1985 *Holy Days*. New York: Summit Books.

Hart, C. W. M.

1930 "The Tiwi of Melville and Bathurst Islands." *Oceania* 1:167–180.

Hartmann, Edward G.

1978 *Americans from Wales*. New York: Octagon Books.

Heilmann, Samuel C.

1977 "Inner and Outer Identities: Sociological Ambivalence among Orthodox Jews." *Jewish Social Studies* 39 (3):227–240.

The Hellenic Chronicle

1985 "How Greek-Americans Help Keep It Burning." The 23rd Biennial Clergy-Laity Congress of the Greek Orthodox Archdiocese of North and South America. Feb. 28, 1985.

Hellman, H.

1978 *Deadly Bugs and Killer Insects*. New York: M. Evans.

Herman, Simon N.

1977 *Jewish Identity: A Social Psychological Perspective.* London: Sage Publications.

Herskovits, M. J.

1958 *The Myth of the Negro Past.* Boston: Beacon Press.

1966 *The New World Negro.* Bloomington: Indiana University Press.

Heschel, Susannah

1983 *On Being a Jewish Feminist.* New York: Schocken Books.

1986 Unpublished remarks at Bryn Mawr College.

Hombs, Mary Ellen, and Mitch Snyder

1982 *Homelessness in America.* Washington, D.C.: Community for Creative Non-Violence.

Honigmann, John J.

1970 "Field Work in Two Northern Canadian Communities." In *Marginal Natives: Anthropologists at Work,* M. Freilich, ed., pp. 39–72. New York: Harper & Row.

Hooker, R. J.

1981 *Food and Drink in America.* New York: Bobbs-Merrill.

Horniatkevych, D.

1963 "Easter Eggs." In *Ukraine: A Concise Encyclopedia,* V. Kubijovyc, ed., pp. 415–417. Toronto: University of Toronto Press.

Hsu, Francis

1983 *Rugged Individualism Reconsidered.* Knoxville: University of Tennessee Press.

Hudson, Charles M.

1976 *The Southeastern Indians.* Knoxville: University of Tennessee Press.

Hunter, J. M.

1973 "Geography in Africa and in the U.S.: A Culture-Nutrition Hypothesis." *Geographical Review* 63:170–195.

Jackson, L.

1969 "Soulin'." *Synergy.* Oct.–Nov., pp. 7–8.

Jacobs, Glen (ed.)

1970 *The Participant Observer: Encounters with Social Reality.* New York: George Braziller.

James, William

1958 *The Varieties of Religious Experience.* New York: New American Library.

Jeffries, B.

1970 *Soul Food Cookbook.* Indianapolis: Bobbs-Merrill Co.

Jerome, N. W.

1975a "Flavor Preferences and Food Patterns in U.S. and Caribbean Blacks." *Food Technology* 29 (6):46–51.

1980 "Diet and Acculturation: The Case of Black-American In-Migrants." In *Nutritional Anthropology: Contemporary Approaches to*

Diet and Culture, N. Jerome, R. Kandel, and G. Pelto, eds., pp. 275–325. New York: Redgrave Publishing Co.

Jimenez, Daniel R.
1980 *A Comparative Analysis of the Support Systems of White and Puerto Rican Clients in Drug Treatment Programs*. Saratoga, Calif.: Century Twenty-One Publishing.

Jones, Delmo J.
1982 "Towards a Native Anthropology." In *Anthropology for the Eighties: Introductory Readings*, J. B. Cole, ed., pp. 471–482. New York: Free Press.

Joyner, C. W.
1971 "Soul Food and the Sambo Stereotype: Foodlore from the Slave Narrative Collection." *Keystone Folklore Quarterly* 16:171–178.

Junker, Bufford H.
1960 *Fieldwork: An Introduction to the Social Sciences*. Chicago: Chicago University Press.

Kandel, R. F, N. W. Jerome, and G. H. Pelto
1980 "Introduction." In *Nutritional Anthropology: Contemporary Approaches to Diet and Culture*, Kandel, Jerome, and Pelto, eds., pp. 1–11. New York: Redgrave Publishing Co.

Kaplan, J. R.
1980 "Introduction: Beauty and the Feast." In *A Woman's Conflict: The Special Relationship between Women and Food*, J. R. Kaplan, ed., pp. 2–14. Englewood Cliffs, N.J.: Prentice-Hall.

Karp, I., and P. Karp
1977 "Social Aspects of Iteso Cookery." In *The Anthropologists' Cookbook*, J. Kuper, ed., pp. 101–105. New York: Universe Books.

Keesing, Roger
1975 *Introduction to Social Organization*. New York: Holt, Rinehart & Winston.

Klose, Megan
1985 "Vecinos Unidos: Changing Ethnicity of Puerto Ricans in Philadelphia." A.B. thesis in anthropology, Bryn Mawr College.

Kluckhohn, Clyde
1949 *Mirror for Man*. New York: McGraw-Hill.

Kochman, T.
1981 *Black and White Styles in Conflict*. Chicago: University of Chicago Press.

Koss, Joan
1965 *Puerto Ricans in Philadelphia: Migration and Accommodation*. Ph.D. dissertation, University of Pennsylvania. Ann Arbor: University Microfilms.

Kottak, C. (ed.)
1982 *Researching American Culture*. Ann Arbor: University of Michigan Press.

Kraut, A. M.

1979 "Ethnic Foodways: The Significance of Food in the Designation of Cultural Boundaries between Immigrant Groups in the U.S., 1840–1921." *Journal of American Culture* 2:409–420.

Kroeber, A. L., and C. Kluckhohn

1952 *Culture: A Critical Review of Concepts and Definitions*. New York: Vintage Books.

Kunstadter, Peter

1967 *Southeast Asian Tribes: Minorities and Nations*. Princeton: Princeton University Press.

Ladner, Joyce A.

1971 *Tomorrow's Tomorrow: The Black Woman*. New York: Doubleday.

Lake, Carlton Jones

n.d. "A Survey of the Music and Music Festivals of the Welsh." Dissertation, Philadelphia Conservatory of Music.

Langness, L. L.

1975 "Margaret Mead and the Study of Socialization." *Ethos* 3(2):97–112.

Langness, L. L., and G. Frank

1981 *Lives: An Anthropological Approach to Biography*. Novato, Calif.: Chandler & Sharp.

Lasker, Bruno

1929 *Race Attitudes in Children*. New York: Collier Books.

Lauria, Anthony

1972 "Respeto, Relajo, and Interpersonal Relations in Puerto Rico." In *The Puerto Rican Community and Its Children on the Mainland*, F. Cordasco and E. Bucchioni, eds., pp. 36–48. Metuchen, N.J.: Scarecrow Press.

Lawrence, J. C. D.

1957 *The Iteso: Fifty Years of Change in a Nilo-Hamitic Tribe of Uganda*. London: Oxford University Press.

L. C. of G. B.

1970 *Challenge: An Encounter with Lubavitch-Chabad*. London: Lubavitcher Foundation.

Leavitt, Ruby R.

1974 *The Puerto Ricans: Culture Change and Language Deviance*. Tucson: University of Arizona Press.

LeBar, Frank, and Adrienne Suddard

1960 *Laos: Its People, Its Society, Its Culture*. New Haven: Human Relations Area Files Press.

1964 (eds.) *Ethnic Groups of Mainland Southeast Asia*. New Haven: Human Relations Area Files Press.

LeClère, Adhémard

1916 *Cambodge: Fêtes Civiles et Religieuses*. Paris: Imprimerie Nationale.

Leeds, Anthony
  1968 "The Anthropology of Cities." In *Proceedings of Southern Anthro-pological Society.* Vol. 2, pp. 31–47.
Leninger, M. M.
  1970 "Some Cross-Cultural Universal and Non-Universal Functions, Be-liefs, and Practices of Food." In *Dimensions of Nutrition,* J. Dupont, ed., pp. 227–240. Boulder: Colorado Associated University Press.
LeVine, R. A., and B. B. LeVine
  1963 "Nyansongo, A Gusii Community in Kenya." In *Six Cultures,* B. B. Whiting, ed., pp. 15–206. New York: John Wiley & Sons.
Levy, Sydelle Brooks
  1975 "Shifting Patterns of Ethnic Identification among the Hasidim." In *The New Ethnicity: Perspectives from Ethnology,* J. W. Bennett, ed., pp. 25–50. New York: West Publishing Co.
Lewin, K.
  1942 "A Group Test for Determining the Anchorage Points of Food Hab-its." National Research Council, Committee on Food Habits. Child Welfare Research Station, State University of Iowa.
Lewis, Oscar
  1963 *Life in a Mexican Village: Tepozlan Restudied.* Urbana: University of Illinois Press.
Lushnycky, A.
  1976 "Ukrainians in Pennsylvania." In *Ukrainians in Pennsylvania,* A. Lushnycky, ed., pp. 17–34. Philadelphia: Ukrainian Bicentennial Com-mittee-Philadelphia.
McCarthy, F. D.
  1958 *Australian Aboriginal Rock Art.* Sydney: Trustees of the Australian Museum.
McDonald, Marjorie
  1970 *Not by the Color of Their Skin: The Impact of Racial Differences on the Child's Development.* New York: International Universities Press.
McGoldrick, Monica
  1982 "Irish Families." In *Ethnicity and Family Therapy,* M. McGoldrick, J. Pearce, and J. Giordano, eds., pp. 310–339. New York: Guilford Press.
Magosci, Paul R.
  1979 *Ukrainian Experience in the United States.* Cambridge, Mass.: Har-vard University Research Committee.
  1980 "Ukrainians." In *The Harvard Encyclopedia of American Ethnic Groups,* Stephen Thernstrom, ed., pp. 997–1009. Cambridge, Mass.: Belknap Press.
Malinowski, Bronislaw
  1984 *Argonauts of the Western Pacific.* Prospect Heights, Ill.: Waveland Press.

Mallowe, Mike
 1983 "Tales of the Main Line." *Philadelphia Magazine*. April, pp. 121–135.
Mandelbaum, David P.
 1958 "Change and Continuity in Jewish Life." In *The Jews: Social Patterns of an American Group*, Marshal Sklare, ed., pp. 509–519. New York: Free Press.
Maquet, J.
 1972 *Africanity: The Cultural Unity of Black Africa*. London: Oxford University Press.
Maranda, Pierre
 1972 *Introduction of Anthropology: A Self-Guide*. Englewood Cliffs, N.J.: Prentice-Hall.
Martel, Gabrielle
 1975 *Lovea: Village des Environs d'Angkor*. Paris: Ecole Francaise d'Extreme-Orient.
Martinez, Aixa
 1984 "Puerto Ricans in Philadelphia: A Study of Socialization Practices in an Urban Community." A.B. thesis in anthropology, Bryn Mawr College.
Mead, Margaret
 1955 *Cultural Patterns and Technical Change*. New York: Mentor Books.
Meier, A., and E. Rudwick
 1966 *From Plantation to Ghetto*. New York: Hill & Wang.
Meiselman, Moshe
 1978 *Jewish Woman in Jewish Law*. New York: Ktav Publishing House.
Mernissi, Fatima
 1975 *Beyond the Veil: Male-Female Dynamics in a Modern Muslim Society*. Cambridge, Mass.: Schenkman.
Miller, Yisroel
 1984 *In Search of the Modern Jewish Woman*. New York: Felheim Publishers.
Millgram, Abraham E.
 1944 *Sabbath: The Day of Delight*. Philadelphia: Jewish Publication Society of America.
Mintz, S. W.
 1970 "Foreword." In *Afro-American Anthropology: Contemporary Perspectives*, N. Whitten and J. Szwed, eds., pp. 1–16. New York: Free Press.
Mokyr, Joel
 1983 *Why Ireland Starved*. Boston: George Allen & Unwin.
Morgan, Prys
 1968 *Background to Wales*. Llandybic, Wales: Christopher Davies.
Morley, Christopher
 1939 *Kitty Foyle*. Philadelphia: J. B. Lippincott Co.

Moskos, Charles C.

1980 *Greek Americans*. Englewood Cliffs, N.J.: Prentice-Hall.

Muecke, Marjorie A.

1983 "Caring for Southeast Asian Refugee Patients in the USA." *American Journal of Public Health* 73 (4):431–438.

Myrdal, G.

1944 *An American Dilemma*. New York: Harper.

Newman, J. L.

1980 "Dimensions of Sandawe Diet." In *Food, Ecology and Culture: Readings in the Anthropology of Dietary Practices*, J. Robson, ed. New York: Gordon & Breach.

New York Times

1982 "Two Western Worlds of Indochina Refugees." October 8, p. 17.

Novak, M.

1980 "Pluralism in Humanistic Perspective." In *Concepts of Ethnicity*, W. Peterson, M. Movak, and P. Gleason, eds., pp. 27–56. Cambridge, Mass.: Belknap Press.

Ó Canainn, Tomás

1978 *Traditional Music in Ireland*. Boston: Routledge & Kegan Paul.

O'Leary, Thomas V. (ed.)

1955 *This Is the Main Line*. Ardmore, Pa.: Main Line Times.

O'Neill, Francis

1973 *Irish Folk Music*. Yorkshire, England: EP Publishing.

Ortner, Sherry B.

1973 "On Key Symbols." *American Anthropologist* 75:1338–1346.

1974 "Is Female to Male As Nature Is to Culture?" In *Woman, Culture, and Society*, M. Rosaldo and L. Lamphere, eds., pp. 67–87. Stanford: Stanford University Press.

Ortner, Sherry, and Harriet Whitehead (eds.)

1981 *Sexual Meanings: The Cultural Construction of Gender and Sexuality*. Cambridge, England: Cambridge University Press.

Ostling, Richard N.

1986 "New Signals about Reunification." *Time*. March 17, p. 71.

Palen, John J.

1979 *Social Problems*. New York: McGraw-Hill.

Pelto, Pertti J., and Gretel H. Pelto

1978 *Anthropological Research: The Structure of Inquiry*. Cambridge, England: Cambridge University Press.

Pettigrew, T.

1976 "Ethnicity in American Life: A Social Psychological Perspective." In *Ethnic Identity in Society*, A. Dashefsky, ed., pp. 12–25. Chicago: Rand McNally.

Pilch, Judah, and Meir Ben-Horin (eds.)

1966 *Judaism and the Jewish School: Selected Essays on the Direction and Purpose of Jewish Education*. New York: Block Publishing Co.

Pisarowicz, James, and V. Tosher
    1982 "Vietnamese Refugee Resettlement: Denver, Colorado 1975–1977."
    In *Voluntary Migration and Resettlement: The Problems and Re-
    sponses of Dislocated People*, A. Hansen and A. Oliver-Smith, eds.
    Boulder, Colo.: Westview Press.
Porter, Judith
    1971 *Black Child, White Child: The Development of Racial Attitudes.*
    Cambridge, Mass.: Harvard University Press.
Prudhomme, Paul
    1984 *Louisiana Kitchen.* New York: William Morrow & Co.
Raphael, Marc Lee
    1984 *Profiles in American Judaism.* San Francisco: Harper & Row.
Report of the U.S. Commission on Civil Rights
    1976 *Puerto Ricans in the Continental United States: An Uncertain Fu-
    ture.* Kal Wagenheim, ed. Washington, D.C.: The Commission.
Richards, A. I.
    1948 [1932] *Hunger and Work in a Savage Tribe: A Functional Study
    of Nutrition among the Southern Bantu.* New York: Free Press.
    1939 *Land, Labour, and Diet in Northern Rhodesia: An Economic Study
    of the Bemba Tribe.* London: Oxford University Press.
Richards, A. I., and E. M. Widdowson
    1936 "A Dietary Study in Northeastern Rhodesia." *Africa* 9:166–196.
Riesman, D.
    1961 *The Lonely Crowd.* New Haven: Yale University Press.
Roberts, R. W.
    1966 *The Unwed Mother.* New York: Harper & Row.
Rosaldo, Michelle
    1974 "Women, Culture, and Society: A Theoretical Overview." In
    Women, Culture and Society, M. Rosaldo and L. Lamphere, eds., pp.
    17–42. Stanford: Stanford University Press.
Rosaldo, Michelle, and Louise Lamphere (eds.)
    1974 *Women, Culture, and Society.* Stanford: Stanford University Press.
Roscoe, J.
    1966 "Agriculture and Food." In J. Roscoe, *The Baganda*, 2d ed., pp.
    426–444. New York: Barnes & Noble.
Rose, P. I. (ed.)
    1970 *Americans from Africa, Vol. 1: Slavery and Its Aftermath.* Chicago:
    Aldine Atherton.
Rosenfeld, Gerry
    1971 *Shut Those Thick Lips: A Study of Slum School Failure.* New York:
    Holt, Rinehart & Winston.
Rottenberg, Dan
    1985 "Summary Report of the Jewish Population Study of Greater Phila-
    delphia." Philadelphia: Federation of Jewish Agencies of Greater Phila-
    delphia.

Royce, Anya Peterson
  1977 *The Anthropology of Dance*. Bloomington: Indiana University Press.
Rudavsky, David
  1984 *Profiles in American Judaism*. San Francisco: Harper & Row.
Sackett, M.
  1972 "Folk Recipes as a Measure of Intercultural Penetration." *Journal of American Folklore* 85:77–81.
Sadie, Stanley (ed.)
  1980 *The New Grove Dictionary of Music and Musicians*. Vol. 9. London: Macmillan Publishers.
Saloutos, Theodore
  1964 *The Greeks in the United States*. Cambridge, Mass.: Harvard University Press.
Sanday, Peggy R.
  1981 *Female Power and Male Dominance: On the Origins of Sexual Inequality*. Cambridge, England: Cambridge University Press.
Sartre, J. P.
  1948 "Anti-Semite and Jew." In *Ethnic Identity in Society*, 1976, A. Dashefsky, ed., pp. 92–95. Chicago: Rand McNally.
Schildkrout, Enid
  1974 "Ethnicity and Generational Differences among Urban Immigrants in Ghana." In *Urban Ethnicity*, A. Cohen, ed., pp. 187–222. London: Tavistock Publications.
Scholem, Gershom G.
  1954 *Major Trends in Jewish Mysticism*. New York: Schocken Books.
Schwartz, Mildred A.
  1967 *Trends in White Attitudes towards Negroes*. Chicago: National Opinion Research Center at the University of Chicago.
Senior, Clarence
  1961 *Strangers Then Neighbors: From Pilgrims to Puerto Ricans*. New York: Freedom Books.
Shack, D. N.
  1978 "Taster's Choice: Social and Cultural Determinants of Food Preferences." In *Diet of Man: Needs and Wants*. J. Yudkin, ed., pp. 209–224. London: Applied Science Publishers.
Shack, W.
  1976 "A Taste of Soul." *New Society* 37 (July 15): 127.
Sharman, A.
  1977 Interview suggestions and outlines provided by Ms. Sharman to her research assistants in the field in conducting "A Study of Food Planning and Children's Daily Nutrition." This study took place among low-income black families in Philadelphia. Unpublished.
Sharot, Stephen
  1980 "Hasidism and the Routinization of Charisma." *Journal for the Scientific Study of Religion* 19(4):325–336.

1982 *Messianism, Mysticism, and Magic.* Chapel Hill: University of North Carolina Press.

Smith, M. G.

1982 "Ethnicity and Ethnic Groups in America: The View from Harvard." *Ethnic and Racial Studies* 5(1):1–22.

Snyder, Charles R.

1957 "Culture and Jewish Sobriety: The Ingroup-Outgroup Factor." In *The Jews: Social Patterns of an American Group*, M. Sklare, ed., pp. 560–594. New York: Free Press.

Soniat, L. E.

1981 *La Bouche, Creole.* Gretna, La.: Pelican.

Spindler, George, and Louise Spindler

1983 "Anthropologists View American Culture." In *Annual Review of Anthropology* 12:49–79. Palo Alto, Calif.: Annual Reviews.

Spiro, Melford E.

1967 *Burmese Supernaturalism: A Study in the Explanation and Reduction of Suffering.* Englewood Cliffs, N.J.: Prentice-Hall.

Spradley, James

1970 *You Owe Yourself a Drunk: An Ethnography of Urban Nomads.* Boston: Little, Brown.

1972 "Adaptive Strategies of Urban Nomads: The Ethnoscience of Tramp Culture." In *The Anthropology of Urban Environments*, T. Weaver and D. White, eds., pp. 21–28. The Society for Applied Anthropology Monograph Series. Monograph No. 11. Washington, D.C.: Society for Applied Anthropology.

1979 *The Ethnographic Interview.* New York: Holt, Rinehart & Winston.

1980 *Participant Observation.* New York: Holt, Rinehart & Winston.

Spradley, James, and M. Phillips

1972 "Culture and Stress: A Quantitative Analysis." *Journal of The American Anthropological Association* 74:518–528.

Spradley, James, and M. Rynkiewich

1975 *The Nacirema: Readings on American Culture.* Boston: Little, Brown.

Stack, Carol B.

1974 *All Our Kin: Strategies for Survival in a Black Community.* New York: Harper & Row.

Steinberg, David

1959 *Cambodia: Its People, Its Society, Its Culture.* New Haven: Human Relations Area Files Press.

Steiner, Stan

1974 *The Islands: The Worlds of the Puerto Ricans.* New York: Harper & Row.

Stevens-Arrogo, Antonio

1974 "Religion and the Puerto Ricans in New York." In *Puerto Rican Perspectives*, E. Mapp, ed. Metuchen, N.J.: Scarecrow Press.

Stivers, R.
1976 *The Hair of the Dog: Irish Drinking and American Stereotype.* University Park: Pennsylvania State University Press.

Stycos, J. M.
1972 "Family and Fertility in Puerto Rico." In *The Puerto Rican Community and Its Children on the Mainland,* F. Cordasco and E. Bucchioni, eds., pp. 76–88. Metuchen, N.J.: Scarecrow Press.

Styles, M. H.
1980 "Soul, Black Women, and Food." In *A Woman's Conflict: The Special Relationship between Women and Food,* J. Kaplan, ed. Englewood Cliffs, N.J.: Prentice-Hall.

Surmach, Y.
1957 "Ukrainian Easter Eggs." New York: Surma.

Tambiah, S. J.
1970 *Buddhism and the Spirit Cults in North-East Thailand.* Cambridge, England: Cambridge University Press.

Theophano, J.
1982 "It's Really Tomato Sauce but We Call It Gravy: A Study of Food and Women's Work among Italian-American Families." Ph.D. dissertation, University of Pennsylvania.

Thomas, Islyn
1972 *Our Welsh Heritage.* New York: St. David's Society of the State of New York.

Tobin, Joseph, and Joan Friedman
1983 "Spirits, Shamans, and Nightmare Death: Survivor Stress in a Hmong Refugee." *American Journal of Orthopsychiatry* 53(3): 539–548.

Townsend, John W.
1922 "The Old 'Main Line.'" Ardmore, Pa.: Privately printed.

Townsend, John W., and Robert W. Lesley
1929 *The "Main Line" Territory: "Then" and "Now."* Ardmore, Pa.: Historical Addresses Before the Community Health and Civic Association.

Trager, Helen G., and Marian R. Yarrow
1952 *They Learn What They Live: Prejudice in Young Children.* New York: Harper & Row.

Trubowitz, Julius
1969 *Changing the Racial Attitudes of Children.* New York: Frederick A. Praeger.

Turner, Victor
1967 *The Forest of Symbols.* Ithaca, N.Y.: Cornell University Press.

Umesao, T. H. Befu, and J. Kreiner
1984 *Japanese Civilization in the Modern World.* Osaka, Japan: National Museum of Ethnology.

U.S. Committee for Refugees
1985 "Southeast Asian Refugee Fact Sheet." Washington, D.C.: U.S. Department of Health and Human Services.

Van Deusen, John

1982 "Health/Mental Health Studies of Indochinese Refugees: A Critical Overview." *Medical Anthropology* 6(4):231–252.

Vaughn, Mary Ann

1982 "Ukrainian Easter." Coralville, Iowa: Communications Printing.

Vermeer, D. E.

1966 "Geophagy among the Tiv of Nigeria." *Association of American Geographers, Annals* 56(1970):204.

1971 "Geophagy among the Ewe of Ghana." *Ethnology* 10:56–72.

Vermeer, D. E., and D. A. Frate

1975 "Geophagy in a Mississippi County." *Association of American Geographers, Annals* 65:414–424.

Walker, Ralph S.

1980 "The Welsh Indians." *American History Illustrated* 15(4):6–13.

Walsh, D., and B. Walsh

1973 "Validity Indices of Alcoholism: A Comment from Irish Experience." *British Journal of Preventive and Social Medicine* 27:18–26.

Warner, W. Lloyd, J. O. Low, Paul S. Lunt, and Leo Srole

1963 *Yankee City.* New Haven: Yale University Press.

Wax, R. H.

1971 *Doing Fieldwork: Warnings and Advice.* Chicago: University of Chicago Press.

Weber, Max

1968 *Economy and Society: An Outline of Interpretive Sociology.* G. Roth and C. Wittich, eds. New York: Bedminster Press.

Weeks, Stephen B.

1891 "The Lost Colony of Roanoke: Its Fate and Survival." *Papers of the American Historical Association*, Vol. 5., pp. 441–481. New York: G. P. Putnam's Sons.

Weinryb, Bernard D.

1957 "Jewish Immigration and Accommodation to America." In *The Jews: Social Patterns of an American Group*, M. Sahlins, ed., pp. 4–22. New York: Free Press.

Wheeler, W. H.

1973 "The Black Family in Perspective." Ph.D. dissertation, Arizona State University.

Whitaker, Donald P. et al.

1973 *Area Handbook for the Khmer Republic.* Washington, D.C.: U.S. Government Printing Office.

Whitehead, T. L.

1984 "Sociocultural Dynamics and Food Habits in a Southern Community." In *Food in the Social Order: Studies of Food and Festivities in Three American Communities*, M. Douglas, ed., pp. 97–142. New York: Russell Sage Foundation.

Williams, John E., and J. Kenneth Morland
   1976 *Race, Color, and the Young Child*. Chapel Hill: University of North
      Carolina Press.
Winter, E. H., and T. O. Beidelman
   1967 "Tanganyika: A Study of an African Society at National and Local
      Levels." In *Contemporary Change in Traditional Societies, Vol. 1; In-
      troduction and Africa*, J. H. Steward, ed., pp. 57–203. Urbana: Univer-
      sity of Illinois Press.
Wolfe, Anne S.
   1977 "The Invisible Jewish Poor." In *A Coat of Many Colors: Jewish
      Sub-Communities in the United States*, A. D. Lavender, ed. Westport,
      Conn.: Greenwood Press.
Yinger, J. M.
   1985 "Ethnicity." *Annual Reviews of Sociology* 11:151–180.
Zalman, Rabbi Schneur
   1962 *Liquetei Amarim (Tanya)*. Trans. by Nissan Mindel. Brooklyn:
      Kehot Publication Society.

Editors and Contributors

In parentheses after the names of the contributors are the dates of participation in the Senior Conference.

Editors

Philip L. Kilbride is the former head of the Department of Anthropology at Bryn Mawr College, where he has taught since 1969. His
most recent publication, with J. Kilbride, is *Changing Family Life
in East Africa: Women and Children at Risk* (1990).

Jane C. Goodale is the head of the Bryn Mawr College Department
of Anthropology, where she has taught since 1959. Her most recent
published work, with C. W. M. Hart and A. R. Pilling, is *The Tiwi
of North Australia* (third revised edition, 1988).

Elizabeth R. Ameisen (1983–84) earned her B.A. and M.A. in anthropology at Bryn Mawr College and is a doctoral candidate there. She
teaches anthropology and history at the Baldwin School and is a
member of the Upper School administration. She is also on the faculty of The Wagner Institute of Science. Her research interests include racism, ethnic relations, and ethnicity in America.

Contributors

Philip Baldinger (1985–86) graduated from Haverford College; he majored in the Bryn Mawr College's anthropology program. He attends the Pennsylvania College of Podiatric Medicine.

Elizabeth Batten (1986–87) works with the Texas prison system as an administrative assistant. Her work includes interviewing staff throughout the twenty-nine prison units in Texas. She plans to pursue graduate study in creative writing.

Karen Belsley (1984–85) earned an M.Ed. in early childhood education from Boston College. Currently, she teaches and cares for her young daughter, Anna.

Anna Dahlem (1985–86) is a doctoral candidate at the University of Chicago Committee on Human Development. She is conducting field research in Israel.

Carolyn Friedman (1983–84) participated in Bryn Mawr's Ethnography Program in Kenya as an undergraduate. After receiving her M.A. from Bryn Mawr in 1986, she worked for a research firm in Princeton, New Jersey, and in fall 1989 entered nursing school.

Erin McGauley Hebard (1985–86) worked after graduation in Palo Alto, California, in day care, as a teacher's aide and as an art teacher for kindergarten through fourth grade. She intends to continue work with young children.

Jennifer Krier (1984–85) as an undergraduate participated in Bryn Mawr's Ethnography Program in Kenya. She is a doctoral candidate in anthropology at Harvard University and will conduct her fieldwork in Southeast Asia.

Andrew Millstein (1983–84) attended the Department of Anthropology at the University of Southern California, where he studied film technique. He is working on a project for EXPO 1990 in Osaka, Japan.

Lorraine Murray (1984–85) has worked since 1987 as a copy editor and researcher for Encyclopedia Britannica. She intends to pursue a career with a press or journal with a specialty in anthropology.

Rebecca Popenoe (1984–85) spent two years in Niger in the Peace Corps. She received an M.A. from Chicago in 1988 and is a doctoral candidate there.

Monica Schoch-Spana (1985–86) is a graduate student fellow in the Department of Anthropology at Johns Hopkins University. Her areas of interest include the anthropology of health and Latin America.

Gita Srinivasan (1986–87) participated as an undergraduate in Bryn Mawr's Leakey Exchange Program in Kenya. She is a graduate fellow in the Department of Anthropology at Stanford University, where her focus is on South Indian ethnography.

Index

described, 264–65; service in, 265–66

Hispanic Catholic, 268; in Puerto Rican community, 270–71; *personalismo* in, 272, 274–75, 286, 288; described, 276–78; mass in, 278–82; attitudes toward, 289–90; role of priest in, 290–92

Churches: Main Line (*see* Main Line); Ukrainian, 137

Class, 4, 11; upper, 24, 231; middle, 27, 231; on Main Line, 27, 41–43, 76, 79. *See also* Elites

Community, ethnic: church as, 286, 288–89, 292; spiritual, 160, 184; children in, 229; American Indian, 246, 250; Greek-American, 253, 255–56, 266; Jewish Orthodox, 225–27; Lubavitcher, 180, 185, 203, 220; Puerto Rican, 270–71; Ukrainian, 135, 138. *See also* Neighborhood

Crown Heights, 154–218 passim

Culture: concept of, 79; elite, 27; national, 10; transmission of, 225, 239
  African, 79
  African-American, 77
  American, 11, 13
  American and Jewish linked, 228
  Black, 79, 95
  Cambodian, 299
  Catholic, 275
  Jewish, 318
  of *shtetl*, 315
  Main Line, 5–6, 13, 25, 28, 30; racial prejudice in, 26, 66, 75; in literature, 30–31; institutions of, 30, 34; rituals of, 34; religion in, 45–49; wealth in, 49–51; values in, 49–51, 61, 62; traditionalism in, 51–52; deviance from, 74. *See also* Main Line; Prejudice, racial
  WASP. *See* Culture, Main Line
  Welsh-American, 104; preserving, 102; competitions in, 103; music in, 103, 109; in writings, 108–9; in newspapers, 110; as anchor, 111

Dance: as symbol, 7
  Irish, 4, 118–19, 121–22; *gymanfa ganu*, 101, 103–7, 110; ceili, 119, 122–31; festival, 119; history of,

121; types described, 122; as metaphor, 128; competitions in, 129. *See also* Dougherty Irish Dancers; Philadelphia Ceili Group

DeLaguna, Frederica, 329

Dichotomizations, nesting, 299

Diversity, ethnic, 58. *See also* Pluralism

Dougherty Irish Dancers, 122, 125, 127–30

Dress, Lubavitcher, 181, 184–85, 199–200

Easter egg, Ukrainian folk art (psanky), 4, 7, 138; as symbol, 134, 139–40, 146–47; specialists in, 138; in ritual, 140–41; in Philadelphia, 141; made by women, 141, 143; symbols on, 141; new uses of, 142–43; workshops in, 142–45; made by men, 143–44; as tradition, 144, 146; meaning of, 146. *See also* Art: Ukrainian-American

Education
  Jewish Orthodox, 155–56; school described, 227–29; functions of, 231
  Lubavitcher: schools described, 181

Eisteddfod, 101, 103

Elites, Main Line, 27, 44, 65, 76. *See also* Class, upper

Ethnic background, 4

Ethnic consciousness, 135, 301

Ethnic cultural study, 10

Ethnic culture, 7, 9

Ethnic dislocation, 293–94, 325; as homelessness, 294

Ethnic experience, 4, 99

Ethnic group, 1, 2, 4, 11, 18, 27, 40, 66, 74, 79, 81, 93; American, 5; defined, 3, 114, 117, 299; boundaries of, 28, 79; boundary maintenance, 101; as interest group, 102, 114

Ethnic group culture, 3

Ethnic identity, 2, 8, 99–100, 250, 299, 330; calendar in, 235, 239; church in, 268–69, 274, 292; defined, 315; holidays in, 235, 238–39; religion in, 136, 243, 261; self-chosen, 130–31; African-American, 86; American-Indian, 243, 249–51; Cambodian, 299, 311; Greek-American, 254–55, 256, 266–67; Irish-American symbols of,

116–18, 120, 127–28; Jewish, 150,
155, 178, 188, 328; Ukrainian-
American, 133–36. *See also* Ethnicity
Ethnic organizations: Hellenic (Greek),
254, 256, 262; Jewish, 153, 163,
296, 315; Welsh, 101, 103–8, 110,
112
Ethnic populations, 25
Ethnicity, 2, 12, 27, 86–87, 105; affirmation of, 328; as concept, 17, 299; defined, 6, 114; expressions of, 326; ingredients of, 314; music in, 105, 107;
new, 8, 266, 294, 330; racial, 5; and
religion, 223–24; politics, 114; self-
chosen, 99, 131, 330; socialization to,
318–20; study of, 11, 18; theory of, 4,
12, 21; in United States, 3. *See also*
Ethnic identity
Ethnocentrism, 9

Feminine nature, Lubavitcher, 193–94,
197, 199, 212, 215
Feminists, Jewish, 153
Fieldwork, 12–13, 15, 17–18, 26, 34–36,
45, 53, 76, 103, 118, 136–39, 188–91,
331; teaching of, 11; theory of, 12, 17.
See also Informants; Interviews;
Methods; Participant observation
Flag: Irish, 123–24, 127; in Jewish
school, 228; Puerto Rican, 292;
Welsh, 108
Food
    African, 81–85, 93; heaviness of, 83;
        preparation of, 84; eating with fin-
        gers, 86; salt in, 89; sharing, 96;
        and health, 97
    African-American: customs of, 6;
        soul, 80–81, 87–90, 92, 95, 97;
        heaviness of, 84, 97; preparation of,
        84, 91–94; eating with fingers, 85,
        90; and ethnic identity, 86–87; and
        social status, 87; spiciness of, 88–
        90; salt in, 89; and other ethnic
        foods, 89; and making do, 90, 93–
        94; use of fresh foods, 91; as self-
        expression, 92–93; not missing a
        meal, 93; and flexibility, 94; restau-
        rants, 96; sharing, 96; and health,
        97; and beauty, 97
    Greek, 254, 256
    Irish, 125

Jewish, 94, 170–72, 206–8, 221, 227,
236–37; as symbol, 237
Ukrainian-American, 141
Friedman, Rabbi Manis, 192–93, 197–
98, 220

Gender, 11, 184–86; roles among blacks,
96; study of, 150, 184–85; roles in Lubavitcher marriage, 151, 200; ideology of,
185; roles among Puerto Ricans, 273
Gladwyne, 32, 39–40, 62–63, 97–99,
100–101
Greek-Americans: history of, 252–54;
entrepreneurship among, 254. *See
also* Church, Greek Orthodox
Group, ethnic. *See* Ethnic group
Gymanfa ganu. *See* Dance: Irish

Hasidism: development of, 161–62
Lubavitcher: rebbe in, 163, 179–80,
184, 203, 206, 208, 220; thought,
179; secular aspects of, 220–21
Haverford College, xi, 65, 149
Health: attitudes of blacks and whites
toward, 97
Hispanics, 7, 13, 247, 273. *See also*
Church, Hispanic Catholic
Holiday, Welsh: St. David's Day,
104–5, 107, 111–13; dinner speech,
110–11
Holidays, Jewish: in cultural transmission, 225, 227; observed in school,
233–35; teaching of, described, 235–
38; in ethnic identity, 235, 235–38.
See also Jews, Orthodox; Jewish Orthodox school
Home, Lubavitcher: described, 170; as
institution, 206
Homeless: Jews' attitude toward, 313;
person's life described, 320–25; person's ethnicity, 326
Homeless, Philadelphia Committee for,
312, 316
Hughes, Alun, 110–13
Hyphenated Americans, 5

Identity: Catholic, 274; cultural, 134;
ethnonational, 135. *See also* Ethnic
identity
Immigration, 7, 101, 315
Informants, 13, 18–19, 118, 302, 312,

35, 37, 80, 104, 118, 156, 188–90, 201–2, 206–9, 241, 255–56, 263, 268, 275–76, 302, 317
Penn, William, 28, 50, 107
Pennsylvania Railroad, 29, 37
Philadelphia, 12, 36, 60, 63, 104, 184, 189, 201, 206–7, 240, 242–43, 246, 250, 252, 270, 277, 294, 296, 299, 312–13, 318, 331; center city, 105, 111, 270, 276, 317; inner city, 241–42, 250–51; Spring Garden area, 268, 275–76, 289–90
Philadelphia Ceili Group, 112, 119, 124–25, 127, 194
Philadelphia Main Line. *See* Main Line
Pluralism, 10, 294. *See also* Diversity, ethnic
Polish-Americans, 5, 65, 126, 130
Prejudice, racial: function of, 27, 36; transmission of, 26–28, 74, 76; defined, 66; in jokes, 67–68; in pejoratives, 72–73; in conversation, 69; in behavior, 69–72; in interviews, 71–73
Premiere Club, 52, 82, 83, 85
Protestantism, on Main Line, 44, 46–47
Psanky. *See* Easter egg
Puerto Rico, 270, 273, 292
Puerto Ricans. *See* Hispanics

Quakers, 28, 44–45

Race, stereotypes of, 5
Racism, 5, 23, 79; ideology of, 72
Racists, 23, 71
Religion: ethnic, 7, 223; Jewish, described, 232–35. *See also* Church
Research, ethnographic. *See* Methods, research
Rituals: of exclusion, 24; of Main Line, 30, 34; group, 80; hogkilling, 96; handwashing, 207–8; transformation of, 319
  Hispanic Catholic: described, 276, 285; as symbolic system, 284; personalization of, 284; variations in, 288; markers of, 289
Russia, 8, 195, 252, 315

Sacred Heart Society, 278, 280–84, 286
Slavery, 7, 24, 87, 93–94

South Africa, 181, 194, 196, 219
Symbols: ethnic, 7; Jewish, 7; church as, 7, 271; Welsh, 108–9, 113–14; defined, 117; theory of, 135; in psanky, 140; in church building, 264; of ethnic identity, 224; in teaching, 237; *mikvah* as, 210

Tiwi, 2, 17

Ukrainian-Americans, 4, 8, 100; history of, 134. *See also* Art, Ukrainian-American; Easter egg
University of Pennsylvania, 61, 94–95, 164, 173, 176, 188

Values, 9, 11, 95, 151, 330
Virginia, 182, 189, 192, 203

Wales, as homeland, 111
WASP. *See* Main Line
Welsh-Americans: history of, 102. *See also* Music, Welsh
Whites, 81, 87, 245
Women: discrimination against, 53–54. *See also* Gender
  African, 90
  African-American, 90
  Black, 92
  Cambodian, 305
  Jewish, 154, 157–58, 197, 252
  Lubavitcher: status of, 152–53; in Jewish community, 153, 225; in marriage, 154, 158, 163, 169, 178, 213–15; in home, 164, 174, 205, 212; and *mikvah* (ritual bath), 164–68, 209–10; spirituality of, 166–67, 177, 199, 201, 204, 211; role in Sabbath, 171–74, 206–7; and commandments, 172; returnees, 175, 183, 188, 190–91, 193, 195, 199–200, 213; and work, 176; at meeting, 183–84; empowerment of, 183, 186–87, 201, 212; power of body, 186–87, 199; attitude toward body, 200; activities of, 204, 211, 218; value of, 211; not marginalized, 212; compared to men, 215–17; and power relations, 215; as community, 217
  Ukrainian: psanky, 141, 143–44